Cultural Competence in Process and Practice

Building Bridges

Juliet C. Rothman
University of California, Berkeley

PEARSON

Boston   New York   San Francisco
Mexico City   Montreal   Toronto   London   Madrid   Munich   Paris
Hong Kong   Singapore   Tokyo   Cape Town   Sydney

For my husband Leonard, whose support and patience makes all things possible, my daughters, Susan and Deborah, and in memory of my beloved son Daniel.

Senior Series Editor: *Patricia Quinlin*
Series Editorial Assistant: *Nakeesha Warner*
Marketing Manager: *Laura Lee Manley*
Production Editor: *Pat Torelli*
Editorial Production Service: *WestWords, Inc.*
Composition Buyer: *Linda Cox*
Manufacturing Buyer: *Debbie Rossi*
Cover Administrator: *Kristina Mose-Libon*

For related titles and support materials, visit our online catalog at www.ablongman.com.

Between the time website information is gathered and then published, it is not unusual for some sites to have closed. Also, the transcription of URLs can result in typographical errors. The publisher would appreciate notification where these errors occur so that they may be corrected in subsequent editions.

Library of Congress Cataloging-in-Publication Data

Rothman, Juliet Cassuto
　Cultural competence in process and practice : building bridges / Juliet C. Rothman.
　　p. cm.
　Includes index.
　ISBN 0-205-50069-2
　1.　Social work with minorities--United States. 2.　Intercultural communication--United States. 3.　Communication in social work. 4.　Ethnic groups--United States. 5. Cultural awareness--United States. 6.　Multiculturalism--United States.　I. Title.
　　HV3176.R68 2008
　　362.8400973--dc22

2007001435

Printed in the United States of America

10　9　8　7　6　5　4　　　　　　14　13

Credits appear on page 353, which constitutes an extension of the copyright page.

CONTENTS

PREFACE

Over the many years that I have taught diversity courses, both at University of California, Berkeley's School of Social Welfare, and at The Catholic University's National Catholic School for Social Service, my understanding of the meaning of cultural competence, the process by which social workers can achieve a level of knowledge and skill in working cross-culturally, and the dynamic and delicate interplay that forms the relationship between social workers and clients has evolved and refined itself. It has been shaped by my own reading and reflection, by my continued experiences with clients and the ever-deeper exploration of cultures, ideas, and worldviews, by the struggle to develop a process and a teaching method that would be meaningful and effective in communicating the ideal of cultural competence to students, and, perhaps even more, by the process of engaging the students themselves, in sharing in their own experiences and insights, and attempting to understand cultural competence as both a unique and individual, and a communal and thus shared, experience.

My work has been challenged by the sheer quantity of books, papers, articles, exercises, workshop and conference programs, and videos that attempt to explore and explain cultural competence as understood by the social work profession. At times, the stacks and piles were approaching waist height in my small office, towering over me as I sat on the floor trying to arrange, order, and integrate the material in order to understand it more fully.

I found much of great value in my accumulated materials. I found excellent conceptual frameworks, models for culturally competent practice, thoughtful and carefully written descriptions and definitions of terms, professional standards, practice examples, exercises to use with students, information that attempted, with varying success, to inform readers about specific cultures chapter by chapter, books that included only race, or race and ethnicity in their definitions of cultural competence, books that focused on one specific area, such as ethnicity, or sexual orientation. I found relatively little material on diversity and cultural competence as applied to worldviews, religions, spirituality, immigration status, or "special" populations that also have a distinct culture, such as homeless people, adolescents, gang members, or people living in poverty.

I believe that we do not serve our clients well, and, in fact, do not fulfill the mandates of our profession, if we consider "culture" and its current corollary, "cultural competence," in an exclusive manner. Inclusiveness is, after all, supportive of social work's core values of dignity and worth of person, and respect for persons, as stated in our Code of Ethics. To assume that we can choose to define "culture" in a way that excludes some groups from consideration undermines the values we seek to support.

This book, therefore, supports an inclusive view of "culture" as broadly defined and self-affirmed and recognized by members of specific groups. It should be noted, however, that not all cultures function equally well in broader society, are positive influences in people's lives, or even operative within the accepted legal and ethical system. Functionality is one aspect of culture, but does not, in itself, determine the existence of the set of beliefs, behaviors, and practices that we associate with the term "culture." In order to work with clients effectively, and to understand the role that culture plays in their lives, we seek to learn, to understand, to focus our skills in a way that enhances our ability to understand clients and their concerns in their cultural context, rather than our own.

The process of knowledge acquisition forms a foundational part of this book. This process has been developed and refined not only by my own work, but also by that of my students. From an original idea about an "immersion project" as a way of learning about a culture, the process was expanded as students spontaneously added pieces to the experience that they felt would be meaningful. Interviewing a member of the culture was added by students, as was the suggestion for using music as an additional tool for understanding. "Cultural event," an experience in which students attend an activity by, about, or with members of the culture they are studying, was adapted and expanded to the times and conditions relevant to specific populations. Reading a history quickly became doing an Internet search, as the most efficient way of learning about a population's experiences.

When do we have "enough" knowledge to feel we are truly culturally competent in understanding and working with another culture? The answer, of course, is never, for one of the first things the process teaches us is that there is infinite diversity within each diversity, and that each person experiences culture in his or her own unique way. We can only learn enough to begin to see some of the special qualities and characteristics of another culture. It is then our role to help the client to take us on the ethnographic journey to an understanding of her/his culture from her or his own perspective.

The broad cultural strokes we have been able to view provide us with the necessary tools for understanding how clients from "our" culture experience our agencies, the programs and services that are offered, and our own work with them. Providing culturally competent services is essential for effective and professional practice. It is sincerely hoped that the process presented here will encourage readers to be especially sensitive to clients' cultural issues, and that the workbook experiences will help each person prepare for a professional career in which the commitment to cultural competence, and the ability to pursue this goal in a meaningful manner, will always accompany her or his practice of social work.

ACKNOWLEDGMENTS

I am especially grateful for the enthusiasm and dedication of the students whose work is a testament to their personal commitment to cultural competence, and to their dedication to the values of the social work profession. Preparing work for publication during the process of graduate education is a major challenge, and one that each student has met with excellence.

I would also like to thank my colleagues for their support of my work: Dr. Kurt Organista, with whom I have shared both this project and the special work of teaching cultural competence; Dr. Paul Terrell, whose confidence in my work has been inspirational, and my other colleagues in the School of Social Welfare, who have been instrumental in assisting me to explore diversity resources they have utilized and found helpful.

I am appreciative of the comments and suggestions of my reviewers: Najma M. Adam, North Eastern Illinois University; Margaret Elbow, Texas Tech University; and Cecilia Thomas, University of North Texas, whose assistance was helpful in organizing my work, and, above all, to my editor, Pat Quinlin, for her confidence, her support, and her enthusiasm for this project.

We build too many walls
And not enough bridges
Sir Isaac Newton

Introduction

It is an accepted standard of social work practice that services be offered in a "culturally competent and sensitive manner." The literature on cultural competence issues in the profession spans all of social work's existence as a distinct profession, for it was recognized early on as an essential element of professional practice. Literature on cultural competence and sensitivity became more prevalent in the 1960s and 1970s, when the great social movements brought cultural issues, racism and discrimination, and civil rights to the center stage of our national conscience. The need for, and awareness of, cultural sensitivity and competence spans all the contexts of practice, from family and children, through health and mental health, school social work, outreach services, mental health services, gerontology, managed care, adjudication services, and employee assistance programs. It is essential to federal policy advisers, PAC workers, organizational managers, community planners, advocates, case managers, and therapists.

Yet, for an area of practice so pervasively important, so generally accepted as essential to every worker's knowledge and skills base, the concept of cultural competence and sensitivity remains somehow elusive. What do we mean when we talk about "culturally competent practice"? Is it knowledge? Is it skill? Does it involve relationships? Does it apply to certain populations? How does it apply to individual professionals? Is "competence" something you *do*—practice with cultural competence, or is it something you *are*—a culturally competent person. Can you actually *be* culturally competent, or is that only an ideal to which one should aspire?

And, perhaps even more relevant in a professional educational setting, how do we achieve cultural competence? How can we tell if we have it? If we do "have it," does that mean we have it for all of the populations with whom we might work? If we know how to work with competence and sensitivity with Korean-Americans, will we know how to be equally competent with people with quadriplegia? With transgendered people? With Native Americans? With Jain? Is there something that we can learn that carries over from population to population—that is general enough and yet specific enough to be defined as cultural competence?

This textbook is an attempt to answer these difficult questions. Yes, this author believes, it is possible to be culturally sensitive, if not totally "competent," in a variety of settings and contexts, and with any population. Yes, there are concepts, methods, and principles that we can adapt to any population and setting to assist us in the work we do. Part One presents an overview of relevant issues and concepts, as well as specific skills that are essential to sensitive and culturally competent practice. A methodology for attaining and assessing cultural competence and sensitivity will be described in detail: a process that includes knowledge acquisition through cultural immersion, and methods of assessment applicable to agencies, programs and services, and personal cultural competencies. This methodology can be applied to increase one's professional and personal level of cultural competence and sensitivity with any population or group, in any setting, and across single or multiple cultural intersections.

Part Two illustrates the methods for acquisition and assessment of cultural competence and sensitivity through the presentation of "projects," which illustrate the process of cultural immersion through many different populations and from the point of view of social work students whose own exposure and experiences with these cultures varies. With knowledge gained during the immersion process, field placement agencies, services and programs, and personal competencies will be explored and assessed. These projects are meant to serve as examples of culturally sensitive social work practice from the perspective of first-year MSW students engaged in the process of obtaining, assessing, and practicing culturally sensitive social work skills in field placement settings. Projects have been selected to highlight a variety of spheres of cultural competence; in each, the writer has selected a population different from her/his own that is served by the field placement agency, and shares with readers her/his own perception of difference, the process of cultural immersion, knowledge acquisition, and reflection, and her/his assessment of the cultural sensitivity and competence of the practice setting, its programs and services, and personal cultural competencies with the chosen population. Through these "projects," readers will gain both a familiarity with the process of attaining cultural sensitivity and competence, and an appreciation for the uniqueness of each writer's individual experiences, and of her/his own personal effort to understand a culture different from her/his own. Each project also presents the writer's understanding of an aspect of the NASW Standards for Cultural Competence as it applies to her/his "project."

The exercises included with each project provide the reader with an opportunity to explore her/his own personal understanding of the population presented; assess her/his own field work agency's cultural competence in regard to that population; develop programs to meet unmet needs in the areas of training, practice, and resources; reconsider some of the assumptions made; and develop suggestions for enhancing cultural competence with this population on a micro-, mezzo-, and macrolevel.

There is no single "right" way of approaching the immersion experience. Not everyone will gain the same insights, develop the same levels of competence, sensitivity, and ease with the population they have chosen, or pursue cultural immersion with the same ardor and depth. Each writer is, of course, a unique person, who approaches the immersion process, selects activities, and experiences cross-cultural contact from her/his own perspective. Each person is also affected by her/his own culture, worldview, and experiences both with the chosen population and with cross-cultural encounters generally. Readers will note that there are several projects in which students "immerse" in the same population—African-Americans, Chinese, or transgendered people, for example. These have been placed consecutively so that readers can easily compare the different approaches, kinds of immersion experiences, and insights gained.

Part Three guides readers through the process of attaining cultural sensitivity and competence with an individually selected population. The goal is to provide an opportunity for engaging with, and learning, the process of increasing cultural competence through working with each of the steps described in the process defined in Part One. This experience will help to ensure the reader's ability to understand and assess any chosen population's experience with agencies, programs and services, and with the individual practitioner. In addition, the NASW Standards for Cultural Competence, included in the Appendix, will provide the reader with a means of assessing competence through professionally developed standards.

It is this author's belief, however, that cultural competence, and sensitive social work practice, are not goals to be strived for, attained, and filed away for use as needed. Rather, cultural competence is a special worldview, a way of considering self and other in the context of the whole range of human experience. Cultural competence is a lifelong process, and as we grow and mature both as professionals and as private individuals, the depth and breadth of our cultural competence is continually evolving. As we take in new experiences, process life events, understand others, experience history, and develop relationships, each one of these elements adds a piece to our cultural competence. We can never know too much about cultures and differences among peoples. It is the *journey*, and not the *destination*, that we must understand and upon which we must consciously embark. We take with us the tools and worldview of our own experience, and we use those tools to understand the experiences of others.

PART ONE

Cultural Competence in the Social Work Setting

As we begin to explore "cultural competence and sensitivity" as they apply to professional social work practice, it is important to recognize some of the inherent limitations in *any* process of cultural competence acquisition, as well as the ways in which current usage of terms might limit our full understanding. "Competence" in this context may be considered in both an absolute and a relative sense. In an absolute sense, competence is an unachievable ideal: we cannot be fully and completely competent in *any* culture, including the one we identify as our own. We are always limited by our experiences and perceptions—we receive cultural information, and process it, as unique individuals, individuals who may share certain levels of commonality of experience, but who also retain a relationship to our own cultural experiences that cannot be understood by another person in its fullest sense. If we are thus limited in our ability to become fully "competent" in our own culture(s), how much more so are we limited in our ability to be fully "competent" in another culture?

Cultural competence in its absolute sense thus seems an unattainable goal. Though this is essential to recognize, lest we make assumptions that can be harmful to our clients, it does not exclude any possibility of cultural competence in a more relative sense. We can, surely, increase our awareness and sensitivity to a culture, either our own or another's, by exploring the cultural experiences both of the culture as a whole, in an historical and existential context, and of individuals who see themselves as a part of that culture. The historical and existential framework provides us with a general understanding, which may be applicable in certain situations and provide a conceptual grounding for thinking about a culture. The specific experiences of people who see themselves as a part of that culture provide us with an understanding of intra-cultural differences, and of the wide diversity of experiences that individuals may have within a culture.

Because the term "cultural competence" is prevalent in the literature and is accepted in our profession, it will be used in this textbook. However, it is important to recognize that it is used here in its relative, and not its absolute, sense.

Cultural Competence in the Social Work Setting

CHAPTER

1

Understanding Cultural Competence

It is essential, as we begin to address cultural competence, that we recognize that we are really talking about two quite different things when we say "cultural competence." One refers to a process, which can be learned, through which a social worker attains the necessary knowledge and skills needed to practice competently and sensitively across cultures. The second refers to the content, a social worker's knowledge and skills in working with a specific population: Mexican-Americans, new immigrants, lesbians, paraplegics, elderly people, homeless alcoholics, or Muslims, for example. The *process* can be applied to any *population*, but the population-specific knowledge, the content, may or may not make the worker culturally competent in working with *another* population. In this way, we can say that cultural competence is both specific, in that it applies to a specific culture or population, and general, in that its attainment follows a process which remains the same in any context.

A Range of Similarities and Differences

An understanding of diversity and difference is a good place to begin our study, for these complex concepts are the foundation upon which our framework for cultural competence must be constructed.

There is a sense in which each individual is "diverse"—a unique creation of biopsychosocialspiritual elements, different from every other individual not only in terms of genes, but in terms of experiences, influences, perspectives, and world view. It is important, as we seek to understand cultural differences and to develop competence, that we keep this important fact in the forefront, and avoid making sweeping generalizations based upon an observable or nonobservable feature through which our society might classify a person into a particular group or culture. Not all Chinese people like Chinese food, not all African-Americans are good athletes, not all Jews are good students, not all Muslims wear head coverings, not all gays are "out," not all developmentally disabled people seek sexual encounters, and not all Latinos are macho. Stereotyping destroys uniqueness, self-esteem, and creativity in all of us. Bias, discrimination, and oppression based on our group affiliations, and the effects of internalized oppression, do affect us all—but not all in the same way.

We speak of cultural competence as something we do "across" cultures when we look, feel, identify, perceive ourselves, or are perceived, as different from our clients. The list of possible differences is infinite—ranging from our commonly held humanity to our uniqueness as individuals. Some of the most commonly understood and identified differences include:

Gender
Race (a social construct, but a prevalent one nonetheless)
Ethnic Group
Nationality
Skin Color
Language
Religion
Ability/Disability
Sexual Orientation
Age
Social Class
Immigration Status
Region of Country
Size and Appearance

But there are many others that occur in a variety of contexts. In many cases, workers and clients share some groupings, and vary in others. Both the similarities and differences can be used as tools in relationship building, problem definition, assessment, the development of intervention strategies, and methods of evaluating and terminating clients.

Commonly Used Terms

Before we can begin to think about culturally competent practices, it is important to arrive at some understanding of the way in which we use culturally related words. A working definition of commonly used terms may provide some clarification, although readers will be aware that many of the terms may be used interchangeably and confusingly in social contexts, the media, and literature.

Culture

A culture may be a set of values, beliefs, and practices grounded in a common history and experiences shared by a group, which it views as distinct and different from that of other groups. People who share a common culture may share geographic location, religion, ethnicity, and/or common life experiences, but each of these may be perceived as necessary and not sufficient reason to define cultural commonality. Culture is context-sensitive, and may be viewed broadly or narrowly in various contexts and situations. Lum states that "culture includes institutions, language, values, religious ideals, habits of thinking, artistic expression, and patterns of social and interpersonal relationship" (Lum D 2004, 98). Culture, as defined by NASW, also includes the way in which a group of people experience the world around them, and can include thoughts, actions, communications, customs, beliefs, values, and institutions (NASW Standards for Cultural Competence in Social Work Practice, Definitions).

Ethnicity

Membership in a group based on ancestry, nationality, or race (Lum 1999, 80), which shares a common experience and a common set of beliefs and identities, and which is passed through the generations may be defined as ethnicity. "Ethnic groups" are often defined as groups that share a common language, country of origin, belief system, history and experience in the United States, and culture.

Green (1999, 16) suggests that there are four ways in which people tend to think of ethnicity, each focusing on a different quality.

1. *Ethnicity as class* suggests a "distinctive lifestyle," such as that exemplified by ethnic areas in urban centers, like Chinatowns, Koreatowns, or Little Italys. These areas commonly attract new immigrants from the related country, and thus are centers that maintain a close cultural connection with the country of origin in language, tradition, cultural institutions, and social support networks.

2. *Ethnicity as politics* relates ethnicity to a common experience of oppression or stigmatization that a group may have encountered in the United States (Green, Ibid). The focus of this view of ethnicity is the development of an ethnically based political organization, so that the group might have a voice with which to address wrongs. The Civil Rights movements are examples of this kind of definition of ethnicity.

3. *Ethnicity as revival* suggests a consciously focused return to traditions, foods, clothing style, language, and celebrations that a group may have brought with them to the United States (Green 1999, 17). In a sense, the ethnic revival focus seeks to undo the assimilation process that an earlier generation believed necessary. The move from a "melting pot" to a "tossed salad" concept of ethnicity and social structure in the latter half of the twentieth century enabled individuals to, in effect, reclaim any or all of the original qualities a group brought with them upon immigration.

4. *Ethnicity as symbolic tokens* to express an identity that is not lived, but remembered and sentimentalized, is Green's fourth view of ethnicity (Ibid). People who define ethnicity in this way want to maintain a minimal connection to the country of origin, in a nostalgic, rather than an experiential, manner.

Diversity

Diversity may be defined as variations between and among social groups based on the kinds of differences noted above. The United States is a diverse society, and immigration and differing birth rates among groups affect the distribution and experiences of all groups over time (Lum 1999, 81). While it is essential to understand the differences *between* groups, it is equally essential to understand that there is a diversity of experience *within* groups as well. Broad "diverse" groups actually contain a number of subgroups, each of which may have different experiences with regard to such issues as education, assimilation, oppression and discrimination, and opportunity. Each broad group contains all social classes, members who are of different generations from immigration, and members who are of different ages, though the proportions of each may vary dramatically between groups.

There is an enormous body of literature that addresses issues of culture, diversity, and ethnicity in the United States. Readers may be confused by the fact that these terms are often used interchangeably, and don't seem to stand out clearly one from the other in much of the literature. It is important to be aware of this looseness in definition and interpretation, and to understand by examining the context exactly how each author is defining each term.

Cultural/Ethnic/Diversity Competence

NASW defines *competence* as "having the capacity to function effectively within the context of culturally integrated patterns of human behavior defined by the group" (NASW Standards for Cultural Competence in Social Work Practice, Definitions). This would include a conscious ability to perform certain tasks and functions in a way that demonstrates knowledge and skill, and the consistent application of the principles or systems upon which the competence is based. Competence also requires the ability to define and describe the various elements that comprise competence in any particular area, elements that, together, define an individual as competent in a particular area.

Cultural competence involves responding "respectfully and effectively" to "people of all cultures, languages, classes, races, ethnic backgrounds, religions, and other diversity factors in a manner that recognizes, affirms, and values the worth of individuals, families, and communities and protects and preserves the dignity of each" (NASW Standards for Cultural Competence in Social Work Practice, Definitions).

Green states that ethnic competence involves several related but distinct areas: awareness of one's own cultural limitations; openness to cultural differences; a client-oriented, systematic learning style; the appropriate use of cultural resources; and the acknowledgment of the integrity of culture (1999, 87).

Sensitivity

Sensitivity involves an awareness of the feelings and reactions of others to events, crises, stress, and special conditions in the context of their unique set of life experiences and situations. In the professional context, self-awareness about feelings and reactions to crises, stress, events, and special conditions, and of the effect of these on the manner in which communication from others is received and understood, is essential to good practice. In this sense, sensitivity is focused both outward and inward.

Cultural/Ethnic/Diversity Sensitivity

These terms comprise an understanding that the experiences of every individual occur in a cultural context that is often a complex interweaving of the client's culture, as defined by the client and by other members of the cultural group, both with other cultures that surround it and with the dominant culture. This cultural context affects the way in which experiences are understood, and responses are developed. The history and experiences of the client's culture and its relationship to the dominant culture affect the client in powerful ways and also often define the manner in which the client and culture are perceived by others. These experiences include individual, societal, and structural oppression, with resultant possible exclusion and discrimination, which can create a sense of disempowerment.

Diversity impacts both social workers and clients. As Green notes:

> The problem is *not* that it is inherently bad, or good either, that most social workers (and nurses and teachers) are white, or that most speak only English, or that most are middle class. The problem lies in the inevitable limitations of those who are monocultural and monolingual in a society that clearly is not. . . . The challenge of cultural diversity is the future of us all. (Green, 1999 pg 6)

As social workers, we cannot avoid taking up Green's challenge.

The Professional Commitment to Cultural Competence

Vulnerable Populations and Professional Responsibility

A strong commitment to working with vulnerable populations has always been a foundational principle of our profession. From the profession's earliest days, in the settlement house movement and in community service organizations, social workers have worked toward changing and improving the lives of vulnerable members of our population. The commitment to social justice is a core social work value.

What makes people vulnerable? There are several factors that must be considered.

One of the major contributing factors is "minority status"—a position generally ascribed to nondominant groups in our society. Traditionally, the term "minority" described the more limited social, economic, and political opportunities experienced by Latinos, African-Americans, Asian-Americans, and First Nation people (Lum 2004, 3). "Minority groups" at first referred to demographics—the percentage of people belonging to a group relative to the percentage of people belonging to the dominant "majority" group. "Minority" applied only to numbers. In the United States, "minority groups" have often experienced generations of oppression, discrimination, and prejudice, which has created a feeling of powerlessness and vulnerability in members. Groups whose physical appearance or "race" has been perceived as different from that of the dominant group traditionally have encountered the most profound and intractable oppression.

The concept of "race" itself is an evolving and changing one, however. In other centuries, in the United States, Irish, Italians, and Jews were considered separate races and experienced discrimination. In the post-9/11 climate, Muslims and Arabs (two groups that differ in composition but are often viewed as the same) have been experiencing "racial" discrimination as well. Religious minorities and national groups from countries outside of Western Europe also experience oppression.

"Minority status" today does not necessarily imply a numerical minority, though it often does. Women are considered minorities, are vulnerable, have experienced oppression, yet comprise more than 50 percent of the population in the United States. Contrary to many other cultures around the world, the United States is a youth-oriented culture; thus, old age is devalued and older people, often disabled as well, are a large, vulnerable group in our population—a group whose numbers are expected to grow appreciably with the aging of the Baby Boomer generation. People who are divorced or separated, especially women, are also a sizeable group in our society who are especially vulnerable.

Membership in a group that is devalued in the dominant society also creates vulnerability. Gays, lesbians, bisexuals, and transgendered people are minorities in a heterosexually dominant world, and often face severe oppression and even physical violence in our society. People with disabilities often experience oppressive, exclusionary aspects of our society, although the passage of the Americans with Disabilities Act in 1990 has attempted to address these issues. Certain kinds of disabilities, such as AIDS, mental illness, and developmental disability create a special vulnerability.

Poverty creates vulnerability. People in poverty tend to have poorer health and less access to goods and services than others in the United States. They often live in substandard housing, in neighborhoods where crime and violence are more prevalent, and are more frequently victims. Working parents in poverty have difficulty in locating safe and affordable child care, and often work long hours at multiple jobs, leaving children unsupervised alone at home. Poor neighborhoods often have higher drug- and alcohol-related problems, and children may be more readily absorbed into this subculture no matter how hard parents try to protect them from it.

Immigrants, especially those who do not speak English, and those who are undocumented, are also vulnerable groups. These populations are especially likely to be exploited by employers, landlords, business operators, etc., and often have little or no legal recourse, access to healthcare, education, and social or other services. Fear of deportation forces undocumented people to forgo medical treatment, needed social services, and educational opportunities, and denies access to basic civil and legal rights. Proposition 187, which was passed in California in 1994, barred access to nonemergency medical services, public education, and cash assistance from state social service agencies, and also required service providers to report to the state any suspected undocumented clients (Hohm and Glynn 2002, 269). This latter provision created complex and difficult ethical issues for social workers, nurses, teachers, and other professionals whose ethical mandate to provide needed services conflicted with the law. Although this law was later rescinded, in 1998 California voters passed Proposition 227, which in effect eliminated bilingual classrooms by mandating that all classroom instruction for children be conducted in English (Ibid). Public discourse on the "rights" of undocumented people, and the "obligations" of government toward them and toward legal members of the population has become increasingly prominent in our post-9/11 society, and was a major issue in the November 2006 election.

Many people in our society have more than one vulnerability, or belong to more than one "minority" group, and their problems are compounded by these intersections. Being old, and Latina, and poor; being Muslim, and African-American; being a newly disabled immigrant from India; being Vietnamese, and female, and Buddhist—these double and triple vulnerabilities often seem overwhelming, creating a feeling of powerlessness and an uncertainty about how to negotiate for oneself in the dominant society.

Diversity competence is necessary if these vulnerable members of society are to be provided with responsible, caring, culturally congruent service; thus, attaining cultural competence is a necessary commitment to effective social work practice.

NASW Code Of Ethics

Social workers' commitment to competent, ethical service to clients is defined and described in the Code of Ethics. All of the Core Values defined in the Preamble support this kind of effort and commitment, most especially social justice, which is further defined in the Ethical Principles section as:

> Social Workers Challenge Social Injustice . . . pursue social change particularly with and on behalf of vulnerable and oppressed individuals and groups of people. Social workers' change efforts are focused primarily on issues of poverty, unemployment, discrimination, and other forms of social injustice. These activities seek to promote sensitivity to and knowledge about oppression and cultural and ethnic diversity. . . . (NASW Code of Ethics, Ethical Principles)

Ethical Standards also reflect social work's commitment to competence in these areas. Standard 1.05, Cultural Competence and Social Diversity, states:

> (a) Social workers should understand culture and its function in human behavior and society, recognizing the strengths that exist in all cultures.
> (b) Social workers should have a knowledge base of their clients' cultures and be able to demonstrate competence in the provision of services that are sensitive to clients' cultures and to differences among people and cultural groups.
> (c) Social workers should obtain education about and seek to understand the nature of social diversity and oppression with respect to race, ethnicity, national origin, color, sex, sexual orientation, age, marital status, political belief, religion, and mental or physical disability. (NASW Code of Ethics, Standard 1.05)

The Code of Ethics also holds workers responsible for engaging in social and political action in support of social justice. Standard 6.04, Social and Political Action, states that social workers should engage in social and political action to "improve social conditions . . . and promote social justice" (NASW Code of Ethics, Standard 6.04a). Other sections of that standard commit workers to:

(b) . . . [A]ct to expand choice and opportunity for all people, with special regard for vulnerable, disadvantaged, oppressed, and exploited people and groups.
(c) Social workers should promote conditions that encourage respect for cultural and social diversity. . . . [S]hould promote policies and practices that demonstrate respect for difference, support the expansion of cultural knowledge and resources, advocate for programs and institutions that demonstrate cultural competence. . . .
(d) Social workers should act to prevent and eliminate domination of, exploitation of, and discrimination against any person, group, or class on the basis of race, ethnicity, national origin, color, sex, sexual orientation, age, marital status, political belief, religion, or mental or physical disability. (NASW Code of Ethics, Standard 6.04)

NASW Standards for Cultural Competence in Social Work Practice

NASW's National Committee on Racial and Ethnic Diversity has developed standards for cultural competence for the profession. The complete standards have been included in the Appendix so that readers may familiarize themselves thoroughly with the contents. Ten specific standards have been defined:

Standard 1: Ethics and Values

Social workers support the values, ethics, and standards of the profession and recognize how personal, professional, and client values may at times conflict.

Standard 2: Self-Awareness

Social workers must develop an understanding of their own personal values and beliefs as a "first step" to understanding the values and beliefs of others.

Standard 3: Cross-Cultural Knowledge

Social workers shall become knowledgeable about the cultures of the clients they serve.

Standard 4: Cross-Cultural Skills

Social workers' methods, skills, and techniques should be culturally appropriate to clients, and workers should also be aware that culture plays a role in the development of the helping relationship.

Standard 5: Service Delivery

Social workers should be knowledgeable about community resources and access culturally appropriate resources for clients.

Standard 6: Empowerment and Advocacy

Social workers should advocate for clients as needed, and be aware of the impact of social policies and programs on diverse client groups.

Standard 7: Diverse Workforce

Social workers should support diversity within the professional community.

Standard 8: Professional Education

Social workers should participate in programs for education and training in cultural competence.

Standard 9: Language Diversity

Social workers should try to provide services, information, and referrals in the language that is appropriate for each client.

Standard 10: Cross-Cultural Leadership

Social workers should support general cultural competence by communicating information about diverse groups to other professionals.

(NASW Standards for Cultural Competence in Social Work Practice, Standards)

Supporting each of these standards in a meaningful and relevant manner is an ongoing social worker responsibility. Cultures are not static: they change and develop, affecting and being affected by the cultures surrounding them. For the worker, this means staying current and being aware of the often subtle changes that occur culturally between and among generations, over time, and in different areas of the country. Chinese-American culture is quite different from Chinese culture as experienced in China. African-American culture of 150 years ago is quite different than African-American culture today. And deaf culture is quite different from the culture of developmental disability.

While learning about *all* cultures may seem an overwhelming and indeed impossible task, it is important to remember that our focus should be on the cultures of the clients we are serving first and foremost. As we work with different groups, we learn different cultures. Exploring new ways of thinking, of doing things, and of relating to the world can be an exhilarating experience for the worker—something to be welcomed, rather than an obligatory task.

Personal Growth and Professional Growth

As presented in the preceding section, a commitment to cultural/ethnic/diversity competence is an essential component of a social worker's commitment to the values and standards of our profession and to social justice. An ongoing commitment to enhancing cultural competence throughout one's career is an essential component of the professional growth process that continues throughout one's professional life and beyond.

But a commitment to cultural competence is not only a commitment to knowledge about other cultures, and to the development of culturally appropriate social work skills. It also involves another kind of commitment, one which may be infinitely more challenging to each individual worker: a commitment to personal awareness, to personal growth, to understanding, and to unlearning (as possible) any biases, stereotypes, or prejudices that may interfere with the worker's ability to assist the client toward culturally appropriate personal goals. However, we must also understand that the complete elimination of *all* biases within ourselves will remain an elusive, though always worthwhile, goal to pursue.

This personal commitment will engage the worker in solitary reflection, in conversations with family members, friends, and associates, and in a deeper exploration of the way in which values and world views are learned and assimilated. It will engage the worker in the effort of defining a "common ground" with a client who, at first glance, seems to have few commonalities with the worker, and in the effort of finding values and strengths within the client's culture to utilize in assisting the client toward growth and change. Each client, each cross-cultural encounter, is in itself an opportunity for personal growth as well as an opportunity to render culturally competent professional service.

A social worker's personal growth, and personal commitment to cultural competence, may be affected by many factors: personal history and life experiences; cultural affiliations; the social environment; the context of practice; the attitudes and beliefs of colleagues and the "culture" of the agency; and the values and beliefs of the dominant culture. Membership in an oppressed and vulnerable group or "minority" status does not make a worker an instant "expert" in cultural competence, though it may make her/him especially knowledgeable about that particular culture, and about the ways in which oppression can affect people of any diverse group. It also doesn't necessarily "protect" the worker from biases, prejudices, and oppressive beliefs about other groups. We are all vulnerable to assumptions, beliefs, and attitudes about others that can compromise our work with clients, and we must all work, individually and together, to overcome these and to become as open, caring, and competent professionals as we each can be!

Summary

We have begun to explore cultural competence by defining some commonly used terms and by addressing the ethical commitment to cultural competence and social justice that is an essential part of our profession, as stated in our Code of Ethics. As we have seen, diversity competence is, in fact, such an important part of professional practice that NASW has developed a separate ethical imperative to address standards for cultural competence specifically and in greater depth.

It is important to recognize that the attainment of diversity competence has both a personal and a professional component. Professional skills will be presented in a succeeding section; however, without the personal exploration of one's own worldview, life experiences, biases, and beliefs, genuine cultural competence will remain an elusive goal. Cultural competence is a lifelong journey, one that will demand continuous effort and interest, but also will provide many personal and professional rewards.

Because diverse groups all exist within the matrix of society, it is important to consider the way in which U.S. society is organized. In the next section, we will explore some of the major theories that have evolved as political scientists and others have attempted to explicate our social structure.

CHAPTER
2

Group Affiliation and Identity

Social Structures and Affiliation

It is a foundational social work principle that each client is a unique individual—a one-of-a-kind combination of genes, life experiences, social milieu, interests, and abilities. We treat each client with dignity and respect, as suggested by the Code of Ethics, grounding these in the client's humanity and individuality.

So, if we are asked to focus on the individual, how should we consider diversity issues? While it is true that each client's experience is unique, human beings tend not to be solitary and isolated. Rather, we live in families, social groups, and communities—in environments that can sustain us as unique individuals if they are appropriate, but that can also be destructive and negative if they are not.

We are born into our first social environment—our family. We quickly learn the environment of the neighborhood, of the school, of the surrounding community. Sometimes, we need to leave our communities and move out into wider society. In the process, we learn to identify with certain groups partly through our own makeup and choices, and partly because those in the society around us place us as members of certain groups. Sometimes, we are very much aware of the groups with which we are associated, while at other times, group affiliation seems relatively unimportant.

There's a simple exercise you can do to help you think about this.
Close your eyes.
Think about your answer to this question:
When do you feel most like yourself?
(This is a great exercise to do with clients, too!)
At first glance, you might respond:
"At the seashore at night, sitting alone on the beach."
"On a mountaintop at night, looking up at the sky."
"When I'm out fishing by myself on the lake early in the morning."
"When I'm fooling around inventing tunes on my guitar."

Good answers, all of them!
But let's think further: in these places, do you really feel your own uniqueness as an individual? Are you clear about the place where defining yourself ends, and "other" begins? At those times, is what you are feeling your *connection*—to the universe, to nature, to music—rather than your difference, your uniqueness?

17

Thinking about it further, you might respond differently: you might be most aware of yourself as a distinct individual when you are in a crowd of other individuals. Yes, you are aware of your connection, your mutual humanity. But are you also not aware of the edge where you end, and the next person begins? Are you not aware of that which is distinctly *you and no one else?* When you interact with others, you notice differences immediately: differences in appearance, in ways of speaking and expressing, in feelings and attitudes and positions about things. You also notice that there are people who look more like you, think more like you, see the world more like you. These people become parts of the groups with which you might identify, so that you *are* a unique individual, but also a member of a group.

We identify with many groups. We are identified by society with many of the groups we ourselves choose, and perhaps some with which we do not feel part of, or prefer not to be part of, for any number of reasons. Not all identities are the same: we welcome some, and feel burdened by others; some carry power and influence, while others may have more negative connotations.

Affiliations are also context-sensitive, and there are often groups within groups. You may be a student, a member of a huge national group. Within that group, you may be a social work student. Within that group, you may be pursuing a child welfare track. You may see yourself, when you are abroad, as simply an American, but when you return home, you are a Southerner, a Midwesterner, or a New Englander. Among people from New England, you become someone from Maine or Connecticut. Or, your family may have immigrated to the United States from Asia. In some contexts, you may simply be Asian, or of Asian descent. In others, you are Thai, or Korean, or Japanese. If you are with a group of Japanese people, you might narrow your identity further, to the island or city from which you or your family came to the United States. Group affiliation has the amazing ability to stretch and to narrow according to the context.

The United States, as we know, is a "nation of immigrants," and all of us except for Native Americans and in some cases African-Americans, have national identities that relate us to other countries. One of the identities that affect us relates to the distance between each of us and the immigrant generation. We are immigrants, first generation, second generation, and so forth. The Japanese have formal names for each generation: the isei, nisei, and sansei generations (Green 1999, 293). At what point do you become simply American, and not a hyphenated American? The answer to that depends partly on you and partly on your milieu.

There are several theories that attempt to define the way in which our society is structured, and all of them integrate the concepts discussed above. It is very important to cultural competence that you understand these theories, and your diversity textbooks should be reviewed carefully in this regard. Some of the most commonly used theories include those grounded in acculturation and those grounded in ethnic conflict.

Acculturation Theories

Acculturation theories were popular during the last century. It was assumed that each new immigrant group would join the American melting pot and, over time, take on the values, attitudes, behavior, language, and world view of those who preceded them into the country (Green 1999, 21). The culture of the dominant majority was primarily Northern European. Generations of immigrants attempted, with varying success, to melt into the pot, despite difficulties with language and an awareness that, socially and economically, immigrants were often at the bottom of the social structure. It was felt that hard work and a good education would help the next generation "rise" and "assimilate" more easily.

Later in the twentieth century, the nation developed an awareness that the melting pot didn't always work, and, even more importantly, that it was contrary to the desires and needs of many people who wanted to maintain a cultural connection with their countries of origin. Critical masses of immigrants from certain nations tended to live in communities where language, food, cultural activities, and behavioral expectations from the home country could easily be preserved. Communications and air travel supported the maintenance of such a connection. Further, some groups did not desire to melt into what was predominantly a Northern European society for many reasons. Thus, our society moved from the melting pot to the tossed salad concept, where each group could function independently and maintain its culture, and yet still live side by side with other groups. While this system worked well in many cases, members of each group still found themselves having to interact with the dominant society for things such as healthcare, education, social services, recreation, etc., and often were aware that, though separate, they were not equal in all respects (Green 1999, 21).

In addition, not all of the salad ingredients were equally desirable in the mix: the salad tongs were generally in the hands of one group, which determined what ingredients to place where, and in what quantities. Thus, in effect, there continued to be a hierarchy among the salad ingredients, and an unequal distribution of societal goods.

Ethnic Conflict Theories

Recognizing that there is often a struggle between and among groups, ethnic competition and conflict theories explore the reasons and extent of the struggle. One theory suggests that as each new group enters the American society, it displaces the group that entered immediately before it, pushing it upward in the social structure. The more generations a cultural or ethnic group has been in the country, the more groups there are who are lower in social status. Each entering group moves into the lower status jobs, the poorer neighborhoods, the more run-down schools that the previous group abandons for better conditions. When several groups enter the country at the same time, there is competition for the homes, jobs, and neighborhoods available—a competition that may be resolved by the dominant group's determining which entering group is more preferable (Hraba 1994, 186–191).

There are also theories that address the complex issues of jobs and social power, for within each ethnicity there are many differences. Generations of immigration is one difference, but there are also differences in educational levels, English language proficiency, and the job skills needed to achieve success in our society. Early waves of immigration primarily included peasants, farmers, and factory workers, but this is no longer true. New immigrants from Asia, for example, fall into two very different socioeconomic groups: those with education and technical skills and a knowledge of English, who arrive in the United States and immediately find a position in society that is relatively high, and those who arrive with no English language fluency and few skills that can be used in U.S. society (Lum 2004, 2). This "split" is one of the important features of new waves of immigration today.

"Special" Groups

It is important to recognize that two groups have had a special status that affects their place in the social structure. African-Americans who were brought to this country as slaves did not "choose" to immigrate, and did not have the opportunity to rise within the social structure through education and training available to many other groups. Oppressed, often poor, and historically facing severe discrimination, the African-American community does not fit comfortably into the models used for thinking about social structure in the United States. It is only with the Civil Rights movement of the 1960s that this group has been able to take its rightful place in our social structure and to have the educational and employment opportunities that our nation offers (Lum 2004, 27–29). However, it is important to be aware as a professional that both history and continuing experiences with oppression and discrimination have a major effect on many African-American clients.

First Nations people were slaughtered in large numbers during the period of European expansion westward while additional large numbers succumbed to diseases formerly unknown and brought by the European settlers. They were confined on reservations, deprived of rights and freedom, and forced to abandon their cultural practices. Children were sent to boarding schools whose mission was to eradicate any trace of Indian language and culture. While the government assumed a protectionist stance by providing medical care, education, and other social supports, it stripped Native Americans of land, tradition, and the ability to live as *First Nations People* in many parts of the United States. While these policies have been largely reversed, this history continues to have a powerful effect on members, who find that their choice is often to leave the reservation for urban centers where cultural traditions and practices are inaccessible, or to stay on the reservation in often poor housing, jobs, and other conditions. It is especially important to be aware of these issues in working with Native Americans, for the effects of the government's oppressive policies have left deep scars. (Lum 2004, 24–27).

Ironically, the government's system for determining membership in these two groups differs; the differences clearly underscore government policies. Membership in the African-American group has traditionally been based on the "one drop" rule: if you had one drop of African-American blood, you were an African-American and, in years past, thus deprived of many social benefits associated with being an American (Davis 2003, 38–45).

Conversely, membership in the First Nation group is based on percentages. Generally, you needed to be at least 50 percent Native American to be considered a member of this protected group and to receive the federal government benefits associated with membership. In recent years, tribes have taken the right to determine tribal membership into their own councils and away from the federal government (Jaimes, M. A., "Federal Indian Identification Policy" In Rosenblum and Travis 2003, 60–64).

Both African-Americans and Native Americans continue to face a much higher level of oppression and prejudice than other groups in society, and this has a major impact on the way in which these two groups may perceive social workers. It is essential for all workers, whether members of either group or not, to explore cultural issues with these clients.

Another group became much more "special" after September 11, 2001. Immigrants from Middle Eastern countries and Arab-Americans face suspicion and harassment, are regularly profiled at airports and on highways, and are often viewed by both law enforcement and the general public as either potential terrorists or people who support terrorism. Muslim organizations undergo surveillance regarding funding, association with known terrorists, and relationship with Muslims in other countries. While community leaders speak out, individual members fear violence, especially when wearing outward signs of Muslim affiliation (Lum 2004, 335–336).

Invisible Affiliations, "Chosen" Affiliations

Some group affiliations, like race and gender, tend to be readily obvious (though not always so). Others may be much less visible. Sexual orientation, religious affiliation, some disabilities (such as learning disability, MS, or AIDS), ethnic group membership, and social class may be a bit less readily apparent to others. In these cases, individuals may choose to reveal their affiliation immediately, after a relationship of trust has been established, or never.

Having invisible affiliations is often a complex issue. Certainly, it exposes people to bias and prejudice that those with more obvious affiliations and identities may not encounter in our politically correct world. People with invisible affiliations must choose who, when, and under what circumstances certain information will be shared with others. Special issues include sharing with someone you are dating, friends, family members, employers, teachers, and colleagues. Social workers should always be aware that clients may identify with and have issues regarding affiliations that are not immediately obvious.

When there is a perceived conflict between affiliations, individuals are faced with a choice: they can retain both affiliations, or choose one or the other. People who are biracial often face these issues, as do people whose parents are of different religions. Often, choices are made pragmatically: you choose racial affiliation based on physical features, religious affiliation based on exposure, or no religious affiliation. However, it is important to recognize that each person who believes they must make such choices has issues and concerns that appear and reappear depending upon life circumstances.

Invisible affiliations and public identity become even more complex when there is a possible perceived danger, or discrimination, associated with sharing such an affiliation publicly. People who are gay, lesbian, bi-sexual, or transgendered may fear others' reactions and may be concerned for their personal safety under certain situations and in certain areas of the country. Violence, and even death, becomes a concern of the entire community, and cases such as that of 22-year-old Matthew Shepard who was tortured and beaten to death in 1998 (Matthew's Place) have a profound effect on the gay, lesbian, bisexual, and transgendered community.

One Person, Many Identities

Identities develop over the course of a lifespan. Some affiliations are understood early in childhood while others, such as professional, interest, political, disability, or religious affiliations may develop much later in life. Individuals may also retain or lose certain affiliations over the course of a lifetime. Identity is not only context-sensitive, chosen and ascribed, visible or invisible, and stable. Rather, identity is a complex, dynamic intersection whose locus is the individual.

You can try this yourself: On a sheet of paper, list all of your affiliations and group identities. After you have made your list, put them in order of their importance to you.

What can you understand about yourself from your list, and from the order in which you arranged it?

How would you explain the affiliations you have chosen for the top of your list?

Why are they important to you?

What has your experience been as a member of these groups?

Would you always arrange, or have arranged, your list the way you did today?

What impact do each of these affiliations have on your life goals and on your happiness?

(You can do this exercise with your clients as well—after you have engaged with them and if you think it is relevant to the reason they are coming for services!)

Your client, too, has within her/himself a complex and dynamic tangle of affiliations and identities that help define and shape who she/he is individually, help or hinder the achievement of goals, and affect self-esteem, opportunities, and place in society. All of these issues are an essential part of the person who comes to you for help with situations that are defined, understood, and addressed within the context of personal identity.

Summary

The ways in which we define ourselves, our personal identities, are very much related to our group memberships and affiliations. Acculturation theories suggest that we have moved from an assimilationist ideal (the melting pot) to a multicultural vision of social structure (the tossed salad) where each group maintains cultural identity and affiliation. Ethnic conflict theories explore the way in which groups compete for the goods of a society, and the effects of immigrant groups upon one another. While many cultural groups fit into these theoretical frameworks, there are notable exceptions for special groups: African-Americans who entered the United States as slaves, Native Americans who were slaughtered and confined, and, currently, Arab and Muslim-Americans who face special challenges in the post-9/11 environment.

While membership in some groups is immediately apparent, membership in others is often not visible. Invisible affiliations pose special challenges, and social workers should be especially sensitive to these.

Each individual is a member of a number of groups such as age groups, ethnic groups, ability groups, religious groups, sexual orientation groups, and social classes. Membership in multiple groups is a normal part of the way we view our identities. As we shall see in the next chapter, however, not all groups and affiliations are equal. Some groups are given preferential status, while others are discriminated against and oppressed, creating difficult problems for individual members. Oppression and discrimination create vulnerability, and social work's commitment to social justice demands that we intervene on behalf of vulnerable groups and meet needs with appropriate and culturally relevant services.

Vulnerability, Oppression, and Power

The social work profession has a strong professional commitment to social justice, and a special commitment to vulnerable populations. People may be vulnerable because of individual, unique, conditions in their lives; however, many people are vulnerable simply because of their membership in, or association with, certain groups in our society that are devalued and often discriminated against and oppressed. In order to be able to offer competent professional services, it is important to recognize that discrimination and oppression have a major impact on individuals, groups, and communities.

As we have seen in the previous section, our multicultural society is composed of many different groups and subgroups, each of which carries a particular status and occupies a specific place in society. Differences such as race, gender, immigration status, sexual orientation, nationality, ethnicity, ability, social class, and others create persistent inequalities among people. The best efforts at "assimilation" may still force Jewish-Americans and Muslim-Americans to use vacation days if they want to celebrate religious holidays. Mexican-Americans living in large ethnic communities á la tossed salad in Los Angeles may find that they do not have the same access to advancement as other, English-speaking groups. New immigrants from Cambodia may study and work desperately hard, but their children may still experience discrimination and exclusion. Little Havana in Florida, another tossed salad ingredient, may be a "safe" enclave, but residents may experience higher-than-normal rates of violence near its borders. Gay and lesbian couples may be white, and Protestant, and English-speaking, but still be denied the same legal partnership rights as heterosexual couples. African-Americans may be middle-class, college educated, and fourth generation Americans, but are still profiled and followed in department stores. Children living in poverty are less healthy, receive a poorer education, and have less adult after-school supervision than children in middle-class families.

Inequalities based on perceived differences seem to persist in our society despite many legal, ethical, and social efforts to eliminate them. They persist despite the myth of a free, equal, and classless society where everyone is treated the same and everyone has the same opportunities for attaining the goods of the society. They persist for generations in subtle and not-so-subtle ways.

How do these inequalities affect groups and the individuals affiliated with them? Discrimination, prejudice, and bias affect everyone in our society. Membership in certain groups in society carries a stigma of which both members and nonmembers are aware. This stigma is *constructed*: that is, it is defined and used by the society in which it exists to create differences among and between members of that society. Differences that are stigmatized also often carry labels, and are vulnerable to stereotyping. The resultant oppression, powerlessness, and lack of entitlement experienced by stigmatized groups have a pervasive negative effect on group members.

Oppression

Marilyn Frye described oppression in a way that gives it immediacy and a context to which we can all relate:

> The root of the word oppression is the element "press." *The press of the crowd, pressed into military service, to press a pair of pants, printing press, press the button* (Italics hers). Presses are used to mold things or flatten them or reduce them in bulk, sometimes to reduce them by squeezing out the gasses or liquids in them. Something pressed is something caught between or among forces and barriers which are so related to each other that jointly they restrain, restrict, or prevent the thing's motion or mobility. Mold. Immobilize. Reduce. (1983)

How does oppression happen?

> Oppression occurs when a segment of the population, systematically and over a period of time, prevents another segment from attaining access to scarce and valued resources. Oppression is a process whereby specific acts are designed to place others in the lower ranks of society. . . . (Lum 1999, 55)

Individuals and groups are oppressed by other individuals, institutions, and the structures of society as a whole. On an individual level, oppression includes racist remarks, exclusion, stereotyping, and other behaviors. Institutional oppression limits accessibility by not providing materials and services in appropriate languages, physical conditions, or locations. Structural oppression includes the norms, habits, and world views of society as a whole, which create and support a system that privileges some groups and stigmatizes others. Oppression creates conditions of exploitation, powerlessness, and marginalization for stigmatized groups—conditions that foster violence both against and within such groups.

External violence is directed at members of certain groups by those with more power and prestige within society. It can take a physical form but also includes the denial of equal rights and access to opportunities and goods. Members of a group that is subjected to these kinds of violent experiences internalize not only the criticism and negative stereotypes placed upon them by other groups, but also the deep and persistent anger these elicit. Powerless and unable, in many cases, to fight back, members of oppressed groups express their anger through violence and destruction toward members of their own community, and, frequently, through violence and destruction of self through drugs and alcohol and other risk-taking behaviors. Such reactions encourage further stereotyping and oppression.

The experience of oppression becomes a part of the history of a group, and the effects of these experiences can persist for many generations. Even if a particular individual has not experienced oppression directly, she/he is still strongly affected by such a history, which can negatively impact self-perception and self-esteem. A history of extreme oppression, such as slavery, internment, genocide, or torture has a major impact on individual beliefs and worldviews. If the oppression persists, the effects can be cumulative and even more destructive.

Because social workers often work with members of oppressed populations, it is vital to understand in depth the effect of oppression on individuals and communities. Franz Fanon has done much of the seminal work on the subject of oppression. Bulhan's work, *Franz Fanon and the Psychology of Oppression*, will provide the reader a more in-depth exploration of this essential subject (1985). Fanon and others who followed in his footsteps explored the mechanism of oppression and the way it operates and also have attempted to define some effective strategies to cope with the destructive effects of oppression on people.

An individual client may have experienced personal, structural, and institutional oppression, and may have internalized the oppression in ways that limit choices, actions, and opportunities. It is essential to recognize the strengths that have made survival possible for the client, to build on these, and to expand choices and opportunities. The strengths perspective is especially useful in working with oppressed clients, and an ecological framework can also assist client and worker to understand the effect of the client's milieu and life experiences.

Power

In *Understanding Race, Ethnicity, and Power: The Key to Efficacy in Clinical Practice*, Elaine Pinderhughes states:

> Power may be defined as the capacity to produce desired effects on others. . . .
>   It involves the capacity to influence, for one's own benefit, the forces that affect one's life. (1989, 109–110)

Powerlessness is the reverse—thus, the *inability* to achieve such benefits for oneself. Powerlessness is a very painful condition—there is a sense in which one has no control over one's life. We experience the effects of power and powerlessness from our earliest days: as toddlers and young children, we were relatively powerless within our family structures. In school groups, we learned that power could be wielded not only by teachers, but by classmates and friends as well. Power differentials create an awareness of dominance and subjugation of one individual, group, or population over another.

There is also a power that we exercise over ourselves. Competence, achievement, and success are kinds of power and also evidences of the exercise of power in support of personal goals. The ability to focus on our studies, to control our behavior or reactions—these are internalized forms of power. The way in which we exercise power over ourselves and over others is an essential ingredient of self-esteem, of a positive self-image. However, individuals do not always have the same access to power, either over themselves or over others.

The power structure of society affects every individual member. In the United States, power is generally concentrated in the hands of a relatively small group of people: generally white, male, moneyed, middle-aged, and from old and powerful families. This small group dominates politics and the economy, and thus the lives of millions. One of the special "powers" of this small group is the determination of who will be able to move upward in society, and who will remain in the relatively powerless groups. It is also in the interest of this group to maintain the "myth" of equality and classlessness in our society, for the status quo is more easily maintained if the population has the illusion that, through hard work and effort, they too can achieve a powerful position. Though some people pull really hard to "lift themselves up by their bootstraps" all they do is break the bootstraps—access to higher status remains an unrealized ideal.

People who come for social services often experience a power differential between themselves and the social worker, who, simply by being a social worker, is presumed to be educated and middle class, and thus a member of at least two dominant groups. Social workers also have the "power" to provide or deny services, and, in many settings such as child welfare, adjudication, and mental health, often have "power" over major portions of clients' lives. Both the empowerment and the strengths perspective will assist workers to address power issues within the context of the client/worker relationship.

Entitlement and Marks

Rosenblum and Travis (2003, 183) suggest that privileged groups differ from others in at least two significant ways, *entitlement* and *marks*. Entitlement, they state, is:

> The belief that one has the right to be respected, acknowledged, protected and rewarded, and that this right to entitlement is taken for granted by those whose status in society gives it to them. (2003, 183)

Marked and unmarked statuses also confer privilege and stigma. In the examples Rosenblum and Travis use, the word doctor is unmarked. When used as an unmarked descriptor, the reference points in our minds conjure up an image of a white, male doctor. We presume white and male without being told, just through the use of the word doctor. If instead we are referring to a woman, we say woman doctor. If we are referring to a Chinese physician, we say Chinese doctor.

The additional descriptors are marks that distinguish the person being described from the people who are automatically assumed to be in that group. When a word is used without a mark, the underlying assumption is that the person referred to has a *right* to that classification—that she/he is eminently qualified to be a doctor, or a captain of a ship, or a senator, or the coach of a major league baseball team, or a judge, or the CEO of a bank. It also means that the preponderance of people in that grouping share the same privileged status.

For the next few days, listen carefully to the conversations around you, to people in the mass media, and even to yourself. Use of entitlement and marked categories is pervasive, and you will find yourself noticing and acknowledging the implications this holds for groups of people in our society.

People whose groups are both entitled and unmarked share a special *master* status (Rosenblum and Travis 2003, 187). White and male are two important master statuses in our society. These are easily recognized and acknowledged because they are physically obvious. Other statuses, such as sexual orientation, some class differences, and some disabilities may be much less obvious. Each grouping is subdivided again and again until we have sufficient descriptors: African-American, female, lesbian, doctor from Alabama, who is elderly, and has Parkinson's disease calls forth a very different image than the simple word doctor might elicit.

We have considered how some of the differences among and between people are visible, while others are invisible. Given the stigmas attached to some of these groups, it is important to understand the meaning of the choices to reveal or not to reveal membership in certain groups. Having a mark, and keeping it invisible, may be referred to as "passing." In some situations, people may "pass" inadvertently— that is, without conscious choice and decision on their parts. In other situations, a definite, conscious choice may be made. There are many positive and negative implications to "passing" that we need to consider when working with clients.

There are many stigmatized categories where "passing" is much less of a possible choice, and where one's membership in a stigmatized group is obvious and/or assumed. Such membership affects both an individual's interactions with others and her/his feeling about self. When people see themselves as they believe others see them, they internalize supposed harsh judgements and become overly self-critical. They may also feel that they are being watched, or on display, due to the visible marks they carry (2003, 191).

It is also important to recognize that not all marks are the same: some marks carry a greater loss of entitlement, a greater stigma, than others. Race is often considered to be the strongest mark a person can carry, followed by gender. These marks are generally quite obvious, and so easy to use in creating groupings. However, there are also differences *within* groups that impact the way in which individuals are considered.

Within the mark of disability, for example, there are huge differences in the ways in which disabilities are considered. If the condition is perceived to have been caused by some error or personal fault, the mark is greater, the stigma more powerful. AIDS and mental illness are two examples of this high degree of stigma: AIDS—because some people feel that it is caused by willful, immoral behavior; mental illness—because it is often viewed as a personal weakness of will. Other disabilities, such as rheumatoid arthritis, polio, or multiple sclerosis do not carry the same negative connotations. People of color are often stigmatized more strongly according to skin tone: there is more of a mark and more of a stigma when the skin tone is darker than when it is light. And within the community of differing sexual orientations, the mark of being transgendered is much deeper than the mark of being gay.

Summary

Understanding the way in which oppression and power affect both individuals and groups in society is an essential element in diversity competent social work practice. Members of vulnerable populations generally lack power and a sense of entitlement, and experience discrimination, bias, and oppression. These affect self-image and self-esteem, and can be an important factor in the development of the client-worker relationship. In the next chapter, we will consider some frameworks and models that are useful in understanding the experiences of clients and define some of the skills that are essential to competent practice.

CHAPTER

4

Practice Frameworks for Diversity Competence

Before engaging with clients in cross-cultural practice, it is essential that the social worker have some theoretical knowledge of practice frameworks and diversity frameworks as well as some knowledge of history and group experiences, as they relate to the populations with whom she or he is working. It is impossible to become an expert on all cultures. Facile, brief descriptions of cultural differences in diversity textbooks may encourage the worker to seek further knowledge, or give her/him a very false sense of mastery over cultural differences. Effective and accurate communication, and culturally congruent and competent skills at every phase of the social work process are also essential to good practice.

In this section, we will be exploring several helpful and commonly used practice and diversity competent frameworks, as well as suggesting the kinds of population-specific knowledge that will be helpful. You may find that you will be blending elements of several of these frameworks with historical and experiential knowledge in working effectively with clients.

Fong and Furuto echo the general stance of the profession toward the integration of culturally sensitive models of practice into traditional social work frameworks:

> It is important that social workers, operating from an empowerment, strengths, and ecological framework, provide services, conduct assessments, and implement interventions that are reflective of the clients' cultural values and norms, congruent with their natural help-seeking behaviors, and inclusive of existing indigenous solutions. (2001, 1).

It is not the intention here to provide an in-depth presentation of these social work practice and diversity frameworks, but only to include them so that the reader may review and have these models at hand throughout the reading of this book.

In addition to theoretical frameworks, it is also essential for the social worker to have a working knowledge of the population with whom she/he is working. This helps to ensure effective and accurate communication, and an essential part of the recognition of cultural difference is an acknowledgment by the worker that she/he has made an effort to learn about the culture. While not proclaiming oneself an expert, indicating a certain familiarity with a client's culture will help the client understand that the worker is truly interested—interested enough to have made the effort to learn something about the client's cultural milieu. The worker can continue to build culture-specific knowledge through an ethnographic interviewing process so that an understanding of the client's needs is always viewed within an appropriate cultural context.

By blending practice frameworks and diversity frameworks, using the insights gained through the acquisition of knowledge about a population, and ensuring accurate communication, workers develop culturally competent skills for all phases of the social work processes. These are, of course, always rendered within the standards set by the NASW Code of Ethics as well.

General Practice Frameworks

Several general practice frameworks appear to work especially well in cross-cultural practice. Three of these are presented briefly in outline below. It is suggested that the reader refer to a practice textbook for fuller and more in-depth explication of these concepts.

Ecological (Person-in-Environment) Perspective

The ecological model builds upon the conceptual framework of ecology to understand the way in which individuals, families, groups, and communities interact with the larger environment in which they exist.

Germain (1980) states:

> The ecological perspective provides an adaptive, evolutionary view of human beings in constant interchange with all elements of their environment. Human beings change their physical and social environments and are changed by them through processes of continuous reciprocal adaptation. When it goes well, reciprocal adaptation supports the growth and development of people and elaborates the life-supporting qualities of the environment. (5)

According to this model, problems occur when the "fit" between the person and the environment is poor. Both individual and environment are affected, and social work change efforts are thus focused on improving and enhancing the "fit." This may be done through affecting change in the individual, in the environment, or in both.

The ecological model is especially helpful in understanding some of the issues and concerns of members of diverse populations whose members may experience a poor fit due to the oppressive nature of the interactions with the wider environment. It is important for the social worker to understand the cultural context and the effects of oppression in order to begin to focus change efforts appropriately.

Strengths Perspective

Building upon, supporting, and enhancing client strengths supports the commitment to the inherent dignity of every individual that is a core ethical value in the social work profession. Saleeby (2002, 13–17) defines several principles that guide social workers. These include:

1. the belief that every human being, family, group, and community has strengths that can be drawn upon in helping people resolve problems;
2. the idea that even painful and difficult experiences, such as abuse, illness, loss, and trauma can offer opportunities and challenges that enable

growth and problem-solving to occur through the use of internal and external strengths and resources;

3. an understanding that human beings are always in a process of growth and change and are not static—thus, it is not possible to know the upper limits of anyone's capacities;

4. an understanding that we help clients best when we collaborate with, rather than direct, them. Clients know their strengths and their goals best;

5. an understanding that sources of support and strength exist not only within clients, but also in their environment, and that these resources can be drawn upon to assist clients;

6. the understanding that the client's belief in the authenticity and genuineness of the worker's concern and care for the client is an essential ingredient in the helping process.

In order to support and draw upon the strengths of both client and community, it is essential to understand the cultural context. Cultures understand, interpret, give meaning, and respond to events and issues within distinctive cultural world views. A strengths assessment of both client and client's environment can be a valuable tool in both defining and understanding the nature of the problem or concern, and the culturally congruent resources available to address it.

Empowerment

In her foundational book, *Understanding Race, Ethnicity, and Power*, Elaine Pinderhughes defines and describes the way in which both the client and the worker experience power. Traditional social work clients often feel disempowered, and the power differential that is often inherent in the social worker/client relationship reinforces the client's sense of powerlessness, most especially in cross-cultural work (1989, 110). Pinderhughes notes that it is important that workers be aware of the way in which they use power in relationship with clients. Addressing the power differential in the client/worker relationship and assisting the client to develop new ways of responding both enhances the capacity of the professional relationship to help clients meet their goals and assists the client in dealing with power issues in the environment (1989, 174).

Empowerment also assists clients to feel valued, respected, and able to control and affect the course of their lives. Change efforts include both an educational and a political component so that clients may be assisted first, to understand the effects of oppression on themselves and their cultural group and second, to become active in community organizations that seek to change the oppressive societal patterns (1989, 194–195).

Culturally Competent Practice Models

Several models have evolved for the practice of culturally competent social work. Each model provides grounding in a methodology, a view of the world and of human nature, and specific methods by which cultural competence can be achieved.

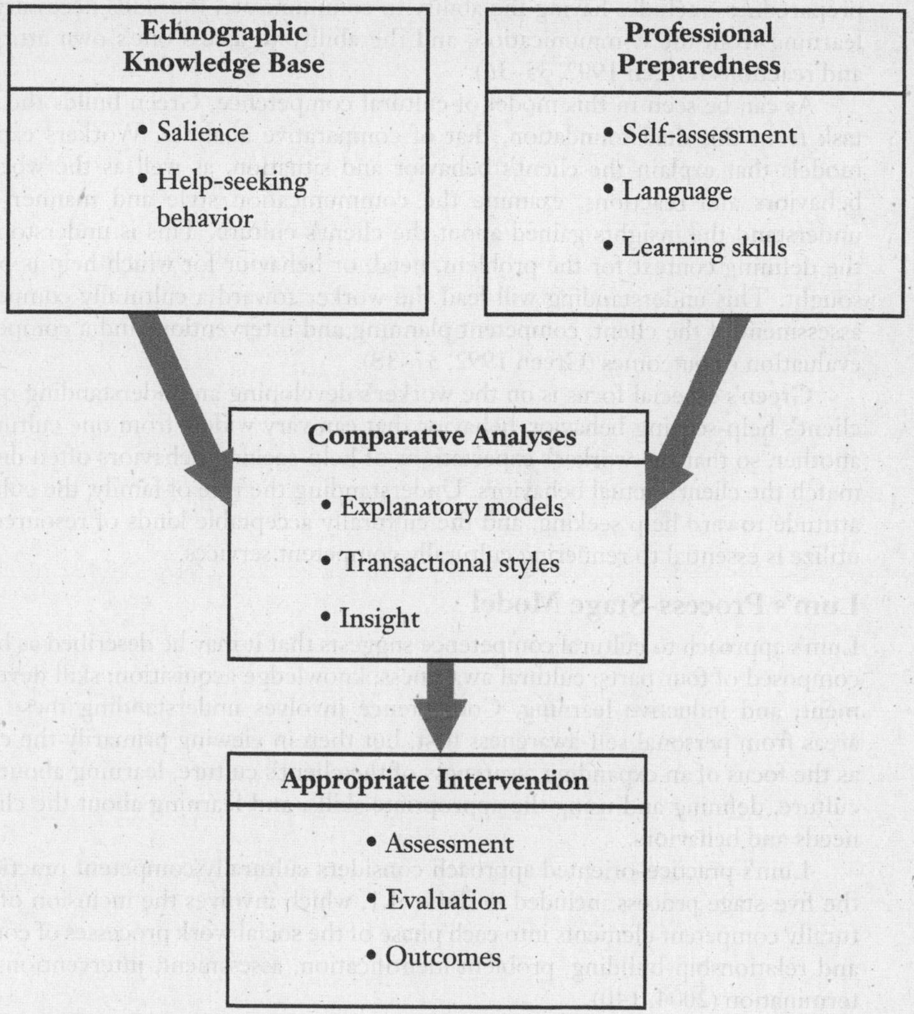

```
┌─────────────────────────┐      ┌─────────────────────────┐
│      Ethnographic       │      │      Professional       │
│     Knowledge Base      │      │      Preparedness       │
│                         │      │                         │
│   • Salience            │      │   • Self-assessment     │
│                         │      │                         │
│   • Help-seeking        │      │   • Language            │
│     behavior            │      │                         │
│                         │      │   • Learning skills     │
└─────────────────────────┘      └─────────────────────────┘
```

```
         ┌─────────────────────────────┐
         │    Comparative Analyses     │
         │                             │
         │   • Explanatory models      │
         │                             │
         │   • Transactional styles    │
         │                             │
         │   • Insight                 │
         └─────────────────────────────┘
```

```
         ┌─────────────────────────────┐
         │   Appropriate Intervention  │
         │                             │
         │   • Assessment              │
         │                             │
         │   • Evaluation              │
         │                             │
         │   • Outcomes                │
         └─────────────────────────────┘
```

FIGURE 4.1 Green's Cultural Competence Model

The models that have been selected for description here are generally accepted by the profession and are applicable to a wide variety of contexts and issues.

Green's Multiethnic Approach

Green suggests that we use an ethnographic knowledge base as a cornerstone of our work toward cultural competence. In order to work effectively in a culturally competent manner, he believes it is necessary to understand not only the important and relevant parts of the client's culture, but also the kinds of behaviors that constitute help-seeking in that particular culture. In addition to the cultural piece, Green places professional preparedness in a foundation role. Professional preparedness includes having the ability to communicate, the skills necessary for learning from the communication, and the ability to assess one's own attitudes and reactions (Green 1992, 35–36).

As can be seen in this model of cultural competence, Green builds the next task from this dual foundation, that of comparative analyses. Workers explore models that explain the client's behavior and situation, as well as the worker's behaviors and reactions, examine the communication style and manner, and understand the insights gained about the client's culture. This is understood as the defining context for the problem, need, or behavior for which help is being sought. This understanding will lead the worker toward a culturally competent assessment of the client, competent planning and intervention, and a competent evaluation of outcomes (Green 1992, 37–38).

Green's especial focus is on the worker's developing an understanding of the client's help-seeking behavior, behavior that can vary widely from one culture to another, so that the worker's expectations of help-seeking behaviors often do not match the client's actual behaviors. Understanding the role of family, the cultural attitude toward help seeking, and the culturally acceptable kinds of resources to utilize is essential to rendering culturally competent services.

Lum's Process-Stage Model

Lum's approach to cultural competence suggests that it may be described as being composed of four parts: cultural awareness; knowledge acquisition; skill development; and inductive learning. Competence involves understanding these four areas from personal self-awareness first, but then in viewing primarily the client as the focus of an expanding awareness of the client's culture, learning about that culture, defining and using the appropriate skills, and learning about the client's needs and behaviors.

Lum's practice-oriented approach considers culturally competent practice as the five-stage process included in Table 4.1, which involves the inclusion of culturally competent elements into each phase of the social work processes of contact and relationship-building, problem identification, assessment, intervention, and termination (2004, 140).

During the contact stage, Lum suggests that the experiences of racism and discrimination affect people as they initially approach the service system, creating mistrust and some shame. Exploring the client's cultural background and family history, including degree of acculturation, may serve both to empower the client and to provide valuable information. He suggests the worker's communication styles display interest, friendliness, and empathy, and that communication occur in a relaxed and comfortable manner (2004, 141–142).

Problem definition may involve the disclosure and description of multiple problems that the client is experiencing, including issues of poverty, unemployment, depression, loss of self-esteem, alcoholism, and child abuse. It is important to place these within the context of the client's reality, and to select an appropriate problem to serve as the primary focus of the work (Lum 2004, 143–144). The third stage, assessment, focuses in more depth upon the problem that has been determined in the previous stage. Client-environmental interactions are vital components of this assessment stage, as well as an exploration of the cultural limitations and resources that can potentially impact upon the problem and its resolution. It is also important for the worker to understand the potential effects of racism and discrimination on the client's perception of the problem and on her/his ability to address it (2004, 145–146).

Interventions mobilize the client and/or elements in the client's environment on behalf of the client and the resolution of the problem. Extended family systems and social support networks can be brought into the intervention process. Interventions may assist in empowering the client and freeing her/him from some of the effects of discrimination, helping the client attain a sense of equality, and maintaining the cultural components that are essential (2004, 147). The termination process incorporates a measurement of change and progress through a process of affirming the positives that have occurred in the client's life as a result of the work (2004, 148).

The process-stage approach is summarized by Lum in the following table:

TABLE 4.1 Lum's Framework for Culturally Diverse Social Work Practice

Practice Process Stages	Client-System Practice Issues	Worker-System Practice Issues	Worker-Client Tasks
Contact	Resistance, communication barriers Personal and family background Ethnic-community identity	Delivery of services Understanding of the community Relationship protocols Professional self-disclosure Style of communication	Nurturing Understanding
Problem identification	Problem information Problem area disclosure Problem understanding	Problem orientation Problem levels Problem themes Problem area detailing	Learning Focusing
Assessment	Socioenvironmental impacts Psychoindividual reactions	Assessment dynamics Assessment evaluation	Interacting Evaluating
Intervention	Joint goals and agreement Joint intervention strategies (planning, selection, and implementation) Micro-/meso-/macrolevel interventions		Creating Changing
Termination	Destination, recital, completion Follow-up strategies		Achieving Resolving

Devore and Schlesinger's Ethnic-Sensitive Model

Devore and Schlesinger's model for ethnic-sensitive social work integrates cross-cultural skills, knowledge, and understanding within the broader framework of general social work practice, suggesting that ethnic sensitivity is one of a number of factors that are necessary in rendering professional services.

Several assumptions underlay the ethnic-sensitive approach to culturally competent social work practice. First of all, there is an assumption that both individual and collective history have an important part to play in the way problems are understood and solutions determined. There is an assumption that ethnicity has influenced the way in which every member of a group has formed her/his identity. There is an assumption that ethnicity can be both a source of strength, cohesion, and identity and a source of strife, discord, and strain. (1999, 139–140) An important final assumption for social work practice is that the present is most important, although it is often shaped by past events and experiences (1999, 143).

Devore and Schlesinger's model, grounded in these assumptions, illustrates "layers" of understanding that contribute to ethnic-sensitive practice as shown in Figure 4.2. Each layer constitutes an essential professional area of knowledge and sensitivity, and these layers apply to competent professional practice with all clients at all times, so that the model is generalizable to any practice setting, population, and need. At the core is knowledge of, and practice within, the NASW standards for ethical practice, followed by knowledge of human behavior, an essential ingredient of competent professional practice. The third layer, agency policy, is a strong determinant of the kinds of services that the worker can provide, and the circumstances under which they can be provided. The fourth, self-awareness, is an ongoing essential ingredient, as it relates to the way in which the social worker understands, relates to, and addresses the issues that are of concern to clients.

An essential layer in providing an ethnic-sensitive practice is the focus upon the client's ethnic reality—a simultaneous focus upon both the problems of the individual and the institutional context within which these occur. Poverty, racism, discrimination, and oppression impact the client's ability to cope with stressors and access resources. Professional responsibility requires that the social worker respond both to the client's individual problems and, through activism, social action, and advocacy, the institutional ones as well (1999, 167).

How do we understand individuals in communities, so that we may respond with sensitivity? In order to be most effective, the social worker may lay the groundwork before the initial encounter with the client, by learning about the community, and some of the customs, practices, values, and world view of that community. Understanding the ethnic reality will help the worker adapt her/his interaction in a way that maximizes opportunity and empowerment for the client within the structure of the client's ethnic reality. By "tuning in" to the reality, the worker is better able to respond appropriately to the concerns the client is expressing. It is especially important for the worker to be sensitive to the client's ethnic reality in terms of the kinds of questions asked, the way in which the

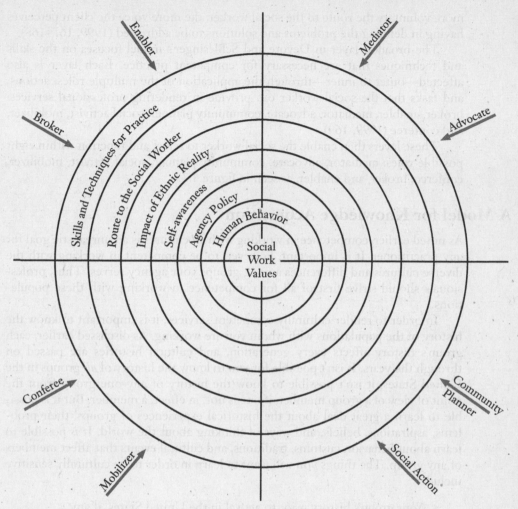

FIGURE 4.2 Devore and Schessinger's Paradigm for Ethnic-Sensitive Generalist Practice

worker responds to the client's sharing, the kinds of services offered, the way in which family and community are brought in to the process, if appropriate, and the client's role in the process of problem definition and resolution (1999, 167–168).

Another important area of competent practice, these authors feel, is to understand the route that the client has taken to reach the social worker for, as we are well aware, the route often affects the way that the problem is defined, the solutions proposed, and the kinds of interventions that are developed in order to attain the desired solutions. The routes are given especial attention because these often help to define the client-worker interaction, which can perhaps best be understood as somewhere between totally coercive and totally voluntary. The more voluntary the route to the social worker, the more voice the client perceives having in defining the problems and solutions to be addressed (1999, 167–168).

The broadest layer in Devore and Schlesinger's model focuses on the skills and techniques that are necessary for competent practice. Each layer is also affected—outer to inner—through the application of the multiple roles, actions, and tasks that the social worker can provide in rendering professional services: broker, enabler, mediator, advocate, community planner, social activist, mobilizer, and conferee (1999, 169)

These layers then enable the social worker to select and function within eight possible roles: mediator, advocate, community planner, social activist, mobilizer, conferee, broker, and enabler, as seen in figure 4.2.

A Model for Knowledge Acquisition

As noted earlier, competence in working with *all* cultures is an unrealistic goal for any practitioner. It is important, however, to be competent in working with the diverse cultures and differences among groups your agency serves. Thus, professionals should strive first of all for competence in working with these populations.

In order to render culturally competent services, it is important to know the history of the populations with whom you are working. As discussed earlier, each group's history affects every generation, and cultural histories are passed on through the years. It isn't possible for you to know the history of *all* groups in the United States; it isn't possible to know the history of any one group from the point of view of a group member, if one is not, in effect, a member. But it *is* possible to learn a great deal about the historical experiences of groups, their problems, aspirations, beliefs, and ways of thinking about the world. It *is* possible to learn about behavior, customs, traditions, and cultural events that affect members of any group. The things you will want to learn in order to be culturally sensitive include:

- Your group's history prior to arrival in the United States, if any
- Your group's experience with immigration and immigration policies
- Your group's experiences with acceptance/integration into the wider U.S. society
- Your group's experience with oppression, discrimination, bias, and prejudice
- Your group's relationship to the country of origin, if relevant, and the relationship of the United States to that country
- Your group's world view and beliefs about child rearing, family relationships, dating and marriage, employment, education, recreation, health and illness, aging, death and bereavement, and other life cycle events
- Your group's relationship with the broader U.S. society
- Intra-group variations and differences
- Roles of the different generations within your population

There are a number of sources to explore for these insights:

A history book

Biographics and autobiographies of members of your group that describe the experience

Films and documentaries that feature or include members of your group

The musical traditions and current music trends

Friends, colleagues, and others who are members of this group

Attendance at cultural or other events where members of your group may gather

Your clients who are members of your group

While understanding a group's history and experiences will enable you to understand some of the general factors that have affected the group, it is important *not* to assume that the experiences of any individual member of a group can be understood from the group's experience in general. It is easy to stereotype from general information. To avoid this, explore the experiences of as many different individuals within the group as possible. Each biography, each film, each conversation, each experience will help you understand the richness and variety of experiences of group members, and help to eliminate rather than develop stereotypes and stereotypical frameworks for thinking about members of the population.

Ensuring Effective and Accurate Communication

When working across cultures, it is not unusual for workers to encounter clients who are unable to communicate effectively in spoken English, either because it is not their native language or because they have a disability. It is essential to address communication needs immediately, for poor communication delays and inhibits relationship-building, leads to errors in understanding, and creates a stressful environment for clients who are already distressed.

If you find that you have difficulty communicating with a client, address this concern with the client directly and ask the client if she/he would like the services of an interpreter. There are several alternatives, each of which has positive and negative features:

1. the client may prefer to struggle with communication and comprehension to ensure privacy. This ensures confidentiality and helps build a relationship, but may result in misunderstanding and may slow the process of resolving the client's difficulties. Extra time will be required to ensure that you and the client understand each other clearly.

2. the client may choose to bring a family member or friend who is able to interpret. This enables the client to select someone who is in a position of trust and with whom they have an ongoing relationship. However, the client may feel uncomfortable raising certain issues in front of her/his friend or family member, and the worker may be uncertain about asking questions or sharing information that might be confidential. It is also possible for the interpreter to interject her/his own ideas or opin-

ions, or leave out or distort certain content without the worker or client's awareness.

3. the client may choose to utilize the services of a professional interpreter, usually arranged through the agency at no cost to the client. Professional interpreters are trained in interpersonal communication and are also bound to a professional ethical code, which includes privacy and confidentiality. Clients can share information with the assurance that it will be kept confidential and that the translation will accurately reflect their content. Some clients, however, may feel that their privacy is violated in having an "outsider" know their personal business.

Although verbal communication is the most obvious form, it is by no means the only, or even the most effective, form of communication. Nonverbal communication between client and worker often creates a subtle but essential link, providing both worker and client with direct insights into the other's thoughts and feelings. When we are working cross-culturally, the nonverbal messages that are routinely sent from worker to client and client to worker may easily be misunderstood and misinterpreted.

Eye contact is perhaps the clearest example of the kinds of difficulties that may occur. In Western cultures, direct eye contact is viewed as an expression of trust, honesty, attention, and interest. So essential is eye contact to communication that social workers are taught to notice when clients do not make eye contact and to consider the possible reasons for this avoidance. It is so essential that, although a blind social worker cannot see her client, she/he is encouraged to look in the direction of the client's voice and face, so that the kind of rapport that eye contact encourages is facilitated.

In many other cultures, including Asian cultures and some Islamic cultures, eye contact represents something completely different. Some cultures consider eye contact between a male and a female inappropriate; others consider direct eye contact a sign of lack of respect for differences in power, age, or other kinds of differences. In these cases, lack of eye contact is not a sign of dishonesty, but of respect and modesty.

Many other forms of nonverbal communication, such as leaning toward a client, patting a client's arm, or nodding frequently can be interpreted differently in different cultures. Learning some of the forms of appropriate nonverbal communication is essential in establishing positive relationships across cultures.

Summary

As we have seen, social workers draw on a variety of practice frameworks and models in order to provide culturally competent services to clients. The three general practice frameworks presented here are not necessarily exclusive of one another: effective practice combines a person-in-environment framework with a focus on supporting and engaging both client strengths and environmental strengths to meet needs. Developing and supporting strengths assists the client to feel empowered, able to make decisions, and to affect her/his own life, that of her/his family, and that of the community.

The models for cultural competence suggest that in the process of using these practice frameworks, we integrate the cultural component as well. The "environment" part of person-in-environment is never culture-free—and neither is the "person." Understanding the role of culture in defining values, accepted behavioral norms, available resources, appropriate interventions, and measures of success and failure is crucial in the development of a plan of action that is realistic and desirable to the client.

Effectively integrating the cultural component requires the social worker have some knowledge of the client's culture. While both you and your client recognize the limitations of your knowledge, and that you cannot have experienced your client's culture in the same way that she/he has, familiarity helps build trust and sends the message that you are a person of good will who cares about her/him and has made the effort to learn something about her/his world. Effective, culturally sensitive communication, both verbal and nonverbal, is an essential ingredient of culturally competent practice.

The Skills of Culturally Competent Practice

Practice skills involve applying the knowledge base you have obtained to specific clients in a culturally sensitive manner. Cultural competence guides the worker in each step of the social work processes. These steps are presented here in general terms only, for it is essential to apply your knowledge of the group with whom you are working and adapt processes in a culturally sensitive manner.

Engagement, Trust, and Relationship-Building

It is best to "do your homework" before initiating a cross-cultural contact. There are many cultural differences that need to be considered, and that will vary between and among groups. Some of these include:

1. manner in which contact is initiated—and with whom. In some cultures, it is important to consider the family hierarchy and structure in deciding with whom contact should be initiated.
2. persons to be included in interview. Certain cultures may have strong taboos against male workers working with female clients alone, or with pregnant women making decisions without a spouse present, or with parents not being present when children are interviewed, or with ill clients making decisions without family input.
3. formality and form of address. Americans tend to be casual and informal in social relationships, but, in many cultures, this is seen as disrespectful and inappropriate.
4. eye contact. We tend to use eye contact as a measure of relationship and to demonstrate attention, interest, and empathy, and think of its avoidance as a withdrawal and a refusal to engage. Eye contact means different things in different cultures: in some, it is a sign of disrespect, in others, it is considered aggressive. When a client does not make eye contact, it is important not to assume that this indicates a lack of interest or connection.
5. physical distance. The physical distance between a client and a worker is also culturally variable. In some cultures, the distance appears to be farther, while in others it is closer, than our usual habit. It is important to take your cues from your client—if a client seems to back away from you, it may mean that more distance is needed.

6. physical contact—such as handshaking or patting an arm. Norms for physical contact also vary between cultures. In some, a pat on the arm or on the shoulder indicates empathy, care, and concern. In others, it is an intrusion. There are also differences between genders in different cultures regarding what is acceptable. Handshakes may be acceptable in some cultures, while in others bowing or nodding is the acceptable form of greeting.

People who are members of diverse cultural groups, many of whom have a history of oppression and discrimination, are especially vulnerable during initial contacts. There is a presumption that the social worker has power and expertise, while the client feels powerless and vulnerable. For this reason, it is important to immediately demonstrate respect and consideration for clients. It is generally best (unless you are working with children or adolescents, or unless your client tells you otherwise) to use formal titles in addressing new clients.

Clients may also be very sensitive to issues of privacy and confidentiality: there is a shame associated with asking for help in many cultures, which creates an additional need to ensure privacy. Other clients prefer the sense of security and safety that comes from having other people in the area in which the interview is being held.

Asking for help is viewed differently in different cultures and situations. In some cultures, it is considered not only shameful but also a violation of family tradition to turn outside of the immediate family for help. There may also be an expectation that families take care of their members, and that going for help immediately implies some failure of the family structure. In other cultures, there are strong taboos against sharing personal information with an "outsider." For all vulnerable clients, asking for help can further decrease self-esteem and self-respect, and increase the feeling of powerlessness. When the route to the social worker is not voluntary, as Devore and Schlesinger note, these feelings may impact the client-worker relationship (104–105).

In some cultures, the imbalance in the relationship created by one party giving help, and the other taking help, creates a sense of discomfort and a need to adjust this situation. Clients may bring gifts to the worker as a concrete symbol of appreciation, and also to lessen the sense of indebtedness. Refusing such gifts may be culturally offensive; accepting them is often contrary to agency policy. It is sometimes possible to accept the gift "in the name of the whole agency"—but in any case it is helpful to discuss this issue with a supervisor.

As noted above, one of the important sources of information about the client's culture is the client. Ethnographic interviewing is the process through which a worker can learn about the client's culture from the client's perspective. The worker asks the client to be her/his cultural guide, to explain and explore the dimensions of the client's culture, which impact upon the problem in the eyes of the client. Leigh notes that "the expert on the construction of meanings of any culture is a member of that culture, not a social worker" (2002, 12). In addition to the obvious benefits of learning about the client's culture from the client's perspective, ethnographic interviewing also empowers the client by acknowledging her/him as the expert in this area.

> Ethnographic interviewing is a method of cultural discovery that requires the social worker to move beyond professionally bound methods of conversation with those who request assistance in solving personal or social-generated problems. The person being interviewed becomes the social worker's cultural guide, and this notion has impact on the professional relationship. In some aspects the person is a teacher guiding the social worker as a student through the intricacies of the contrasting culture. The social worker has to become a skilled listener. (2002, 12)

Assessment

Consonant with social work philosophy and frameworks, assessments can be more productive and beneficial if they are performed in the language of "strengths" and "needs" rather than in the language of "problems" and "deficits." The former is a strong tool for empowering the client, for strengths speak to positive abilities and qualities and focus on these rather on the negatives associated with powerlessness to resolve "problems."

Individual assessments should include the way in which the client is situated relative to culture, ethnicity, religion, and other group affiliations. Positive affiliations provide support and nurturance, and enhance self-esteem. Clients may also be able to utilize their cultural affiliations as resources in addressing their needs in a culturally relevant manner.

Environmental assessments include the positive assets of the populations, strengths that can include resilience, cohesiveness, mutual support giving, social networks, language and educational resources, community activities, etc. It is also important to recognize that a group's history and experience with oppression, exclusion, and prejudice negatively impact groups and communities, limiting the resources and fracturing the community in the efforts of individual members to survive. Eco-maps can be important assessment tools cross-culturally as well: these define relationships with individuals and community institutions which can assist in understanding the cultural milieu.

In understanding the experience of the individual in the context of immigration, Lum's "culturagram" can provide helpful information by focusing on the experience, the access to community resources, and the support network of the family or individual. In addition to the categories Lum defines in Figure 5.1, another piece of information can be helpful: understanding the current political relationship between the country of origin and the United States. People whose nationality of origin is a country with whom the United States has strained relations may have very different, and more difficult, experiences socially as well as in relation to government agencies and services.

Traditional biopsychosocialspiritual models of assessment focus on considering the person, family, group, or community holistically by addressing four separate though overlapping spheres in-depth to provide a multidimensional view of the client(s). However, when working with immigrant families of any generation,

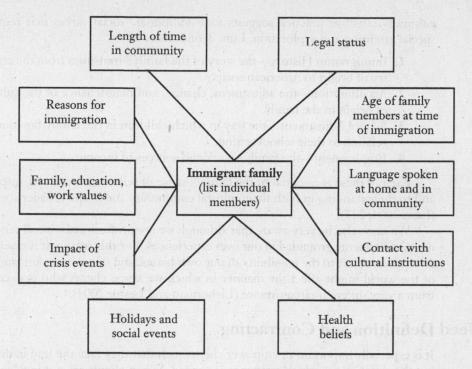

1. **Reasons for immigration**—why immigrants leave their country of origin
2. **Length of time in the community**—provides information on the degree of adherence to the original cultural beliefs and acculturation
3. **Legal or undocumented status**—legal immigration, student or work permits, secret arrival, remaining in this country after the expiration of visas
4. **Age of family members at time of immigration**—provides information on the degree of individual acculturation (e.g., learning the new language) and family conflict caused by the rate of acculturation
5. **Spoken language**—native language, English, or bilingual ability
6. **Contact with cultural institutions** (ethnic churches, schools, social clubs)—provides information on cultural identity
7. **Health beliefs**—native attitudes of health, illness, and treatment that differ from those of American medical practice

8. **Holidays and special events**—religious and life cycle transitional events (birth, marriage, death)
9. **Crisis events or stressors**—losing a job, death of a grandparent, rape, relocation to a different country or geographic area
10. **Family, education, and work values**—provides information on family patterns of support, education, and career selection

The completion of a culturagram reveals important differences among family members in terms of acculturation and family functioning. As a result, family stress and conflict areas are identifies.

The following questions might be asked in completing the culturagram:

1. What brought you to the United States? Why did you decide to leave your country of origin?
2. How long have you lived in the United States—particularly in this community?

FIGURE 5.1   Culturagram

culturally sensitive practice suggests four additional "social" areas that require special attention and exploration. Lum defines these as:

1. Immigration History—the story of the family's transition from the country of origin to American society.
2. Acculturation—the adjustment, change, and maintenance of the culture of origin in the family.
3. School Adjustment—the way in which children in the family function in relation to their school setting.
4. Employment—the family's work and sources of income.

Each of these is essential to the family's sense of self-esteem and self-respect, and to their standing in both their cultural community and in the broader society (Lum 2004, 227).

We must also be very aware that although we are professionals, we all tend to make assessments grounded in our own experiences. For this reason, it is essential to be always alert to the possibility of our own biases, and our own understanding of the world might affect the manner in which we assess clients who may come from a very different circumstance (Lieberman and Lester 2004).

Need Definition and Contracting

It is especially important to empower clients such that they take the lead in defining the situation for which assistance is needed. When clients are not involved in this determination, the entire process of assessment and intervention may not be relevant, and thus will more likely fail. Clients will define problems in cultural terms: if the worker is familiar with the culture, it will be easy to recognize and assimilate these cultural components into planning. Workers can use the material obtained in ethnographic interviews to assist them in couching the problem in a manner that is culturally congruent for the client, and in developing a contract that supports the values and norms of the client's culture as well as those of the wider society (Lieberman and Lester 2004, 60).

Intervention

If the social worker and client have worked together and defined needs and goals, and grounded these in a culturally congruent manner, if together they have explored the resources and strengths of the client and the cultural milieu, the development of culturally appropriate interventions will proceed naturally. It is important to recognize, however, that "culturally appropriate" is not a static term: clients differ in their levels of acculturation, their motivation toward or away from cultural ties, and the specific form that their relationship with their culture assumes. Thus, the client must define culturally appropriate interventions, rather than the worker impose outsider knowledge of norms and cultural expectations. The worker's knowledge and skills, and awareness of the client's culture, may serve to guide and inform, but not in itself to determine, culturally appropriate interventions to meet the client's needs.

Evaluation and Termination

Success or failure, and the reasons for either, should be understood from within the cultural context. The methods used to evaluate interventions and outcome may be defined differently in different cultures. Standards of measurement, degrees of flexibility, and values attributed to specific accomplishments are all culturally determined.

Similarly, clients' approaches to termination, to ending the professional relationship, will vary culturally. Some clients may feel that the worker has become an integral part of their lives, and may attempt to redirect the relationship into a purely social one. Some may terminate abruptly, or be uncomfortable with discussions about termination. Others may want to thank the worker with gifts, dinners, or other acknowledgments. As in other aspects of cross-cultural work, it is important to consider the cultural meaning of each situation individually prior to responding.

Utilization of Cultural Resources

Culturally competent social work and the ecological perspective also demands that workers be aware of family and community resources that can be utilized to address the client's needs and concerns. Family support networks are often very powerful in other cultures, and extend not only to blood kin but also to close family friends who are considered integral members of the family. Family members as resources should be considered during the assessment process, and may have a direct role in interventions. In certain cases and cultures, family members may have been a part of the social work process throughout the client's contacts. Using eco-maps can assist the worker to understand the nature of family relationship and to identify potential resources.

The degree of connection clients feel toward their cultural community should also be a part of the assessment process. Where many members of a group live in close proximity, there are often excellent community support networks available to assist community members. It is important to ensure that your client desires to utilize these resources; depending upon the nature of the need, the relationship of the individual and family to the community, and the relevant available resources, referrals to community networks and services may or may not be appropriate for the client at any given time. As the work progresses, however, these circumstances could change, and it is important for the worker to reserve these for potential future referral. Where identification and connection to a group are more tenuous and uncertain, the worker and client may explore cultural community resources and determine whether these would be appropriate and desirable.

Advocacy

Clients from diverse cultures, as noted earlier, often have experienced oppression, bias, exclusion, and discrimination, which has left them with a feeling of powerlessness. Individuals are not alone in this regard: whole communities and populations often feel disenfranchised and marginalized due to their diversity in our society. It is important to recognize that these conditions affect individuals on many levels, and that the goal of empowerment is vital to communities as well as to individual clients.

In our professional roles, social workers both advocate for clients and assist clients to empower themselves and their community members to advocate for change and for social justice.

Summary

The traditional general practice frameworks—the ecological, strengths, and empowerment perspectives—are especially applicable and constructive in working across cultures, and can easily be adapted to any group. Within these, it is helpful to adopt a culturally sensitive practice model, or to use a combination of practice models to suit the individual client situation and need. The acquisition of knowledge about a population from a variety of sources will increase cultural competence and also decrease any tendency toward facile stereotyping. The acquisition of this knowledge is the individual worker's responsibility, and can enable a general orientation to the client's culture, which will facilitate the development of professional rapport. The wider the variety of sources of information, the richer and fuller will be the worker's understanding of both the culture in general and the variations of individual experiences within that general understanding.

Effective cross-cultural practice is essential at each step in the process: from engagement across cultures and understanding the cultural context of help-seeking to termination expectations, and gift-giving, cultural issues must guide and inform effective practice. Both general practice frameworks and frameworks for culturally competent practice should be utilized at every stage.

Cultural resources should always be considered as especially helpful if applicable to the client's situation, and can be explored as a part of the assessment process. Advocacy is often helpful as well especially when clients are members of oppressed groups.

Thus, effective practice involves the utilization of both practice and diversity frameworks, knowledge about the client's population, effective and accurate communication, the application of social work skills consonant with these, and the appropriate use of community resources and advocacy.

Effective cross-cultural practice involves not only clients and workers. The social service environment can support or hinder the individual practitioner's cultural competence in rendering service. The agency's community, the ambiance within its offices, and the cultural sensitivity of its programs and policies all have an important role to play, and understanding this role is essential to cultural competence. In the next chapter, we will present some of the major factors that determine the cultural competence of an agency and its programs and services.

CHAPTER

6

Cultural Competence in the Context of Practice

Much as we sometimes think our service universe is composed only of ourselves and our clients, in reality our agencies determine who becomes our client, the services we offer, and the conditions under which we offer them. Understanding the agency's culture and its environment renders culturally competent service possible. Both the agency's external environment (in terms of location and community, and linkages to other resources), its internal environment (in terms of receptivity, staffing, and other parameters), and its policy and programs all have a direct impact on the worker's provision of culturally sensitive and competent services.

The Agency Environment: The Community

The agency's community refers to the neighborhood in which the agency is located, and the broader institutional community of which it forms a part. Using the eco-systems perspective, the agency's environment consists of all the surrounding entities with which the agency interacts, or does not interact. These include other agencies and institutions, government systems, community groups, and individual community leaders and members. The agency's client base is often drawn from its surrounding neighborhood, although this is not always the case when an agency serves a specific and special population, group, or concern.

The broader area from which the agency's clients are drawn is called its catchment area. The agency's catchment area may be the city or town in which it is located, the country, the state, or even, in cases of federal agencies and programs, the nation as a whole. Within the catchment area, the agency provides a range of services to meet specific client needs.

It is important to explore both community and catchment area in order to understand the agency's target population and some of the important cultural dimensions of that population. Agencies may serve in specific catchment areas one special group: they may be located between two communities or neighborhoods, or may provide services that meet the needs of more than one group.

Exploring the Neighborhood

Perhaps the most simple method for learning about an agency's milieu is to take a walk or a drive around the blocks surrounding it. Note the location of supporting neighborhood institutions such as schools, hospitals, banks, police station, health clinics and clubs, public transportation, and government offices. It is helpful to explore shopping areas and shops as well. Do the foods and goods they carry reflect the surrounding population? Are there large shops, or a preponderance of mom-and-pop stores that offer less selection but more personal service? Does the neighborhood reflect the surrounding cultures through decor, posters and advertisements, and signage? Would a member of a group living in this community feel welcome in this neighborhood? Would the person feel as though it was *her/his* neighborhood, and that it reflected her/his values, interests, and activities? If a person were not a member of the neighborhood's groups, would she/he feel comfortable and accepted, ignored, or regarded with hostility? These latter considerations are important in understanding clients' experiences in getting to services, as well as their possible perceptions about the agency.

Community Mapping

Using a map of the agency's neighborhood and catchment area is a helpful way to further knowledge. Maps can be used to indicate the location of an agency and of all the neighborhood institutions and shopping areas. Using different colors to indicate different groupings, it might be possible to define the cultural groups in the area by outlining these on the map. Some clients might be able to access an agency without crossing any cultural boundaries, while others must cross one or more boundaries, and still others might need to use public transportation.

Community Profile

Another helpful tool in understanding an agency's external environment is the community profile. The profile explores history, geography, characteristics of the people who live in the community, and community resources. A clarification of community strengths is also important to understanding your agency's milieu. Devore and Schlesinger have developed an outline for gathering this helpful information that can be used as a guide.

Devore and Schlesinger's Community Profile

Identification

1. Name of community (e.g., "The North Ward," "Watts," etc.)
2. City (or township, borough, etc.)
3. County
4. State
5. Traditions and values

Local History

1. When settled
2. Changes in population
3. Major historical incidents leading to present-day development
4. Principal events in the life of the community, etc.
5. Traditions and values

Geography and Transportation

1. Location—is it located near any of the following?
   a. Principal highways
   b. Bus routes
   c. Truck routes
   d. Railroad routes
   e. Airports/air routes
   f. Rivers, oceans, lakes
2. Do any of the above facilitate/hamper residents' ability to get to work, major recreational centers, community services?

Population Characteristics

1. Total size of population
2. Breakdown by
   a. Age
   b. Sex
   c. Minority groups
   d. Other ethnic groups
   e. Religious affiliations
3. Educational level
   a. Median educational level for total adult population
   b. Median educational level for women
   c. Median educational level for each of the major ethnic and minority groups
4. Have there been major shifts in the population composition over the past five to ten years (e.g., in migration of minority groups, departure of sizable numbers of people in any one population group)?
   a. Are there any major urban renewal or other redevelopment efforts?

Employment and Income Characteristics

1. Employment status
   a. Major sources and types of employment for total adult population
   b. Major sources of employment for women
   c. Major sources of employment for each of the major ethnic and minority groups
2. Median income
3. Income characteristics below poverty level
4. Type of public welfare system (e.g., state, county jurisdictions; state involved in Medicaid program?)

Housing Characteristics

1. Prevailing housing type (apartments, private homes, mix)
2. Percentage of population owning, renting homes
3. Housing conditions (e.g., percentage characterized as "dilapidated" by the census)

Educational Facilities and Level

1. Types of schools available
2. Do the schools have bilingual programs?
3. Are minority and ethnic group members found in the members of staffs, school boards?
4. Are the schools aware of the particular problems and strengths of minority and ethnic group members?
5. Do the schools promote cultural awareness and sensitivity programs?

Health and Welfare Resources

1. Important resources available
   a. Health and medical (hospital, clinics, public health facilities, "folk healers")
   b. Recreational and leisure time facilities
   c. Social agencies
2. Are staff members bilingual where appropriate?
3. Is there adequate representation of minority/ethnic group members on the staffs of hospitals and social agencies?
4. Do these facilities develop cultural awareness and sensitivity programs?
5. What are the prevailing formal and informal community networks?
   a. "Swapping networks"
   b. Church-supported health and welfare groups
   c. Ethnic-based lodges, fraternities, benevolent societies
   d. Union-sponsored health and welfare facilities
   e. Self-help groups of people with special problems (e.g., alcoholics, the physically handicapped)

Special Problems and Strengths

1. What are the major social problems (e.g., prevalent health problems, housing, schools)?
2. Is there a particular concern with crime, delinquency, underemployment?
3. Are there particular intergroup tensions, efforts at intergroup coalition?

Evaluation

1. What do you consider are some of the major problems of this community?
2. Does this community have a positive identity, loyalty? Describe.
3. What are the major strengths and weaknesses of the health and welfare community?
4. What are the major gaps in services?

Strengths Perspective

In determining the strengths and possible needs of the surrounding community, it is also helpful to use the Strengths perspective, as outlined on p. 31–32. This can easily be applied to communities and population groups as well as to individuals.

Discussion with Supervisor and Colleagues

In addition to exploring, mapping, and profiling an agency's community, it is also helpful to share impressions with other professionals for additional insights and information.

The Agency Environment: Cultural Factors

Route of Access

Consideration should be given as to the route of access of clients to agency services. Is there convenient public transportation? Is there a way for people who are disabled or frail to reach the agency for service? Is the agency located near other health and social services, so that clients can move easily from one to the other? If clients must cross cultural boundaries to reach the agency, how can the effect of this be understood and discussed? Often, the relationship between the client's group affiliation and the groups through which the client must pass will impact their relationship to the agency and its services. If the agency is located in one community, do members of other groups feel alienated from it? How can the agency address this issue?

Public Areas

The agency's decor and waiting room atmosphere should be culturally congruent to the population it serves. Colors, wall hangings, and furniture styles can be welcoming by mirroring clients' culture and activities, or alien and off-putting. Because the waiting room is the client's first exposure to the agency and its services, it is important to consider its effects.

Brochures, fact sheets, and information packets should similarly reflect the culture of the agency clients and be in a form that is accessible to them the information contained. This may mean having material available in a number of languages, or on tape, or in Braille.

Staffing Patterns

Diversity in staffing is an essential part of culturally competent agency services. In some agencies, the professional staff tends to be predominantly from one group, usually the group that is dominant in society, and the nonprofessional staff tends to better reflect the community from which the client base is drawn. This can send a message to the client: I, and people who look like me, can only have secondary positions in this place. This message may negatively impact client/worker relationships. Some agencies do not have any staff members who reflect the agency's population, and here the problems can be even more severe. If the agency's population is primarily immigrants, or speaks another language, it is essential to have both professional and nonprofessional staff who reflect those languages and cultures. If an interpreter is needed, someone from within the agency will be more readily acceptable than someone from outside. It is also possible to assign monolingual clients to workers who can provide services in their language.

Education and Training

Culturally competent social service agencies provide ongoing education and training in diversity competence, and encourage discussion of cultural issues and concerns at staff meetings and in supervision. There is a great variation in the levels of culturally sensitive expectations between agencies: some do not address the subject at all, others address it minimally and do not consider the in-depth issues raised, while others endeavor to educate and train members carefully and thoroughly. Some agencies have special task forces or committees to monitor diversity competence.

Sensitivity to Client Culture

Agencies may vary in their sensitivity to client cultures. Use of formal or informal means of address; sensitivity to gender, age, and cultural differences; understanding family structures and communication patterns in terms of decision-making and contact with the agency; and respect and consideration for special needs all have a major impact on the way the client perceives her/himself in terms of the need for services. A culturally competent agency provides sensitive services that are evidenced through the respect and consideration accorded to clients by each member of the agency's staff.

Funding

Cultural competence within agencies often requires adequate funding for training, hiring, and service provision. Many agencies are limited in their ability to provide culturally competent services by funding restrictions that force difficult choices and overburden workers, thus limiting cultural effectiveness.

Agency Services and Policies

In order to provide culturally sensitive and relevant services, agencies should be viewed as active, caring, and involved members of the communities they serve. To be effective, it is helpful if not essential to involve members of the community in identifying needs and developing services. Agencies that invite community members to participate in service and policy decisions also have community members who are invested in the agency and advocate for the services that it can provide to members of their group.

While community member insights will enhance agency services and develop a positive image of the agency in the community, social workers must remain aware that there are some limitations in the degree and type of community involvement that can be solicited. Agencies are professionals offering services: there is a professional knowledge base that must always be respected. Also, agencies have contracts and agreements with other agencies, with funding sources, and with licensing bodies that may place some limitations on the kinds of services that can be offered and the conditions under which the services are rendered.

Identifying Community Leaders and Institutions

Familiarization and mapping efforts can provide several tools for identifying community leaders and institutions. There are other sources of information as well: colleagues, clients, educators, and members of community groups. The head of the local elementary school's PTA, the Neighborhood Watch chairperson, the Ethnic Festival chairperson, the church Volunteer Services coordinator, the After-school Program mother, the Boy Scout leader, the kids' sports coach—all these and many others are potential leaders in the local community.

Integrating Community Leaders into Policy Development

Once leaders are identified, an agency representative, often the agency's director, may reach out to individuals and asks for their involvement and assistance in program development and policy formulation. Community members may serve on boards, be committee advisers, review policies on an individual basis, develop links between the agency and their own organization, provide some volunteer services and involvement, or serve in other helpful capacities.

While this system works well in the private, nonprofit sector, it is more difficult to involve the local community in providing input and direction for services offered by government agencies. More difficult—but not impossible! With good will and creativity, it is possible to involve communities in public agencies as well!

Assessing Community Needs

The community leaders are an excellent source of information for assessing community needs and preferred methodologies for meeting these needs. Agencies may also hold focus groups with community members, send outreach workers to interact with other agencies, provide speakers who will explain the agency's mission and services to community groups, and provide a community forum for input and feedback. Written suggestions can be elicited as well.

Utilization of Community Resources

An individual agency cannot provide all of the services that a community identifies. In order to ensure that community and catchment area needs are met, agencies develop relationships with other community resources that can be contacted to meet specific client needs. Linkages with these resources can be formal, with written agreements and terms and referral systems, or informal, with social workers contacting relevant community services on a needs basis.

In either case, it is essential that the agency be familiar with the resources being used, the kinds of services the clients receive, and the professionalism of the resources in terms of privacy and confidentiality and the kinds of services rendered. The importance of agency linkages and use of community resources is especially noted in providing services across diverse cultures. To meet the service needs of clients, agencies may also utilize the services of other, ethnically based community resources (Lum 2003, 160)

Formulating Policies and Services

All of the available resources and the advice of community leaders should be utilized in the development of culturally competent services and policies. It is especially important to ensure that community support networks are utilized, and that services are culturally accessible and sensitive to the help-seeking behaviors of the populations served. Where needed, professionals who are bilingual, and bicultural, should be available to meet client needs. Requirements for services should be culturally sensitive, especially in the area of gender roles and intergenerational relationships, and consideration should be given to decision-making patterns.

Measuring Cultural Competence

The suggestions above will promote the development of culturally competent services and policies. These can also be explored and evaluated by examining:

Effort—are the "type and quantity" of program activities (Rothman and Sager 1998, 265) culturally congruent to the focus population? Is there a consistent effort made to be culturally sensitive to client populations? Given the overall resources of the programs and services, are a sufficient number specifically directed toward the focus population in a culturally congruent manner?

Quality—measuring "accessibility, assurance, communication, competence, conformity, courtesy, deficiency, durability, empathy, humaneness, performance, reliability, responsiveness, security, and tangibles" are all included in an overall assessment of quality of services rendered (Netting, Kettner, and McMurtry 1998, 267). Focusing on the most relevant issues for cultural competence, it is important to consider if the programs and services offered are accessible, if communication is open, if the services are culturally competent, if empathy is rendered in a culturally competent form, and whether the services are responsive to cultural differences. One way to measure this is through a feedback system for clients to provide input into the quality of services provided by the agency.

Effectiveness—are services being utilized by clients in the focus population such that "they are better off after coming . . . than they were before they came?" Do the services "resolve the client problems they are funded to address" in this population? (Netting, Kettner, and McMurtry 1998, 267). Are clients accepting services in the forms in which they are being provided? What "intended benefit outcomes or unintended consequences" (Rothman and Sager 1998, 265) have, or have not, occurred for clients who are members of the specific population?

Efficiency—are services provided in a way that maximizes resource utilization? What is the "ratio of volume of service provided to dollars expended" (Netting, Kettner, and McMurtry 1998, 266)? What are the "relative costs" (Rothman and Sager 1998, 265) of providing services to this population?

Summary

Agencies are the context within which services are provided to clients. Agency practices and policies, ambiance, staffing, and other factors can have an impact on client's willingness to access and utilize services. It is, first of all, important to understand the community that is served by the agency. This can be accomplished through mapping, profiling, consultation, and a simple walk around the neighborhood.

Waiting rooms, decor, attitude of staff and employees, cultural competence training, and sensitivity all impact upon clients as well. Each agency has its own unique combination of factors that welcome clients, or discourage them. Cultural competence reveals itself in staffing policies, the way in which clients are greeted and attended to, and the inclusiveness of literature and wall decor.

In order to develop culturally competent services, agencies need to utilize outside resources such as community leaders, other agencies, community needs assessments, and client feedback mechanisms.

While agencies' services, policies, receptivity, and sensitivity impact strongly on clients, it is most essential to culturally competent service that each individual worker make a commitment to self-awareness, the acquisition of knowledge, and the thoughtful and sensitive application of theories and frameworks. It is only when agency settings, services and policies, and individual workers practice with care and sensitivity that our obligation to social justice, client empowerment, and social work values can be fully met.

CHAPTER 7

Process and Practice Integrating for Cultural Competence

We have explored both theoretical frameworks and the specific kinds of information that social workers need to become culturally competent. As we have seen, acquiring cultural competence is an ongoing, lifelong process to which professionals are personally committed. However, it is also possible to gain cultural competence in working with a specific population by learning about the population in depth, and then considering the way that this knowledge can be used to offer culturally congruent and sensitive services to clients through social agencies, programs and services, and professional relationships. Knowledge about any group or population is a necessary prerequisite to culturally competent service delivery at every level from individuals, to groups, organizations, communities, state and national policies and programs, and international health and social programs and interventions.

The process of preparation for practice through knowledge acquisition can be applied to any group in any context. The steps defined here address many major areas of competence, but in working to acquire competence with a population, practitioners should be open to a wide variety of learning tools and methodologies, which may augment or supplement those included here. The process of applying the knowledge to understand and assess, and possibly to improve, the cultural competence of agencies, programs and services, and individual practitioners may also be expanded and adapted to meet special needs and circumstances.

The basic structure provides for two separate but related efforts:

1. knowledge acquisition relative to a specific group or population through cultural immersion in that population.
2. the assessment of agency, programs and services, and personal cultural competence grounded in the knowledge acquired from the immersion experience.

The outline provided below serves as a general guide to the Projects presented in Part II as well as to the project that will be suggested for readers in Part III. Although it is suggested that this process be done in conjunction with a field placement, it is also possible to acquire the knowledge suggested below in regard to any population desired at any time.

Part I Knowledge Acquisition

The knowledge acquisition process defined below can be utilized with any population group; in any context of practice, at the micro, mezzo, or macro level, at any time in any professional setting. It is portable, easily applied, and practical in any context.

Each step is designed to provide another dimension of knowledge. Steps in the knowledge acquisition process can be adapted, augmented, or re-defined to meet professional needs and circumstances.

- Select a population that is *served by your agency*, and is *different* from you in race, ethnicity, gender, sexual orientation, religion or worldview, social class, ability, or other difference.
- Explore the history of your selected group, especially, the history in North America or the United States. Journal articles, books, the internet, and any other sources may be used. If possible, include information from the Census to provide specific demographic data.
- Read an autobiography, a biography, or a story based on true experiences by or about a member of this population.
- View a film by or about the chosen population.
- Attend an event that is culture-specific. Ethnic fairs and festivals, religious services, gay or straight bars, support group meetings, and community meetings are examples of the kinds of events to select. While at the event, observe the reaction of others to you, and yours to them. Look inward to your feelings about this group, and be aware of your sensitivity to others' reactions to your presence.

Caution: Don't place yourself in a situation where you are uncomfortable—you may choose to do this activity with a classmate or a friend if you prefer, though it will dilute your experience somewhat. Select an activity at which you will be at least somewhat at ease—and *always safe*

- Interview a member of your population. You may choose a classmate, a colleague, a friend, someone you meet at the event, or someone you contact for this specific purpose. Ask them about being a member of this population and about their experiences. Please *do not* use a client as your interviewee as this will affect the client-worker relationship.
- Listen to music by or for members of your population. You can choose current and/or historical selections.

When you have completed these activities, you may want to organize and synthesize your experiences and insights regarding the population you have explored. The experiences suggested should enable you to gain an overall understanding while also increasing your awareness of intragroup differences and variations. If you are writing these experiences, ensure the privacy and confidentiality of people you have interviewed by disguising names, identities, locations, and any other identifying information.

Part II Application of Knowledge: Assessing Agency, Programs and Services, and Personal Cultural Competencies

With the knowledge you have gained through your immersion process, you can now explore your chosen population's experiences with social work services with more insight. You can use your knowledge to assess the cultural competence of your agency, its programs and services, and your own competence to work cross-culturally with "your" group or population. As you follow the steps in the assessment process, you will need to keep your focus on your population specifically, rather than broadening your assessment to include other groups. You may find that your agency serves all of the needs of your population very effectively, somewhat effectively, or not effectively at all. You will also become aware of your agency's strengths and resources, which could be developed to meet the needs of clients in your population more effectively. Your assessment of your own practice competencies will validate your learning and also clarify areas that need further effort.

Field Work Agency:

- Agency's Community: Walk around your agency's neighborhood and describe the "feel" and appearance of the community. What do you note as the population groups that are included in your agency's community and catchment area?
- Access: What is the route of access to your agency for members of your population? Must they use public transportation, cross ethnic or cultural boundaries, or travel long distances? Can they view your agency as a "neighbor"? Does your agency provide outreach services to the population you have studied that are culturally sensitive?
- Receptivity: Does the agency decor, color scheme, entrance, and waiting room appear to welcome clients from your population? Does the agency's literature, reading materials, and other written material include members of your population? If your population might need these, are interpreters, signers, communications boards, tty (teleTypewriter), TDD (telecommunication device for the deaf), TT (text telephone), or other facilities available? Are there staff members who are members of the population?
- Administration and Staff Training: Does your agency have an ongoing program to train staff members, both professional and nonprofessional, in culturally sensitive and competent practice? Are there meetings, lectures, or retreats where issues related to diversity are addressed?

- Staff Sensitivity: From your direct observation, is the staff of your agency respectful of differences, sensitive to special client needs, and nonjudgmental? Do they use stereotypes or "they" language when speaking about members of your population? Do they use formality/informality and expressions consistent with client's culture?
- Funding: Does your agency have adequate funds to serve members of your population in a culturally sensitive manner? Does funding allow for cultural variations in programs and services?

Program and Services:

You can explore your program and services by reviewing the mission statement, policy manual, and procedure manual, and by talking with directors, administrators, and supervisors using these parameters.

- Effort: Do your agency's programs and services reflect an effort to be sensitive to cultural differences, to secure input on program delivery from members of your population, and to include members of your population in formulating and designing culturally sensitive policies and programs?
- Quality: How do policies and programs ensure that the quality of services provided are culturally competent, equitable, respectful, and accessible to your population and to employees of the organization that are members of the population? Do the expectations and criteria for service take into account cultural variations between your population and the dominant society?
- Effectiveness: Do the numbers of clients from your population being served by your agency reflect their numbers in the agency's catchment area? From what you have experienced, how do clients from your population feel about the quality and quantity of the programs and services available to them? Are there unmet needs that are not included in your agency's policies and program formulations?
- Efficiency: Do agency programs reach out into your population's community? Set up linkages with existing community institutions? Use alternative service delivery systems to support clients from your population?

Personal Cultural Competencies:

You can assess your personal cultural competency skills in working with your chosen populations using the major social work processes as a framework and describing the ways in which you might use your knowledge of your chosen population to ensure that your approaches to your client are culturally competent:

- Engagement, Trust, and Relationship-Building: How does your population, in general, feel about using social agencies for addressing problems and needs? What help-seeking behaviors indicate needs for individuals, families, groups, and communities? What might be the culturally appropriate forms of address, distance, eye contact, touch, empathic responding? Does your population expect to be guided and directed, to make all major decisions individually, to consult with family and community members? How would you utilize ethnographic interviewing to learn about your clients' individual and cultural group experiences?

- Assessment and Problem Definition: What specific tools would be effective and applicable in assessing your client's needs and resources? How would you engage your client in the assessment process? How might your client identify problems grounded in cultural norms, beliefs, and expectations? How do you understand the relationship between your clients' culture and that of the dominant society in the lives of your clients?
- Contracting and Goal Setting: How would you define some culturally appropriate goals for clients in your population? How would you engage the clients in goalsetting and contracting? How might you need to adapt and adjust the contracting process to be culturally sensitive to your population?
- Interventions: Describe several culturally appropriate interventions, and some appropriate resources that may be called upon on behalf of the client within the client's cultural community.
- Evaluation and Termination: What are some of the ways that your population understands success or failure in dealing with issues? Is the focus on solutions, on diminution or elimination of symptoms and conditions, on inner change that may not be immediately visible? Who determines whether an intervention has been helpful and successful in addressing a problem? What is your population's cultural norm regarding separation and ending a relationship? Are there specific adaptation and adjustments, in time, in manner, in degree, that might be helpful in terminating services to members of your population?

Evaluation Using NASW Cultural Competence Standards

Review the NASW Standards for Cultural Competence. In considering the assessments you have completed, how do you feel that your agency, its programs and services, and your own personal cultural competencies support the NASW Standards? What suggestions might you have for improvement, if any?

Part II will offer examples of this knowledge acquisition and assessment process. These have been developed by first year MSW students using the guidelines suggested here. As you read these projects, you will notice that there is much variation between them. Some of this is a reflection of the approaches, personalities, and interests of the writers, but some is also a reflection of differences among agencies, programs and services, locations of the agencies, populations served, and the population the writer has chosen as the focus of study. When you begin your own work, in Part III, you will notice that you too will develop unique approaches to the challenge of developing cultural competence.

Summary

This chapter has provided a summary guideline that you may use in your effort to attain cultural competence with a selected population. In Part II, you will be sharing in the experiences of first year MSW students, who have used this process to explore and achieve a level of cultural competence with a population served by their field work agencies. In Part III, you will be asked to "practice" this "process" on your own as it applies to a population your agency serves. This summary chapter may be used to review and in preparation for your own work.

Personal Growth and Cultural Competence—A Final Word

It is quite possible to complete a course in culturally competent social work practice as an intellectual exercise only, and not to engage in the often difficult and painful process of reflection and exploration of one's own personal values, world view, biases, and prejudices. It may feel "safer" not to engage, and easier to remain within the world view that is comfortable. Awareness of personal prejudices and biases in oneself is usually not possible in isolation—it is only a small step from self-awareness to awareness of the attitudes of others: family members, friends, coworkers, and fellow students. And with that awareness may come a discomfort and a disillusionment, and the anxiety associated with making decisions about when to ignore, when to confront, when to accept statements and attitudes by others that may have been heard before, but are now heard with new ears— new awareness and new sensitivity.

Yet, it is with these new ears that we can listen to clients, families, groups of people, community members, and others and really begin to understand their life experiences within *their* framework, *their* milieu. Professional and competent social work asks that we always consider the client and the client's life situation from within the lived experience of the client, that we hear not only the individual pain, the individual need, the individual problem, the individual sorrow, but also the experience and history of the community or group of which our client is a part.

To develop these new ears, it is important to make a genuine commitment to cultural competence, despite the discomfort in varying degrees that this may engender. Social justice, our Ethical Code, and our professional Cultural Competence Standards ask that we make this commitment.

The students whose projects are included in this text have made this commitment. It is the author's sincere hope that, in experiencing their struggles and their conflicts, the reader will recognize the importance of engaging her/himself fully in the effort.

BIBLIOGRAPHY

Barker, R. I. 1999. *The Social Work Dictionary*. 4th ed. Washington, DC: NASW Press.

Bulhan, H. A. 1985. *Franz Fanon and the Psychology of Oppression*. New York: Plenum Press.

Davis, F. J. Who is black? One nation's definition. In K. Rosenblum and T. M. Travis. 2003. *The Meaning of Difference*. Boston: McGraw Hill.

Devore, W., and E. Schlesinger. 1999. *Ethnic-Sensitive Social Work Practice*. 5th ed. Boston: Allyn & Bacon.

Fong, R., and S. B. Furuto, eds. 2001. *Culturally Competent Practice: Skills, Interventions, and Evaluations*. Boston: Allyn & Bacon.

Frye, M. 1983 oppression. In Frye, M. *The Politics of Reality: Essays in Feminist Theory*. Freedom, CA: The Crossing Press/ TenSpeed.com

Germain, C., and A. Gitterman. 1980. *The Life Model of Social Work Practice*. New York: Columbia University Press.

Gibelman, M. 2003. *Navigating Human Service Organizations*. Chicago: Lyceum Books.

Green, James W. 1999. *Cultural Awareness in the Human Services*. Boston: Allyn & Bacon.

Hohm, C., and J. Glynn. 2002. *California's Social Problems*. 2d ed. Thousand Oaks, CA: Pine Forge Press.

Hraba, J. 1994. *American Ethnicity*. 2d ed. Itasca, IL: F.E. Peacock.

Jaimes, M. A., Federal Indian identification policy. In K. Rosenblum and T. M. Travis. 2003. *The Meaning of Difference*. Boston: McGraw Hill.

Kettner, P. M. 2002. *Achieving Excellence in the Management of Human Service Organizations*. Boston: Allyn & Bacon.

Kirst-Ashman, K., and G. Hull. *Generalist Practice with Organizations and Communities*. 2d ed. Belmont, CA: Brooks/Cole.

Leiberman, A., and C. Lester. 2004. *Social Work Practice with a Difference*. New York: McGraw Hill.

Leigh, J. W. 2002. *Communicating for Cultural Competence*. Prospect Heights, IL: Waveland Press.

Lum, D. 1999. *Culturally Competent Practice: A Framework for Growth and Action*. Pacific Grove, CA: Brooks/Cole.

Lum, D. 2004. *Social Work Practice with People of Color: A Process-Stage Approach*. Pacific Grove: Thomson/Brooks/Cole.

Matthew's Place, "Matthew's Life," Matthew's Place, http://www.matthewsplace.org

Miley, K., M. O'Melia, and B. DuBois. 2004. *Generalist Social Work Practice: An Empowering Approach*. Boston: Pearson.

National Association of Social Workers. 1996. *NASW Code of Ethics*. Washington, DC: Author.

National Association of Social Workers. 2001. *Standards for Cultural Competence in Social Work Practice*. Washington, DC: Author.

Netting, F. E., P. M. Kettner, and S. L. McMurtry. 1998. *Social Work Macro Practice*. 2d ed. New York: Longman.

Pinderhughes, E. 1989. *Understanding Race, Ethnicity, and Power*. New York: The Free Press.

Rosenblum, K., and T. M. Travis. 2003. *The Meaning of Difference*. New York: McGraw Hill Publishers.

Rothman, J. and J. S. Sager. 1998. *Case Management: Integrating Individual and Community Practice*. 2d ed. Boston: Allyn & Bacon.

Saleeby, D. 2002. *The Strengths Perspective in Social Work Practice*. Boston: Allyn & Bacon.

PART TWO

Projects in Cultural Competence in Practice

Introduction

In this Part, first-year MSW students will share with you their experiences with using the process presented in the previous Part. In each instance, students were asked to select a population that their field placement agency served, and of which they were not a member. After acquiring knowledge of the population through a process of cultural immersion, students applied their knowledge to an assessment of their agency, its programs and services, and their own practice skills in rendering culturally competent service to that population. They also explored at least one of the standards in the NASW Standards for Cultural Competence in Social Work as it applied to their assessments.

Students chose their specific population for many reasons: some had studied that population in previous course work and wanted to deepen their knowledge, others had always been interested in learning more about a group of people, or had always felt an affinity toward them. Some students chose a population that they felt would require some specialized relational skills. Still others chose to learn about a population that was unfamiliar to them, or which had made them uncomfortable. In each case, students were aware of needing to leave their cultural "comfort zone"—of needing to be open to the new experiences, ideas, and contexts they would encounter.

Grouping the cases used here presented a major challenge. As was discussed in Part One, each of us belongs to a number of groups, and affiliates with many populations. Sometimes affiliations are self-selected, while at other times they are ascribed by others. Affiliations can also be very context-sensitive. In addition, a particular affiliation may be of major importance to one person, while the same group membership may appear of marginal interest or value to another.

In trying to arrange the cases, an attempt has been made to focus on the "master statuses" referred to in Rosenblum and Travis (Rosenblum & Travis (2006) p. 2): gender, race, ethnicity, sexual orientation, social class, etc. However, there were times that a choice had to be made between two or more master statuses—such as African-American, male, and on the down low; working class and caucasian; undocumented and Mexican. In each instance, the choices that were made were dictated by a desire for variety—diversity—rather than by any assumption of the value or importance of any one affiliation over another.

Many of the student projects included here focus on a racial or ethnic group, and racial and ethnic differences are often among the most obvious and most challenging that social workers can face. Perhaps more than any others, perceived racial and ethnic differences are both value-laden and emotionally charged, and affect relationships not only with clients, but also with colleagues and agency staff. Practitioners work across racial and ethnic differences in all practice contexts, in macro as well as micro practice, and both self-awareness and knowledge of other racial and ethnic groups are essential to competent practice.

Readers will note that there are two students who chose African-Americans, and two who chose Chinese Americans. These projects were grouped together in order to highlight the uniqueness of each writer's perspective, interests, and choices, the influence of their personal experiences, and the way in which different settings addressed cultural competence for the same groups of clients. There is no single, "right" way to seek to acquire cultural competence. At each step, many choices are made, choices that will lead to different insights and different awarenesses. Although they are all in the biographical genre, Richard Wright's *Native Son* will read differently from Maya Angelou's *Wouldn't Take Nothing for My Journey Now*, which will read still differently from a biography of Martin Luther King. *Real Women Have Curves* will explore a different world from that of *Raising Victor Vargas*, or *The Buena Vista Social Club*, or *Y Tu Mamá También*. Using various sources of information helps in understanding the wide range of experiences within populations, as well as some of the common threads.

Two projects focus on immigrant groups: Iranian Americans and Filipino Americans. Although both groups share the experience of leaving a country behind and going to a new country where the language, customs, and everyday life are quite different, the two groups' immigration experiences differ markedly. The reasons for immigration, the conditions experienced during the process, and degree of difference from the culture of the United States all affect the way in which population groups relate to the immigration experience. A third project explores some of the special circumstances people face whose status in the United States is a major political issue—undocumented Mexicans. Another project focuses on caucasians who are members of the working class, a largely invisible population whose status and role in our country is still largely unexplored.

Three projects address gender identity and sexual orientation. The two students who study transgender populations begin their work from very different personal perspectives, but both demonstrate their care, sensitivity, and empathy in the way that they approach their interviews. The study of African-American men on the down low thoughtfully explores some of the cultural differences in the way that sexual orientation is understood and experienced.

Although every adult has experienced adolescence, and the major tasks of adolescence remain the same in terms of establishing affiliations and identities, each generation's adolescents also face some very unique experiences. The life course perspective teaches us that we are strongly affected not only by our own biology, and by our families and communities, but also by the events in the world around us. To understand some of the experiences of adolescents today, a student studies this age group in depth. At the very other end of the spectrum, another student explores some of the challenges and complexities of aging in our society, one that devalues old age and prizes youth, beauty, and strength.

Two of the students whose projects are included here explore disabilities: one focuses on deaf culture, the other on mental health consumer advocates. Although these are clearly "populations," in the sense that they self-identify, recognize an affinity to others who share their culture, and share certain values and worldviews, reading these projects will clearly illustrate the differences in perspectives and challenges each faces. Deaf culture is valued: for many people, it is a chosen culture which provides cultural supports that enable people to live rich, full lives. Yet, one can be deaf and not identify with Deaf culture.

The other project's population presents a special challenge to the social work student: consumers of mental health services who advocate for consumer-driven services, rather than services professionals provide. Planning a career as a mental health practitioner, the student who selected this population finds herself challenged in considering how clients with mental health needs should best be served, and, through this immersion, is led to a deeper understanding of the "culture" of consumer advocates in mental health.

Four projects that focus on special populations that social workers serve, each of which are especially vulnerable in different ways, help us to explore the various ways in which "culture" can be conceptualized and lived. Homeless people, incarcerated women, alcoholics, and veterans of the Vietnam War each experience different challenges in our society, and each have special long-term needs that must be addressed. Each of these populations experience a society in which they are, or have been, devalued as individuals, and where programs, funding, and societal priorities often have not considered their needs and circumstances thoughtfully.

Each of these selections will enable the reader to gain some insights into different populations, and also to see the ways in which the starting point, unique and different for each writer, may lead each one down unique and different paths toward the knowledge and sensitivity necessary for cultural competence.

CHAPTER

8

Cultural Competence with Racial and Ethnic Groups

Culturally Competent Social Work Practice with Black Women

Diversity Project by Cheryl Pascual

My field work placement is at a county adult mental health clinic, located in a traditionally diverse working-class neighborhood that is in the process of gentrification. The population my agency serves includes many diverse groups of people who are either mentally ill or homeless, or, in many cases, both mentally ill and homeless. Though there is a special program in my agency to serve Filipino Americans, the agency also serves many black clients.

It seems as though I have spent much of my life contemplating what it means to be a Filipina woman, a daughter of immigrants, living in the United States. This past decade I have intentionally surrounded myself with a community of Asian American women friends—my best of friends being Filipina American with similar struggles and dreams. Through this experience, I have only begun to understand what womanhood and sisterhood means in my life and in my community. This led me to ask: *What does this journey look and feel like for other women of color?* So with the chance to explore this question, knowing

that such a short-term immersion experience is limited for many reasons, I wanted to begin to understand more fully the joys and struggles of the black woman. In short, I saw this as an opportunity not only in developing a model for culturally competent social work, but as a creative and personal way to understand people.

I recognize that what I share cannot be a comprehensive picture of the experience of black women in the United States, but only a tiny glimpse, a slice, filtered by my own eyes and colored by my own experiences. What I am about to share are the facts, the stories, and the feelings that struck me as meaningful and telling.

KNOWLEDGE

Data—The Census: What's the Story Beyond the Numbers?

According to a March 2002 U.S. Census Bureau Report, blacks made up 13 percent of the civilian population, or 36 million people, in the United States, with most living in the South. In general, blacks are younger, less likely to be married, have larger families, participate in the labor force at a lower rate, and have higher rates of unemployment than the non-Hispanic white population. Overall, data specific to black women indicate that more black women than black men have earned at least a bachelor's degree. Yet, 35 percent of black families headed solely by a female with no spouse present lived in poverty as compared to 19 percent of non-Hispanic white families.

I recognize that the U.S. Census could be viewed as controversial because it "counts what the nation wants counted" (Davis 2003, 43). Nevertheless, leaving the politics of "counting" behind, I found myself hearing the struggles of black women and how poverty, education, marriage, family, and history have all closely intertwined in their stories.

Two distinct pictures of black women emerged—one who successfully finished college, and one raising her family alone and living in poverty. Yet, I came to see that these two different women know each other well, for both probably come from families and communities that instilled courage and strength. Though I am reminded that "women of all races and black people of both genders are fast filling up the ranks of the poor and disenfranchised," (hooks 2000a, 8) the experience of hardship, marginalization, and injustice of black women remains.

Finally, returning to the census, I saw that incarcerated people are not included, many of whom may be the women's brothers, husbands, and sons. These men, made literally and politically invisible, may not be counted or valued by the census-takers, but are not forgotten by their black sisters, wives, and mothers.

Autobiography: *All About Love:* Visions from bell hooks

All About Love is a collection of thoughts by bell hooks rooted in her personal experiences about the nature and dimensions of love.

Conceptualized by hooks as "care, affection, responsibility, respect, commitment, and trust," (hooks, 14) love has the ability to transform humans. One of the most striking discussions was hooks's encouragement of self-love. hooks writes:

> When we can see ourselves as we truly are and accept ourselves, we build the necessary foundation for self-love. The confusion arises because most people who think they are not lovable have this perception because at some point in their lives they were socialized to see themselves as unlovable by forces outside their control. (hooks 2000b, 53)

Women who do not fit the white, blond, blue-eyed profile of beauty, such as black women, have been raised to feel ashamed of their appearance. In addition, the effects of slavery and rape have severely and devastatingly damaged the self-perception of black women. hooks inspires *all* women to reclaim unconditional love for themselves first and foremost, allowing them to recognize the beauty of self-worth, and knowing that it can be done without tinges of selfishness or narcissism.

Film—A Love Story of Peace: *Their Eyes Were Watching God*

I first read Zora Neale Hurston's 1937 novel *Their Eyes Were Watching God* more than ten years ago as a teenager in my high school English class. *Their Eyes* is considered by some, such as Alice Walker, as Hurston's masterpiece. My recollections about the novel are simply that it is a story about a passionate woman who is in search of true love. And Oprah promotes the now made-for-TV movie as her "favorite love story" (Boyd 2005). Thus, I was drawn to watch *Their Eyes*, asking myself, "What does *Their Eyes* reveal about black woman and love?" With two of the most powerful and prominent black women in the United States as its executive producer (Oprah Winfrey) and its star (Halle Berry, the first black woman to win a best actress Oscar), this story certainly has much to reveal.

Set in the 1920's South in Eatonville, claiming to be the first all-black town, *Their Eyes* is about the life of Janie Crawford, a woman who marries three different men and finds different parts of herself in the process of the experience of falling in and out of love. Though the TV movie adaptation received criticism for the absence of the lyrical beauty of the novel, I watched for the strengths of Janie's character, and heard her lessons about being true to freedom, expression, and peace in ourselves, by example and by our authenticity, facilitating the growth of this perspective in others.

I was struck deeply by the scenes of Janie gazing toward the sky in the midst of the Everglades watching God. In Hurston's own words:

> It was a spring afternoon in West Florida. Janie had spent most of the day under a blossoming pear tree in the back-yard. She had been spending every minute that she could steal from her chores under that tree for the last three days. That was to say, ever since the first tiny bloom had opened. It had called her to come and gaze on a mystery. From barren brown stems to glistening leaf-buds; from the leaf-buds to snowy virginity of bloom. It stirred her tremendously. How? Why? It was like a flute song forgotten in another existence and remembered again. What? How? Why? This singing she heard that had nothing to do with her ears. The rose of the world was breathing out smell. It followed her through all her waking moments and caressed her in her sleep. It connected itself with other vaguely felt matters that had struck her outside observation and buried themselves in her flesh. Now they emerged and quested about her consciousness. (Hurston, 2. (1937) p. 71)

The quiet wonderment seen in Janie's character illustrates the peace that the black community and black women long for. The struggle against injustice is tiring, but through Janie, one can revel in moments of peace that are present in nature and in the every day.

Music—*Waiting to Exhale* Soundtrack: Music of Sisterhood

Music is one of the creative expressions of the black community. Whether it is hip-hop, gospel, jazz, or soul, music serves as both a lifeline and a voice that connects the experiences of the black diaspora in the United States

Waiting to Exhale, a novel written by Terry McMillan, is about four women's relationships with each other, their struggle with men, careers, and love—a process of coming into their identity as strong black women. The sister-celebratory novel was adapted in a major motion picture released in 1995 starring actresses Angela Bassett and Whitney Houston. The movie was a box office success, and had mixed reviews from being considered a movie presenting a negative view of men to being a true celebration of black sisterhood. I enjoyed the movie, but it was the soundtrack that struck me.

The soundtrack included songs of all dimensions: sensuality, friendship, anger, pain, and joy. The music, predominantly soul and R&B (Rhythm and Blues), felt like a spirit linking the experiences of love, rekindling old memories, and expressing eloquently the longings of the women's hearts. *Waiting*'s title track spoke to the hardships of love and life and the need to "exhale" in order to not only to endure the suffering, but to thrive through it all. Out of this deep connection with the music came inspiration, strength, and ultimately transformation.

Interview—Amy: A Beautiful Black Woman

I begin sharing about my time with Amy with appreciation. I am so grateful for this woman, and for her willingness to engage with me so that I might share in her perceptions and experiences. She is to me a beautiful black woman—intelligent, strong, and warm.

Amy grew up in California and was raised by her mother. Her maternal family history goes back to the early 1900s, with her grandparents, who lived in a poor rural farming community in North Carolina. In search of gainful employment, the family moved north to Connecticut, to a black working class neighborhood. The black Baptist church was a strong influence on her grandparents, and values of education and hard work were instilled from childhood. Her family believed "education was the way to the American dream." And, moving to California, her mother found a way Amy could attend high school outside her own low-performing school district.

Because her mother encouraged multiethnic friendships, Amy did not think too much about her identity as a black woman, and was first confronted with racism and oppression during her freshman year in college. Her stories of how white women would treat her and her biracial roommate, and how she felt watched, sounded reminiscent of bell hooks's experiences. hooks expressed it clearly: "We (the white women and I) did not reside on the same planet," (hooks 2000, 26).

Amy believes that it is hard for an educated black woman to find a man. Her cousin joined in our conversation at this point, saying that it is also difficult for a self-educated intelligent black man (like himself) to find a black woman willing to be with him. They both agreed that the drama in the game of relationships could lead to interracial dating. Still, her cousin keeps searching and admires Amy and her husband, who "made it, rare in our community."

At times, Amy finds it hard to be the only black woman in so many daily social and work-related settings, and to "have to educate" others about the black experience. I resonate with that experience—of the internal struggle of wanting to say something, but wondering if it would be taken the wrong way, or of being tired of explaining, or being seen as "the one voice" to represent your entire community.

Event—Spirituality and Cornel West: A Hope for True Change

My experience at a talk given by Dr. Cornel West, a Princeton professor, theologian, activist, and prolific author, sponsored by Laney's Black Student Association to celebrate Black History Month was personally and communally inspirational. West has been touted as "present[ing] the facts of today's world in terms and forums not only directed toward academia, but also to those of us in everyday life that actually live it" (West). His words were accessible, deep, and poignant, challenging us to think about and hope for change in radical ways. West spoke about the aspects of community life in the context of the black experience: class, politics, race, family, and economics.

I was overwhelmingly struck with West's infectious spirit, engaging us to believe hope exists. He called us all to believe in "hope and not optimism" for optimism is based on change of the status quo, but hope is based on the creation of a brand new paradigm. As I reflected on his words, bell hooks's writing on class came to mind:

> When growing up, most people believed that the poor had lives full of hardship, but rightfully we saw the poor as victims of an economic system that did not create structures to enable all citizens to adequately provide for themselves and their families. In those days, I never heard anyone suggest that people wanted to be poor. (hooks 2000a, 122)

Thus, applying the hope that West defines would mean creating entirely new systems that enable citizens instead of disabling them. This model of "keeping hope alive" in the words of the famous Rev. Jesse Jackson is a familiar anthem, rooted in the black church. "You can't escape the church," West says. "You may want to leave, but you turn on the radio and hear Stevie [Wonder] and there it is. You hear Marvin [Gaye] and there it is." The church is an integral part of the black experience and history because it "fuel(s) a cohesion and social identity" (Edwards 1996, 180)—a unity that fueled the Civil Rights movement.

Though blacks made up three-fourths of the audience, West touched upon important issues across racial lines and spoke to the entire congregation. Because of his presentation style, I felt included and invited to be in communion with all who were there to be inspired. At times, I did sense that his message was particularly for the black community, but I truly respected this connection because West spoke from his experience. And there's something so respectable about an individual taking the risk of being real. Such authenticity seems to come with wisdom and maturity.

Reflection—A Refreshing Dip

My reflection began with a vision of the black woman's experience as a colorful and rich piece of knitted fabric—if stretched taut, the fibers become strong and resilient and, at the same time, if left free, the fibers are loose and unrestricted, with each strand revealing in its uniqueness. Each piece of string represented to me all the stories of struggle, love, beauty, spirit, and strength told here and beyond. These stories are woven together to form a bond of sisterhood and womanhood that becomes stronger when stretched by poverty, injustice, and oppression. Yet, when given the opportunity to be free and at peace, each fiber still remains connected to the others.

This knitted fabric comes of academics like Cornel West who want to break down systems that stretch blacks too strenuously,

music like that of *Waiting to Exhale*, which gives voice to feelings, characters like Janie of *Their Eyes Were Watching God* who call to be more free and expressive, writers like bell hooks who offer self-love as a way to find strength in ourselves and the community, and women like Amy who make these stories come to life for me. Throughout all the mediums I have explored, I see that all of the stories speak out of personal experiences, so authentic and real.

Because the limits of time and the reality of being an outsider, I admit I had doubts about being asked to "immerse" myself in a population that was different from my own. As a person of color living in the United States, many of these experiences are my reality. They are not an immersion. They are life. Still, I knew that I needed to be open to learning.

I feel as though this journey has been more like a refreshing "dip" that has helped me see just how connected the experience of people of color is in the United States. It all came together when interviewing Amy, and seeing the similarities in our families' perceptions of the American dream, the development of our ethnic identity, and struggle of our elders to make a better life for themselves, their families, and their children. Recognizing these similarities in no way takes away from the uniqueness of being who we are—a black woman or a Filipina American. It just makes loving each other much easier.

In closing, I have indeed learned much about the experience of the black woman in the United States and a model to use to do cross-cultural social work. I have also learned that doing social work is inherently cross-cultural, for each individual brings her/his unique history and experience. Furthermore, being able to recognize strengths in communities different from our own takes practice and also a looking inward, to draw from the strengths in ourselves and our own community.

Applying the Knowledge Base: Agency, Programs and Services, and Personal Competencies

FIELD WORK AGENCY: A COUNTY ADULT MENTAL HEALTH CLINIC

The Agency

My placement is at a Mental Health Service clinic located in a major urban county. The clinic is part of the Community Behavioral Health Service, which itself is part of the county's Public Health Department. The agency provides mental health services, including individual and group therapy, clinical case management, psychiatric medical evaluations, and information and referral. Clients are referred by (1) the county mental health hotline; (2) other county agencies; (3) drop-in (or self-referred); (4) community-based organizations; and (5) outreach to the homeless.

Community Agency services are primarily for residents who live in the neighborhood. There are three main service teams to serve specific populations. These include (1) a Filipino American service team, (2) a linkage program with the local hospital's psychiatric patients and other adults for out-patient treatment, and (3) a Mobile Outreach and Support Team that serves mentally ill homeless people.

This section of the city has historically been a low-income, high crime area, but has changed dramatically over the years due to commercial and upscale residential redevelopment.

Access The agency is fairly accessible by public transportation, and the majority of clients use public transit or walk to the clinic because it is neighborhood-based. Because it is a county-funded clinic, the facility is equipped with ADA-compliant ramps, restrooms, and hallways. Outreach materials and resources in the waiting room are primarily in English and Spanish. Resources on black support groups in the county are also provided and posted on the community bulletin board in the waiting room.

Receptivity The agency seems very receptive to the black community. There are currently six black staff members in different disciplines (clinical social work, health workers, and administrative staff), with one black female in a director position. In the agency as a whole, 17 percent of providers are black and 24 percent of the client population served is black. Although a disparity still exists, the county is making efforts to recruit staff to close the gap through the Multicultural Student Stipend Program that offers stipends to interns of color.

Although the waiting room lacks warmth and is, at most, clinical and functional, the hallways display consumer artwork, and each staff member is able to decorate his or her office creatively. For example, one of the black female social workers has decorated her office with pictures of her family, African art pieces, and quotes of her personal black heroes.

Administration and Staff Training The Behavioral Health Services Department offers free, ongoing training for its staff across disciplines. Training is also offered at no cost to the staff of contract agencies, many of which are community-based mental health non-profits. During my time as an intern, I have attended training on domestic violence, the elderly, women coming out of incarceration, depression in children and adolescents, and reducing stigma. However, although issues around cultural competence are addressed during the sessions, they are not covered comprehensively. No theoretical framework about diversity was part of the training.

Staff Sensitivity From direct observation at meetings and through my interaction with staff, I believe that the staff is reasonably respectful of differences, culturally sensitive, and nonjudgmental. I do not recall any instances when staff spoke with a "we versus them" mentality regarding black women. I am only aware of staff poking fun of Axis II clients, particularly those who were diagnosed with borderline personality disorder. Most of the time, the joking was fairly lighthearted and was focused on the eccentric behavior of Axis II clients.

Funding As the agency is a county-run and publicly funded clinic, managerial staff is constantly on alert for ways federal and state legislation will affect the county, and how the mayor's office will address budget shortfalls. Managerial staff feel there is not enough mental health funding "out there," and take reimbursement protocols and any type of audits seriously. With the passing of Proposition 63 in California, many clinicians are encouraged to be part of county working groups forming to give input on the strategic plan. Social workers and other clinicians are encouraged to identify and involve consumers as well.

Policies and Programs

The Department of Public Health has special programs specifically targeting the black population in the arenas of health promotion, education, and infant mortality, many of which address women's issues and concerns specifically. These programs are open to all eligible county residents and the clinic is able to make appropriate referrals within the system.

Effort A review of the county's Mental Health Plan provider manual reflects a serious and conscious effort to care for the needs of its diverse and multicultural population. Its mission statement is "to provide high quality mental health care which is community based, culturally competent, and consumer guided." This statement is also published in the consumer services guide that encourages consumers to submit their comments and ideas to the county in order to help themselves and other consumers become and stay healthy. The county's system goal is "to promote recovery, positive functional outcomes, and reduction in the symptoms of mental

illness for consumers. System goals will be defined by consumers themselves and their family members." Lastly, the values of the mental health system are based on a number of guiding principles that recognize the importance of consumer collaboration, language accessibility, and cultural competence.

I was personally impressed with these policies and the attention given to include consumers at many points of the continuum of care in the system. I feel there is a historical commitment to community mental health. I learned from informational conversations that African American consumers (some who are now on staff at the clinic) have participated in different county committees that review grievances, create contracts, and seek consumer input.

Quality In addition to its mission and vision statements, the Cultural Competency Task Force and the Office of Cultural Competence and Client Relations work to ensure that the quality of services provided are culturally competent. The task force was charged with creating and reviewing polices around cultural and linguistic issues while the office facilitates the implementation. According to county policy, the definition of culture refers to "integrated patterns of human behavior that include the language, thoughts, communications, actions, customs, beliefs, values and institutions of racial, ethnic, religious, or social groups" (***Department of Public Health). And competence is defined as "having the capacity to function effectively as an individual and an organization within the context of the cultural beliefs, behaviors, and needs presented by consumers and their communities" (***Department of Public Health). It is also mandatory that programs receiving monies from the county submit an annual cultural competency report for review.

Effectiveness and Efficiency African Americans comprise 24 percent of the entire client population under the county's Mental Health Plan. According to an approximation by staff, roughly 40 percent of clients my specific agency's clinic serves are black, and more of these are males than females. The clinicians I spoke with were hesitant to say if this was reflective of the neighborhood population, because it is a district that is historically transient, aged, and low-income. The agency also serves a predominantly black community, as well as other communities with a strong black presence.

Workers agreed that the MOST (Mobile Outreach Suppport Team) program served a large majority of black clients (both male and female). MOST consists of a mix of mental health professionals and peer outreach workers that provide intensive clinical case management services. MOST is extremely effective in outreaching to the mentally ill homeless (which is not specifically my population, but inclusive of it) because staff members literally meet their clients where they are—they go out on the streets to provide the homeless with medical and mental health services. All three programs at my agency also link clients to housing resources, substance abuse treatment, public assistance programs, and support groups. Representative payee and vocational training resources are also located at the clinic. Though these programs operate separately, the co-location of services is convenient to many clients.

Personal Cultural Competencies

Engagement, Trust, and Relationship-building Conversations with black psychosocial staff at my agency suggest that there still remains a large stigma attached to receiving mental health services, or any kind of public assistance, in the community. bell hooks states, "Women who received assistance from the state—women on welfare—were pitied not because they did not have jobs but because they did not have men to provide for them, men who would make them respectable" (hooks 2000a, 20). Thus, I believe that the engagement process, especially building trust in the "system," is key to retention.

In the engagement process, it is important to address clients in a more formal manner using "Mr." or "Ms.," as this helps to create a sense of professionalism and respect.

I feel that a most important aspect of building a relationship with black clients is to recognize that many may subscribe to a worldview—an Africentric perspective—that gives priority to the collective over the individual (Edwards 1996). Furthermore, pride in the successes of individual group members and concern about failures could make sharing problems and seeking help complex tasks. Social workers also must acknowledge how religion and biculturalism shape both clients' understanding of problems and needs and the formation of goals and objectives. Using ethnographic interviewing techniques, I could engage my client in asking her to share about her community in geographic, familial, spiritual, and friendship terms. This would help me understand the dynamics of the matrix of support that the black community employs.

Assessment and Problem Definition Tools that would be helpful with my population include the person-in-environment model and the strengths assessment. These can help identify the strengths and needs of clients, informal networks, and the broader community. They can also facilitate the discussion and validation of the client and community's experience with racism, and acknowledge the lack of access and resources that continue to plague the black community today. Both environmental and personal struggles could have played a major role in turning these many strengths into problems and stressors. For example, the notion within families about collective responsibilities (e.g., older children taking on parental tasks) has the potential of turning into resentment or pressure. The worker can also affirm the strengths of being bicultural and acknowledge that society has refused to recognize the inherent biculturalism of groups who must function in both societies—theirs and that of the dominant culture.

Contracting and Goal Setting It is important to instill a sense of hope during the contracting and goal-setting stage. I hope that clients in a therapeutic relationship would see that our meetings to discuss goals could alleviate stress and increase self-awareness and functioning. Treatment goals should be client-driven within self-identified contexts, and support an Africentric perspective if this is the client's choice. Goals should be appropriate and meaningful within the cultural context, and should be expressed in the client's terminology within that context.

Interventions In general, interventions should be implemented at the family and community levels as well as the individual level. Workers should be careful to structure interventions in a culturally appropriate manner. It is important for the client to view the intervention as a joint effort between client and worker. Including worker tasks and responsibilities creates and supports a mutual alliance.

Resources that a worker can utilize include kinship circles, and the client's informal network/system of care, such as neighbors, relatives outside the area, and church friends. Because the black community values collective responsibility and collective sacrifice, these resources would be appropriate and relevant in working with clients in a variety of settings.

Evaluation and Termination During this process, workers should be especially aware that the entire black community takes pride in the success of its members, and suffers from their failures. Thus, the experience of problems and how they are dealt with is felt at many levels in both the family and the community. It is important to assist the client to determine what has been accomplished through the helping process. Endings are generally viewed as something positive because they mean a step toward self-sufficiency and self-determination, as well as community-sufficiency and community-determination. I believe progress and moving forward instills a greater sense of hope for present and future generations.

NASW Standards for Cultural Competence

Agency As an agency that is part of the county system, my field placement's major

strengths are the focus on culturally competent service delivery (Standard 3) and professional education (Standard 10) (National Association of Social Workers 2001). Since the primary charge of county government is to deliver services to the most vulnerable and at-risk populations, the county tries to cultivate a workforce that is able to deliver services both in a professional and culturally competent manner.

When I was able to participate in administrative meetings and system-wide training, I saw that the county makes good attempts to ensure that services are provided with client and culture in mind. Black women and their problems are considered with care, concern, and empathy.

Services and Policies I believe that the services and policies of my agency strive for excellence in cross-cultural skills (Standard 4), empowerment and advocacy (Standard 6), and diverse workforce (Standard 7). Members of the black community, especially black women, are well-represented in my agency at all levels in a proportion fairly close to that of the client population. Through observation at staff meetings, policies and protocols, and instruction by my supervisor, I believe that programs are created and implemented to support culturally competent services to black women. The focus on people—both staff and consumers—is what makes my agency a unique place to work and receive services.

I feel there is a commitment to sharpening skills (e.g., staff are encouraged to attend training), to the empowerment of clients and consumers (e.g., consumers work as interns in the clinic), and to maintaining a diverse workforce. As no training specific to cultural competence or to black women has been offered to my knowledge, it might be beneficial to include this in future workshop planning.

Personal Competence I believe my greatest strength is my self-awareness (Standard 2), and I have made a personal commitment to gain additional cross-cultural skills (Standard 4) while in school and during my internship.

Though at times I feel anxious about my skills in general as a beginning professional, I know that it will take years to acquire and sharpen cross-cultural skills. I also know it takes willingness and a certain amount of humility to be open to making mistakes, learning from them, and looking to my clients to be my guides.

REFERENCES

Babyface (producers). 1995. *Waiting to Exhale* [soundtrack]. United States: Arista Records.

Boyd, V. 2005. Our Eyes Were Watching Halle: Can Oprah Winfrey and Halle Berry Turn Zora Neale Hurston's Classic Tale into a Prime-time Winner? *Essence* (March 2005)

***County Mental Health Plan, Online Services Guide.

Davis, J. Who is black: One nation's definition. In K. Rosenblum and T-M. Travis. 2003. *The Meaning of Difference.* New York: McGraw Hill.

***Department of Public Health. Cultural and Linguistic Competence Policy. No. 102

***Department of Public Health. Provider Manual.

Edwards, V. Clinical case management with severely mentally ill African-Americans. (Chapter 7). In P. Manoleas, ed. 1996. *The Cross-Cultural Practice of Clinical Case Management.* New York: Haworth.

hooks, b. 2000a. *Where We Stand: Class Matters.* London: Routeledge.

hooks, b. 2000b. *All About Love: New Visions.* New York: William Morrow.

Hurston, Z. 1937. *Their Eyes Were Watching God.* New York: Harper Collins.

Martin, D. (director). 2005. *Their Eyes Were Watching God* [made-for-TV film].

National Association of Social Workers (NASW). 2001. *NASW Standards for Cultural Competence in Social Work Practice.* Washington D.C.: Author.

U.S. Census. 2000. http://www.census.gov/main/www/cen2000.html

West, C. http://www.cornelwest.com

Whitaker, F. (producer). 1995. *Waiting to Exhale* [motion picture]. United States: 20th Century Fox.

Worksheet

1. The author suggests that, as no cultural competence training has been offered through the agency, it might be helpful to plan such a workshop. What are the elements you believe to be most important in training for cultural competence in working with black women? Develop an outline for this training.

2. Black colleagues interviewed during this project have suggested that there is a stigma associated with asking for mental health services in the black community. From your knowledge of black communities and values, develop an outreach program to help black women find the services they might need.

Culturally Competent Social Work Practice with African Americans

Diversity Project by Richie Zevin

My field placement during the past year has been with the Community Aftercare Program at the Family Care Project located in an urban setting, and providing clinical case management services for adults with severe mental illness. Because of the diversity of the city's population, my agency serves clients from many different cultural groups. I've chosen to focus my work on learning more about the African American population. As a white, Jewish kid growing up in an almost unbelievably homogeneous New Jersey suburb, I had very little contact with anyone from cultural and ethnic backgrounds different from my own. At the same time, my physician father has had his medical practice in the inner city for the past 35 years, and he's estimated that 95 percent of his patients are African American and working class. Yet we only rarely discussed issues of race in my house, and I feel that I learned some skewed lessons in childhood: residential segregation is acceptable; most people living in poverty are black; we live in a meritocracy.

I've since gained an understanding of the pervasive hegemony that preserves the status of the cultural elite; realized that the mainstream media's portrayal of impoverished African Americans ignores the fact that a majority of impoverished individuals in the United States are children and caucasian; and created my own social circle to include people from a variety of backgrounds and ethnicities. Despite my broader understanding of the concepts and policies and perspectives that historically dictated and currently influence the treatment of African Americans, I've never had the opportunity to synthesize this information through a more detailed study of the direct experience of African Americans in our society. By reading histories and memoirs; watching a movie that addresses with wit and intelligence the con-

temporary, urban African American experience; interviewing a member of the African American community; and attending an event during Black History Month, I've been able to piece together for myself a more complete awareness and appreciation of the adaptations, struggles, triumphs, and tragedies that have influenced and continue to influence the African American experience.

KNOWLEDGE OF POPULATION

History

According to the 1998 World Almanac, 33.8 million African Americans live in the United States, comprising about 13 percent of the overall population. But the Almanac's statistics have little to do with the actual experience of these individuals in the United States. It says nothing of the way in which white slavetraders shipped innumerable Africans to the Americas, nor does it discuss what happened to the Africans once they arrived on U.S. soil. This past summer I read a novel of historical fiction called *The Known World*, by Edward P. Jones (2003). The book describes the diversity of experiences among African Americans within one county in Virginia during the years leading up to the Civil War. There are slaves, people who bought their freedom from slavery, people who bought their freedom only to be unjustly forced once more into slavery, people who look like whites but are not, African American slaveowners, and slaves who wish to be slaveowners. It seems that there is no single common experience that defines a culture, but rather a broad variety of experiences that occur within a culture.

An Autobiography and a Film: *The Color of Water* and *Who's the Man?*

I can only begin to understand the larger developments that affected African Americans when I study the personal experiences of those individuals—real or fictionalized—who lived through them. The Civil Rights movement, perhaps the foremost example of such a larger development, did not arise spontaneously on a timeline, but rather grew out of the struggles of educators and leaders over the course of decades whose "hard work . . . seemed far more heroic in the hour of harvest than it did during the years of cultivation" (Anderson 1988, 278). In order to ascertain the products of that harvest, I read James McBride's *The Color of Water: A Black Man's Tribute to His White Mother* (1996).

McBride writes about being one of 12 children in a family, all of whom appear black to the outside world, and all of whom have a white, Jewish-turned-Christian mother who encourages them to look beyond color, and to rely on religion and education to guide them through the world. His mother had left her family in the South, married and had eight children with an African American man in New York, was widowed, married another African American man, had four more children, and became a widow yet again. McBride states that "during the rare, inopportune social moments when I found myself squeezed between black and white, I fled to the black side, just as my mother had done. . . . Given my black face and upbringing it was easy for me to flee into the anonymity of blackness, yet I felt frustrated to live in a world that considers the color of your face an immediate political statement, whether you like it or not" (262).

When McBride visits his mother's home-town of Suffolk, Virginia, after he's grown up and finishes college and decides to write a book about his history and his mother's history, he stands in front of the town synagogue trying to figure his next move. He realizes that he's been looking "up and down the street every couple of minutes lest the cops come by and wonder why a black man was loitering in front of a white man's building in the middle of the day. . . . This is, after all, the nineties, and any black man who loiters in front of a building for a long time looking it

over is bound to draw suspicion from cops and others who think he's looking for an open entrance so he can climb in and steal something" (220). Although the Civil Rights movement gave an "official" voice to the African American community, it takes more than a law and nearly half a century to change public perceptions, no matter the strength of the values and achievements of individuals who identify as members of the community.

In addition to reading *The Color of Water,* I watched a film called *Who's the Man?* (1993), starring Ed Lover and Dr. Dre, the erstwhile hosts of the now defunct Hip-Hop television program *Yo, MTV Raps!* The plot centers around two African American barbers who join the police force and uncover the ruthless scheme of a white businessman who is buying large amounts of property in Harlem. When I first watched the movie about ten years ago, I laughed at the jokes and smiled at the cameo appearances by some of the luminaries of Hip-Hop, like Ice-T and Busta Rhymes.

Watching the movie again, I realized that although it has many funny scenes, the story actually addresses four major issues that the African American community faces: the gentrification of working class African American neighborhoods by white capitalists; class struggle and division within the African American community; the limited number of careers that young African Americans growing up in poor, urban environments can pursue; and the problems that drug trafficking and addiction can bring to neighborhoods that were once safe.

In *Who's the Man?,* a greedy white capitalist pays members of the African American community to convince small business owners to sell him their property, thus undermining the solidarity of the community by bankrolling the class ambitions of a susceptible few. Meanwhile, the movie's protagonists are faced with the choice of enrolling in the police academy and joining the force—which they and their community view as "The Man"—or sitting around watching reruns of the *Beverly Hillbillies.* The film also implies that white capitalists are either directly or indirectly behind the drug trade in Harlem, and that once the property values have decreased as a result of the crime associated with the drug trade, white corporate business-men can and do swoop in and act as if they're doing the African American community a favor by buying their property at "reason-able" rates and building astronomically-priced condominium complexes. The ease with which white America is able to subvert the united efforts of black America indicates that cultural hegemony is alive and kicking, and the film presents a very negative picture of the dominant culture.

A Cultural Event: A Tribute to Black History Month

It is a testimony to the resilience of the African-American community that, despite being treated as second-class citizens or worse throughout much of U.S. history, the com-munity's artistic achievements are incredi-bly rich. Within the past several years, I've seen exhibits of the work of the painter Jacob Lawrence and the collage artist Romare Bearden, and I've been captivated by the intensity of colors and the striking posture of the human figure as expressed on canvas. Lawrence and Bearden capture the power and strong emotions of the Civil Rights struggle in their artwork. The viewer's immediate recognition of their understanding and inter-pretation of that struggle marks their work as both powerful and innovative.

However, for this particular assignment, I tore myself away from the Lawrence and Bearden monographs in the library and attended the Fillmore Nights Tribute to Black History Month at the African American Art and Culture Complex. The performances in the first act were meant to recreate the life of San Francisco's Fillmore District in the mid-1940 through mid-1960 nightlife scene, taking the audience for a walk down Fillmore Street, stopping first in a blues club, then in a jazz club, and then in an after-hours club. During the second act, cover bands per-formed songs by Gladys Knight and the Pips, and by Smokey Robinson and the Miracles.

The majority of both performers and audience was African American, and during the second act I realized that many of the audience members were relatives or friends of the performers. As a female singer in her twenties finished a song, a middle-aged man in the front row yelled, "She's so fine!" The woman next to him laughed and yelled to the rest of the audience, "It's okay, he can say that 'cause he's her Daddy!" Though I was alone, I did not feel unwelcome. Some people sitting around me were friendly during the inter-mission, some were indifferent, and nobody seemed hostile or apprehensive. However, although I appreciated the show artistically and intellectually, I could only imagine the nostalgia that people were expressing for the old Fillmore experience, and listen while many audience members sang along to songs I'd never heard.

It wasn't until the end of the show, when a cover band called The Best Intentions sang Smokey Robinson's *The Tracks of My Tears*, that I was able to join in. For me, it was a matter of finding that piece of common ground and shared experience that could allow me to connect with the group. Com-mon ground and shared experience are strong bases for any relationship, and it might be a matter of searching a little harder and deeper for them when interacting with members of disparate cultures.

A Personal Interview: Bernie

While attending a Youth Activism panel dis-cussion in which my 16-year-old niece was participating at the library, I found myself sit-ting next to an African American woman who made several insightful comments about the role that schools play in helping connect stu-dents to community activist organizations. During a break in the program, I asked her about herself and her experiences in schools when she was younger, and eventually asked if I could interview her for a school project.

Bernie explained to me that she moved to this city from Texas when she was in ele-mentary school, and that she never knew that desegregated schools existed until she stepped into her classroom and found that her teacher was white. She talked about how the Japanese Americans the U.S. government placed in internment camps during World War II took years to resettle with any level of comfort or financial stability, and shared that she was always filled with guilt as well as relief during that time as the brunt of racism was directed toward Japanese Americans instead of toward her and the African American community. She was later shocked when a Jewish friend of hers admitted that she felt the same way when racism toward African Americans moved the spotlight away from the Jews. Over time she found herself developing more sympathy for Native Americans than for her own people—"after all," she said, "the government came in uninvited and stripped from the Native Americans all of their land and rights, and the population still hasn't recovered."

Bernie talked about a special experience she had at a high school football game. The other school had bussed in Samoan students from other neighborhoods to help the football team, and Bernie had her first experience of seeing black people who were not of African or Caribbean heritage.

The most sustained racism Bernie ever felt was while she was taking classes at a university following the Kent St. University shootings during the Vietnam War protest there. There was a palpable tension on campus, and she thought that the police officers stationed there expected her to do horrible things simply because she was young and African American.

Bernie believes that education is the only way to prevent racism—education for the perpetrators of racism, and for herself as well, so that if someone approaches her with stereotypes based on her skin color, her knowledge of subjects from chemistry to current events will help to contradict them.

Conclusions

The African American clients with whom I currently work not only must contend with the underlying stereotypes that influence many people's beliefs about them based on their skin color, but also with the stigma associated with major mental illnesses. One of my clients, a 60-year-old African American woman with schizophrenia, told me recently that she feels as if she's been "three different colors" in her life, apparently based upon the different ways others have treated her at different stages of her life. I think that's an appropriate metaphor for the African American experience in a more general sense—during slavery and for many years after it, African Americans were not treated as the equals of whites in most parts of the country. Then, during the Civil Rights movement, African Americans were often feared by the white community for their potential to usurp power from the traditional white establishment. Finally, in the post–Civil Rights movement era, the diverse and culturally rich African American identity began to take its rightful place in the larger community.

I gained several insights from my interview with Bernie that I think will help me in working with African Americans, but also with many other groups. Recognizing the relief mingled with guilt that a member of a group that has experienced oppression and discrimination feels when the "spotlight" of racism becomes focused on another group is a consequence that I had not previously considered. The spotlight moves from group to group as the media dictates, and it is important to be aware of the effect of the spotlight not only on the group it highlights, but on other groups as well. Bernie also indicates that, as an African American, she has to be prepared to respond to racism at all times, and that it continues to be a regular part of her everyday life. Though many positive changes occurred as a result of the Civil Rights movement, racism is still a part of her experiences today. In her concern for Native Americans and their experience, she expresses an empathy that may come in large measure from her own experience. Perhaps, then, it is important for social workers to be in touch with some of their own experiences of oppression and powerlessness—

even if in other contexts and circumstances—so that they can tap into their clients' emotions and be more fully able to empathize authentically.

Historically and presently, Jews also experience oppression and discrimination, and I feel that there are elements of common experiences that Jews share with African Americans. I chose to read *The Color of Water* in part because it blended some of these parallel experiences, and Bernie's sharing her insights about her Jewish friend's experience with the "spotlight" helped me to see some of the commonalities between the two groups. However, I also know that it is important for me to recognize that there are many differences, and that each group often considers its own experiences to be quite unique.

Applying the Knowledge Base: Agency, Services and Policies, and Personal Competencies

FIELD WORK AGENCY PROGRAM: CASE MANAGEMENT FOR CLIENTS WITH MENTAL ILLNESS

The Community Care Project in which I am placed within my agency provides case management services to mentally ill clients who live in Board and Care homes in the city. Because this is a field agency, it is the case manager's responsibility to visit his or her clients in the variety of neighborhoods in which they reside. An interesting facet of this system is that CCP's clients do not necessarily live in their communities of choice, but rather in a house in a neighborhood where there was an available bed at the time the client was designated for the corresponding level of supervised care. Therefore, clients are often geographically disconnected from others in their ethnic communities, and instead find themselves in extraordinarily diverse households whose managers and staff members do not necessarily employ culturally sensitive methods of care.

Around 15 to 25 percent of the clients my agency serves are African American.

The Field Work Agency

Community The office is located across the street from an ornately domed Russian Ortho-dox Church. The neighborhood is largely Russian and East Asian, and the agency is situated inconveniently for any clients who wish to visit—many of the clients live in homes in various neighborhoods close to the center of the city, while the agency is located on the city's outskirts. African American clients would probably travel through various ethnic communities in order to reach our agency.

Access Public bus transportation is available but far from ideal, as buses can be quite slow during peak hours. Clients rarely visit the agency's office, and times for visits are arranged by the case manager. If a case manager does not own a car, traveling to see a single client at a remotely located house can consume an entire day—not a particularly efficient use of time. Furthermore, many of the clients have cognitive impairments significant enough to limit their abilities to contact their case managers, even in times of crisis—the ability to remember or locate a case manager's phone number, have immediate access to a telephone, and the ability to dial the number are often impaired.

Receptivity The staff is an ethnically diverse crowd, and I commend the management for hiring case managers who come from various cultures (Korean, Nicaraguan, Venezuelan).

However, African Americans are under-represented among the staff, which consists of 12 people in all, including two interns. The two individuals on the staff who are African American are the Office Manager (a position that consists almost exclusively of receptionist duties and data entry) and a Case Manager whose excellent clinical skills belie her lack of formal education (she never received a college education, much less a graduate degree). These two employees are presumably among the lowest-paid staff members, and as a direct result of their relatively low positions in the agency hierarchy they are certainly two of the least influential in the agency's decision-making processes. Therefore, it seems to me that African Americans are not proportionately or appropriately represented among staff members in light of the number of African American clients that the agency carries. However, on the rare occasions when an African American client visits the agency, he or she is greeted by an African American receptionist.

Upon interviewing the supervisors and case managers at my agency, I found that their backgrounds are overwhelmingly *not* grounded in social work, but rather in clinical psychology, counseling, and even philosophy. While I trust that many of my colleagues are aware of issues of diversity, I saw little evidence that they had ever formally studied culturally sensitive methods of practice. This gap in training highlighted for me *outside* of the classroom the precise lesson that the School of Social Welfare impresses upon its students *inside* the classroom: what makes social work special is its focus on person-in-environment—physical, social, and cultural as well. Each of these has an essential role to play in our work with clients.

Administration and Training The case managers use a client-centered approach to develop goals in conjunction with the client, no matter the severity of the client's cognitive impairments. But the client-centricity only covers the realm of mental illness, and does not readily extend to cultural sensitivity. Staff trainings, to the best of my knowledge, acknowledge the diversity of the symptoms of disorders like schizophrenia, but not the diversity of the ethnic backgrounds of the individuals who suffer from schizophrenia. Supervision sessions also focused on clinical techniques to address the client's mental illness, rather than on interventions that would reconnect the client to his or her ethnic community.

Staff Sensitivity The staff is generally respectful to clients, regardless of ethnicity or severity of impairment, but they are markedly less formal than I had expected. Many clients are older adults, often in their fifties or sixties, and the majority of the staff is under the age of 50. Yet I rarely heard a client addressed by anything other than his or her first name. The only occasion during which a client was introduced to me in a more formal way (as "Mr. H—") occurred when I shadowed the African American Case Manager, and she introduced me to a client of hers who was an older African American man. This simple form of deference seemed appropriate, and I believe that it would have been appropriate in other cases, as well.

I certainly felt odd when addressing several of my clients by their first names without their explicit permission, but they were introduced to me as "Gertrude" and "Karl" and "Gary" (pseudonyms, for purposes of confidentiality), and I had little opportunity to alter that system. More importantly, even the clients who come from cultures in which the elderly are traditionally treated with deference and respect had no choice but to accept that their case managers would address them by their first names, no matter the age difference or cultural distinctions. I never once heard a discussion at my agency about the disempowering effects that this culturally insensitive practice could potentially create.

Funding The irony inherent in the Community Care Project (CCP) structure is that, despite its expressed commitment to client-centered services, the supervisors constantly complain that funding is so sparse during today's unforgiving economic climate that there is little petty cash on hand to reimburse employees or clients for fees associated with connecting clients to community organizations. Because the clients themselves are limited to incomes derived from Social Security and the occasional part-time job, and because most of that income pays for their rent at the Board & Care facility, they are usually left with about $100 each month of spending money.

For many clients, that translates into the guilty pleasures of a cup of coffee and a pack of cigarettes each day, and there's no money left over to attend an event at the African American Arts and Culture Complex, for example. The case managers—even if they had more funds at their disposal to connect their clients to culturally appropriate events and organizations—have caseloads of 45 clients, and thus can only give attention to clients who are in crisis or who require interventions to maintain their current levels of functioning. Clients who are interested in connecting to their cultural community are often the clients who receive the least amount of consideration from a case manager, because they are the most stable, and assisting clients in this way does not seem to be a high priority.

Agency Services and Policies

Effort The agency's mission statement describes 65 percent of the clients it serves as "cultural or ethnic minorities." Of the 16,076 clients that the agency supports, 3,066 are African American, which by my calculations is about 19 percent of the overall clientele. The percentages of African American and other minorities within the Community Care Project have either not been compiled or not been made available publicly, but as mentioned earlier, they appear to fall into these same ranges.

CCP has made gestures to include its clients in the design of its services, but not necessarily from a standpoint of cultural diversity. The agency invited one of its clients to be the consumer representative during directors' meetings that would formulate the policy and nature of services in the future, but there seems to have been little thought given to including consumers from minority groups; the client who serves on the committee is caucasian, highly functioning, and has been an active consumer advocate for many years. The agency made no attempt to reach out to its more underserved clients for this position, and instead chose to congratulate itself for including a single client in its decision-making processes. While I believe it is a nice start for the Community Care Project to gain insight into what services its clients actually want, I think the agency has much work left to do in terms of incorporating the needs of its diverse consumer base into its program model.

Quality Because the clients who comprise CCP's caseload have such severe mental illnesses, culturally sensitive practice becomes secondary. Culturally competent practice is present, but it is like a wallflower: the staff members are only peripherally aware of its existence, and they only acknowledge it if it gets in the way of a primary objective. In fact, some of the interventions that CCP's employees use in order to address psychotic symptoms in clients serve to persuade the client to act according to societal norms, and fail to address the diversity piece entirely. For example, I asked my supervisor for advice regarding a client of mine who routinely stood outside his door yelling about CIA/Communist conspiracies and the assassination of John F. Kennedy, and who was beginning to frighten and bother the neighbors. My supervisor told me to ask the client if he sees anyone else yelling to themselves outside, and what the client thinks he looks like to others when he acts that way.

I worked with my client using the intervention my supervisor recommended, and while the intervention achieved its objective, I began feeling very uncomfortable using a technique that convinced my client to act like everybody else and conform to societal standards. While this particular client is caucasian, I thought about how I would feel using this style of intervention with an individual from a minority culture that has been oppressed in the United States for, say, hundreds of years. If I, as a white male case-worker, encourage an African American female client to conform her behavior in a specific way in public, am I simply reinforcing centuries of cultural hegemony? Am I helping this individual to function in a society dominated by a select few who wish to limit her opportunities and silence her voice? What agencies that I link her with will respect her and accept her for who she is, with her mental illness and minority status? These questions motivate me to provide culturally sensitive services, and they allow me to assess whether I'm actually succeeding.

Efficiency As discussed earlier, it is perhaps the desire to efficiently see 45 clients every month that poses an obstacle to a more profound degree of culturally sensitive services at CCP. In the interest of keeping a single client out of the hospital, a Case Manager has little time to spare to learn about the unfamiliar cultural background of a different client, who would benefit from such attention, but not decompensate without it.

Effectiveness My definition of effectiveness encompasses not only the provision of appropriate treatment for a client, but also the degree of genuine time devoted to each client. As social workers, we are effective if we help to empower a client, not just maintain him or her at a functionally impaired level when there is more potential for growth. However, the county government allots a limited number of billable hours to a Case Manager per client, at the "level of service," which this agency is contracted to provide. Therefore, Case Managers often do not have the luxury of exploring their clients' cultural backgrounds or developmental experiences. With a rubric so slanted toward crisis intervention, the agency's services fall short of their full potential for benefitting their clients.

Personal Cultural Competencies

During my time as an intern at CCP, I found that only in rare cases had my clients been previously provided with culturally appropriate services. One extraordinarily high-

functioning and independent client of Jewish heritage, for instance, had had a brief connection with Jewish Family Services several years back, but had not been in contact with that organization for quite some time. In my population of study—African Americans—I found that there was a great desire among clients to reconnect with their families, rather than with organizations set up for the explicit purpose of providing resources to African Americans with mental illness.

Trust and Relationship-building I noted a great deal of anxiety and concern about the client's impairment becoming known in the cultural community, which seemed to contraindicate linking clients with mental illness resources within the African American community. One 60-year-old African-American client explained to me that she only "wants white people" providing services for her until she links up once again with the husband and children she has not seen for decades. Another African American client in his late fifties said that he doesn't leave the house for weeks at a time because he's scared that younger African American males would hurt him because he is mentally ill.

I think there is a certain amount of shame, especially among some members of the older generation of African Americans with mental illness, around what they perceive as their failure to uphold the dignity of the community. As a result, some members might not want to reveal themselves to their communities of origin, and therefore miss out on some of the most culturally sensitive treatment they could receive. Instead, they rely on services rendered by the same dominant culture that has oppressed them. I think that this issue is not limited to the African American population, but extends across many ethnic and cultural minority groups in the United States for quite similar reasons.

Assessment In the Knowledge Base section of this case presentation, I discussed one client who explained that she feels as if she's been "three different colors" in her life, because of the ways that others have viewed her at different times. I only understood what she meant after using the Life Course Perspective tool, and matching up her life history with historical events, especially with those that specifically affected the African American community. She grew up while segregation existed throughout much of the country; she reached adulthood during the height of the Civil Rights movement and the Feminist movement; she is a member of three minority groups— African-Americans, women, *and* the mentally ill—that continue to struggle for equality and fair treatment in an unequal and unfair society.

Perhaps because they have lower expectations of what the mental health system can help them accomplish, my African American clients seemed surprised by the interest that I took in them. I hesitate to generalize about the population based on my experiences, but I sensed a degree of independence and pride among these particular clients that, on the one hand, allows them to survive, but, on the other, often limits their incentive to reach out to other individuals and groups in the community that would benefit them greatly.

Contracting and Goal Setting It is important for African American clients to feel empowered and to have a sense of control over the process of receiving help. For this reason, it is essential that the client take the lead in goal setting and in developing objectives. My African American clients seemed to prefer goals that were somewhat tentative, and strongly educational. This would support Bernie's statements about the value that education holds in the African American community.

My clients were interested in understanding their surroundings and becoming familiar with their neighborhoods. Together, we explored their neighborhoods of residence and the organizations and resources within them. However, my clients did not seem willing to engage with their surrounding, even to the extent of joining a church or simply obtaining a library card. There seemed to be a hesitation to engage with the greater community. This may have been due to a combination of factors: the frequent moves and

hospitalizations may have made connecting to any community seem pointless, the shame about mental illness within the African American community, and a lack of trust in other ethnic communities grounded in past experiences with racism and prejudice. It is important for the worker to be sensitive to these concerns, and to work with the client to develop goals and objectives that reflect their values, and not those of the worker.

Interventions In accord with the client-centered model that my agency utilizes in working with clients, my role in developing interventions is offering choices and options for courses of action and resources rather than taking a strong initiative in suggesting interventions to clients. The client-centered model is especially appropriate for working with African American clients as it is strengths-based and empowering. My clients' experiences will guide them in choosing interventions that are reasonable and acceptable to them.

It is also important to remember that African American clients consistently express the desire to reconnect with family, if not necessarily to the African American community as a whole. Helping a client to establish, or to reestablish, a relationship with a family member may be a very meaningful intervention. Helping to arrange visitation and supporting the client and the family member in maintaining contact is also very valuable.

Evaluation and Termination Reviewing the case management experience with clients is helpful in affirming the progress that has been made, and also in looking ahead to the next steps. Using the assessment tools and the contract enables worker and client to focus clearly and thoroughly on validating the client's achievements. It is important to ensure continuity and to support gains by assisting the client to make the transition to the next worker, and to assure the client that you have shared with the next worker your client's accomplishments, aspirations, and goals.

Upon visiting my clients of African American ethnicity for the final time, I found that our farewells were not as emotional as I had expected. I realized that they have said good-bye to many people in their lives, especially to many helping professionals. I think there's a cultural element, too—a certain understanding grounded in cultural history that life goes on even when sad things happen, and that *much* worse can happen and has happened than simply saying goodbye to someone whom you've known for a relatively short period of time. There is often a resiliency in long-term African American clients with mental illness that can be one of their greatest strengths.

Evaluation Using NASW Cultural Competency Standards

In evaluating the distinctions between agency, program, and practitioner I have encountered many differences in standards of cultural competence. My agency states that it espouses a diverse clientele, a diverse workforce, and a client-centered approach. In its agency description are references to several of the Cultural Competence Standards developed by NASW—Empowerment and Advocacy, Cross-Cultural Knowledge, and Ethics and Values (2001). I believe that the agency makes a sincere commitment to cultural competence, but I think that this commitment is not communicated effectively to the specific programs under the agency's umbrella.

The Community Care Project demonstrated a strong commitment to client-centered

services for adults with severe mental illness, but there was rarely a mention of the NASW standards with regard to cultural competency. The workforce is diverse, but diverse leadership is lacking. Several different Case Managers are bilingual, but there is no emphasis on culturally sensitive service delivery. Case Managers might be aware of cultural and ethnic perspectives, but they are rarely included in professional discourse. It is left to the individual practitioner to develop a standard of personal cultural competence in the provision of services. There is little support for such efforts on an agency-wide basis.

I was well aware of the importance of being sensitive and accommodating the needs of my diverse clients, African American as well as others. I was aware that my age and ethnicity might be off-putting to those clients who might prefer someone older and more accustomed to their respective cultural practices, and I tried to address these concerns with sensitivity as soon as I became aware that a client seemed uncomfortable with me. I made sure that I learned as much as I could about the cultures of the clients I was serving. What my agency taught me most is that there are gaps between what *could be* and what *is*, and that only by way of constant vigilance and self-assessment can I make sure that I am meeting the client not only where he or she currently is, but also where he or she came from.

REFERENCES

Anderson, J. D. 1988. *The Education of Blacks in the South, 1860–1935.* North Carolina: The University of North Carolina Press, Chapel Hill.

Demme, T. (director). 1993. *Who's the Man?* [motion picture]. United States: Newline Cinema.

Famighetti, R., ed. 1997. *The World Almanac and Book of Facts: 1998.* World Almanac Books.

hooks, b. 2000. *Where We Stand: Class Matters.* New York: Routledge.

Jones, E. P. 2003. *The Known World.* New York: Amistad.

McBride, J. 1996. *The Color of Water: A Black Man's Tribute to His White Mother.* New York: Riverhead Books.

National Association of Social Workers (NASW). 2001. *NASW Standards for Culturally Competent Social Work Practice.* Washington D.C.: Author.

Worksheet

1. The author suggests that shame, based on a possible perceived dishonor to the African American community as a whole, serves as a major barrier to African American clients with mental illness in seeking assistance and resources within the African American community. In order to address this problem, it may be essential to reframe mental illness in terms that are more culturally congruent.

   If you were a community practice social worker within an African American community, what are some of the steps you might take to begin to address this important issue?

2. The Community Care Project appears to be working effectively to meet the salient needs of this special client population. Frequent crises, difficulties in cognitive functioning, instability, and the need for close monitoring make strong demands on the time and energy of individual practitioners, who must continually prioritize clients' needs in terms of urgency. This may be contributing to the seeming lack of concern for cultural sensitivity and competence among the staff.

   If you were the director of this agency, and if you were concerned about cultural competence of your staff, how might you begin to address this issue? Possible options to be considered might include: developing a brief, mandatory training for all practitioners, providing literature on cultural competence for each practitioner to read and learn on his or her own, raising funds to hire more workers and decrease the caseload (thus allowing for time to address cultural issues with clients), hiring a cultural competence trainer who works with the staff on a regular basis, or other approaches.

   Consider each of these options by doing a cost-benefit analysis. Remember that funds in and of themselves are not the only "costs." Worker time, stress, turnover, and other hidden "costs" also need to be considered.

Culturally Competent Social Work Practice with Filipino Americans

Diversity Project by Rosa Solorzano

My current placement is at a major hospital's Social Services Department. The hospital is located in a city with a population of over 60,000 residents, but also serves patients from neighboring cities. While the majority of patients the hospital sees are insurance members, many patients with no insurance also arrive through the emergency department. Due to the diversity of the area, patients represent all income levels and ethnic backgrounds, however members generally tend to be working class or middle-income. Because of its location, the hospital has a large number of Filipino, Filipino American, and Latino patients. As a Latina, I chose to focus on Filipino Americans to develop cultural competence with this population.

KNOWLEDGE BASE

History

Filipino Americans are the second largest Asian group in the United States, having a population of nearly 2 million (U.S. Census 2000). Their history in this country reaches back to the late 1500s when Filipinos sailed to the United States on Spanish galleons (Minato 2004). Some escaped and built communities off the coast of Louisiana and California. In the year 1896, the United States claimed victory over the Spanish in the Spanish-American War and gained control over the Philippines. As a result, the Philippines were a commonwealth of the United States until the year 1946 (Minato 2004). In his essay, *Filipino Americans*, Ryan Minato (2004) describes two main waves of immigration from the Philippines since 1906. Between 1906 and 1946, 5,000 of the best students from the Philippines were provided small stipends to attend universities in the United States through the U.S. Pensionado Act of 1903, while over 100,000 were recruited to work on sugar and pineapple plantations in Hawaii and in California's farmlands (Minato 2004; Sharlin and Villanueva 2000).

When in 1946 the Philippines was granted independence, Filipinos went from an automatic U.S. national status to alien status, and immigration to the United States was abruptly restricted (Sharlin and Villanueva 2000). It was not until the Immigration Act of 1965 that Filipinos were again allowed to immigrate to the United States in large numbers. Filipino professionals entered the country in order to meet high labor demands (Minato 2004), and as economic and social unrest grew in the Philippines, other non-professional Filipinos and their families soon followed.

Filipino Americans have made significant, largely unacknowledged contributions to their adopted country through their struggles for social justice, by founding labor movements, and by joining forces with other groups to address discrimination. For example: by 1930, Filipino Americans were 15 percent of all the agricultural workers in California (Salomon 1994). Although companies expected the large incoming group of Filipinos to be docile and accept lower wages, they soon learned that these farm workers were quick to organize when faced with unfair labor practices. When they were not welcomed in the mainly white Agriculture Workers League, they formed the Filipino Agricultural Laborers Association (FALA), effectively organizing worker strikes and growing to over 30,000 members by 1940 (Salomon 1994). Eventually, they began to work collectively with Caesar Chavez and Mexican workers in the National Farm Workers Association, which led to their combined efforts under a new name, United Farm Workers (Salomon 1994).

Another contribution made by Filipino Americans involves military service. Filipinos were considered U.S. nationals and were called to active military duty during WWII (Minato 2004). Over 140,000 Filipinos served in the United States military and were promised benefits equal to those offered to all military. However, after the war, Filipinos were excluded from the benefits provided under the GI Bill. To this day, Filipino American veterans continue to fight for the full benefits they were promised and rightfully deserve for the sacrifices they made for this country (Minato 2004).

Stories and Biographies

Going Home to a Landscape, (Villanueva and Cerenio 2003) is a collection of short stories and poems by Filipinas and Filipina Americans that deals with many of the issues, including those of farm workers and veterans, that Filipinos have faced throughout the history of their relationship with the United States. One of the consistent themes is the pain caused by separation felt by families and individuals as they, or loved ones, left the Philippines to seek a more financially stable life in the United States. One of the short stories, "Mang Tomas," written by Victoria Sales Gomes (Villanueva and Cerenio 2003), an ICU nurse born in the Philippines, but now living in San Francisco, had a great impact on me. She shares her experiences as an immigrant woman working as a nurse when an elderly Filipino veteran, Mang Tomas, is hospitalized with terminal lung cancer. Her longing to be with her father and this veteran's lack of family lead her to form an intense bond with him. She also shares her frustration with her lack of power in her workplace, and her inability to give voice to the injustices this man encountered.

Because my current field placement is in a hospital ICU, where the majority of nurses are Filipina, this story gave me a great amount of insight into the power dynamics in hospitals and the expectations placed on nurses to support, but never contradict, physicians, who tend to be white males. Additionally, Mang Tomas's advanced stage of illness is directly related to the lack of the medical benefits to

which he was entitled as a veteran. Mang Tomas represents the thousands of Filipino veterans that were emotionally damaged by the war and were left to face a lonely, poverty-stricken existence in the United States.

Another very beautiful, yet heartrending story in Villanueva and Cerenio's collection (2003), *Cold*, by Noelle de Jesus, involves a young woman, Katrina, who comes to the United States to pursue a master's degree at a small Midwestern university. The writer relates the physical assaults Katrina's body experiences when acclimating to the intensely cold weather and the emotional and psychological pain she feels as she encounters discrimination, ignorance, and homesickness. Having left the Philippines full of hope and excitement, she soon begins to struggle to find her voice and battle insecurities over her Filipina appearance—dark hair, skin, and eye color—in contrast to her white classmates. Invited by well-meaning but insensitive friends to a traditional Thanksgiving dinner, she is introduced to a Korean student. Due to their shared status as "Asian students," their hosts expect them to instantly have many things in common. Katrina is frustrated and humiliated by the disregard for two unique cultures with entirely different histories, languages, and traditions. In the last paragraph of the story, she declines an invitation to have a drink with "friends"; she is alone in her room shaking from being cold. "She breathes to warm her skin, and waits for her heart to make the proper adjustments" (Villanueva and Cerenio, 93).

Film

While the two stories highlighted above focus on the experiences of immigrant Filipinas, I was able to gain more insight into the lives of second generation Filipino Americans through the film, *The Debut* (Cajayon 2001). This film depicts the life of the Mercados, a working class Filipino American family living in Los Angeles, as they prepare for a party celebrating their daughter's entrance into womanhood. Acculturation, the importance of family, Filipino traditions, and Filipino struggles are all addressed as the main character, Ben Mercado, the 17-year-old son who is ready to graduate from high school, faces identity confusion while attempting to assert his individuality. We gain insight into his feelings of shame about his family and the culture they represent through his attraction to a white schoolmate, his reluctance to introduce his white friends to his family, and his unwillingness to participate in, or learn any, Filipino traditions. Intergenerational conflict between Ben and his father due to expectations to accept a scholarship to UCLA instead of pursuing his dream to attend a prestigious art school highlights Ben's inability to recognize his father's motivations and sacrifices he has made for his family.

Because his friends insist on remaining at Ben's sister's debut, Ben experiences his culture and family in a new context. He is introduced to several young Filipinos who befriend him despite his reputation as a "coconut," brown on the outside, but white on the inside. Ben's awareness and appreciation of his culture grows as he watches his sister perform traditional Filipino dances, and learns about his father's own artistic aspirations and sacrifices for his family. Through one of his new friends, Ben also receives some brief, but poignant lessons on Filipino American history that force him to reassess his views and previous attempts to discard his Filipino identity in order to assimilate into American mainstream culture.

A Culture-specific Event: A Theater Production

I attended a theater production named *The Woman Monologues* at the Bindlestiff Studio, a small and welcoming venue with a focus on Filipino American theater and art, with a goal of promoting dialogue regarding issues facing the community. It also houses a community center, which encourages intergenerational communication and activities. *The Woman Monologues* included monologues performed by their Filipina writers addressing sexual abuse and its effects, a daughter's loving thoughts of her father, a young Filipina's embarrassment and pride as she encounters her "All American" crush while selling live

chickens at a local flea market, an undocumented Filipina working as an in-home aide and her responsibilities to her family in the Philippines, and a college student's speech to her sorority sisters before she gets deported to the Philippines due to her illegal status.

Because I attended this event alone, I was slightly concerned about how my presence would be perceived. When I arrived at the theater, I found small groups of young Filipinos and families gathered outside the theater discussing their friends' and family members' involvement in the production. I was welcomed at the front door and thanked for my support, but mainly went unnoticed during the 20-minute wait before the doors were opened. As we entered and chose our seats, I found that I was truly the only non-Asian audience member. I never felt any hostility, and while no one spoke to me, I felt at ease with the situation. Throughout the performances, I found myself laughing with other audience members, and because so many of the issues presented were universal to young women of all races and ethnicities, I was able to find connections to my life as a Latina. At the same time, I was still able to identify how these stories were specific to Filipino American culture through the manner in which they were told and subtle references to Filipino history.

As the production ended and the lights in the theater came on, I sensed that everyone was brought closer together through our appreciation for these young artists and their willingness to share their intimate thoughts and sometimes painful experiences with us. Several young Filipino Americans sitting next to me asked for my opinions, which led to a discussion about growing up in the United States and the importance of supporting positive community events. As I left, several theater volunteers thanked me again for my support, and encouraged me to come to the next month's production, called *F.O.B*, "fresh off the boat"—a slang term for recent immigrants. My final interaction with a fellow audience member occurred as I walked to my car. A young man was interested in my reasons for coming. I chose not to tell him about the assignment, and instead stated that San Francisco had a lot to offer in the arts, and I was curious to learn more about events that promoted cultural awareness. He smiled and said I should bring my friends the next time. That had been exactly what I was thinking before our conversation began!

Personal Interview

A Filipina friend was kind enough to recommend the book, film, and event I chose for this project. I asked her what she thought were the most important things for me to know about Filipino Americans. She began with her own family history, and her experiences as she left a predominately immigrant community and moved to a wealthier and predominately white neighborhood. She discussed the challenges she faced as she went to a school where there were very few Filipino students.

One comment that I had never encountered before was her thought that within some Asian communities, Filipinos were viewed as the "black" Asians. She said that although Filipinos are identified as Asian, they are very different from other Asian groups: their history involves Spanish colonialism, they have darker skin, more animated behavior, and strong connections to the Catholic Church. While these differences have sometimes led to discrimination, she also felt most connected to her "open, friendly, and warm" culture through them. She described Filipinos as very hospitable, vocal about feelings, and having a deep love for the performing arts. In addition, Filipino's have "soul." She explained how children are always encouraged to sing popular Filipino songs, or do traditional dances at Filipino gatherings, and how this positive attitude toward performing and celebrating led her to become involved in a cultural event known as Philipino Cultural Night (PCN) while in college, enabling her to form solid friendships with other Filipino students based on their deep appreciation for their culture and their desire to celebrate and share their heritage.

My friend feels that the Filipino community is still extremely tied to the Philippines and tends to view all Filipinos as extended family due to their shared experiences as immigrants. Good friends soon become cousins, and family friends are uncles and aunts. Filipinos introduce themselves by sharing their place of birth and if they speak Tagalog. There is a willingness to accept others into the group on the condition that they attend family and social gatherings and display culturally appropriate behavior such as greeting everyone present, being *carinoso* (affectionate), and being able to take a joke. A large number of Filipinos maintain close ties to the Philippines as *balik bayans*, or Filipinos who come to the United States for the opportunity, but return to their home country on a regular basis, or for retirement. Families also often pack large boxes filled with American products, candies, and food to bring to relatives, symbols of generosity and remembrance.

However, oppression and colonialism have led many Filipinos to form an "internalized colonial mentality" that, she feels, tends to idolize American culture and values and often results in internalized self-hate and a desire to adopt behaviors such as individualism and consumerism with a focus on material wealth. Her family and her college experience gave her the opportunity to learn the real history of the Philippines and taught her to be proud of her heritage. However, she is also concerned that her parent's generation has a higher percentage of individuals with college degrees than hers.

Conclusions

The project has provided me with the opportunity to learn a great deal about a culture in which I have always been interested. I was able to leave my comfort zone and ask questions that I would have been too shy or embarrassed to ask, and I feel that I can truly walk away with greater insight into many of the challenges and struggles Filipino Americans face. I also realize that now that I have this knowledge, my understanding will continue to grow as I encounter other Filipino Americans.

Applying the Knowledge Base: Agency, Service and Program, and Personal Competencies

FIELD WORK AGENCY: THE ICU UNIT OF A MAJOR HOSPITAL

The Agency

Access The hospital is centrally located in a major urban center. Public transportation is available; it is close to the freeway and parking is free. The hospital also offers taxi vouchers or assistance with Redi-Wheels enrollment, which provides low-cost transportation to those unable to utilize public transportation due to disabilities. The hospital is located in a neutral area of the city and many patients arrive via ambulance.

Receptivity Many culturally competent services are offered. A diverse staff of volunteers are "greeters" and help direct patients and their visitors. The hospital provides professional translators and signers as mandated by Title IV of the Civil Rights Act. The building provides easy access to wheelchairs. Elevators, wide hallways, and accessible restrooms are located throughout the hospital. The hospital's decor celebrates diversity and a commitment to customer service. Art work by artists of different cultures lines the hallways. Photographs of staff representing different positions and ethnic backgrounds with statements regarding patient care are near the entrance. Two of the six employees shown in these photographs are Filipino. The waiting rooms tend to be comfortable with literature in different languages, including Tagalog. Filipino patients will find that many members of the Filipino community make up the nursing, pharmacy, administrative, and custodial staff. However, while Filipinos are represented in several high earning positions such as nursing and upper management, to my knowledge there are no Filipino physicians. Additionally, the signage used throughout the hospital is only in English.

Administration and Staff Training While the staff at the hospital is very diverse, there is no ongoing diversity training available to all employees. When hired, employees are given small booklets with information regarding culturally sensitive practices and cultural differences they may encounter.

Staff Sensitivity During my field placement, I attended a training open to all staff where hospice services and palliative care were discussed. A Chinese-born social worker addressed death and dying from a traditional Chinese perspective. While most in attendance respected the information she provided, one particular physician attempted to discredit her thoughts. In her defense, several other physicians argued that staff needed to be open to suggestions in order to be culturally competent. The conversation made me realize that despite the hospital's efforts to promote cultural competency, key providers still may not have a basic grasp of the concepts. Apart from this one incident, I did not directly witness disrespect or insensitivity toward patients based on ethnic or cultural background. However, I did sense that the medical staff was often less empathetic toward patients with substance abuse-related medical problems, or who were young men hospitalized due to stabbing or gunshot wounds.

Funding The hospital's funding allows for Filipinos, as well as other cultures, to be served in a culturally sensitive manner. Literature is available for staff in the hospital library. As I mentioned, translation services are also readily provided and patient literature is available in various languages. However, social workers are expected to balance the medical approach of the hospital by providing psychosocial interventions, and therefore have more resources for outside training on cultural competence available to them than most medical staff.

Agency Services and Policies

Effort Because the approaches that different programs take vary throughout the hospital, I will focus only on social services. Within the Social Service Department, management has made consistent and serious efforts to deliver services that are sensitive to different cultures. The director of Social Service is Filipina, and throughout my placement has shared ideas with staff on how to improve the quality of services provided to patients from diverse backgrounds.

Effectiveness There is no system in place that includes patients in the process of formulating and designing culturally competent polices. Instead, individual plans are created for each patient. Patients' needs and strengths are thoroughly assessed, and they and their families then have a great amount of input in creating long-term plans for their care. Depending on the skill level of the social worker assigned to provide services, the quality of these plans can vary. However, providing culturally competent services is an important goal for all the social workers I shadowed and worked with, and patients ultimately have control over following recommendations.

One area that could be improved concerns the amount of time given to each particular patient. The Social Service Department has very limited staff resources, so social workers may be required to see up to 20 patients a day. Because patients that have large families who participate in decision making often take more time and coordination, there is a possibility that their needs may not be met as effectively. This is a particular disadvantage for Filipino patients due to the important role family plays in many of their lives.

As an intern, I had more flexibility in my schedule and could spend more of my time working with family systems as opposed to simply the patient. While I feel that other social workers would do the same if given the same opportunity, the reality of their work environment kept them from spending much time with each patient. As a result, workers used creative alternatives to support Filipino patients with these needs, and included contacting a local priest or chaplain to meet with religious families in need of emotional support, or assigned these patients to me because I had a smaller caseload.

Quality Evaluation surveys returned to the hospital from patients demonstrate that patients receiving social services tend to have positive views on social work services. While these evaluations are encouraging, it must be noted that not all patients returned surveys.

The Social Service Department is planning to hire two more social workers by the end of the summer, which will enable more time to be spent with patients and families. One of the requirements for both positions is that the social workers be bilingual.

Efficiency Patients are usually referred through other hospital employees such as physicians and nurses, but any patient who wishes to utilize social services is encouraged to do so. Generally, Filipino patients tend to be very open to social workers and the idea that someone is there to assist them. This is especially true when social workers approach patients in a caring and friendly manner and engage families and loved ones as well as the patients themselves.

It is common for Filipino patients to have rooms crowded with relatives and friends ranging from small children to elderly grandparents. This can cause problems due to noise level, lack of a consistent family representative, and confidentiality. However, social workers encourage these visits because they appear to have positive effects on the patients' morale.

Personal Cultural Competencies

Being hospitalized can have a major effect on the emotional and mental health of individuals. In general, patients can feel they have very little control over their situation and the clinical language medical staff uses can often be intimidating, impersonal, and lack emotion. In addition, many patients find that everyday stressors become amplified as the reality of obligations at work and home are considered. For these reasons, medical social work is generally viewed as a more "human" aspect of hospitalization that patients welcomed.

Engagement, Trust, and Relationship-building Through my immersion project, I learned that Filipino culture tends to be very open to speaking to new people. However, there can be an initial period of relationship-building that must occur before deeper concerns and problems are expressed. Therefore, I have found that the first contact is very important and should consist of a warm and friendly conversation that does not probe deeply into the private lives of patients too quickly. Family members must be greeted in a manner that displays an understanding of their importance. Because patients are receiving medical care and can be susceptible to infections, they are generally not touched, but I have found that some elderly patients feel more comfortable when they can hold your hand. All adults in the room receive business cards, and everyone is encouraged to contact social services with any questions. If a Filipino patient is alone, I ask about their home life and important people using open-ended questions and empathy.

Assessment and Problem Definition Assessing Filipino patients usually begins with a clear explanation on the role of the Social Service Department. It is imperative that they understand the reasons why we may need to ask personal questions, and that the information they share will be kept confidential. As with all patients, Filipino patients are encouraged to define their own problems and concerns. The role and importance, as well as the location of family members, is an essential ingredient of assessment with Filipino patients.

Contracting and Goal Setting Goal setting should focus on the problems they have identified as most pressing, and the desired outcomes. With the patient's consent, family members are invited to participate, and often contribute greatly to enabling patients achieve their goals.

Interventions Culturally appropriate interventions are also extremely important when serving Filipino patients in the ICU. Religious beliefs and language barriers must be taken into account. For patients and families seeking emotional support, empathy and sitting down with the family and discussing their feelings can be very helpful. Offering patients and their families a visit from a Catholic priest can be comforting. A Filipino priest from the local church is open to meeting with patients on very short notice, speaks Tagalog, and is also able to administer Last Rites. The sacrament of Last Rites or Extreme Unction can be very soothing to families and patients, helping alleviate anxieties, regrets, and the fear of death.

Placing a family elder who needs high levels of ongoing care can be extremely difficult for Filipino families, due to the high value placed on family cohesion and views on intergenerational responsibilities and obligations. By suggesting the family visit long-term care facilities that have a large number of Filipino residents and staff, families and patients feel more at ease with this difficult decision. Placement in these facilities also increases the likelihood that patients will adjust more easily. Familiarity with the food served, activities provided, and languages spoken have a positive effect on care.

Evaluation and Termination Because patients in hospital settings are referred to social services for a wide variety of reasons, success or failure is based on individual factors. Universal goals ensure that patients' psychosocial and concrete needs are met and that they will have needed resources available upon discharge. While services usually end at discharge, patients are encouraged to contact social services if questions or problems arise. Social workers meet with patients the day of discharge to review the established long-term plan and address any last minute concerns. Generally, patients look forward to leaving the hospital, and termination is viewed as a positive experience. Filipino cultural norms regarding separation usually consist of acknowledging the relationship and showing a high degree of appreciation. It is the social worker's role to then inform the patient and family how much they have enjoyed working with them and demonstrate a sincere desire for the patient to remain healthy.

Evaluation: NASW Standards for Cultural Competence

The Hospital This hospital demonstrates cultural competence in several areas according to NASW (2001) standards. It actively looks to promote and hire a diverse workforce that represents the population it serves. In compliance with Standard 6.04 (c), the hospital promotes policies and practices that "demonstrate respect for difference and support the expansion of cultural knowledge and resources." It also provides social workers with the opportunity to receive further education on diversity in respect to race, ethnicity, age, religion, and disabilities as required by section 1.05 (c). In addition, as stipulated by Title IV of the Civil Rights Act, the hospital provides free language assistance to all non-English speaking patients.

Additional attention could further increase the level of cultural competence. Implementation of mandatory training on cultural competence for all employees, including physicians, would enhance cultural competence across disciplines. The hospital could work harder to meet standard 6.04 (a) by engaging in social and political action that addresses inequalities in access to healthcare and other resources for the entire community, and not just insurance-plan members. In addition, it could invite the public to participate in shaping hospital policies and practices (6.02).

The Social Service Department The Social Service Department has gone to great lengths to meet NASW standards. In particular, the social work management team consistently provides and arranges for its staff to receive diversity training (1.05 (c)). It also requires all social workers to have a solid knowledge base of the cultures it serves, and expects them to be sensitive and respectful of differences (1.05 (b)). Social workers are also required to understand the concepts of culture and oppression, and recognize that strengths exist in all cultures (1.05 (a)). In accordance to standard 6.04 (c) the department also emphasizes the social workers' role as patient advocates that work toward promoting conditions and practices that support cultural and social diversity. This is particularly important during daily rounds, where social workers meet with medical staff to determine the needs of each patient.

However, like the hospital, the Social Service Department could still improve in becoming more culturally competent through how it approaches its obligation to global issues. At this time, the Social Service Department does not work toward promoting equal access to healthcare through political and social action. It also works within the hospital system and rarely advocates for system-wide change.

Cultural competency is extremely important to me. As a Latina, I have encountered discrimination in various forms and feel obligated to participate and support practices and policies that promote self-awareness, the development of cross-cultural knowledge and skills, and advocacy for patients and clients (1.05 (a)). I am also committed to working for the empowerment of disenfranchised and marginalized communities. During my field placement, I actively sought out opportunities to expand my knowledge base through discussions with patients and social work staff, as well as trainings (1.05 (c)). I have treated all of my patients' and their cultures with respect and an understanding of the various struggles they may have faced in life. I also see the MSW program as an opportunity to learn more about the issues surrounding access to medical care and what actions I can take to become more politically and socially involved.

Conclusion

No matter to what population or group a patient belongs, it is vital that as social workers we understand that cultural competency is based on effective cross-cultural communication, which includes empathy and a willingness to explore and learn. Within medical settings, this is demonstrated through the availability of effective services for diverse populations that emphasize respectful interactions and strong relationships between patients and hospital staff. While working with Filipino patients, respectful interactions and building strong relationships often entails recognizing the importance of family and being sensitive to the patient's emotional and spiritual needs. Through my field placement, I have learned that I have the ability to bring warmth to what patients often view as an intimidating and impersonal environment, which can have a big impact on how patients' perceive their overall care. I have also been able to advocate on behalf of my patients when I feel that the medical staff is overemphasizing their medical condition and ignoring cultural and social aspects of their care. I realize that becoming truly culturally competent is a process that requires time and experience, but I look forward to encountering challenges and growing to become a more sensitive practitioner.

REFERENCES

Minato, R. 2004. *Filipino Americans*. Commission on Asian Pacific American Affairs. http://www.capaa .wa.gov/filipinoamericans.html

National Association of Social Workers (NASW). 2001. *NASCO Standards for Cultural Competence in Social Work Practice*. Washington, D.C.: Author.

Salomon, L. 1994. Filipinos build a movement for justice in asparagus fields. *Third Force 2* (4), 30.

Sharlin, C. and L. Villanueva. 2000. *Phillip Vera Cruz: A Personal History of Filipino Immigrants and the Farm Workers Movement*. Seattle: University of Washington Press.

Cajayon, G. (director). 2001. *The Debut* [motion picture]. United States: Sony Pictures.

U.S. Census. 2000. http://www.census.gov/main/www/cen2000.html

Villanueva, M. and V. Cerenio. 2003. *Going Home to Landscapes: Writings by Filipinas*. St Paul, MN: CALYX Books.

Worksheet

1. Providing diversity competent and sensitive social work services can be very challenging in an ICU, where the patient may be unable to communicate, visitation time is limited, family members may be distraught, and confidentiality and privacy are luxuries not often readily available. How might you approach engagement and relationship-building in this setting?

2. Family relationships and support are extremely important to Filipinos. However, as is true for all cultures and groups, there are also people with a Filipino culture who do not have actively engaged and supportive families. Some of the WWII veterans mentioned in the history section might be examples of this. What might be some culturally congruent approaches for working with Filipinos who have no known active family members?

Culturally Competent Social Work Practice with Iranian Americans

Diversity Project by Greg Cohen

My field work agency is a county out-patient clinic located in an urban area that serves adults with mental illness. While my agency's community is primarily European American, with some Latino and African American members, it also serves a substantial Iranian and Iranian American population. I have chosen to focus my work in cultural competence on the Iranian American population because this group has long been of special interest to me, and also because current events have focused national interest on Iran.

KNOWLEDGE OF POPULATION

Historical Context and Distribution of Iranian Americans

To understand where Iranian Americans came from and why they are here, we must return to Iran, and a history heavily influenced by foreign domination. Shah Mohammad Reza Palhavi's father had been forced to abdicate by the British and Soviets, in reaction to his favorable relationship with Germany during WWII, leaving his son to assume power. In 1951, following years of protest against foreign domination of Iranian oil, the democratically elected Prime Minister nationalized Iranian oil fields. In 1953, prompted by the United States, the Shah attempted to dismiss the Prime Minister, who resisted this action with the force of his popular support. The Shah fled the country, but was soon returned to power in a coup organized and directed by the CIA.

Discontent with the ruling regime's aggression and failed economic reforms began brewing in the 1970s. Nationals who had lived in more open societies abroad, along with other secular elements, formed an organized, directed opposition to the Shah (Keddie 2003). Religious factions in Iran had also grown increasingly contemptuous of this very secular regime (Ibid).

Paralleling the mobilization of protests against the Shah was an increase in the popularity of Muslim cleric Ayatollah Khomeni, who was able to gain the support of the secularists, the urban poor, and disaffected Muslims with assurances of democratic rule (Ibid). Protests in 1978 culminated on Black Friday, as government troops opened fire on hundreds of thousands of demonstrators in the streets of Tehran, killing 3,000 (Sullivan 2001). Workers began to strike, and Iranian citizens roundly defied bans on public demonstrations. In early 1979, the Shah was forced into exile, and Ayatollah Khomeni became the ruler.

Many middle-class secularists believed at first that the revolution would cure the social ills they had experienced under the Shah (Eshagian 2001). "Many of the older men and women, particularly those who had been students abroad, were stunned to find themselves marginalized, imprisoned, and finally exiled by the event they helped create" (Sullivan 2001, 125). Pre-revolution factional unity faded as Khomeni took power. As Keddie (2003) notes, "The decade of Khomeni's rule was marked by the ever-growing power of his followers and elimination, often by violence and despite resistance, of opposition groups, and by increasing enforcement of ideological and behavioral controls on the population" (241).

In this climate, the option of leaving Iran became an obvious choice for many. As Sullivan (2001) notes in a qualitative study of the Iranian Diaspora:

> Each narrator remembers a slightly different moment that tolled the death knell of her or his particular notion of revolutionary possibility and its narrative of universal freedom. Months before the taking of hostages and the occupation of the American Embassy (which was for

many the last straw), there were other signs and portents. For some women, the moment was July 12, 1979, the day on which four women charged with prostitution were executed ... For some, it was the naming of new and imagined "enemies," followed by attacks on Kurdistan. For many it was the day the government closed the offices of the leading liberal newspaper, *Ayandegan*. For one woman, it was the day on which women bathers in the sea were flogged. For another, it was the day on which coeducation, even in elementary schools, was banned (summer 1979); for Lily, it was the day she saw "Zahra Khanum" who cursed her and all women like her. For Afsaneh, it was the killing of prostitutes, then the women's march on March 8, 1979, then the hostage crisis, and finally the Iran-Iraq war. (132)

Following his exile and Khomeni's rise to power, the ailing Shah sought health care in the United States, where he was granted entry. In response, the "Students Following the Line of the Imam" seized the U.S. Embassy in Tehran and took personnel hostage. With Khomeni's support, the hostage crisis lasted for 444 days (Keddie 2003).

In the wake of these events, hundreds of thousands of mostly modern, middle-class Iranians fled their home country, settling in the United States, France, Germany, and Turkey, among others (Keddie 2003). The 2000 U.S. Census identifies approximately 340,000 citizens of Iranian descent residing in the United States. (It should be noted that this figure categorically distinguishes Iranians from persons of Arabic ancestry.) The highest concentration of Iranians is in Los Angeles—often referred to as "Tehrangeles." Primary places of settlement include California generally and Washington D.C. There is a striking diversity of religious backgrounds among American immigrants, including Muslim, Jewish, Zoroastrian, Armenian Christian, Persian Christian, and Bahai.

With the hostage crisis came the demonization of Iranians and Iranian Americans, as American society began to widely apply an image of Islamic fanaticism to all Iranians. Threats of fingerprinting arose in the United States and Iranian exiles were subjected to hatred and alienation (Eshagian 2001). As a result of the stigma and shame that became associated with Iranian ancestry, many Iranian Americans began to distinguish themselves by identifying as Persian, or in some cases through their non-Muslim religion (Eshagian 2001).

Biography: *To See and See Again*

This beautifully written memoir by Tara Bahrampour provides a unique glimpse into the life of an American-born person who spent most of her childhood in Iran and her adolescence in the United States. Her parents met and married in Berkeley in the late 1960s. Her father was an architecture student and son of an Iranian landowner, her mother a singer and European American native of Los Angeles. They moved to Tehran, but fled during the revolution to Portland, Oregon, and then California. As Tara grew older, she yearned to reconnect to those pieces of herself she had left behind. She spent time in Iran as a college student in the 1990s, later returning to the United States, where she is currently living. Binational and bicultural, Tara provides a unique glimpse into the borderlands between personal and collective cultural identity, and the open spaces in between.

While living and attending an American school in Iran with her American mother and liberal, American educated father, she was aware that she enjoyed an independence other family members did not have. Yet, although she was part of two different communities and warmly accepted by both, she felt a certain distance from each.

Returning to the United States in adolescence, her family's financial difficulties and the moves from one community to another were trying for Tara. Her struggle to assimilate came at a time when many in the United States hated Iranians. It was especially difficult to fit in and find a sense of self or home, as she made new friends and strove to join her new community only to be cut loose each time her family moved. She reflects on her struggles:

> Didn't I feel just as displaced when we left Iran; didn't I look back just as longingly at my old life and disparage the new one—the American public schools that could never provide the Renaissance lectures and science classes I'd left behind, the series of houses that would never live up to Sharak, my parents' American jobs that were pale substitutes for the careers they would have thrived on in Iran. At age three I felt stolen away from one kingdom; by age eleven I had adapted so well to the new one that moving was like being stolen all over again. (Bahrampour 1999, 357)

As she grew older, Tara seamlessly navigated between family members, passing easily enough as Iranian, American, or a combination of the two, depending on circumstance. Tara is equally the product of Iran and the United States, and seems to relish this, despite her sense of being perpetually out of place.

> Now, on the Web site and everywhere else where I find Iranians, I see a similar sense of displacement. Strangely it seems strongest in Iranians my own age. Those young enough to have adjusted to America but old enough to still remember Iran seem to have the most difficulty choosing their cultural allegiances, perhaps because they were too young to have made their own decisions about staying in Iran or leaving. (348)

While Tara's experience is unique to her, it is also universal for many of those who left when she did.

Cinematic Immersion—*The House of Sand and Fog*

The House of Sand and Fog is a Greek-style tragedy that weaves the stories of three tortured parties into a grim tale of desperation and happenstance. It takes place in the San Francisco Bay Area and focuses on an Iranian American family—a husband (masterfully played by Ben Kingsley), wife, an older daughter, and younger son. Kingsley's character, Behrani, had been an eminent general prior to the revolution and flashbacks give viewers the insight that in fleeing Iran he left behind not only an illustrious career, but also an incredibly lavish lifestyle. This seems to be one of many common threads for Iranians who came during or directly after the revolution. Indeed, those who were able to afford transport out of Iran were, by definition, on the wealthier end of society.

Themes of loss and struggle pervade this film, as we see Behrani and his family plummet in social status and experience deep separation from community. The film opens to one of the major events in a parent's life—a daughter's wedding. In the Iranian community, marriage is a shared experience among family and extended family, who traditionally participate in the selection process and are intimately involved in the ceremony along with friends. On this most auspicious of occasions, the family is thoughtfully presented, their carefully painted veneer just beginning to crack.

The beautiful marriage ceremony and Behrani's glory days as an upper-class general are juxtaposed with the day-to-day reality of the two working-class jobs (CHP worker and convenience store clerk) he was forced to take to support his family. To return home after work in his Mercedes Benz, Behrani daily changes into a suit, a physical sign of the psychological and emotional life to which the family still clings. In spite of all of his efforts, the family still feels some resentment toward Behrani, who bears the heavy burden of sole breadwinner. These themes surface in the shame the family experiences with respect to their peers, who are presumably doing well, or at least feigning it well enough.

Their financial reserves dwindling, Behrani finds a real estate deal: a house that would ensure the family's socioeconomic status, comfortable lifestyle, and emotional well-being. In the context of this transaction, they enter the life of another vulnerable soul, the former owner of the house. Kathy is the victim of city negligence that allowed Behrani and his family to buy the home her father had bequeathed her at a fraction of its value. Kathy, who is already very depressed, desperately pleads with Behrani for her home. Confronted with these ethical choices, Behrani resolutely determines that his family's welfare must come first, and keeps the house. Following a series of inexorably tragic events, Behrani's son gets killed. Devastated, Behrani and his wife choose suicide, having lost everything for which they had lived.

This film illustrates the extreme displacement and alienation of Behrani's family, while touching on a number of common Iranian American themes such as family roles, the importance of appearances, hierarchical decision-making patterns, and the struggle to adjust to a new country, new culture, and new social position.

Cultural Immersion Experience: Masters of Persian Classical Music

Filing through a crowd of exquisitely garbed Iranian Americans to my balcony seat for the concert, I was aware that the mood was quiet and reverential, as before an elegant storm. Through an often-turbulent history, Persian classical music has often been a source of continuity (Nooshin 2002), transcending the realm of aesthetics to the spiritual, invoking in song the poetry of such mystics as Rumi. "Rooted in a rich and ancient heritage, this is a music of contemplation and meditation which is linked through the poetry to Sufism, the mystical branch of Islam whose members seek spiritual union with God" (Nooshin 2002).

Mohammad Reza Shajarian exemplifies the beauty and spirituality of traditional Persian singing, with a style of singing considered most difficult to master. Kayhan Kalhor played the kamancheh (spiked fiddle), Hossein Alizadeh the tar (long-necked plucked lute), and Homayoun Shajarian, Mohammad Reza Shajarian's son, played the tombak (goblet drum) and sang. M. R. Shajarian, K. Kahlor, and H. Alizadeh are nationally and internationally renowned as composers and instrumentalists.

At the core of Persian classical music lies the notion of creative performance. As noted by Nooshin,

> The importance of creativity in this music is often expressed through the image of the nightingale (bol bol). According to popular belief, the nightingale possesses the most beautiful voice on earth and is also said never to repeat itself in song. A bird of great symbolic power throughout the Middle East, the nightingale represents the ultimate symbol of musical creativity. To the extent that Persian Classical music lives through the more or less spontaneous re-creation of the traditional repertoire in performance, the music is often described as improvised. (2002)

Rigorous training, including a canon of songs known as the radif, passed by oral tradition from teacher to student, is also required. The performer infuses his individual creativity into this canon, which becomes a driving force for the music (Nooshin 2003).

Although at moments I felt an outsider intruding upon a communion of initiates, those around me were exceptionally polite, and greeted me with a warm smile. I felt worthy of this experience in part because I gave their music its deserved sacramental respect. At 15 to 45 minutes in length, each song was a meditative journey into the unknown. The concert began with the vocalist and kamancheh player and gradually added the other two ensemble members. Delving deeply into the songs, there came points at which everything disappeared but the music *in that moment*—a very powerful sense of oneness shared among the audience and performers. This unity, embodied in the music and initiated by the performers somehow brought us all to a higher plane of being. It allowed us all to transcend material experience and reach a timeless realm devoid of physical space. I felt that we had also transcended cultural differences, as all sense of identity disappeared for a cosmic moment. Music is one of the few forms of expression that is universally understood and experienced, because of its highly visceral nature. As the concert ended, I was in an ecstatic state, having shared this experience with so many others—to have entered their world, and to have experienced the boundaries between us disappear so completely.

Personal Interview: "Lily"

Lily is a 30-year-old woman who moved from Tehran to Washington D.C. at the age of 5, in 1980. At 12, she was sent to a boarding school, where she lived until she was 17. We spoke of the struggles she faced in attempting to integrate two very distinct cultures into her own unique identity, highlighting the clash between the values of her family and the larger American culture. She talked about the confusion she and so many others faced as they fled to America: extremely vulnerable, open to the promise of this refuge, then subjected to the hatred and racism of an American public consumed with the hostage crisis.

Reactions to the hostage crisis in the Iranian community ranged from self-hate and a desire to assimilate to isolation and fear. Lily's family lived near an Italian community; and many of her peers wanted to change their names to Italian ones and "pass" as European. In the context of this fear and confusion, she explained the "Persian" verses "Iranian" distinction. "Persian" came into use by expatriates from Iran around the time of the hostage crisis and its backlash, enabling them to distance and distinguish themselves from the hated "Iranians." Many people from Iran also distinguish themselves from Arabs, identifying more as Europeans. Both are not only reactions to the hostage crisis, but also a questioning of racial and ethnic identity upon immigration to a society dominated by European ancestry. Accompanying these semantic and ideological differentiations was a measure of self-hatred and racism toward Arabs.

Growing up in the United States, the values of Lily's more collectivist family and culture came into conflict with those of the larger society. Assertions of independence or freedom were seen as disrespectfulness, and actions were always evaluated in the context of their effect on the group. Positive actions increased the strength or power of the collective, whereas unacceptable or negative acts weakened it.

Lily also spoke of a double standard that favored males, and often associated shame with a linked grouping of femaleness and sexuality. Lily feels this gender-based double standard highly sexualizes women, infusing shame into behaviors that are socially inappropriate for females but unquestioningly accepted in males. For example, a female teen's going out with friends to a movie might be thought of as sexually provocative behavior, bringing shame to her family, while male teens are free to socialize or go to the movies as they wish. Independence is often equated with promiscuity or sexually provocative behavior. In such an environment, Lily remembers having to be self-conscious about her social behavior in order to avoid shaming her family.

The autonomy Lily yearned for during adolescence was often in conflict with her family's expectations, where femaleness is positively associated with purity, submissiveness, and chastity. She mentions having to wait until she got out of the house and away from her parents to put on even an eye-liner's worth of make-up. The expectation, tacit and explicit, was that she would marry someone within the circle of intimate friends, and independent dating was not acceptable.

Although the rigidity of these cultural norms could be overwhelming when imposed by the collective force of her family, there is also a beauty in this sense of community, which Lily feels is generally lacking in American life. With the passing of older generations, and the dilution of tradition in the face of modern alternative American lifestyles, there is for her a sense of loss and mourning.

Synthesizing the Lessons

Iranian Americans have often been thought of monolithically as Arabic, Islamic, and repressive. They are in fact an incredibly diverse group with a rich, storied history. Iranian Americans each have their own story and unique identity. Recognizing this will help ensure respect and facilitate meaningful interaction.

Deep in this story of exile and diaspora is the stark reality for most there was no hope of return to a homeland that was a haven until the time of the revolution. For many of those who left when they were very young, there can only be fragments of home in different places. The connection to the Iran that was, and the mourning for what it might have been like live only in the hearts of the older generation. Though there is a fear that the connection will weaken with the years, younger Iranian Americans too feel a sense of loss— loss of a particular lifestyle, loss of friends, loss of a more communal way of life.

Because many who fled were wealthy, or at least middle-class, it is easy to believe that they continue to reside comfortably in the middle and upper classes of the United States. This can mask the pain and loss, and ignore the highly subjective nature of cultural values and struggles for adjustment in an often unwelcoming environment. It also ignores the prime issues of language and employment many face.

Many people in the United States believe most Iranian Americans were not only ecstatic to escape Iran, but would never want to go back to that hated, repressive, rigid society. In truth, many Iranian Americans miss the beauty and collective spirit that characterized their lives in Iran. It is important to learn their stories and validate their pain. A beautifully composed exterior can easily betray internal struggle.

**NOTE: Out of respect for my chosen population, I shall use the term *Persians* instead of *Iranian Americans* in referring to this group for the remainder of this project. I do this because it is the term they self-apply, and so supports cultural competence.

Applying the Knowledge Base: Agency, Service and Program, and Personal Competencies

FIELDWORK AGENCY

Agency

My field placement is an out-patient adult mental health clinic serving a suburban county. My agency serves clients who have severe mental illness and/or severe and persistent mental illness, offering case management, medication management, brief psychotherapy, and vocational rehabilitation. Our clients most commonly receive SSI/SSDI benefits for a mental disability, are homeless, or have income around the poverty line. We provide for those with MediCal or Medicaid and cover the residual cost of diagnostically qualified patients who lack such supplemental insurance.

Agency's Community Based on the 2000 Census, there are approximately 2,500 Per-

sians within our catchment area, which is dominated by European Americans (approx. 70–80 percent), followed by Latinos of mostly Mexican descent (approx. 15–20 percent), and then by African Americans (approx. 5–10 percent). Although there is no outwardly Persian area, there are small, loosely connected communities. According to my field instructor, they are largely offshoots of a large, neighboring Persian community. Members of this population must cross through the mostly Latino and so-called "white" areas to get to our clinic.

Access As Persians originated from more middle- and upper-class backgrounds, entering a public clinic that predominantly serves clients of a lower SES is very stigmatizing at the outset. Most of these clients cross the ethnic boundaries by car, with their families. As it would be culturally dystonic to display information about mental health issues in public places frequented primarily by Persians, my agency does little public outreach directly to this population, though outreach through health venues is practiced. Persians learn of our services largely by word of mouth. In terms of accommodating people who have a physical disability, my agency has specialized ramps, restrooms, and an elevator.

Receptivity The clinic's family-like atmosphere and the services of a couple Persian staff members are welcoming to this population. Waiting room signs and brochures indicate the availability of interpreting services in about 25 languages, including Farsi, and the decor appears culturally neutral.

When the intake staff identifies a client as Persian, referral to Persian staff is initiated. The clinical psychologist who manages my team as a clinician and case-manager is a Persian immigrant, as is one of the clinic psychiatrists. Both speak Farsi. They can appreciate and communicate about many of the personal struggles clients have experienced. Their offices are adorned with Persian tapestry and artwork. It is important to note here that Persian clients primarily identify their relationship as being with these individuals, not the agency itself.

Administration and Staff Training At the county level, the Cultural Competence Training Committee directs trainings in cultural competence quarterly at the very least, but, although most agency staff attend, attendance is not mandatory. Issues related to diversity are often discussed in team meetings at my clinic and highlighted by team leaders, both of whom are women of color.

Staff Sensitivity The staff members at my agency represent a variety of ethnic, social, and cultural backgrounds, facilitating a socio-culturally conscious, aware, and tolerant atmosphere. Generally, the staff is very sensitive to special client needs and regards each person as a unique individual within their socio-cultural context. I have not heard stereotypes or "they" language in reference to Persians. This population is well represented on staff, and there is awareness of major cultural issues and experiences.

Funding Funding allows for cultural variations in that interpreting services are guaranteed for nearly all clients, regardless of language. Funding has also allowed for recruitment and retention of Persian practitioners within our clinic. Funding additionally allows for contracting appropriately tailored services for Latinos and Asian/Pacific Islanders.

Program and Policies

Cultural Competence Mission Statement

- Create a therapeutic milieu that supports the individual's/consumer's culture, values, beliefs, life ways, and lifestyles.
- Educate the workforce to be culturally competent, through a strategic plan which encompasses a set of congruent practice skills, attitudes, policies, and structures which come together in a system of agencies and professionals that enables the system to work effectively in cross-cultural situations.

Cultural Competence Vision Statement

- The Mental Health Division will continue to develop an environment which embraces and embodies acceptance and which values the full range of the diversity of human experience; particularly recognizing the culture of the mental health consumer (***Health Services Department 2004).

Effort The county and agency's policies are rooted in a commitment to culturally competent service and corresponding oversight. Under the umbrella of cultural competency is a commitment to representing the views and needs of diverse ethnic and cultural groups, including those of mental health consumers and their families. The Diversity Work Group, which is composed of clients, caretakers, staff, and members of the general population, oversees and directs design and delivery of culturally competent programming. Additionally, mental health consumers are represented in our staffing as support workers and counseling professionals.

The Mental Health Division formed the Diversity Work Group to "discuss, advise and approve the development of a Cultural Competence Plan which meets State requirements and . . . sets a high standard of care for consumers." The workgroup seeks to reduce disparities in mental health utilization and provision, reporting annually on findings and directives. It is subdivided into the following committees: (1) Cultural Competence Training, (2) Linguistic Access, (3) Research and Evaluation, (4) Retention and Recruitment, and (5) Best Clinical Practices. Minorities under-represented both in the mental health system and the general population are specially targeted for inclusion. These minorities may include client groups with dual-diagnosis (mental illness and substance abuse) or those of under-represented ethnic groups. Institution of the annual Cultural Competence Plan is carried out in program design, direct practice standards, agency, and staff composition.

Due to the high intra-cultural level of stigma associated with mental illness, Persians have largely stayed away from the Diversity Work Groups. Nonetheless, a strong effort is made to include them. The gap left by such consumers and their families is filled somewhat by Persian practitioners, while the door remains open to consumers, families and the general population (***Health Services Department 2004).

Quality To ensure culturally competent service for Persians and for employees of the agency, a county-designed Diversity Assessment Tool is implemented in survey form. These survey forms address issues of equitable, respectful, and equal access to all clients and staff. The Diversity Assessment Tool was designed to be directive in terms of staff training, hiring, and retention needs as well as service provision. Equal access is further addressed in utilization review proceedings. Culturally competent practice encompasses a wide range of individualized services. With Persian clients, client-practitioner, cultural, and linguistic matching is provided, as supported by policy-directed practice.

On the policy level, the county strives to be inclusive of a variety of worldviews, values, and belief systems. The Diversity Work Group is continuously adapting to the changing needs of the community. Though it does an excellent job including African Americans, Latinos, and Asian Americans/Pacific Islanders, Persians are not nearly as well represented at this policy level, perhaps due to the difficulty inherent in discussions of mental illness, as well as their relatively recent growth as a target population. Special attention to the provision of culturally competent services to Persians includes expectations and criteria that take into account cultural variations between Persians and the dominant white culture, while tailoring service to each Persian client and family.

Effectiveness As of 2004, the number of Farsi speaking clients in the clinic totaled 172. Both Persian and Afghani people speak Farsi, and the utilization review does not differentiate between these two groups. Identifying effectiveness of utilization is a difficult, complicated process, due in part to the taboos on mental illness within the Persian community. The stresses associated with the Iranian Diaspora may increase the risk of mental illness, and true determination of need versus utilization would warrant an in-depth study.

There have been no formal quality assessments specifically targeting services to Persians. From an informal assessment, I feel that clients from my population are very satisfied with the nature and scope of services provided them. It is rare to find a psychiatrist and clinical case manager that speak Farsi and fully understand Persian culture, while also being rooted in an understanding of the larger umbrella of public mental health. From direct observations and clinician reports on retention, it appears that they are very satisfied with the services they receive. The only unmet need I can identify is a lack of culturally competent staff of Persian descent within in-patient services.

Efficiency Most clients find out about our clinic by word of mouth. To improve utilization, the clinic might have area Persian medical doctors reach out to clients with brochures and recommendations. In the case of this population and agency, I feel that alternative delivery systems are not necessary.

Personal Cultural Competencies

In discussing personal competencies utilized in micro practice, it is important to make clear that working with Persians involves working with three distinct groups—(1) the generation of elders that grew up in Iran and moved to the United States as adults, (2) the generation of adults that grew up in both Iran and the United States, and (3) the generation of children and young adults who grew up wholly in the United States. The first generation of immigrants who grew up in Iran embodies pure traditional Iranian mores and customs. The immigrants who grew up both in Iran and the United States straddle both worlds, but have largely assimilated. Finally, first and second generation American-born Persians live mainly by American mores and consider themselves primarily American.

The above distinctions made, it is important to know that working with Persians is a "family affair." That is, in most instances of working with this population, a caseworker will in some way be working with all three distinct cohorts.

Engagement, Trust, and Relationship-building
For the elder generations of Persians, mental illness holds an especially high level of stigma. For all of the generations, the use of government institutions (i.e., county mental health) and supplemental services (i.e., SSI) is thought of as "lower class." Therefore, most Persians who enter our clinic experience stigma around both mental illness and government benefits/services. Persians generally resist the use of mental health services and attempt to deal with the problem in the family. Failure reflects negatively on the patriarch, whose role is to take complete care of his family. For the patriarch, there is not only a loss of face, but also a personal feeling of inadequacy.

If a Persian family or client comes to our clinic, it is likely because they have already tried private services and become overwhelmed by the costs. County mental health is an option of desperation and last resort. It may be important to validate this decision.

Introducing oneself in a very formal manner, including one's title and credentials, is important as a culturally syntonic gesture for professionals, according the family respect and establishing authority. Shaking hands is not appropriate between very religious Muslim men and other women. In the case of a greeting gesture, it would be important to take cues from the client system. Additionally, it is important to always walk behind the family and allow them to pass through doors first as a sign of respect. Finally, with the older generations it is important to avoid eye contact in the public spaces of the clinic because it will force an acknowledgment of their shame and loss of face. In private confines, eye contact is more appropriate and acceptable. Verbal validation of pain and suffering is important for clients in this population, who may feel blamed by family and community for their illness. It is important to take cues from the client system to be sure such an action will not threaten the caregivers. It is important to avoid being too intrusive in expression of empathy.

In the process of engagement and throughout, the therapeutic relationship may need to be structured and negotiated through the family patriarch. At the very least, consultation with the patriarch would be essential, as caring for women and children is considered his responsibility. The matriarch's participation is also very important.

When working with licensed professionals, this population expects to be directed. If the family/client trusts you, part of the expectation is that you will guide them with your expert opinion in their search for a cure.

Pathways to understanding and interacting with each Persian client system will be further illuminated through ethnographic interviewing. In doing this it will be important to place members along the lines of generation, immigration experience, and religious background, and to understand the relative change in SES over the lifetime of the client system. Finally, it will be important to get a sense of their understanding of mental illness generally and the specific problem at hand.

Assessment and Problem Definition In Persian culture, mental illness is understood not through etiology but rather in terms of aberrant behavioral manifestations. If a family member fits DSM diagnosis for a mental disorder and is acting inappropriately, but such behavior can be contained, the family may not define the problem as mental illness. However, if a psychotic family member makes inappropriate sexual comments at a party, the family will be mortified beyond words and much of the local community will know before dawn. This will acutely speed up the family's drive to seek services.

While the DSM may be initially effective in some cases, it may be difficult to get the ethic definitions required to identify certain diagnostic symptomatology. Internal experience may be eschewed or expressed in a very paradoxical way due to the stigma around mental illness and religious folkways. Observed and expressed external behavior is much easier to address, and can be revealed over time or reported at the outset. Finally, in assessing, it will be important to get information from numerous family members, all of whom might have unique insight or knowledge.

Mental illness may be most palpable to Persians in the identified inability to fulfill the important social roles of marriage, patriarchy, and matriarchy. I would engage my client in assessment and problem definition around the issues of social role fulfillment and observable behavioral manifestations.

Contracting and Goal Setting Given that most Persians seek help around mental health issues on the basis of poor social functioning, it may be best to define goals around gains within this sphere. This would be especially true of practice with older generations. I would avoid defining mental

illness too directly, focusing instead on the behavioral as opposed to intra-psychic components unless the client and family initiate such discussion.

Generally, this population expects a practitioner-directed process. If the family trusts me, they will feel very comfortable with my setting the goals, and would feel uncomfortable having too much control over the process. They might say, "You're the expert, you tell us!" This is of course less true for more Americanized generations.

Interventions Medication management is a central intervention for those who face mood disorders and/or psychosis. Generally speaking, the Persian community has a great deal of respect for doctors and a medical model of healing. Accordingly, psychotropic medication is a highly appropriate intervention for this population. The watchful eye of the patriarch and matriarch could be well utilized to help ensure medication compliance.

Supportive psychotherapy can be a very useful intervention, both individually and with the family. It should be conducted without challenging family mores and role definitions, including the patriarchal family structure. To achieve the balancing act of working with multiple generations, the social worker may have to ask the younger generation family members to make concessions that conform to the process, and facilitate the respect of elders. It is important to enable Persian clients to "take you there" with deeper issues.

Although recognizing mental illness as such is very taboo within Persian culture, psycho-education may be very helpful and successful. It is essential to gain the family and client's trust. Once it seems appropriate, it is important to educate the family about mental illness, especially because they tend to expect a quick fix with medication.

Linking Persian clients with higher education and vocational programs are excellent culturally syntonic interventions, if the client is ready, interested, and able. Educational and professional progress are of great importance in Persian communities, and in this context can foster social acceptance and the development of social skills, while helping facilitate reintegration into the community.

Finally, if the family is religious it is important to understand the religious interpretation of the client's problem. With the family's consent, it might be helpful to explore their religious leader's insight into the problem.

Evaluation and Termination As stated earlier, older generations of Persians come to mental health professionals looking for a "cure." This population can often be impatient and view success or failure in all or nothing terms. This dichotomy is supported by the avoidance of defining mental illness. As a result Persians may grow easily impatient with a lack of quick success in mental health service provision.

Success may be defined in terms of social functioning and the ability to fulfill social roles, or in terms of their ability to marry and take part in social functions. For males especially, success may be the ability to take care of the family by providing physical and emotional support.

While outward appearances might point to the family patriarch to decide the success or failure of an intervention, true power may reside with the family matriarch. If a practitioner is able to intervene successfully, the client and family will be very grateful and may view that practitioner as part of the family. When ending a successful therapeutic relationship, Persians often gift social workers, and it is important to either accept such gifts or to have prepared a really good explanation as to why a gift cannot be accepted. Otherwise, the refusal of a gift may be viewed as a result of the gift not being good enough, and taken as a rejection and loss of face. The initial major separation from the family or client should be accomplished through incrementally less frequent session spacing. In some cases, the relationship may continue indefinitely on an infrequent basis.

Evaluation—NASW Standard for Cultural Competence

Standard 4 *Cross-Cultural Skills—Social workers shall use appropriate methodological approaches, skills, and techniques that reflect the workers' understanding of the role of culture in the helping process (2001).*

My agency fulfills this standard well with respect to Persians. My agency and its respective Persian psychiatrist/clinical case-manager team utilize methodological approaches tailored specifically to Persians. Their understanding of the role of the helping process in Persian culture, and their experiences and identities as Persians, serve as an adjunct to their respective training in methodology and techniques.

The county's mental health services as a whole are moderately highly proficient in cross-cultural skill competency. Trainings support such skill competency, but are not mandatory. Staff diversity, especially with respect to management positions, helps foster appropriate cross-cultural skills. Cross culturally competent services are ensured for Latinos and Asian/Pacific Islanders through contracting. The county's Diversity Workgroup supports proficiency in cross-cultural skills with its Best Clinical Practices and Cultural Competence Training sub-committees. Because my clinic has a Persian clinical team, Persian clients are referred to us whenever possible. To provide services in all areas of the county, our Persian clinical team could hold countywide inservice trainings on best practices with Persian clients for both out-patient and in-patient staff. Though culturally challenging, including Persian consumers/families in quality assessment would be helpful. Finally, including Persian/Afghani specificity in utilization review would provide specific demographics to inform service program planning.

Through the in-depth exploration, discussion, and interviewing this project has required, I feel that I have attained much of the necessary skills and knowledge for working with Persians. It was possible to complete this practice section only with the extensive help of a Persian clinical team, whom I interviewed at length. They believe it is not necessary to be Persian or speak Farsi (in cases where the client's English is good enough) to be effective with this population. My skill-set would certainly need practice and ironing out, as working with a Persian family can be a balancing act of sorts. I am certainly up to the challenge.

REFERENCES

Bahrampour, T. 1999. *To See and See Again.* New York: Farrar, Straus and Giroux.

Eshagian, E. I. (executive producer), and T. Eshaghian (director). 2001. *I Call Myself Persian: Iranians in America* [documentary]. New York: Third World Newsreel.

***Health Services Department. 2004. Mental Health Division. Annual Update. 2004.

***Health Services Department. 2004. Mental Health Division. Cultural Competence Plan.

Keddie, N. R. 2003. *Modern Iran: Roots and Results of Revolution.* New Haven, CT: Yale University Press.

National Association of Social Workers (NASW). 2001. *NASW Standards for Cultural Competence in Social Work Practice.* Washington D.C.: Author.

Nooshin, L. 2002. Liner notes. *Without You—Masters of Persian Music* [compact disc recording]. World Village Label.

Nooshin, L. 2003. Improvisation as 'other': creativity, knowledge and power—the case of Iranian classical music. *Journal of the Royal Musical Association* 128: 242–296.

Perelman, V. (director/screenwriter). 2003. *The House of Sand and Fog* [motion picture]. United States: Dreamworks.

Sullivan, Z. T. 2001. *Exiled Memories: Stories of Iranian Diaspora.* Philadelphia, PA: Temple University Press.

U.S. Census. 2000. http://www.census.gov/main/www/cen2000.html

Worksheet

1. Labeling is a very sensitive issue in all cultures. It is an especially sensitive issue for the population in this case study, because of the often negative associations many Americans have with their country of origin. As a result of his cultural study, the writer has changed from the term "Iranian" to the term "Persian," which he believes is preferable to members of this population. What associations do you have with the word "Iranian"? With the word "Persian"?

2. Persians (to use the author's preferred terminology) are not the only cultural group that has difficulties with issues of mental illness in families and communities. Other populations also have strong taboos against talking about, acknowledging, and seeking treatment for mental illness. Of the personal competency strategies and techniques the author has developed, which would be applicable to another, or other, population(s)? Which might not work well? Why?

Culturally Competent Social Work Practice with Chinese Americans

Diversity Project by Kenya Sullivan

My agency, a division of the health and human service agency in a major urban center, serves a very diverse group of clients with mental illness who are living in the community. I have several Chinese clients, and, as an African American, I have chosen to focus on the Chinese population in order to become more culturally competent through understanding some of the historical perspectives and experiences of Chinese and Chinese Americans. I have made no explicit distinction between "Chinese" and "Chinese Americans" because the decision to hyphenate has historically been such a personal and private one; the Chinese descriptor is meant to include all levels of personal and cultural identity. I have made an attempt to include broad and varied perspectives on the "Chinese experience." Economic, legal, and social factors in the United States have affected this population in many ways, and relations between Chinese Americans and "American society" have been quite complex. One of the major issues, immigration, has engendered both hostile resistance and exploitation. In common with other Asian cultures, Chinese Americans' worldview may be quite different from that of the dominant culture. Asians tend to emphasize circularity over linear progress, self-sacrifice over independence, and cooperative over individual achievement. Within the context of the dominant Western culture, this antithetical view has had a profound effect on the experiences and history of the Chinese in the United States. Rather than focusing on acculturation issues per se, I will attempt to highlight both the challenges and the special strengths of this population.

KNOWLEDGE BASE

History

Asian Americans are increasing in numbers, but are still a relatively small group when compared to others ethnic minorities in the United States. According to the 2000 Census, there were 11.9 million self-identified Asians, with Chinese as the largest group. Most Chinese immigrants came to the United States for economic opportunities and/or to escape the hostile political environment of China. However, as early as the nineteenth century, racist, anti-Chinese sentiments in the private, legal, and political sectors had a strong negative effect on the immigrants' experiences. In an 1871 Los Angeles incident, a white male was accidentally shot and killed in a crossfire between two Chinese gangs. Hundreds of whites went to the city's Chinatown, destroying property and randomly attacking the Chinese residents. Twenty Chinese were killed in indiscriminate attacks, suggesting that the anger was directed toward the population as a whole rather than toward the gunman, and no action was taken against the perpetrators of the violence. This example seems to reflect both private sentiment and public policy. Another attack occurred in 1885 in Wyoming where a labor union staged an attack on 600 Chinese employees who refused union membership. As in the Los Angeles incident, no legal action was taken against the perpetrators.

In a series of incidents during the 1800s, California attempted an ethnic cleansing of Chinese immigrants in the state called "yellow pearl." Physical attacks, lynchings, and humiliations drove people out of regions of the state, almost halving the Chinese population. The passage of the Chinese Exclusion Act in 1882 prohibited the entry of Chinese laborers for ten years with the exception of a small quota of workers. Trade unions who organized in support of its passage used the slogan "Asians stealing American jobs." Chinese immigration was permitted only during the gold rush, when their labor was needed.

119

The Scott Act of 1888 prohibited the reentry of all Chinese laborers who left temporarily. In 1892, the Geary Act extended the exclusion law for an additional ten years. California's Alien Land Laws, which specifically prohibited land ownership by Chinese were enacted in 1913, 1920, and 1923, and similar laws were passed in Washington, Arizona, Oregon, Idaho, Nebraska, Texas, Kansas, Louisiana, Montana, New Mexico, Minnesota, and Missouri.

In 1923, the courts excluded Asians from naturalized citizenship, and in 1924 the National Origin Quota Act limited immigration from all Asian countries, affecting immigration levels until 1952 (U.S. Immigration Policy). This history still informs and influences contemporary Chinese families, often manifesting as conflicts between generations, and affecting cultural identity development. The film *The Joy Luck Club* captures the history of immigration, intra-generational conflicts in cultural values, and self-identity.

An Intergenerational Account:
The Joy Luck Club

I asked Chinese classmates to suggest movies with which they most identified. Their recommendations were *To Live* and *The Joy Luck Club*. I chose *The Joy Luck Club* because I was especially interested in its emphasis on the transgenerational disparities in cultural views, perspectives, expectations, and individual desires.

The story is told from the perspective of three matriarchs who had been subjected to arranged marriages, subservient gender roles, professional immobility, and financial dependence on the husbands. They immigrated to the United States to escape the oppression of traditional China, and to ensure what they believed would be a better future for their daughters. The mothers intended to raise their daughters to reach their full potential without being subservient to either their future husbands or tradition. However, the daughters perceived their mothers' intentions as pressure to conform (though in a different way), setting in motion a dynamic similar to what the mothers had experienced.

The movie provides insight into the constant back-and-forth of this process, as Chinese women take steps to distance themselves from the oppression of Chinese culture, and to ensure that the next generation of women have the freedoms that had been denied them. The themes of intergenerational differences in experiences and perceptions, in goals, and in the acculturation process are woven throughout the film. In his essay, *The Accidental Asian*, Eric Liu addresses another sensitive issue: the submersion of the individual cultures of the varied countries of Asia into one monolithic identity: that of "Asian."

Autobiographical Essay:
Being "Chinese," Being "Asian"

Eric Liu has been both a correspondent and a commentator on MSNBC. He was also a speechwriter for Bill Clinton during his presidency. He shares with the reader some of the defining moments in his understanding of his own identity, and how it is shaped not only by his Chinese heritage, but also by the emerging concept of something that seems to both unify and transcend that: his identity as an "Asian." Because race seems to matter so much in the United States, people who look somewhat the same, and whose ancestors came from the same part of the world, tend to be lumped together in our society. The individual differences of language, customs, foods, and beliefs that distinguish a Korean from a Japanese, to use his example, are submerged in what is viewed as dominant: the similarity of race and racial features. Originally a category the U.S. Census created, the identity "Asian American," was embraced by Asian student activists who were strongly affected by the positive achievements of the Black Power movement. Asian Americans, too, were concerned about discrimination and bias, and they too were aware of the history of oppression that defined the experiences of immigrants from Asian countries well into the twentieth century.

In order to work together to affect policy, defend against threats, and support the needs of "Asians" in every sphere, it was necessary to submerge both cultural differences and the history of wars and animosities that characterized the relationships between the various countries in the past. To invent the identity of "Asian" required cooperation and a new understanding of common interests and concerns. Liu suggests that instead of one "melting pot"—a now discredited concept—what we really have in the United States is a series of multicultural melting pots, where differences within racial groups are "melted," and relationships within groups strengthened.

Liu suggests, however, that this relatively newly forged identity may not last more than a generation. Fifty percent of Asian Americans are marrying non-Asians. Clearly, this will have a major impact on the way in which race is viewed in the future. He ends with suggesting very positively that the future of any one "race"—in his case "Asian Americans"—will reflect the changes that will come to the concept of "race" itself.

In exploring this "future," I chose to attend an event that focused on racial tensions between two groups of students: Chinese and African Americans.

Event Immersion: The Chinese Community Center Meeting

The invitation came about as the result of racial tensions on a high school campus between Chinese students and African American students. The racist epithets from African-American students were the typical Asian stereotypes: being model students, being asexual, or being homosexual, just to name a few. The Chinese students had responded to these in anger, and had begun to isolate themselves and express their own stereotypes about African Americans as well as other non-Chinese groups.

As an African American social work student, my charge was to present a political, social, and economic history of blacks in America to a group of teenagers on a Friday night at a Chinese community center, a very daunting proposition since the students' wounds were fresh from the recent incidents on campus.

As I walked on the campus, I felt anxious. I could not see the students, but I heard their voices; the louder the voices got, the more anxious I became. And when I saw the size of the crowd, I was overwhelmed by the sheer number of students who had come to hear me speak on this Friday night. I felt as if everyone stopped and stared at me as I made my way to the door of the community center. To get into the building, I had to walk up a stairwell with students on both sides of me. I began an internal monologue, trying to understand why I was feeling so anxious in a situation that was not an unusual one for me—being around crowds of students. This time, I realized, I was more aware of my difference. I rarely experience those sorts of feelings, so I sort of laughed at myself and attempted to rationalize my thoughts and feelings (mostly projections). That walk seemed to take forever. Although my hosts offered me food and drink, and helped me feel comfortable, my anxiety seemed to increase exponentially with each succeeding second.

I watched the students take their seats, wishing I could just leave. The chairs were set up in a circle with my chair—of course—being dead-center. One of the hostesses initiated a check-in with the students, but my tension and anxiety were so great that I could not make out the words, and I just watched as the circle made itself around to me and I was introduced. My mind raced thinking of how I might control the situation to make it into something more familiar to me and, therefore, less anxiety-producing. Recognizing I would be more comfortable in a therapist role than in a guest-lecturer role, I switched roles in my mind.

I began the *session* by asking the group about stereotypes that they had (or had heard) about African Americans to get the group engaged and give them a sense of empowerment. They mentioned the standard ones, but then one teen turned the question around and asked me the same question. My response was that I had none, and that I respected their culture. Many of the students went into detail about how painful the stereotypes were to them, and I responded authentically. I felt my presentation was successful, considering the teenagers' level of participation and their emphatic request that I "come back just to hang out."

I left the community center really feeling their hurt, and identifying with their pain. I was keenly aware that the African American students had the same kind of hurt and pain, and I wished I could have addressed them as well, and maybe facilitated a group dialogue and educational opportunity. The intimacy of this experience helped me see and understand the struggles that being Chinese in a racist America can create, even when the racism comes from another oppressed group. It also helped me see the similarities between African Americans and Chinese Americans, especially in terms of the identity struggle. Like African Americans, Chinese Americans vary in how they identify themselves. Sometimes self-identity is not the same as ethnic identity or nationality, as is the case with my interviewee, David Wee. His story is one of seeking an identity that was separate from Chinese, within the context of China's history of war and immigration and the racism he experienced as a youth during the tumultuous years described earlier.

Interview with David Wee

David Wee is a 50-year-old social work clinician and educator. Although he was born in America, his father's traditional Chinese upbringing informed his parenting style. Mr. Wee is not certain when his family immigrated from China to America, but he does recall that his paternal grandparents moved to America, and his grandfather was a restaurateur, hoping to work to make enough money to move back to China and live well. Mr. Wee notes that his grandfather's was "the trend at the time," and that he wanted his children to have a Chinese education. They were able to accomplish these goals, and returned to China.

Eventually, the threat of World War II and the Japanese invasion loomed, and prompted the family to immigrate back to America. Because of tighter immigration laws at that time, Mr. Wee's grandmother, uncle, and aunt remained in China with the expectation that they would join the family later—but "later" never came as immigration laws were tightened and entry restricted. The family members died before the immigration laws were changed, and Mr. Wee never got to know these relatives.

Around the mid-to-late 1960s, his grandfather and children returned to live in the area where he was born and raised. He was keenly aware that he was *different* amongst his white neighbors and childhood friends. He was aware of his Chinese identity, but didn't feel he belonged to any particular group; not belonging felt "awkward" to him. He describes his journey toward an individual identity that would be meaningful to him. Very much aware of Japanese relocation efforts, he describes feeling that "it could be me at any time, so I was hyperaware of my difference and my lack of power."

Mr. Wee describes his father as traditional Chinese, whereas his mother was more acculturated, and he watched his parents struggle with acculturation issues. His family's social circle was predominantly Chinese, and they belonged to a traditional Baptist Chinese Church, which further reinforced his sense of *difference*.

Today, Mr. Wee feels more tied to his Chinese identity than ever. He is also in an interracial marriage with a white woman and has had interesting conversations about identity with their two daughters and son. Mr. Wee says that "race is a constant discussion in our house. . . . The children care, actually care, that their Chinese blood is recognized and acknowledged." His daughters and their friends refer to themselves as H.O.P.A's (pronounced Hop-a), an acronym with which he is not familiar. They have said that the name refers to anyone with any percentage of Asian blood—similar to the one-drop rule that defined African American identity. The acronym is compounded by the "percentage" of Asian blood: a biracial person would be considered "one-half H.O.P.A," and another fraction of that may be considered "one-fourth H.O.P.A." Mr. Wee responds to his children with laughter, fascination, and pride. He simply stated that "it's good that they hold their Chinese heritage close to their hearts." This seemed to be very important to him.

Author's Comments

In my search for some cultural competence in working with Chinese Americans, I sought to research a wide range of experiences with tradition, immigration, education, and identity-formation. In order to make this task comfortable, I started with the easiest—the film *The Joy Luck Club*—and ended with the most challenging, the personal interview. My insights, and my appreciation for the challenges of the Chinese experience in the United States increased as I became more engaged with the material.

Being from an oppressed group, I could see the similarities between our respective collective experiences of oppression in America. I had not been aware of how closely our experiences paralleled in terms of physical, legal, and political hostilities, in-group fighting, whether to flame or not, the one-drop rule, and the fight to self-identify.

While all of my experiences were very meaningful, my most profound understanding came from the stories by the Chinese women in the film, who shared their feelings about female oppression in their culture. The conflict between cultural values, self-identification, intragenerational battles, and in-group fighting seems to characterize every oppressed group's experience in the United States. My exploration of this topic has made me more empathic toward other oppressed cultures, and toward people who experience oppression due to gender, immigration status and language, and other kinds of difference.

Applying the Knowledge Base: Agency, Services and Policies, and Personal Competencies

My field placement agency's mission and vision statements reflect a philosophy of culturally responsive practice, and best-practice standards are used throughout its programs, training, and service delivery. As an intern, I had the good fortune of being trained by a cutting-edge agency and dedicated practitioners, who supported my personal goal of becoming a culturally competent practitioner.

While many other cities use county agencies to provide services to residents, my agency is unique in that it receives special city funding and provides services specifically targeted at city residents. Their mission is to protect and improve public health and quality of life for individuals and families in the city through innovative, effective services, and strong community partnership. The purveyors of services envision a city that will remain constantly alive and responsive to the welfare of its people, where diversity is valued, acknowledged, and respected. The agency serves families, teenagers, children, and students.

AGENCY

Access Demographics, configuration, and spirit have created a city where there are no areas that are predominantly Chinese American, and there are no racially or culturally homogenous areas. Consequently, there is no specific issue of access for a particular ethnic group. However, socioeconomic differences might render it more difficult for upper-class residents to utilize agency services. A sliding-scale fee enables access to services for clients with financial considerations.

The agency is well positioned for public transportation access. For clients who are unable to utilize public transportation, the agency contracts with four services—Paratransit Services for senior citizens and persons with disabilities: Taxi/Scrip Program, Wheelchair-Van Program, and Ticket Price-Discount Services. The Taxi/Scrip Program provides temporary paper money (scrip) to pay for taxi rides, ramped-van vehicles, and other specialized vehicles for citizens 70 years or older. The Wheelchair-Van Program provides vouchers for specialty van rides, and the Ticket Price-Discount Services provides tickets at a discount to individuals who meet the criteria established in the Americans with Disability Act. There is also a supplementary free Social Service Bus for the more severely and persistently afflicted clients.

Specifically to ensure access to Chinese clients, brochures are written in Chinese, and there are clinicians who speak both Mandarin and Cantonese. Agency representatives attend many community events and/or town hall meetings, or participate by having a booth at various community and city events, which target all citizens, including Chinese residents.

The agency offers services 15 hours a day, 365 days of the year. The outpatient clinic is open from 8 a.m. to 5 p.m. Monday through Friday and the Mobile Crisis Team is on duty from 9 a.m. to 11 a.m. 7 days a week. The clinic has a wheelchair ramp at the front entrance, and the doors, hallways, offices, and restrooms are wide enough to accommodate wheelchairs. However, the agency appears to be more responsive to the mental than the physical limitations of its clients.

Receptivity The agency is attentive to "respecting the unique qualities of each individual and family, and believe that human diversity is our most valuable community asset." (City of ***, Vision Statement 2005) In addition to Chinese language brochures and Mandarin and Cantonese-speaking staff, there are various posters that portray members of the Chinese community.

Administration and Staff Training A Cultural Competence Team has been established by the administration. The team is charged with identifying the strengths and weaknesses in the agency's cultural responsiveness. The team meets monthly for an hour and has annual three-day retreats where ways to improve or introduce new cultural training for the staff are discussed. Culture is defined broadly and includes race, ethnicity, culture, gender, sexual orientation, socioeconomic class, and other differences. The front-line staff attend weekly three-hour didactic programs focusing on specific diverse groups, including the Chinese.

Staff Sensitivity I have not noticed any staff member being disrespectful or negative about clients from the Chinese community. Chinese clients are welcomed into the agency.

Funding A wide range of services for adults include Crisis Services, Community Treatment, Homeless Outreach, Mobile Crisis, Social Service Transport, Breakfast Programs, and Family, Youth, and Children Services.

However, financial limitations seem to have inhibited the recruitment of more culturally diverse clinicians, as well as the provision of adequate support services for people who are blind and/or deaf. These concerns have been raised in meetings during my internship, and the agency is aware of the need for greater diversity among staff.

Programs and Policies

Effort The agency makes a concerted effort to provide a comprehensive approach to serve diverse cultures including Chinese. Agency policies reflect that effort in print and practice. As noted above, many of the shortcomings result from limited and/or specialized funding, and are not due to lack of agency effort. Their commitment and efforts are evidenced by their creation of a Cultural Competence Team, comprised of each diverse group, that meets regularly.

Quality Quality of services is measured in a number of ways. A designated staff member reviews charts and service delivery for quality control. Supervision, both individual and group, offers opportunities for exploring and strengthening culturally competent practice skills through check-ins, peer case review, and supervisor's input. A resident psychiatrist provides consultation, case conferencing, and pharmacologic assessments. Agency records are subject to periodic and random chart reviews as a means of quality control. Clients can participate in the quality of services through client evaluations and a grievance process.

Agency policies reflect a sensitivity to diverse world views, values, and beliefs, and individual clinicians are able to respond to individual cultural needs of all clients, including Chinese clients.

In addition, the program's expectations and criteria of services take into account variations from the dominant culture by enabling the clinicians to have autonomy in their practice, comprehensive training on cultural responsiveness, and emphasis and support on client-centered treatment.

Effectiveness Clients are using the resources as effectively as their limitations and crises permit. Comprehensive and high-quality services cause clients to travel from their places of residence to qualify for agency mental health services. The number of clinicians appears to match the numbers of the Chinese population, in that only a small percentage of the client population is Chinese. Because of the low numbers of Chinese clients and the multiple sites where clinicians work, it is too difficult to assess the Chinese client-population's level of satisfaction. However, overall client satisfaction appears to be high based on the low rate of canceled appointments, failures-to-attend treatment, and the low number of poor client-clinician relationships.

Efficiency The breadth of agency services reflects the cutting edge social work theories and practices. The agency also participates in an interagency network, meeting monthly to facilitate continuous communication of needs and services. Members of this network include every social service program in the city, including police, drug treatment programs, shelters, gender specific shelters, sexual orientation specific organizations, shelter-plus care, and city council members. It appears that the agency is efficient in maximizing their resources and opportunities.

Personal Cultural Competencies

Engagement, Trust, Relationship-building The Chinese population, in general, has a negative attitude toward social services. Culturally, there is shame around needing assistance. The Chinese tend to rely heavily on family members for support. However, when a member of this population does seek help, she or he somaticizes emotional problems and personal and family difficulties. Often, Chinese clients conceptualize psychological disturbances as a loss of *Chi* (Qi) and *Ching-Lo* (Meridian)—the balance between self and the surrounding environment. The loss of Chi affects both physical and psychological health, and is countered through ritualistic healing behaviors that are believed to restore balance. Other Chinese cultural remedies include herbal medicines and nutritional balancing. It is important to me as a clinician to affirm the client's representation of their illness and attempt to strike a balance between Chinese and Western conceptualization of the affliction.

When initially engaging a Chinese client, it is appropriate to be formal until the client prompts the clinician to the contrary. As a male clinician, eye contact and touching may be appropriate with other men, but not with women, and is often inappropriate with both. Empathetic responding is critical to validate and support the family members of a person who suffers from a mental illness. It is important that the clinician acknowledge the sacrifices of the caregiver. Chinese people hold professionals in high regard, and are especially desirous of the social worker's advice and direction. This runs counter to the general professional stance, which supports a self-determined, decision-making, and action-planning process.

To assist me in understanding the client, building a relationship, and enhancing the client's sense of control and power, ethnographic interviewing questions are helpful. Examples might include: What do you call the problem/condition/situation? What do you think has caused the problem/condition/situation? Why do you think it started when it did? What do you worry about the most when you think about this problem/condition/situation?

Assessment and Problem Definition The challenges of cross-cultural assessment and problem definition make it essential for me to rely on tools that minimize the cultural gaps. The tools that would be helpful are the Ethnographic Interview Schedule and the construction of an eco-map. The interview schedule would enable me to gain a better understanding of how the client relates to their culture while the map would identify the client's support system.

I would seek to understand how the client identifies and conceptualizes the problem for which they are seeking services. To this end, I would ask the more open-ended questions in the interview schedule emphasizing *furthering questions* for at least the first two sessions before becoming more active in the third and subsequent sessions. Chinese clients often describe their emotional problems in somatic terms. This is understood as being rooted in the Chinese culture's conceptualization of Yin-Yang and the connection between one's spirit and the environment (Chi). For many clients, mental illness is the consequence of an *imbalance* in the Chi or Yin-Yang, and could be corrected through ritualistic rebalancing practices.

The differences in cultural practices between Chinese and Western cultural norms have historically been complex and problematic. As we have seen, the Chinese experience in the United States has been fraught with social, political, and legal tension. Thus, it is not inconceivable that Chinese clients perceive their relationship with the dominant culture as being hostile and approach it with some trepidation. However, rising immigration figures would seem to suggest that many people believe that the "quality of life" is much better in the United States than in China.

Contracting and Goal Setting Contracting and goal setting with Chinese clients require a precarious balancing of client-autonomy and therapist-directedness. While good practice standards suggest that goal setting be guided and framed by the client, the client may prefer, and may even expect, that the social worker will plan and guide the process. It is important to be sensitive to client cues and to

frame goals in a culturally congruent manner. To supplement the client's autonomy, my level of directedness would be limited to contributing to the development of goal-setting options to be discussed with the client. Additionally, I would strongly consider asking the client if she/he would like to include someone from her/his informal social support system, perhaps someone viewed as a family decision-maker, in the planning process.

Interventions Interventions with Chinese clients are most effective when grounded in Chinese cultural norms. Additionally, including the informal social support network in the development of interventions and tasks is important because the literature suggests that Chinese clients tend to use formal agencies second to family and friends. As a clinician from a different culture, my primary goal would be to work cooperatively with the client in negotiating intervention options. Once again, one of my roles is to provide a Western understanding to supplement the client's Eastern conceptualization in order to minimize barriers to services in the United States. In recognition of my client's spiritual needs, and depending on the wishes of the individual client, I would include spiritually based organizations and practices as well as culture-specific organizations in the intervention plan.

Evaluation and Termination The evaluation and termination stages of therapy present several challenges as the result of differing cultural perspectives. There are different cultural definitions of success and failure in Chinese culture and Western culture. In the Chinese culture, *achieving and maintaining balance* is a measure of success and effective intervention. There is a great deal of stress associated with mental illness among Chinese Americans, at least in part because of the negative cultural associations with mental illness. Research has found that culturally Chinese people have more associated stress as the result of the negative social attitudes toward mental illness, and that the stress can affect both client and family member. Success can be achieved through the elimination of symptoms; anything short of that is considered failure. The elimination of symptoms would enable the individual to appear in society without the stigma and shame of mental illness, and this is an important and valuable measure of success.

At the point of termination and separation, the client often will present the worker with a gift of appreciation both to show that the services have been valued, and to give the social worker something tangible in return for the service provided. It would be considered an insult if the therapist declined such a gift. The separation process often appears unemotional and matter-of-fact. This may be reflective of a general discomfort with asking for and accepting help, as well as some lingering shame related to the mental illness. Based on what I learned in the process of developing some measure of cultural competence, it would appear that needing the services of a formal social service agency is both a matter of shame, and an indication of a failure on the part of the client's natural support system, her/his family and community.

NASW Standards of Cultural Competence

I view both my agency and the programs and services it offers as culturally competent and sensitive. I have chosen, therefore, to focus on my own cultural competencies in working with Chinese clients in order to assess myself more fully.

Standard 2 addresses the importance of self-awareness in cross-cultural work. In the process of doing the activities required to increase my knowledge and sensitivity, I have become more aware of the similarities between the Chinese and the African-American experience in the United States in terms of oppression and discrimination. While this has given me greater understanding and empathy for the experiences of my chosen population, I am also aware that there are differences as well as similarities. I must be careful not to assume that the experiences of my Chinese clients are all similar to my own, while using some of the commonalities to help me to build a relationship of trust within which my client can grow and change.

Standard 3 presents the importance of cross-cultural knowledge. I consider myself to be a work in progress, with much progress having been achieved as a result of this project and cross-cultural studies. I would assess my level of cultural competence in working with Chinese clients as marginal before undertaking this project. I know that I could have avoided at least some of the errors I made in serving the Chinese population had I been more aware of Chinese history, experiences, and culture. I know that I may still make mistakes in working with Chinese clients, but the knowledge I have achieved through cultural immersion is very helpful in rendering culturally sensitive service.

Standard 4 addresses cross-cultural skills specifically. I have developed skills as a result of the knowledge I have gained, and also through learning ethnographic interviewing techniques, and culturally sensitive skills at each step in the social work processes, as detailed in the preceding section on personal cultural competencies. As with cross-cultural knowledge, I am a work in progress in skills as well, and I look forward to continuing to develop these.

In conclusion, although my overall competence level in working cross-culturally with Chinese American clients has improved, I shall continue to strive to attain the high level of competence that is expected of me as a professional: self-monitoring and self-awareness, demonstration of cross-cultural knowledge, exhibition of cross-cultural skills, client advocacy and empowerment, and cultural sensitivity.

REFERENCES

Brammer, R. 2004. *Diversity in Counseling Asian-Americans*. Belmont, CA: Thomson Brooks/Cole, 83–111.

City of *** Core Values, 2005.

City of *** Health & Human Services Mission Statement, 2005.

City of *** Vision Statement, 2005.

Health and Human Services—Division of Mental Health. http://www.ci./***Ca.us/mental health

Liu, E. The accidental Asian. In K. Rosenblum and T-M. Travis. 2003. *The Meaning of Difference*. 3d. ed. Boston: McGraw Hill

National Association of Social Workers (2001) *NASW Standards for Cultural Competence in Social Work Practice*. Washington, D.C.: Author.

Segal, U. Social work practice with immigrants and refugees. In Lum, D., ed. *Cultural Competence, Practice Stages, and Client Systems: A Case Study Approach*. Belmont, CA: Brooks/Cole, 230–272.

U.S. Immigration Policy, Historical Overview (1790–1996). http://www.uscis.gov/graphics/shared/aboutus/statistics/leghist/index.htm

Wang, W. Director/Producer, and Tan, A. Producer/Book Author (1993) *The Joy Luck Club* [motion picture] USA: Hollywood Pictures.

Worksheet

1. Because of the shame associated with mental illness, and because of the religious and spiritual understanding of health and illness in Chinese culture, there is often a tendency to somaticize mental problems. What might be some culturally appropriate and sensitive approaches to address the needs of clients who, you believe, have somaticized their mental problems?

2. Gift-giving in appreciation for social work services is a common practice of Chinese clients. However, many social agencies have carefully thought out policies that do not permit social workers to accept gifts from clients for many reasons, including possible manipulation by clients, the burden such expectations place on clients, the disparity that may be created both within and among client groups, and a number of other relevant concerns. Your agency has such a policy, and you have been advised that you are expected to adhere to it.

You have been working with a newly immigrant Chinese family for six months. During this time, you have engaged the family patriarch in culturally appropriate services for seniors, helped parents find their way through a complex maze of needed services for a developmentally disabled child, helped the parents locate and enroll in English-language classes, and assisted the family with generational concerns around a 15-year-old daughter. As you terminate with the family, all in attendance to say good-bye: grandfather, parents, and children. The grandfather offers you a beautifully wrapped gift, expressing the family's gratefulness for your kind services to them.

Should you accept the gift? In making your decision, consider the NASW Code of Ethics, your agency policy, common agency practice, and your personal moral code.

Culturally Competent Social Work Practice with Chinese Americans

Diversity Project by Caroline Cangelosi

My interest in Chinese Americans is both professional and personal. Professionally, my current field placement is in an urban public hospital's Emergency Department, which serves a diverse group of patients including Asians and Pacific Islanders, who comprise 20 percent of the patients (General Hospital 2003). While this is a substantial percentage of the patients served, it is notably lower than the percentage of Asian Americans in the hospital's catchment area, which is 33 percent. The hospital serves a large number of Chinese American patients, and I hope to learn more about this population in order to provide more effective and culturally appropriate social work services. Personally, after reading *Wild Swans* last summer, an autobiography and biography by Jung Chang that beautifully tells the story of three generations of women in China, I became aware of both how very little I know of Chinese history and how impactful that history is on individuals' lives. Finally, my partner is Chinese American and this project offered the opportunity to learn more about his family's culture.

History and Statistics on Chinese Americans

To understand the history of Chinese Americans one must look at both the history of China and the history of Chinese Americans in the United States. During the early part of the twentieth century, China was enmeshed in conflicts and civil war between the ruling Nationalist Party and the growing Chinese Communist movement. During World War II, Japan attacked China, and when the United States joined the war after the attack on Pearl Harbor, China and the United States became allies. In 1949 the Chinese Communist Party took over China, and Mao Zedong

proclaimed the establishment of the People's Republic of China. Party leaders recognized that they needed guidance in transitioning China's huge urban areas to socialism and industrialization, and turned to the Soviet Union (*Encyclopaedia Britannica* 2006). In 1950 the two countries signed the Treaty of Friendship, Alliance, and Mutual Assistance, which would stay in effect until 1979. This alliance was troublesome to the United States, which was opposed to Communist rule in the Soviet Union. A priority of the Party was to raise China to the status of a great power that would lead the world to Communism (*Encyclopaedia Britannica* 2006). The new leadership helped restore the economy, pushed for a return to normality after decades of war, and quickly gained mass popular support. Several reforms took place, including land reform, which virtually eliminated landlords, and social reform. Initially the Chinese government modeled their version of Communism after that of the Soviet Union, and effectively organized the vast majority of peasant households into collectives (*Encyclopaedia Britannica* 2006).

By the late 1950s, the Chinese government's social reform, meant first calling for criticism of the Party, and then punishing those who spoke out (*Encyclopaedia Britannica* 2006). China wanted to become its own power, separate from the influences of the Soviets, and from 1958 to early 1960, Mao pressed the Great Leap Forward. This was a push to use China's massive manpower rather than modern machinery to forward industrialization, and resulted in the organization of the rural population into communes. The program was hastily implemented and China's problems were exacerbated by natural disasters and the withdrawal of Soviet technical expertise. This enormous experiment disrupted the country's agriculture so greatly that 20 million people died of starvation from 1958 to 1962 (*Encyclopaedia Britannica* 2006).

After this political failure, Mao Zedong launched the Cultural Revolution in 1966, an upheaval intended to renew the spirit of revolution in the country (*Encyclopaedia Britannica* 2006). He used China's youth, the Red Guards, as his troops, and had them shut down schools and attack traditional values and anything considered "bourgeois." When these groups began to fight amongst themselves, Mao sent millions of students to rural areas to learn to live like the peasants. The Cultural Revolution also resulted in fighting within the government and resulted in the physical abuse, verbal attacking, deaths, and purging from the Party of millions of members.

In the midst of this, and of the Vietnam War, Mao organized a secret meeting with United States national security adviser Henry Kissinger in 1971, and the United States and China took steps toward reducing their mutual animosity. The Cultural Revolution ended in 1976 after Mao's death, but left lasting problems, including a generation of youth who lacked an education, a loss of public image of Party legitimacy, and corruption and factionalism within the Party (*Encyclopaedia Britannica* 2006). It is important to understand the vast historical and political differences between China and the United States and the influence of Communism and Mao. As described by *Encyclopaedia Britannica* (2006), "Perhaps never before in human history had a political leader unleashed such massive forces against the system that he had created. The resulting damage to that system was profound, and the goals that Mao Zedong sought to achieve ultimately remained elusive."

After Mao's death, millions of political prisoners were released from labor camps and the role of the police forces was cut back dramatically. In the late 1970s China began opening its economy to the outside world, which proceeded through the 1980s with pressure from the public. In the late 1980s in China, the government was demonstrating its continued desire to silence public criticism, though the opening of China to television crews made this more difficult. Thousands of people were killed or injured when the government brought in military force to end public protests in Tiananmen Square. This incident set back China's emerging foreign relations as the United States, the European Union, and Japan imposed sanctions (*Encyclopaedia Britannica* 2006). By the 1990s, the countries had taken steps towards improved relations and were trading again.

Like that of many minorities in the United States, the history of Chinese Americans is full of incidents of discrimination. Few Chinese Americans lived in the United States prior to the discovery of gold in California in 1848, which led to the recruitment of Chinese labor. From 1850 to 1870 the Chinese American population in the United States grew from 4,000 (out of 23.2 million) to 63,199 (out of 38.5 million) (Public Broadcasting Service 2003), representing less than .2 percent of the entire population. In 1865 the Central Pacific Railroad Company began recruiting Chinese workers to build a transcontinental railroad, which was completed three years later. From the early days of their settlement in California, Chinese Americans took part in mutual protection associations to defend themselves against prejudice, but in 1871 anti-Chinese violence erupted in Los Angeles and other U.S. cities, continuing through the 1870s (Public Broadcasting Service 2003). As recently as 1982, racial bias still very clearly existed in the courts. Vincent Chin, a Chinese American, was killed by two white Americans, and when his killers were sentenced only to probation and a fine of $3,000 plus court fees (Public Broadcasting Service 2003). Public perception goes both ways, of course: in 1987 *Time* published a cover article titled, "The New Whiz Kids," which caused many Chinese Americans to express a concern about a "model minority" stereotype.

Immigration policy for Chinese people has been influenced by discrimination. In 1882 Congress passed the Chinese Exclusion Act, which forbade Chinese from becoming citizens. In 1910, the Angel Island Immigration Station opened, as a place to process potential Asian immigrants. Angel Island has had a long and troublesome history, as it was often used as a detention center where new immigrants were held for years with no help. In 1943 the U.S. Congress repealed all Chinese exclusion laws and granted Chinese the right to become naturalized citizens; however the effect of this was minimal as only 105 Chinese were initially allowed to immigrate to the United States each year (Public Broadcasting Service 2003). In 1950 the Chinese American population was 150,005 (out of 151.3 million), still a tiny .1 percent of the population. Since then, the Chinese American population has slowly continued to grow, although a peculiarity of U.S. immigration and refugee policy is that even though China is a Communist state, the Chinese are not considered refugees, but immigrants (Potocky-Tripodi 2002). Today, only 1.0 percent of the U.S. population has come from the world's most populous country (U.S. Census 2000).

The 2000 Census reports that there were 11,898,828 Asian Americans[1] in the United States in 2000, representing 4 percent of all Americans. Of these, 2,865,232 were Chinese Americans, representing 24 percent of all Asian Americans and 1 percent of the total population. Chinese Americans matched the general population in several ways: average age, average household size, and family size. In others, however, Chinese Americans looked quite different. Overall, they appeared to have a higher education level and higher family income than the general population—of adults over the age of 25, 47 percent of Chinese Americans had a bachelor's degree or higher compared to 24 percent of all Americans. The median household income in 1999 of Chinese American families was about $10,000 higher than the average of all Americans ($51,119 compared to $41,994), and the median value of owned homes was significantly higher than

the average. Sixty-four percent of Chinese Americans were foreign born, and 73 percent spoke a language other than English at home—well above the averages for all Americans. It is notable and representative of Chinese American history that 35 percent of all Asian Americans and 39 percent of all Chinese Americans live in California, which has only 12 percent of the total U.S. population.

Book—*China Boy*

China Boy, by Gus Lee, came recommended by an elderly friend, who said it gave him a new appreciation of the Chinese American experience. It certainly did the same for me. The fictional book is the story of a boy, Kai Ting, whose upper-class family fled China during World War II and the civil war in China, and found themselves living as relatively poor residents of the Panhandle neighborhood in San Francisco, an area with few Asian Americans. The book eloquently describes the family's transition to America.

> Mother and my elder sisters had lost everything—extended family, ancestral home, conventional roles, tradition, friends, teachers, wet nurses, cooks, wealth, servants, advisers, tailors, nation, customs, continuity, harmony, status. I do not think I have left anything out. (Lee 1994, 34)

Lee describes Kai's mother's high expectations for her children—that Kai become an accomplished musician, that his sister become an engineer—as well as her anguish over her inability to fulfill her familial duty to care for her father across the sea. He describes the familial roles each of the children play—the eldest daughter is the most responsible, the second and third daughters are forever scorned for not being wanted boys, and Kai is revered as his mother's only and long-awaited son. At age 6, his mother dies and is soon replaced by a caucasian stepmother, who attempts to beat everything Chinese—

[1]For this paper I have chosen to use the more inclusive category "Asian alone or in combination with one or more other races" rather than "Asian alone." For statistics of Chinese Americans, I have similarly used "Chinese alone or in any combination," which includes people of Taiwanese and mixed ancestries.

which she associates with "poverty, exclusion, isolation" (Lee 1994, 71)—out of Kai and his sisters. Hers is a very different perspective on children and on Chinese culture—one from privileged white American eyes.

Although he is technically born an American, Kai still experiences an assimilation process. This takes place partly by force— from both his stepmother and the neighborhood kids, who routinely beat up young Kai, giving him his name "China Boy"—and partly through a loss of customs in the absence of extended family and long-time Chinese friends, especially after the death of Kai's mother and other protectors and conveyors of the culture. Kai's mourning over the loss of his mother, his cherished place in the family, the family structure, and his native tongue is portrayed.

The book provided both a fascinating story and a wealth of cultural information. Lee frequently says things like, "This was tradition . . ." or "The Chinese do . . ." He also incorporated those cultural beliefs into the character of Kai Ting, who, for example, was convinced that fighting the street bullies back would be bad for his *yuing chi*—his karma. Lee provides both an adult's objective description of Chinese culture and traditions, and a fascinating look at the subjective world of a young Chinese American, who has internalized beliefs from both immigrant Chinese American and traditional caucasian American cultures.

Film—*The Joy Luck Club*

I chose this film because although I read the book years ago, I could remember little of it besides the fact that it told a beautiful story of Chinese American women. In fact, it told eight beautiful stories—four of young Chinese American women who grew up together in the United States, and four of their mothers, who had very different immigration and family stories. The mothers' stories gave glimpses into the diversity of Chinese society. One mother had been a low-ranking concubine and committed suicide in order to improve her children's status. Another woman

was sold at a young age into an arranged and unhappy marriage and then physically punished for not having children with her husband, who secretly refused to sleep with her. Another woman married a dashing and wealthy young man who blatantly cheated on her and abused her, leading her to drown their child in a desperate attempt to hurt her husband the way he hurt her. The final woman, the later founder of the Joy Luck Club, was forced to walk a great distance to freedom, and to leave her twin daughters on the side of the road. She did this so that they wouldn't be cursed by dying with their mother, then went away to die, but was instead taken to a hospital and never learned the fate of her daughters. All of these stories involved great loss, and formed these women's characters as they immigrated to the United States. The women came together weekly in the Joy Luck Club, where they shared mahjong, tea, and stories of their growing daughters.

The daughters' stories gave insight into their experiences growing up in the United States with Chinese-born mothers. They each struggled with parents who expected them to be English-speaking, high-achieving Americans, but to still think like the Chinese. A common theme was the mothers' struggles to have their daughters understand where they came from, and the daughters' endeavors to understand their mothers' high expectations and love for them. Their stories are of breakthroughs as the four women finally relate to their mothers' stories and their connection to past generations. The movie portrays these women's Chinese American experiences in a way that left me crying at their losses and touched by the strength of family bonds. *The Joy Luck Club* gave glimpses of the diversity of life in both China and the United States and at the same time brought the stories together to show commonalities and ties.

Event—Dim Sum in Oakland's Chinatown

After reading Kim Severson's *Chronicle* article, "Taste more than China in Oakland's Chinatown," a walk through Oakland's Chinatown and a Sunday dim sum brunch seemed to be an appropriate cultural event. I went with a Chinese American friend as my guide. He explained that the tradition of dim sum started because people would get together for tea, and it evolved into a weekend tradition of going out to eat followed by many people in China, Hong Kong, and Taiwan as well as many Chinese Americans. I suggested we go to the Restaurant Peony, as the article said that many consider it the most authentic Hong Kong-style dim sum spot in the Bay Area, to which he replied that he wouldn't go anywhere else—it was *the* place to go for dim sum. Indeed, the restaurant seats 800 people (though I don't know if all of the sections were full) and there was a wait. Approximately 80 percent of the patrons were Chinese American and most were family groups.

According to Severson, Oakland's Chinatown is roughly a 12-block square in downtown Oakland where Chinese immigrants have been living since the 1860s. There one can find traditional Chinese produce (such as bitter melon) and other Asian cooking ingredients, imported pottery, and Chinese apothecaries offering dried roots and herbs for time-honored medicinal soups. Today there are also other Asian influences, including Vietnamese, Filipino, and Thai. Severson notes that the food in these restaurants has to be good to stay competitive, because there are plenty of creative immigrants vying for space, and locals frequent the restaurants.

My impression of others' reactions to me was that I was mostly bypassed—staff members glanced at me and then spoke to my Chinese friend. I don't think the staff said anything directly to me the entire time we were there. I was mostly relieved to have him take over the ordering, as the practice of ordering and the food items themselves were different than I am accustomed to. I was content to have someone else who knew how to flag waitresses down or deflect them, who knew what the food items were and how to eat them, and who knew how to get the bill. I asked my friend if any of it were gender-related, that is, if people were looking to him to order because he is male. But he said no, if I were Chinese they would have spoken to either of us. He noted, however, that like in American restaurants, they would have given him the bill.

I'm sure that I would have felt much less comfortable had I gone alone or with a non-Asian friend. When I scanned the room, it seemed that most of the other non-Asians there were with at least one Asian, who, like my friend, seemed to handle the ordering process! The event was a reminder of the strengths of Chinese American family bonds.

Interview with a Chinese American

I choose to interview a 28-year-old friend who was born in Taiwan and moved to the United States at age 2, becoming part of the "one and a half generation." Although I have spoken with him many times about his experiences, this gave me an opportunity to do so in a structured, formal manner. My friend spent most of his childhood in Florida in a community with few other Chinese Americans. As he described it, he wasn't blatantly discriminated against. "I had the 'FOB' (fresh off the boat) bowl-cut haircut and glasses, so everyone made fun of me. I spoke English fine, but I looked different—there were few minorities living near us growing up." His parents had high academic expectations of him and little concern for his social life. Still, he did very well in school and does not begrudge them. He describes his academic experience below.

> I remember learning Chinese at home—it was additional homework, so I didn't like doing it. My parents, being traditional Chinese, were pretty conservative and didn't let me do much at all—I wasn't allowed to date. So for a while I didn't like being Chinese—I thought it was a burden.

Moving to California was a refreshing change—suddenly being Asian wasn't so different. He said that now, when he goes somewhere where he is the only Asian, he doesn't pay attention to other people's looks and impressions. It surprised me that he was able to simply ignore people's responses and struck me that others cannot so easily do so.

My friend described his parent's immigration story. His father first came to the United States to obtain higher education, and my friend and his mother soon joined him. Both of his parents spoke English when they arrived, as they learned it from third grade on in Taiwan. The family struggled financially at first, living in married student housing and using Food Stamps and babysitting jobs for extra income. Life became easier when they moved to Florida for his father's teaching job. His brother was born there, and when he was in tenth grade, my friend and his parents became U.S. citizens (retaining dual citizenship with Taiwan). His parents currently live in Hong Kong, where they are closer to extended family, all of whom still live in Taiwan. It was interesting how my friend compared his family's immigration story those of others. He noted that although as he was growing up, most of the other families he knew had similar stories, he has since met many others with very different immigration histories. He knows many people his age whose parents are first-generation and do not speak English, and did not enjoy some of the advantages that made his family's immigration easier.

My friend is very knowledgeable of both Chinese and Taiwanese history. When I asked him about the role of Communism in his family's history, he told me that the beginning of Communism was the reason his grandparents, who were merchants and didn't want to live under Communist rule, moved from China to Taiwan. He noted that although he is very aware of the historical and current troublesome aspects of Communism, he generally has good thoughts about China. My friend said that there have been times when he has been blatantly discrimi-

nated against by people who think he doesn't speak English, but that these experiences have been largely confined to rural areas. Finally, he noted that older Chinese people he meets expect him to speak Chinese (which he does—Mandarin).

Concluding Thoughts

The combination of these experiences and ways of learning about Chinese American culture as effective in giving me a new perspective. The learning was cumulative—as I undertook later parts (reading *China Boy* and watching *The Joy Luck Club*), I was able to recognize and integrate things from the earlier parts of this project. As I read in *China Boy* that "Chinese food is complex artistry in preparation, and simple, unrestrained celebration in eating," (Lee 78) I thought of my outing to dim sum and how true that statement was for that event, which appeared to my outsider eyes as a gratifying event for families. As I watched *The Joy Luck Club* I thought of *China Boy*'s and my friend's stories of traditions fading over time. As I witnessed through the interview, reading, and film all different and often difficult immigration stories, I thought of the experiences of Chinese Americans once they reached the U.S. coast. And I noted the common themes of parents' high expectations for their children, and the importance of family.

Each medium provided a different angle into Chinese American culture, and each expanded my knowledge base, yet this exercise was again a lesson in how small that knowledge base is and in the importance of continual learning. It provided an opportunity to appreciate the multiplicity of stories and cultural practices of Chinese Americans and served as a reminder that this diversity precludes generalizations or stereotypes about populations, even my own. Both this broader knowledge base and important reminder are valuable to social work practice.

Applying the Knowledge Base: Agency, Programs and Services, and Personal Cultural Competencies

My field work placement is in the Emergency Room of the largest public hospital in a major city. As a public hospital, it serves all of the city's diverse residents.

Agency

Agency's Community The hospital serves nearly 100,000 patients annually, providing comprehensive emergent, urgent, and nonurgent care. Patients are a diverse group, but only somewhat represent the demographics of the city—20 percent of patients are Asian or Pacific Islander (compared to 31 percent of city residents), 25 percent are white (compared to 50 percent of city residents), 21 percent are African American (compared to 8 percent of city residents), 29 percent are Latino (compared to 14 percent of city residents), and 6 percent are Native American, other, or of an unknown race (compared to 11 percent of city residents) (***General Hospital 2004; U.S. Census 2000).[2] Ninety percent of patients are low-income or indigent, and 9 percent were homeless at some point during the past year. The Emergency Department (ED) is the Level I Trauma Center for the county, as well as for parts of two neighboring counties. Any significant traumas (car accidents, falls, shootings, stabbings, etc.) are brought to the ED by ambulance. Over 50,000 patients visit the emergency room every year, an average of more than 150 daily. Of these, 3,000 are serious traumas, averaging nine per day (***General Hospital 2003).

The hospital's population reflects the neighborhoods it primarily serves—the majority of patients reside in six nearby city neighborhoods, none of which has a large number of Chinese American residents. The majority of Chinese Americans in the city live in three neighborhoods that have other healthcare providers. There is a Chinese Hospital, an acute care hospital with a 24-hour Emergency Department in the city's Chinatown, and there are public and private community clinics both in Chinatown and elsewhere that are aimed specifically at the Chinese American community, as well as other healthcare resources.

Providing culturally competent services is not optional for a hospital serving a population as diverse as the residents of this city, where almost 50 percent speak a language other than English at home, and 37 percent were born outside the United States. Among the over 150,000 Chinese Americans living in the city in 2000,[3] 70 percent were foreign born, and 84 percent speak a language other than English at home, although the percentage of these who are monolingual Chinese speakers is unknown (U.S. Census 2000).

Access The hospital is located in a neighborhood that is home to a large Latino population. Chinese American patients who come to the Emergency Department must cross ethnic boundaries, and some have to travel relatively long distances. Although there are numerous bus lines that run to the hospital, it is likely that many residents of outlying neighborhoods choose closer Emergency Departments for nontrauma injuries and illnesses. Chinese Americans from these neighborhoods might choose to come to this hospital if they are uninsured or if they already received other care there.

---

[2]Please note that these statistics are not ideal comparisons, as the hospital data allowed "Latino" as a separate category, and the U.S. Census requires that Latino individuals choose a race and then add on "Hispanic or Latino" as an ethnicity.

[3]Again, statistics are using the Census category, "Chinese alone or in any combination."

Receptivity The waiting room in the ED is not particularly welcoming to Chinese Americans or to other patients, with its linoleum floors, fluorescent lights, buzzing soda machines, ever-running TV, and constant stream of people. It is currently under construction, which has made patient flow more confusing, and resulted in a smaller seating area. At times it is quite crowded. Although signs near the registration area are in English, Spanish, and Chinese, temporary signs made for the construction period are either in English and Spanish or only in English. A patient coming to the ED will encounter many people, including a security guard, a triage nurse, a registration staff member, numerous doctors, nurses, medical students, nursing students, and aides, and at times a social worker and interpreter.

Some of the doctors and a few of the nurses and aides speak Chinese; however, none of the ED social workers do. If the patient speaks primarily a Chinese dialect, he may be lucky, and have a Chinese-speaking practitioner, but even in this case he will encounter numerous other staff who will speak to him in English. Obviously if a patient brings a family member or friend along to translate, they will have someone who speaks their language the whole time. Otherwise, they may have one practitioner who comes and goes, or may have a hospital interpreter who comes down for brief interactions. Interpreters who speak Mandarin and Cantonese, or other Chinese dialects are on call 24 hours a day. Some of the literature patients receive is in Chinese; however much of it (such as their discharge summary) is only in English.

The hospital makes other efforts to serve Chinese Americans in a culturally sensitive manner, including an in-patient unit with an Asian focus, where special emphasis is given to providing culturally appropriate services in Asian languages. ED patients are given only a standard meal; elsewhere in the hospital patients are given more choices, although a representative from the Inpatient Nutrition Department told me that the "Asian meal" simply means the addition of a bowl of juk (rice porridge).

Administration and Staff Training The hospital is a large institution and has a wide variety of forums for training staff in culturally sensitive and competent practice. There are numerous Grand Rounds each month on a variety of topics, some of which address issues of diversity. Some of these Grand Rounds are aimed specifically at social workers, but they are not mandatory and are usually offered during the day shift, which means that they are available only to a select number of staff. Informally, ED social workers frequently discuss issues of race, language, and cultural differences that come up with clients, and such considerations were a regular part of my supervision as a social work intern.

Staff Sensitivity ED social workers are generally respectful and nonjudgmental of cultural differences with Chinese American patients and family members. I have not observed stereotyping or "they" language. However, in many cases the language barrier remains a major obstacle. Many Chinese American patients seen in the ED speak only a little English, or are monolingual Chinese speakers. In my experience, social workers have been more likely than other disciplines to ask patients about their preference in using an interpreter, or to request an interpreter to speak with a patient or family.

Cultural differences can pose another barrier to ideal service delivery. Upon questioning several ED social workers about hospital and social work treatment of Chinese Americans, I was surprised at the range of their answers. I believe this variance reflects individual differences in knowledge of Chinese American culture and culturally sensitive practice. However, all ED social workers generally use formalities in addressing patients and family members, attempt to talk with all family members present, and address all parties with respect and empathy.

Program and Services

I worked with the Emergency Department Social Work Team. ED social workers provide psychosocial support to patients seen in the ED and their families and friends. They are involved in cases such as trauma, domestic violence, substance abuse, referrals to community services, and death in the ED. There are usually one or two social workers on duty from 8:30 a.m. until 3:00 a.m. daily. The ED social work department is one aspect of the broader mission of the hospital, which is clearly aligned with providing culturally competent services.

The hospital's mission statement includes delivering culturally competent services in its first line. It goes on to say that part of this means eliminating barriers to care, including linguistic barriers (***Dept. of Public Health (2003). Along with numerous community medical clinics, mental health clinics, and social service programs, the hospital is run by the city's Department of Public Health, which similarly states its commitment to culturally competent services in its mission statement. The Public Health Department has a task force on cultural competency and has adopted the federal Culturally and Linguistically Appropriate Services (CLAS) standards for healthcare standards. These standards outline specific standards for Health Care Organizations (HCOs), from the broad expectation that HCOs ensure that patients receive effective, understandable, and respectful care in a manner compatible with their cultural healthcare beliefs, practices, and language, to more specific mandates that HCOs provide no-cost language assistance at all points of contact and have a strategic plan for cultural competency (***Department of Public Health 2002b).

Effort Programs and services reflect a commitment and effort to be sensitive to cultural differences in patients, including Chinese Americans, however, gathering feedback and adjusting new programs can take time. As an example, the ED social work department recently started a bereavement program for family members and friends of patients who die traumatically shortly after coming to the ED. This program was designed to fill a gap in available bereavement services by offering support specific to the sudden and distressing nature of traumatic death. Participants receive mailings and phone calls, and attention is paid to cultural and individual differences in grieving styles. The program is in a pilot stage and is being adapted through formal feedback. Initially, it is only being offered in English, which limits its usefulness to Chinese Americans who are not proficient in English. English language also limits feedback from this population, however it is hoped that in the future the program will be expanded to multiple languages.

Quality, Effectiveness, and Efficiency It is difficult to formally evaluate the quality of social work services provided in the ED. Because of the brief and often stressful nature of visits, it is often not feasible nor is inappropriate to request feedback from patients and family members. Patients do, however, often give feedback through verbalized appreciation or frustration, or through nonverbal cues. My experience with Chinese Americans has been that it is even harder to obtain feedback from them, due to both the language barrier and the cultural practice of politeness. Most Chinese Americans I have worked with have been exceptionally polite and expressed appreciation for my services and those of the medical team.

Additionally, the ED social work department does not currently have a good supervisory structure, so social workers receive little direct feedback on their performance in the absence of complaints. By default, responsibility for assessing and improving cultural sensitivity lies with individual social workers, and the result is a staff with varied levels of sensitivity and commitment to cultural competency.

Overall, the number of Chinese American patients utilizing hospital services does not reflect the number of Chinese Americans in the city. This may be due to their use of other Western healthcare resources, to their use of traditional healthcare services, or to the fact that most Chinese Americans in this area immigrants and immigrants generally underutilize services.

Personal Cultural Competencies

Engagement and Assessment Chinese Americans are often interested in using both Western and Eastern medicine; thus, a visit to the hospital might be only part of the healthcare plan for a patient. It is important for social work and medical staff at Western institutions to be familiar with healthcare usage patterns and barriers for Chinese Americans; there is literature to support this. Grace Ma (1999) notes that because the majority of Chinese Americans are foreign-born, strong Chinese cultural beliefs, values, and traditional health practices still play a big role in their health-seeking behavior. Barriers to using Western medical care found in her study that are applicable to looking at ED social work services at the hospital include: a lack of understanding of the United States healthcare system, miscommunication, a lack of understanding of traditional medicine on the part of Western practitioners, and a distrust of Western practitioners (Ma 1999). The study found that most Chinese immigrants preferred a combination of Western and traditional health services and remedies. Chinese immigrants seeking Western healthcare preferred to consult physicians of their own ethnic background, who were believed to have sympathy, common language, flexible appointment schedules, and a familiarity with Chinese medicine principles. Western medicine was generally avoided for nonserious conditions, but was believed to work more quickly in urgent situations (Ma 1999), which of course represents the majority of care provided in the ED.

Chinese Americans often expect to make decisions as a family. J. Tanner (1995) reports that in contrast to the Western medical model, which places responsibility solely with the physician, the entire Chinese American family feels directly responsible for care of the patient. If a patient is admitted to the hospital from the ED, difficulties with communication, medical decision-making, and the strict visiting hour rules may occur. Although the ED is not a setting that lends itself to extensive ethnographic interviewing, politely asking the patient or family member about healthcare beliefs and practices is important. In a social work role, it is important for social workers to assess the cultural aspects of family dynamics in order to begin considering the impact of the patient's illness or injury on the family.

Finally, the social work role in the hospital setting might be unclear to Chinese Americans. Tanner (1995) points out that in traditional Chinese medicine, practitioners provide support with both physiological and psychosocial problems for the patient. Many Chinese Americans feel uncomfortable expressing feelings in front of strangers (Tanner 1995), so it may be important for the ED social worker to explain his or her role and, as with all patients, to offer emotional support at the patient or family's comfort level.

Goal Setting and Interventions Tanner (1995) suggests that the most important area of concern in providing care to Chinese Americans in a healthcare setting is continued family involvement; thus an important area for consideration in goalsetting with a family might be ways to maximize their involvement in the patient's care. If a patient is admitted to the hospital, the social worker might do this by ensuring that the family is kept updated and involved in medical decision-making. If a patient is discharged from the ED, the social worker can similarly ensure that family members are involved in after-care planning. In addition to supporting the patient and family, the social worker can educate other medical staff on Chinese-American patterns of communication (Tanner 1995).

Evaluation and Termination: As noted earlier, Chinese Americans generally use Western hospitals for urgent and serious medical problems. If these are addressed and resolved in the ED, this is viewed as a satisfactory outcome. Engaging the family in planning followup care, whether inpatient or outpatient, is essential. Chinese Americans will also express appreciation for the personalized care and attention they have received from the social worker.

Evaluation Using NASW Standards

Standard 9: Language Diversity—Social workers shall seek to provide and advocate for the provision of information, referrals, and services in the language appropriate to the client, which may include the use of interpreters (NASW 2001).

Agency The hospital has expressed a commitment to providing services in multiple languages through their policies and practices. Currently, hospital interpreters provide language assistance to patients in over 35 languages, handling 150 language interpretations per day (***General Hospital 2003). The hospital should evaluate on an ongoing basis whether existing interpreter services are sufficient, especially after-hours. Although services are available, I have seen practitioners express frustration at having to use a translator and attempt to speak with the patient or family members in English first, to see if they can get by. The hospital should evaluate this and consider how to provide education on the importance of using interpreters to provide culturally competent care. Finally, the hospital should improve the availability of signs and written materials in Chinese and referrals to agencies that target Chinese Americans.

Program: ED Social Work The ED social work department could improve services to Chinese Americans in several ways, including training on cultural competency and the use of interpreters. Like the whole hospital, the ED social work department could evaluate and expand its own use of interpreter services. Hospital interpreters are busy and are on call for the entire hospital, so they generally remain in the ED only briefly when called. Because the social worker's interaction with a patient or family often consists of ongoing, short check-ins, and because it is not feasible to call an interpreter for each of these, some of the empathy and support the social worker is trying to convey is lost.

Additionally, when using a hospital or informal translator, most social workers talk directly to the patient, but some talk directly to the interpreter instead. When a young adult family member is serving as a translator, this mistake can disrupt the power balance in the family, as it makes the young person the source of information and power.[4] Additionally, the social work department could provide more referrals in Chinese on existing community resources for Chinese Americans, including traditional healthcare resources, as my experience is that the English materials are updated much more frequently than those in other languages. Finally, it would be helpful to recruit a Chinese-speaking social worker for the department.

My Cultural Competence My role in providing and advocating for the provision of information, referrals, and services in Chinese is parallel to that of the ED social work department. I can evaluate and expand my use of interpreters. My experience with interpreters has been mixed—some have interpreted quickly both ways, and have made suggestions about what to say and how to say it in a way that is culturally sensitive, while others have had lengthy conversations with patients and family members and reported little back to me. It is important that I both build good relationships with interpreters and provide feedback both to individual interpreters and to my supervisor. Additionally, I can advocate for the use of interpreters by other practitioners for patients I am serving. Finally, I can advocate for assistance in translating existing resources, or in obtaining new resource materials in Chinese. These responsibilities represent only a small part of an ongoing commitment to providing culturally sensitive social work services.

---

[4]There are multiple other components to effective translation in healthcare settings that are beyond the scope of this paper but can be found in the literature.

REFERENCES

Chang, J. 1991. *Wild Swans*. New York: Simon & Schuster.

***Department of Public Health. 2002a. *Resolution 2-02: Amending the Department of Public Health's Policy Directive 24, Contractors' Compliance with Antidiscrimination Protections and Cultural Competency, and Adopting Guidelines for Culturally and Linguistically Appropriate Services (CLAS) in Health Care*. Retrieved on April 17, 2006.

Department of Public Health. 2002b. *Cultural and Linguistic Competency Policy*. Retrieved on April 17, 2006.

Department of Public Health. 2003. ***General Hospital: About Us*. Retrieved on May 1, 2006.

Encyclopaedia Britannica. 2006. S.V. "China." Retrieved on April 23, 2006, from Encyclopaedia Britannica Premium Service, http://www.britannica.com/eb/article-9117321

General Hospital Medical Center Foundation. 2003. ***General Hospital Medical Center Annual Report*. Retrieved on April 26, 2006.

General Hospital Medical Center Foundation. 2004. ***General Hospital Medical Center Annual Report*. Retrieved on April 2, 2006.

Lee, G. 1994. *China Boy*. New York: Penguin Books, Inc.

Ma, G. X. 1999. Between two worlds: The use of traditional and western health services by Chinese immigrants. *Journal of Community Health* 24 (6): 421–437.

National Association of Social Workers. 2001. *NASW Standards for Cultural Competence in Social Work Practice*. Retrieved on May 1, 2006, from http://www.socialworkers.org/sections/credentials/cultural_comp.asp

Potocky-Tripodi. 2002. *Best Practices for Social Work with Refugees and Immigrants*. New York: Columbia University Press.

Public Broadcasting Service. 2003. *A Bill Moyers Special: Becoming American: The Chinese Experience*. Public Affairs Television, Inc. http://www.pbs.org/becomingamerican/index.html

Severson, K. 2000. Taste more than China in Oakland's Chinatown. *The San Francisco Chronicle*, 9 August, FD-1.

Tanner, J. 1995. Death, dying, and grief in the Chinese-American culture. In Parry, J. K. and A. S. Ryan, eds. *A Cross-cultural Look at Death, Dying, and Religion*. Chicago: Nelson-Hall, 183–192.

U.S. Census Bureau 2000. *American Fact Finder*. http://factfinder.census.gov/home/saff/main.html?_lang=en

Wang, W., A. Tan, R. Bass, and P. Markey. (producers), and W. Wang (director). 1993. *The Joy Luck Club* [Motion picture]. USA: Hollywood Pictures.

Worksheet

1. Social workers generally support empowerment and individual rights, especially in terms of healthcare decision-making. However, this may not be culturally congruent for Chinese American patients, who often either prefer to follow the position taken by the family elder, or prefer to make decisions as a family unit. How might you support self-determination if you were working with a Chinese American patient in a medical setting?

2. As the author notes, Chinese American patients often use a mixture of traditional Chinese medicine and Western medicine. (a) What are some of the issues of which the social worker should be aware in working with Chinese American clients who use both kinds of medical interventions? (b) Where would you go to learn more about Chinese medicine, in order to become competent in working with patients who use it?

Culturally Competent Social Work
Practice with Undocumented Mexicans

Diversity Project by Rosailda Perez

For this project, I chose to study undocumented Mexican individuals living in the United States, with a particular focus on California. Being a child of Mexican immigrants myself, I have seen the difficulties faced by aunts, uncles, and even cousins for not having legal status in the United States. Although I am a member of the same family, my experiences in life are tremendously different from the experiences of my undocumented family members. In addition, my agency also represents minors who are undocumented or are children of undocumented parents. I encounter undocumented Mexican immigrants every day, and feel the need to learn more about them in order to better serve them in my profession.

KNOWLEDGE ACQUISITION:
CULTURAL IMMERSION

History and Current Status of Mexicanos Indocumentados

Immigration of Mexican people to the United States has been occurring since the existence of this country; however, the number of immigrants from Mexico has steadily been on the rise ever since the implementation of the Bracero Program in 1942. The United States established this labor contract system for Mexicans in order to fill labor shortages in agriculture created by World War II. Participating Mexican workers were granted temporary visas and labeled *braceros* (hired hands). During its existence, about 5 million Mexican workers entered the U.S. labor force as legal seasonal workers (Aguirre 2001, 147). The U.S. Congress also used the Bracero Program as a way of reducing the number of illegal immigrants from Mexico. By extending the program beyond World War II, Congress sought to provide some relief for the struggling U.S. Border Patrol, which had been rel-

atively ineffective in its control of the illegal immigration (Aguirre 2001, 147). Congress today still has been unable to control illegal immigration.

In 1954 with the approval of Congress, the Border Patrol launched Operation Wetback, with the full authority to stop and search any "Mexican-looking" person. Between 1954 and 1959, 3.8 million people were returned to Mexico (Aguirre 2001, 148). This operation reinforced the perception among Mexicans that their presence in the United States would always be insignificant and questionable.

Today, over 50 years later, the problem of illegal immigration from Mexico to the United States has not been resolved; instead, it has worsened. According to the Pew Hispanic Center, about 6.3 million undocumented immigrants from Mexico live in the United States, and an average of 485,000 more arrive every year. About 57 percent of undocumented immigrants in the United States are from Mexico, 24 percent are from other Latin American countries, and 19 percent are from other countries. Estimates show that in the early 1990s about 2 million undocumented immigrants were from Mexico; in 2000 that number jumped to 4.8 million, and in 2006 the number has increased to over 6 million (Thornburgh 2006, 38). *Time* magazine reports that one out of every ten people born in Mexico now resides in the United States, and that 80 to 85 percent of new immigrants from Mexico lack legal documentation (Thornburgh 2006, 38).

The majority of undocumented immigrants come to the United States seeking economic advancement. Immigrants come in hopes of making enough money to provide a better life for themselves and their families. According to *Time* magazine, the median hourly wage of Mexican-born workers in the

United States in 2004 was $9.00/hour, while in Mexico the average hourly wage in 2004 was $1.86 (21 pesos). The estimated combined annual gross income of all U.S. workers born in Latin America, with both legal and illegal immigration status, in 2004 was $450 billion; 93 percent of that money was spent in the United States, while people in Mexico receive 1.7 billion a month from U.S. immigrants (Thornburgh 2006, 39).

These numbers illustrate the tremendous impact undocumented Mexican immigrants have on this country; they literally are its backbone. The need to recognize these individuals and address their issues is a strong imperative. I was surprised to find that undocumented Mexican immigrants play such an extensive role in the United States: they are resilient hardworking individuals who do nothing less than help out this country.

Biography: *Morir En El Intento* (*Dying to Cross*)

In order to get a true life perspective on the hardships of entering the United States illegally, I read *Dying to Cross*, by Jorge Ramos, a well-known and respected Mexican anchorman and journalist for Univision. The book describes the tragic story of 73 immigrants, 19 of whom lost their lives after attempting to enter the United States illegally. On the hot and humid evening of May 13, 2003, at least 73 people boarded a tightly sealed trailer truck in what they hoped to be the final leg of an intricate journey toward their dream of living and working in the United States. The trailer in which they were riding was to take them from Harlingen, Texas, to Houston, about 300 miles away. The trailer never made it past Victoria, Texas, a place that would become the site of the single worst immigrant tragedy in U.S. history. Nineteen immigrants died of asphyxiation, dehydration, and heat exposure, trapped inside the trailer truck. Among the dead was a 5-year-old child. Never before had so many undocumented immigrants died in one single incident.

Through various interviews with the survivors and other people involved in the tragedy, Ramos powerfully describes the stressful events leading up to these tragic deaths. The "coyotes," people who arrange for illegal border crossings, overcharged the immigrants, crammed them all into a trailer truck, and even lied to the driver of the truck about the number of people he would be transporting. It was utterly demoralizing and disgusting to see that the immigrants were treated like objects of no significant value.

While reading the book, I found myself battling feelings of rage and sadness at the same time. Should anyone have to put their life on the line, just to enter another county in search of a better life? How can we as legal citizens of the United States, the land of opportunity, be so blinded by the harsh realities that immigrants face daily, just to be a part of our society? How can something so inhumane be happening in the twenty-first century?

One section that stood out from the book was when Ramos was trying to determine the real culprit in these terrible events. I found myself agreeing with him when he stated that the "coyotes" involved in this incident were not the only ones responsible for the 19 deaths; severely flawed U.S. immigration policies, as well as the dire economic and social conditions in Mexico are also to blame for what happened (Ramos 2005, xvi). Individuals resort to this "profession" of trafficking human bodies, to becoming "coyotes," due to inadequate economic opportunities, and not for the fun of it. It often seems that they are all victims of both the U.S. and the Mexican government's shortcomings and their inability to fix these problems; this is a saddening reality people are forgetting when pointing the finger at one another.

Film: *The Gatekeeper*

I viewed the film, *The Gatekeeper*, for this project. The movie was written, directed, and produced by John Carlos Frey, a Mexican American who was born in Mexico and raised in San Diego, California. This film was an extremely powerful and moving depiction of undocumented immigrants' journey to the United States. The film clearly depicts the current civil unrest occurring at the U.S./ Mexico border. Adam Fields is a border patrol agent who is focused on preventing Mexican undocumented immigration from Tijuana to San Diego, and who takes this on as his personal mission. Without permission from the United States Border Patrol, Adam goes undercover to expose and publicize the criminal nature of Mexicans entering the United States illegally. However, his plan goes terribly wrong, he ends up trapped within a well-organized crystal-meth drug ring in central California, and is forced to work among the people he so furiously hated. The film shows scenes portraying the hardships endured by undocumented immigrants. Eva Ramirez, the only female immigrant in the film, is raped by the white meth-lab owner, and is subjected to further humiliation and mistreatment. Her son is forced to go through similar experiences: having very little food, sleeping in shacks, and being mistreated by the Americans.

It was a shocking experience to see how difficult everyday life is for undocumented workers in this country: their lives are much harder than any of ours, as U.S. citizens. Adults, let alone children, should not have to endure these hardships especially when in pursuit of freedom. Is it humane to deny freedom for those that seek it, to turn our backs and exploit those who seek it?

Cultural Event: La Gran Marcha 2006

On March 25, 2006, I attended the Mass March against Sensenbrenner's HR Bill 4437 in Los Angeles, California. I do not think I will ever be able to describe the full impact this event had on the immigrant community, as well as on my life. It was an amazing experience to see the numbers of people, a large percent undocumented immigrants, who came to show their disapproval of such an extreme anti-immigration bill. Spanish radio stations had been announcing the need for the Latino community to come together and protest the bill in a peaceful manner weeks before the March 25th event. They instructed the participants to wear white, a color that

would show the peaceful nature of the event, and, at the same time, the solidarity in the immigrant community. Although the media would later say that over 500,000 people came together to rally against proposed HR Bill 4437, most of us who were there believe over a million people were gathered in downtown Los Angeles. It is speculated that because of liability issues, the number was said to be just "over 500,000." *Los Angeles Times* reported that the attendance at the demonstration far surpassed the number of people who protested against the Vietnam War and Proposition 187.

My 17-year-old sister and I boarded the train in our hometown of Simi Valley, a predominantly white, suburban, middle-class community. Not having thought that other members of my community would go to such an event, I was immediately surprised when I saw other Latinos at the train station wearing white t-shirts that read "Stop HR 4437." It was an eye opening experience to see other members of my community taking time out of their schedules to go and support the immigrants.

When we arrived at Union Station in downtown Los Angeles, I was struck by the tremendous numbers of people that were gathered. Never had I expected there to be such a large turn out. Ordinary immigrants alongside labor, religious, and civil rights groups stretched more than 20 blocks chanting, "Si, se puede!" (Yes we can!) and "El pueblo unido jamas sera vencido!" (A united community shall not be overcome!). I was very grateful that I was able to participate in such a powerful movement. It was uplifting to see the community united. Because our Mexican features are apparent, my sister and I were not regarded as outsiders, but rather as members of the Latino community who were advocating for justice. Although having legal status in this country, I felt it was my duty to go out and support the undocumented workers because my parents had once been in their situation as well. At one point I did worry that my presence would be rejected simply because of the fact that many would consider me "Americanized," but those feelings were put at ease when I felt the strong unity vibe. My sister and I were welcomed in that demonstration in the same manner that any person, of any color, with an interest in immigrants' rights would have been welcomed.

It was just a beautiful experience witnessing the unity and peaceful nature of all those gathered in Los Angeles. People were there with flags from their countries as well as with flags of the United States. Homemade posters and banners were seen throughout the crowd, many advocating for amnesty, and others recalling the history of this territory, as it became a part of the United States.

One of the most powerful signs I saw was held by a man who appeared to be an undocumented worker. It read,

> "Please U.S.A. Political, Be smart. Just check how much you can get and how much you can loose. We be here because we think American Dream. Just give us a chance."

This sign moved me in particular because of its sincerity and its authenticity. It was obviously written by an immigrant who was voicing his opinion without reservation or shame, and symbolized the great effort made, and the strong desire immigrants have, in obtaining a better life. The importance of the demonstration was clearly stated: immigrants are here to work and ameliorate their status, not to cause trouble and wreak havoc on society. To criminalize immigrants is to deny their individual human rights.

Interview: La Historia de Un Immigrante

In order to get a closer insight on the immigration experience, I interviewed a family friend who, for purposes of this project, I will call Roberto, a 23-year-old male born in Jalpa, Zacatecas, Mexico. I was reluctant at first to interview him, due to the sensitive nature of the subject matter; I did not know how he would react to some of my questions.

To get a comprehensive look at Roberto's immigration experience, I first asked him about his lifestyle in Mexico, and what it was that had prompted him to come to the United States. Roberto explained to me that life in Jalpa was very difficult for him as a child. His mother had been in an abusive relationship with his father. Before he was born, his mother left his father, took her eight children, moved to another home, and began to work to try to provide for them as best she could. Roberto lived in poverty for most of his life, and it wasn't until he was a teenage boy that his family was elevated to the status of the working class in Mexico. Roberto revealed to me that this was a period of great sadness for him, because he saw how much his mother struggled to move the family ahead in life. Roberto stated that life was difficult for them, and that he decided that he would follow in his brothers' footsteps, and come to the United States one day to make money and have a better life.

Roberto's manner of coming to the United States is somewhat different from the "typical" undocumented immigrant's experience involving "coyotes" and life-threatening situations. He did not hide in the trunk of any car, nor walk great distances in the desert. Instead, Roberto came to United States by airplane. At the age of 17, he was fortunate enough to get a student visa, which proved to be his golden ticket to entering the United States legally.

Upon arriving, Roberto was picked up by one of his brothers, who had been living in the United States for quite some time. He recalled that he was intimidated by the huge city around him, and was wary of what life was going to be like in such a foreign land. Not knowing anyone except his family, and not speaking any English, Roberto spent the better half of two months locked up in a room in his brother's house. Roberto confided that those were two of the loneliest months in his life. "I felt isolated. I did not have any friends. It felt weird. I wanted to go back (to Mexico) so badly." He stated that he would call home every weekend, and that it was those phone calls that kept him sane and provided him with the strength to stay in the United States. At this point in the interview I found myself relating Roberto's story to the book I had read, to the film I had watched, to so many other stories of immigrants coming to the United States. The feelings of isolation and homesickness are often, if not always, present in the immigrant experience.

As Roberto had not been able to find employment, his brothers began to push him to enroll in high school. Roberto recalled that the same day he was going to enroll in school, one of his brothers telephoned him and told him he had found him a job in a prestigious camera house. "I was excited because I was going to be making $7.50 an hour, when, at the time, the minimum wage was $5.75 an hour," Roberto said. "I was very nervous at the same time; I was scared that no one there was going to speak Spanish. My brother told me that there was *raza* working there, but when I started I found out that there was only one other person who spoke Spanish," he said.

Although he had found employment, Roberto still had to face the challenges of everyday life as an undocumented immigrant. Having no car, and being unfamiliar with the city, Roberto's brother taught him how to use the bus system. "I was very scared that I was going to get lost," stated Roberto. On his first day of work, Roberto rode the bus for an hour and 40 minutes, and continued to do so everyday afterwards. He would wake up at 4:00 a.m., in order to be at the bus stop at 6:00 a.m., and would not return home until 8:30 in the evening. He began going to night school after work to learn English, but after two months of getting home at 11:30 in the evening and waking up at 4:00 in the morning, his body grew exhausted. "It got to be overwhelming," stated Roberto. The resilience and dedication Roberto had was impressive.

I was curious to find out the nature of interaction between Roberto and his coworkers and boss so I asked him about his feelings of being one of two Mexicans at work.

> I was nervous in the beginning but soon grew accustomed to working with the gringos. They were all really nice and welcomed me with open arms. My boss and I get along really well, he has always helped me and has never discriminated against me; he is a great man, I am glad he gave me a chance to prove myself.

Roberto informed me that his boss would sign him up to attend trainings and conferences that would teach him new things and enhance his job performance. It was wonderful to hear that his boss had so much confidence in him, and that he saw Roberto's potential at such a young age. However, in reality not all undocumented immigrants get treated this way by their employers. I was reminded of all those individuals who are exploited, overworked, and earn very little money.

Today, six years after his arrival, Roberto is in his fifth year of employment at the same camera house, and is fluent in English. Having started out cleaning the camera equipment, he is now a camera and electronic technician, making over $20.00 an hour. After two years of living with his brother, and another year with his cousin, Roberto now rents an apartment where he lives on his own. In addition, Roberto sends his mother money every month, something extremely important to almost all immigrants from Mexico. I asked Roberto how he felt about his accomplishments. Roberto replied (in English), "I am very happy. I am making my own money, I can send money back to my mother, and I am taking care of myself." I realized that it was the notion of being self-sufficient and independent that made Roberto happy. I was extremely amazed at the tremendous accomplishments Roberto had achieved in just six years of being in this country.

Although Roberto's story appears to be a successful one, it is plagued by harsh realities that hold true for all undocumented immigrants. Despite the fact that Roberto entered the country legally, Roberto today is just like any other undocumented immigrant; his student visa expired in 2003. "When I realized that my visa had expired, I was very sad. I did not know what to do. I was scared to tell my boss, because I thought he would fire me for sure, and I would lose everything I gained," stated Roberto. With the advice of his brothers, Roberto sat down with his caucasian boss and explained his situation. His boss was very understanding and cooperative. "He did everything he could to help me, just like he had been doing all along. We sat down together, made up a social security number, and spoke about moving past this hardship."

Roberto is at a disadvantage because he is undocumented. He has no identification, cannot get a driver's license, cannot register to vote, cannot purchase a car, and lives in fear of being deported. He feels very sad to be contributing to a society that will not return anything to him; he is unable to attend school, and, hardest of all, he is unable to return to visit his family in Mexico, especially his mother, who is dying of cancer. Roberto's story illustrates the harsh realities faced by the 6.3 million undocumented Mexican individuals living in this country.

Conclusion

This immersion project has provided me with the opportunity to take a closer look at a population with which I am closely associated, and inspired me to think critically of the grave political issues surrounding immigration in the United States. Immigration reform is desperately needed in this country in order to provide better treatment to such valuable members of our society such as Roberto, and the people at La Grande Marcha. As Los Angeles Mayor Antonio Villaraigosa has stated, "We cannot criminalize people who are working, people who are contributing to our economy and contributing to the nation."

The book, *Dying to Cross* and the film *The Gatekeeper*, both provided powerful insights into the horrors immigrants face when entering this country illegally. Although I had heard numerous stories of my family members crossing the border, and their experiences when first arriving in this country, I had never placed these into the broader context I gained from the book and the film. La Grande Marcha further heightened my awareness of the imminent need for immigration reform, and was an opportunity to see activism and advocacy in action. It was an inspiring feeling seeing all of the Latinos come together for a common cause. Unity is highly valued in Mexican culture and this was very apparent at the rally.

What must it feel like to leave one's family, heritage, language, and even country all for a menial job in a country where you are not wanted and not received with open arms? The sad part of this is that most of us that were privileged to have been born here will never know the answer, and will never care enough to learn the answer. I do not see how this country, which prides itself in being the land of opportunity and the land of the free, can have immigration policies that are so closed minded and insensitive to the social and economic conditions of other countries. Would it not be smarter for neighboring countries to be friendly and at peace with each other?

The immigrant population has been and still is of great importance: aside from the monetary contribution they make, they provide a valuable piece of the rich culture, language, and heritage. The United States is founded on immigration, and it is the immigrants that make that United States what it is. Undocumented immigrants are a vital part of that, and their presence cannot be ignored nor their value denied. Our policies and laws should recognize their contribution and provide for their well-being.

Applying the Knowledge Base: Agency, Programs and Services, and Personal Cultural Competencies

FIELD WORK AGENCY

The function of the county's Juvenile Dependency Unit is to represent the legal interests of children who are in the child welfare system. Law enforcement personnel have placed children that this agency serves into protective custody as a result of the potential for endangerment and the high risk of emotional and physical abuse and/or molestation. My agency is one of the many parties who have legal standing in the matter of each child.

Agency

Community The Juvenile Dependency Unit is located in a major urban center, and serves the city and surrounding county. The city has a population of just under a million, of whom 30.17 percent are Hispanic according to the U.S. Census (2000).

As of 2000, the county's residents were approximately 54 percent white, 26 percent Asian, 3 percent black, 0.3 percent Native Hawaiian or Pacific Islander, and 17 percent of the population was of some other race or two or more races. The Hispanic or Latino population consisted of 24 percent of the total population. Out of a million and a half county residents, almost one-fifth were Mexican. Approximately 34 percent of this population was born outside of the United States with an estimated 100,000 of them being undocumented immigrants (County Official Website 2006).

Access My agency is located in the city's downtown, and clients can access the agency by car or by easily available public transportation. As the county is such a culturally diverse community, undocumented Mexican immigrants must cross several ethnic and cultural boundaries before reaching my agency. Because our clients are children, their caretakers or parents usually bring them to our office and court when needed. If their caretakers are undocumented Mexican immigrants, they usually get rides from family members or friends, or opt to take public transportation. Due to the nature of the agency itself and the type of service it provides, there are no outreach services. Neither undocumented Mexican immigrants nor the majority of the surrounding population view our office as a "neighbor." Our clients are automatically assigned to a lawyer in our agency once a child abuse report has been substantiated. Fear of deportation can become an issue for parents once their children are involved in juvenile dependency court, espe-cially if they are found to be the perpetrators of the abuse.

Receptivity The office is receptive to all populations, including undocumented Mexican immigrants. The only minors this agency does not represent are those who are not in dependency court or those who are involved in the probation system.

There are no staff members in the agency that are undocumented Mexican immigrants; all employees are citizens of the United States. However, there are Mexican individuals working in the office, including myself.

The agency waiting room is decorated in a manner that appeals to children and caretakers; however, it does not cater to Spanish-speaking individuals. The agency's mission statement is hung on the wall in the waiting room, but it is only written in English. Furthermore, the magazines and announcements in the waiting room are all in English.

Although the literature and reading materials do not explicitly include undocumented Mexican immigrants, the material is available in Spanish so that Spanish-speaking clients and families may read it. An activity book for children who are going to court entitled *What's Happening in Court?* is also available in Spanish, and is given to children when they meet with the Dependency Investigator. The activity book provides information on everything from who's who in the courtroom, to family law court, adoption, emancipation, and other special laws that affect children. It is an obvious effort to reach out to those clients who are not fluent in English or familiar with the court process in the United States.

All of the court forms, petitions, and pamphlets are available in Spanish. My field work instructor said that the only thing not in Spanish were the court reports because of the nature of the court system. Interpreters, however, are also available for those clients who need them.

Administration and Staff Training The office has an ongoing program to train staff members, both professional and nonprofessional, in culturally sensitive and competent practices that include working with undocumented Mexican immigrants. My field work instructor participates in training child advocates, attorneys, and social workers six times a year in various continuing education unit classes (CEUs) that teach cultural competency. Although training is provided, there is no follow up, meetings, lectures, or retreats where issues related to diversity or undocumented Mexican immigrants are addressed. Should one have a question regarding these issues, one is expected to consult with the supervisor.

Staff Sensitivity During my internship I have noticed that most staff members are respectful of differences when interacting with clients who are of different cultures. With the exception of a newly hired female attorney, the rest of the attorneys in the agency are caucasian. Although the staff strives to do its job objectively and interact in a culturally sensitive manner, the power differential is both seen and felt. Although the staff members do not use "they" language per se, they do not seem to be culturally sensitive in the conversations they have with one another. Some staff members have made generalizations and expressed negative judgments on members of minority populations without thinking twice about their statements.

In many instances, the attorneys do not meet with their clients before the scheduled court date, but only meet them seconds before they represent them. They do spend a great deal of time reviewing their client's legal files, but they rely on the social workers and the social work interns to meet with the clients. Clients who are undocumented Mexican immigrants have confided in me that they feel more comfortable speaking and interacting with me, a native Spanish speaker, because they can identify with me and speak to me in Spanish.

Funding The District Attorney's office has adequate funds to serve undocumented Mexican immigrants in a culturally sensitive manner. Spanish interpreters are available whenever clients may need them and pamphlets, brochures, and legal forms are all available in Spanish. Cultural variations in funding occur when paying differentials to Spanish-speaking interpreters. If a client requires an interpreter of a different language, he or she is referred to the main office.

Programs and Services

Effort The agency does make an effort to be sensitive to cultural differences in general, and also to undocumented Mexican immigrants. Because this is a government agency, and therefore laws, regulations, and policies are not written by staff, I am quite certain that undocumented Mexican immigrants are not consulted in formulating and designing culturally sensitive policies and programs. However, services to all county residents are available regardless of their race, class, ethnicity, or residential status.

Quality Due to the nature of its mission, my agency only provides legal representation for its clients, a service that cannot be specifically culturally tailored—except for the provision of interpreters for non-English speaking clients. The legal representation of clients is completely objective and leaves little room for subjectivity: in theory everyone receives the same standard and quality of representation, regardless of race or ethnicity. The office supports equitable, respectful, and equal access to all clients.

The nature of legal representation does not allow for the inclusion of worldviews, values, religions, and belief systems that vary from the dominant cultural norms; representation is provided as dictated by law and does not deviate from the set standards. While my agency recognizes that outcomes for their undocumented Mexican immigrant clients are less favorable than the outcomes for clients who are from the dominant group in society, caucasians, there is very little they can do to ensure cultural sensitivity aside from providing materials in Spanish and referring clients to outside agencies that can provide culturally competent services. Undocumented Mexican immigrant youth and their undocumented parents are ineligible for social security, Medicare, Medicaid, Healthy Families, Income Support Services, Food Stamps, and vocational counseling services, which puts them at a serious disadvantage in society.

Effectiveness Clients who are undocumented Mexican immigrants are utilizing the services effectively. Although they do not seek my agency's services on a voluntary basis, they do seem to be partaking in all aspects of the process once mandated. According to my field work supervisor, many agency clients are undocumented Mexican immigrants.

Based on informal assessment, clients who are undocumented Mexican immigrants feel at ease with the services the agency provides. Because the majority of our clients are young children, they rarely speak out to voice their opinions on the services they receive. Older children do state their confusion with the representation processes and their unfamiliarity with its formalities. However, because of their lack of legal status in this country, they feel intimidated, so they tend not to speak out. Although involvement in the juvenile dependency system does not justify deportation, many of the clients and their parents do not know this, and opt to silence their concerns.

Several needs remain unmet for undocumented Mexican immigrants that are agency clients. However, my agency makes it a point not to dismiss dependency until the child has obtained legal status in this country. As a general rule (county policy), all children who enter the juvenile dependency system and who do not have legal status in this country obtain legal status by the time their case is dismissed. The parents of these minors who are undocumented Mexican immigrants do not receive any type of assistance in the legalization process, nor are they deported. In cases where the undocumented Mexican immigrant youth is in the United States without a caretaker, it is the role of the county social worker to contact the social welfare agency in Mexico to assess whether or not the child has a stable family environment in Mexico that can meet basic needs. Once the assessment has been made, it is the role of the attorney to advocate for the best interest of the child, whether to remain in this country in a foster home setting, or to return to Mexico.

Efficiency As noted, because of its mission and function, my agency does not make efforts to reach out to the community. Clients are referred to the agency because they are in need of legal representation. Aside from having an official county website, there is no outreach done to target any specific population.

Personal Cultural Competencies

Engagement, Trust, and Relationship-building Undocumented Mexican immigrants are hesitant to use social agencies for addressing problems and needs. Because of their legal status in the country, many members of this population are hesitant to speak to any service professionals and opt to resolve their problems themselves with the help of their families and friends. Because of this, it is important for practitioners working with a client of this population to speak Spanish, and preferably be of the same culture; otherwise, it might be very difficult to engage the client and to gain trust. Addressing the client in a formal manner, shaking hands and referring to her or him using "usted" instead of "tu," is of the utmost importance when working with adult Mexican clients. When working with children however, it is more appropriate to use the "tu" manner of addressing individuals because it lessens the sense of formality and allows the child to become more comfortable in working with the practitioner.

In the Mexican community there is a strong reliance on friends and family members to provide advice and support. A social worker working with undocumented Mexican immigrants should be very open, take the time to explain all processes of the legal system to ensure that the client can trust them, and be comfortable in disclosing personal information. Because of the attorney client privilege law, confidentiality of information is ensured. It is essential to describe this privilege to the clients so that they can rest assured that there is no risk in disclosing personal information to the attorney.

Pathways to understanding and interacting with undocumented Mexican immigrant clients will be further highlighted through ethnographic interviewing. When conducting this, it will be important to place members along the lines of generation, immigration history, religion, and socioeconomic status.

Assessment and Problem Definition Identifying and assessing the needs of an undocumented Mexican immigrant might best be done using ethnographic interviewing and a culturagram. While the obvious problem for members of this population is the lack of legal status in this country, there are many more pressing issues that can stem from that problem. By using ethnographic interviewing, the practitioner will enable the client to identify the problem, and to share his or her perspective, rather than the worker making assumptions about what the problem might be. By employing this method, an undocumented Mexican immigrant might feel empowered, and more willing to engage, because she or he will feel that the practitioner is listening to them and will genuinely attempt to assist them.

Using a culturagram when working with an undocumented Mexican immigrant might also be beneficial in assessing and defining the presented problem. The culturagram enables the practitioner to get a sense of the client's experiences and family history, length of time in the community, reason for immigration, the language spoken at home and in the community, legal status, family, education, work values, and the relationship between the country of origin and the United States. It also encourages the client to share her or his personal immigration story with the worker.

Living as an undocumented Mexican immigrant is in itself a stressful situation, and this can contribute to the conditions that make children of undocumented immigrants at special risk in our society. Issues surrounding acculturation, displacement, and adjustment all arise and pose struggles for these immigrant youth and their families who have

very limited resources available to them. It is not uncommon for family tensions to rise because of the pressure of environmental stressors. Youth often turn to delinquency to cope with the stressors of being an undocumented minority member of society.

Contracting and Goal Setting Being a child of Mexican immigrants myself, I have grown up with many members of this population. I have dealt with the harsh realities undocumented Mexican immigrants face, although I myself have not experienced them. I would use this knowledge to meet the client where she or he is. I would speak in Spanish, and answer any and all questions the client may have in order to gain their trust, gauge their level of engagement, and build a strong rapport. Once having established the rapport, my client and I together can define some culturally appropriate goals. Because there is a strong emphasis on family unity in the Mexican culture, goals should support keeping the family intact, or reunifying it, whichever the case may be. An example of a goal for a parent might be to comply with all aspects of their case plan, so that overnight weekend visits with their child can be approved on the next court date. Although it is impossible to ignore the issue of the client's legal status, it is best if the topic is addressed separately, aside from goal setting. Rather goals should be focused on concrete tangible achievements.

Interventions Interventions for undocumented Mexican immigrants should be culturally appropriate. Because undocumented Mexican immigrants are hesitant to leave their communities, and are wary of caucasian professionals, an attempt should be made to provide them with a practitioner who is of the same culture, who speaks the same language, and whose office decor and arrangement is welcoming to undocumented Mexican immigrants. If the practitioner is not skilled in Spanish, then he or she should be very familiar with the Mexican culture and adhere to its practices by being respectful to the clients' traditions and customs. Practitioners should be aware of the great importance Mexican culture places on the male headed family structure and its strong adherence to tradition. Interventions should be focused around the family and take a family systems-based approach rather than an individual approach.

Referring a client to a support group of undocumented Mexican immigrants might also prove to be beneficial, because the client will have the opportunity to develop a source of support from individuals who are experiencing the same life issues. Because there is generally a strong reliance on friends and family members to provide support in the Mexican community, initial concerns about privacy and exposure issues can be diminished by utilizing a social context to help group members get to know each other, learn of their similar experiences, and regard each other as friends.

Evaluation and Termination In the Mexican community, resolving issues within the family, friends, and the community is a sign of success and the preferred way of addressing problems. Failure to resolve issues within the scope of the home is looked upon as failure. However, this is not to say that an individual will be looked at as a failure if he or she receives aid from an outside agency. Should a child of undocumented Mexican immigrants become involved in the juvenile dependency system, the parents as well as the client (the child) would measure success in terms of reunification. Family unity is of such great importance in the Mexican culture that dismantling the family structure would be severely detrimental to the well-being of each family member. This should be carefully considered in planning and goal setting, in the development of interventions, and in considering the success of services to the client and family.

Based on my experience, focus on solutions in the Mexican community tends to be on the diminution or elimination of symptoms and conditions instead of inner change, and it is the client that determines whether an intervention has been helpful or successful in addressing a problem. The practitioner should be in tune with the needs of the client and ask the client how effective she or he views the intervention.

Termination in the delivery of services in the Mexican culture does not entail any specific rituals or practices. Because separation and relationship-ending are common occurrences, only termination of meaningful relationships requires something out of the ordinary. Should the client feel grateful and indebted to the practitioner, it is not uncommon for them to present the worker with a parting gift that is meaningful to them.

Evaluation Using NASW Standards for Culturally Competent Social Work Practice: Standard #9—Language Diversity

Agency While the majority of the attorney's and social workers at my agency are caucasian, the office does an adequate job of providing information, referrals, and services in the language that is appropriate to the client, including Spanish. In instances where there is not a staff member that speaks the language, the office makes it a point to hire an interpreter from an outside agency to accommodate the client. Improvement can be made in hiring more diverse staff, as to represent the clientele it serves.

Programs Language diversity is visibly being utilized throughout the District Attorney's office and the agencies to which they refer clients. Programs that target non-English speakers are available for those individuals to attend, and provide a support network with other members who are like them. For example, Spanish-speaking counselors, therapists, classes, foster parents, etc., are available for monolingual, Spanish-speaking clients. By referring clients to programs such as these, the District Attorney's office promotes language diversity.

Personal Competence Using my personal experience and the knowledge I have acquired in my graduate studies, I have developed a strong sense of awareness for the need of language diversity in the social work profession.

Because of the fact that I am a native Spanish-speaker, I believe it is my responsibility to utilize my Spanish and work with those individuals who are non-English speakers to ensure that they are provided with effective and culturally competent treatment. Although I am cognizant of the fact that Spanish is just one of the many diverse languages our clients speak, I will continue to utilize it in order to eliminate communication barriers. In my future endeavors I hope to learn other languages and perfect my Spanish in order to assist vulnerable clients, and thus become a more competent professional.

REFERENCES

Aguire, A. J. R. and J. H. Turner. 2001. *American Ethnicity: The Dynamics and Consequences of Discrimination.* 3d ed.

***County Office ***Website. 2006.

***County Official Website. 2006.

Frey, J. C. (director). 2002. *The Gatekeeper* [motion picture]. United States: Universal.

National Association of Social Workers (NASW). 2001. *NASW Standards for Cultural Competence in Social Work Practice.* Washington D.C.: Author.

PewHispanic.org

Ramos, J. 2005. *Dying to Cross.* New York: HarperCollins.

Thornburgh, N. 2006. Inside the life of the immigrants next door. *Time Magazine,* 6 February, 34–36.

U.S. Census 2000. http://census.gov

Watanabe, T. and H. Becerra. 2006. *500,000 Pack Streets to Protest Immigration Bills.* Latimes.com.

Worksheet

1. The issues around the status of undocumented immigrants have become political "hot topics." These are complex, and it is important to consider the interests and well-being of all parties. What do you believe is an appropriate approach to addressing these issues?

2. If a child who is living in the United States, but is not a resident or citizen of this country, is perceived to be endangered and/or at high risk for abuse or molestation, do you feel that it is appropriate for the United States alone to plan for and adjudicate matters pertaining to this child, or do you believe that the child's country of origin also has a stake, as well as a responsibility to the child? If you believe that the child's home country has a role to play, what might be an effective way to engage that government, addressing the problem and arriving at an appropriate course of action?

Culturally Competent Social Work Practice with Working Class Caucasians

Diversity Project by Eva Wexler

Growing up as a child of cultural anthropology majors, I was continually exposed to other cultures. By the time I was 10, I had walked the streets of Morocco, watched a kickboxing match in Bangkok, and sipped horchata in Madrid. Living in the Bay Area also provided me with the opportunity to appreciate the rich backgrounds of individuals different than myself. Some of my most vivid memories as a child include holding my father's hand as we squeezed through the produce markets of Chinatown, slurping *pho* at our favorite Vietnamese restaurant in Mountain View, and gazing wistfully at the brightly colored *pi tas* and frilly *quinceanera* dresses in the windows of Mexican shops in Redwood City.

In the public schools I attended in an affluent Bay Area suburb, my teachers made great efforts to provide exposure to other cultures, particularly those who had been historically oppressed. Instead of an in-depth view of the founding fathers, the vast majority of our history curriculum was devoted to discussing Japanese internment, the forced displacement and extermination of Native Americans, and most of all the atrocity and current implications of the enslavement of African Americans. Thus, by the time I was in high school, I felt a certain preferential ease with those who were culturally different than myself; subsequently, my peer group read like an advertisement for the United Colors of Benetton. However, with all of my exposure to other cultures, all of my international travels, exotic foods, and diverse friends, it wasn't until I was in college in upstate New York that I remember first seeing a working class white person.

I was eating lunch in the food court at a mall in Ithaca, New York, with friends I had recently made as a new transfer student at Cornel when I was struck by a family that was sitting a few tables away from us. A weary looking couple struggled to maintain control of their five blond children who were swarming over a table full of fast food kid meals. As the children's fingers grabbed at a pile of French fries, I examined the mother and father with awe. Though I had seen plenty of white people in my life, for some reason this family was different, and so incredibly foreign to me. As I stared, a flicker of compassion was soon overshadowed by a lifetime of preconceptions. They hate Jews, I thought. They are Republicans, they are conservatives, and probably are racist, and why do *they* have so many children? Finally, it began to sink in that I had spent my entire childhood living in a liberal, upper-middle-class bubble. This family represented a significant portion of the population to which I had been entirely unexposed, and the thought of this made me extremely uncomfortable.

After graduating from college, I returned home to the Bay Area and settled in San Francisco. My experience watching the working class caucasian people in upstate New York soon became a distant memory, as I easily immersed myself back into a life among the educated and ethnically diverse population of the Bay Area. However, in thinking about this project I remembered my experience at the mall and recognized that among all of my experiences, both national and international, I felt the most discomfort during my interactions with working class caucasians. Recognizing my own biases and stereotypes, I realized that immersing myself in the culture of working class whites would undoubtedly be the most challenging project, but also the most beneficial to my personal growth as a social worker and an individual.

My field placement, in a foster care agency located in a diverse urban center, includes working class caucasians as well as many other races and ethnicities as both foster parents and foster children.

KNOWLEDGE AQUISITION: THE CULTURAL IMMERSION EXPERIENCE

History

Though the true definition of "working class" has been the source of much debate, two generally accepted descriptions of the working class are those families who earn in the bottom third nationally (less than $35,000 per year) and/or those families who do not have a college degree.[1] According to the five class model most commonly used by sociologists, the 30 percent of individuals who are classified as working class are actually the lowest section of the 70 percent of Americans who consider themselves middle class.[2] Of this middle-class majority, the middle-middle class (30 percent of the population) and the upper-middle class (approximately 10 percent of the population) are economically above the working class, while the 20 percent of the population considered the lower class make less money than the working class and are typically on welfare. Finally, 1 to 3 percent of the U.S. population is classified as upper class. It is estimated that the wealth of the top 1 percent of Americans is equivalent to that of the lower 95 percent.

Historically, the roots of the white working class in America are evident in the wage labor system of the pre–Civil War industrialism of the North, which was comprised of immigrants from Europe, many of whom were from Ireland. Between 1840 and 1920 approximately 37 million people immigrated into the United States, and it was during this time that the United States became the world's leading industrial nation. While some new immigrants took part in the westward expansion, many others stayed in the East and worked in factories, facing long hours, harsh working conditions, and low wages. In the

century that followed, the working class labor movement experienced a variety of political, technological, and demographic changes. Some of the most notable include the emergence of labor unions in the early twentieth century which successfully lobbied for policies protecting labor, the 1933 National Industrial Recovery Act of Roosevelt's New Deal, and, more recently, the relocation of U.S. corporations overseas and the new waves of immigrants who joined the ranks of the working class. Most recently, it has been recognized that the shifting political affiliations within the white working class have had a monumental effect on the current political climate of the United States, evident in both the election and reelection of George W. Bush, and the subsequent ideological support for the policies of the Bush Administration.

Film: *Country Boys*

In an effort to better understand the values and culture of working class caucasians, and with my special interest in working with young people, I chose to watch a Frontline documentary special, *Country Boys* (2006), chronicling three years in the lives of two young men growing up in the Appalachian hills of eastern Kentucky. The three part special, created by David Sutherland, follows the lives of Chris Johnson and Cody Perkins from ages 15 to 18 as they attend the David School, an alternative high school in David, Kentucky. Though the environment at the David School is one of warmth and personal attention, the families of Cody and Chris are its antithesis. Cody, a punk born-again Christian, lost his mother to suicide when he was a baby, and then his father in his early teens after his father murdered his twelfth wife and then committed suicide. Since then, Cody has chosen to live with his former stepgrandmother (the mother of his father's

---

[1] C. Shea, "Who are you calling working class?" The *Boston Globe*, Feb. 2006.

[2] Wikipedia, *Class in the Contemporary United States*, http://en.wikipedia.org/wiki/Cass_in_the_Contemporary_United_States

fourth wife), instead of his biological extended family, with whom he does not get along. Chris also has his family challenges, though both of his biological parents are alive. Sharing a dilapidated trailer are Chris, his high school drop out mother, his alcoholic father suffering from terminal liver disease, and younger siblings, all struggling to survive, relying heavily on the disability check that Chris receives through a diagnosis of a learning disorder when he was a child.

The three years that the cameras follow Chris and Cody through their daily lives are a riveting journey, chronicling the relationship between cultural environment and the perception of available choices, made at a young age, that impact the experiences of a lifetime. Cody, through the support of his step-grandmother, his girlfriend, and his deep religious faith, emerges with astounding resilience and hope, graduating from the David School as valedictorian with plans to attend college. In contrast, Chris, heavily burdened by the financial pressures to care for his family, the volatile relationship of his parents, and the termination of his disability checks, drops out of school his senior year in order to support himself through working full time at a fast food restaurant. After being strongly persuaded by staff at the David School, Chris takes his GED and passes, enabling him to graduate with the rest of his class. However, the emptiness and lack of support from his biological family overshadows his achievement.

While I am well aware that Chris and Cody's experiences do not represent the norm for my population of working-class whites, watching *Country Boys* and connecting with their struggles altered my views of working class whites in some very significant ways. First, I was unprepared for the fact that despite the chaos of their family lives and the poor odds stacked against them, both Chris and Cody displayed a tremendous amount of intelligence, determination, and insight. Second, through seeing the positive impact of Christianity on Cody, I began to understand

that, for some people, religion has a purpose beyond creating and affirming conservative beliefs. While there were a few points in the documentary where there were hints of Cody's conservative beliefs, they did not arouse my usual negative response; I understood much more clearly the context and importance of Christianity in his life. For me, this has great implications for my work with conservative and religious caucasian clients. Third, through a deep personal connection with Chris and the difficulties of his family situation, I began to understand more clearly the developmental path of an individual who might inevitably have some of the white working class beliefs from which I feel so disconnected. I could especially relate to how the unstable relationship of Chris's parents affected both the choices he made in high school and his sense of self.

I realized that had I been born without the model of educated parents, who truly cared about me, and who supported me financially and pushed me to attend college, my life choices would have been severely constrained. Through examining the potential outcome of these limitations, it is possible to see how conservative white working class values might evolve as potential strengths.

Autobiography: *Nickel and Dimed*

The next stop of my journey through the world of the caucasian working class was reading Barbara Ehrenreich's moving account of her experiment of living as a low-wage worker in *Nickel and Dimed* (2001). In the book, Ehrenreich, an upper-middle-class writer, embarks on a personal experiment to see if she can survive among the ranks of people working for minimum wage. She moves from the Florida Keys to Maine, and later to Minnesota, taking a variety of low-wage jobs including waitress, hotel housekeeper, nursing home attendant, house cleaner, and Wal-Mart employee. She begins at each place with approximately $1,000, and sees precisely how she can survive working low-wage jobs. Though the locations are different in geography and demographics, she encounters similar obstacles in each place. The first is that with a wage of $7.00 an hour, she has to take more than one job simply to survive, even without any major financial emergencies, such as health or car issues. The second is a struggle with housing. At a $7.00 hourly wage and a two-week pay cycle, Ehrenreich finds more than once that her only option is to find weekly housing, as she does not have enough to pay an entire month's rent at once. The weekly and nightly housing options she finds range from dormitory style rooms to cheap motels, and at $60 per night to $200 per week they are invariably much more costly in the end than the monthly rentals. This is one instance of how life ends up being more expensive for low-wage workers, who end up paying more for things because they don't have the resources to live more cheaply by cooking meals in their kitchens, driving cars to a discount store, or having prescription medications covered by health insurance. Furthermore, the physical labor involved in waitressing and cleaning houses in back to back shifts creates a huge, cumlative physical toll. Lack of healthcare and an unhealthy diet that is quick and cheap are often the only options for those working multiple jobs. Finally, Ehrenreich finds that, as a highly educated individual possessing a PhD and years of experience as an author, she is no more prepared or able to face the tasks and challenges of each low-wage job than anyone else; there are in fact no "unskilled" jobs.

In reading *Nickel and Dimed* I found some very salient themes that illustrated the psychological impact of working low-wage jobs, enabling me to develop greater insight into how the conservative values of the white working class might evolve. Many of the people Ehrenreich encountered in her journey demonstrated a fierce determination, an independence, and a strong work ethic, which help them remain fully engaged in multiple low-wage jobs, despite the grueling hours, the terrible conditions, and the fact that they were making barely more than those on welfare. In their unwavering commitment to support themselves, it is not difficult to imagine how resentment toward those on welfare might evolve.

Another significant theme of the book was the utter invisibility that Ehrenreich experienced as a low-wage worker, especially when she worked as a house cleaner. After years of this type of discrimination, anyone might feel desperate for affirmation, or simply for acknowledgment. For a working class white person, this could manifest as a perceived superiority to people of color, and a subsequent contempt for policies such as affirmative action that might threaten her or his position on the racial hierarchy. Finally, in reading Ehrenreich's account of the innumerable hardships of low-wage work there is an understandable hostility that arises towards those who are economically better off; an "us versus them" attitude. For working class whites, this could evolve into a fierce opposition to things associated with those who are wealthy, even if they might be beneficial, such as the resistance to the natural food co-op in Vermont, in the PBS documentary *Class Matters*, the distaste for critically acclaimed art films depicting the corruption of large corporations where they might be employed, or presidential candidate John Kerry, with his seemingly more educated and thus condescending manner of speech.

Personal Interview

In searching for a person of a caucasian working class background whom I could interview, I was extremely lucky that my friend Darren was willing to candidly discuss his experiences growing up in the white working class area of Sioux City, Iowa. Darren was a particularly helpful interview candidate because he was not only comfortable with discussing his childhood and family background, but was also willing to share his thoughts on how some of the conservative values of the white working class might have developed.

Darren characterizes his family as caucasian working class farmers and described how his father quit school in the ninth grade to help out his grandfather on the family farm in Iowa. Darren had more contact with his mother's family while he was growing up. His grandfather, a milkman and union member, was quite racist toward blacks and Jews and expressed his views very openly. His mother continues to work as an administrative assistant, even at the age of 67. And, though Darren admitted feeling like somewhat of an outsider growing up, as he did not fit the ideal Midwestern image of a strong athletic working man, he maintains that he still carries some of the working class values of his childhood with him today. Most prevalently among these: an unwavering work ethic.

In describing how the ethic of hard work was an omnipresent force within his family and community, Darren explained what he believed to be the fundamental roots from which a predominant number of white working class values emerge. Throughout our talk, the ideologies of hard work, responsibility, and picking yourself up by your bootstraps as mechanisms for realizing the American dream were mentioned again and again. While I had noted this theme in *Nickel and Dimed* as perhaps the only explanation of why individuals would endure such horrendous, poverty level working conditions rather than seeking public assistance, with Darren I was able to clearly see this as the guiding force behind all of the values of the caucasian working class, and, perhaps most directly, the way that they interface with politics and religion.

When I asked Darren why the working class have such faith in the very large corporations that oppress them, he speculated that these companies are viewed as having worked hard to achieve the American dream. The existence of the McDonald's, and the Sam Waltons of the world affirms the possibilities that hard work, determination, and the American spirit can achieve, and thus their own personal possibilities. Darren also confirmed that such values have political implications, manifesting as disapproval for the expansion of public assistance programs and race-based affirmative action.

Finally, he shared his thoughts about how the work ethic of the caucasian working class is manifested in religious beliefs, and subsequently in support for political candidates espousing similar spiritual values and beliefs. Religion, Darren said, is viewed not only as a mechanism for affirming the existence and often thankless labor of the working class, but is also an instrument of hope and faith that something better is possible, much like the belief in the American dream.

Cultural Event: A Predominantly Caucasian Working Class Mall

Locating a cultural event that was predominently attended by members of the caucasian working class was a challenge! After consulting with friends and classmates, I traveled to a nearby working class suburb to hang out at a local shopping mall. I felt reasonably certain of having made a good choice when I arrived and noticed the preponderance of "God Bless America" bumper stickers in the parking lot.

Caucasians were, however, the ethnic minorities as patrons at the Subway and the Dollar Tree on the afternoon of my visit. Nonetheless, I was able to observe some of the activities, and even observed a disagreement between a white and Latina lady in line at the Dollar Tree nearly evolve into a physical altercation, perhaps evidencing some of the racial tensions that exist within such communities. In any case, I do plan on attending a Rodeo next month, and have great hopes of finding a white working class majority there.

In the end, my experience of immersion into world of the caucasian working class was a truly unexpected journey with both personal and professional implications. While I now have a greater comfort with the white working class on a very basic level, I also feel I have gained insight into their deeply held values and convictions. I hope that this understanding will contribute to my abilities as a social worker, and most importantly, to my humanity.

Applying the Knowledge Base: Agency, Programs and Services, and Personal Cultural Competencies

FIELD AGENCY

The agency where I am interning this year is a private, nonprofit organization that is licensed by the state as a Foster Family Agency to provide casework services for children in the foster care system. In addition, the agency recruits and trains foster parents and also certifies foster homes for placement. My agency is one of the largest private providers of foster family-based care in the area, and is contracted by neighboring cities and counties for placement of abused and neglected children with safe and loving foster families. The agency's mission statement is to foster nurturing family environments within the community for children in need, including preserving families at risk, providing short-term and long-term substitute families, preparing foster youth for adult independent living, and responding to needs in the community as they arise.

Agency

Agency's community My agency is located in a major urban center. It is convenient to public transportation, and there is a parking lot for clients and foster parents who drive to the agency. The city is very diverse, both racially and in social class. There is a large working class community, and the agency is generally regarded as a neighbor, providing needed services to the community.

My agency serves 90 children in foster care. Approximately 15 percent are caucasian, while 27 percent are African American, 24 percent are Latino, 19 percent are Asian/Pacific Islander, 13 percent are biracial, and 2 percent are Native American. Of the foster families that the agency recruits, certifies, and with whom it places children, 2 percent are caucasian, 65 percent are African American, 15 percent are Latino, 16 percent are Asian/Pacific Islander, and 2 percent are other/biracial.

Access All of the children receive case management services and their caseworker visits approximately three times per month. These visits may take place in the foster home, the child's school, at the agency, or another off-site location, but for all visits the caseworker travels to meet the foster child in placement or facilitates transport for the child. The caseworker also visits the foster parents, who are additionally required to attend foster parent training meetings once a month at the agency. For these required meetings, the foster parents must find their own transportation.

Receptivity It does not appear that the agency is particularly receptive, nor is it overtly unfriendly or unwelcoming, to caucasian clients, or specifically caucasian clients from a working class background. However, there is a lack of presence or representation of working class whites among the agency's staff and in its décor. Of the eight full-time caseworkers, only one is caucasian, and she is not from a working class background. Of the remaining staff, there is a caucasian receptionist, but she is also not from a working class background.

While the agency décor is warm and inviting, there is a similar lack of representation of caucasian individuals or working class whites. Upon entering the agency, clients are greeted by a huge brightly painted mural depicting the faces of children and families. However, all of the people in the mural are Latino, African American or Asian; there is not one caucasian depicted in the painting. Throughout the rest of the agency there are posters including a beautiful photo of an African child and an inspirational quote and photo of Malcolm X, but again, there are no images of caucasian individuals. However, the agency's literature does include several images of caucasian foster children and also seems to present an ethnically neutral message to potential foster parents.

Administration and Staff Training While the agency does not have any formal training regarding culturally competent practices, there are several other ways in which the agency communicates a commitment to serve culturally diverse populations. First, the agency strives to hire a culturally diverse staff, including caseworkers who are African, African American, Mexican, South American, Filipino, and Korean. Second, the agency prioritizes the hiring of staff who are bilingual in English and Spanish, so that native Spanish-speaking clients will receive better service. Third, the agency produces literature in both English and Spanish. Fourth, the agency has weekly meetings in which cultural differences and culturally competent practices are informally, but regularly, discussed.

However, in all of the agency's activities and practices that illustrate a commitment to serving culturally diverse clients, it does not appear that caucasian working class people have been included, or are even considered to be a population in need of awareness and culturally competent practice.

Staff Sensitivity The agency's staff is overwhelmingly sensitive and respectful to all clients, and especially so when interacting with foster parents. The staff is particularly sensitive to members of historically oppressed populations, as staff who are members of these populations often use their own cultural background and experiences to explain or support a client behavior. However, this is not true for caucasian or working class white clients, whose cultural differences from staff members and other clients are largely ignored.

Funding The agency has sufficient funding to recruit a diverse group of foster parents and also provide bilingual clients with services. However, I am not aware of any funding being targeted specifically for potential caucasian working class foster parents.

Agency Programs and Services

The agency's three major programs and services include: the recruitment, training, and certification of foster parents; the placement of foster children with an appropriate foster home; and the case management for the foster children and parents after placement.

Effort For recruiting, the agency has recently tried a few media campaigns including advertisements on buses and other public transportation. However, when I asked about the agency's recruiting practices in the past, I was told that the agency had made efforts to recruit a diverse group of foster parents by going into some area churches. The agency was especially successful in recruiting foster parents from several African American churches, who then referred their friends to the agency, thus resulting in the large percentage (65 percent) of African American foster parents currently at the agency.

In addition, the agency has made special efforts to recruit Latino foster parents through printing recruitment materials in Spanish and having Spanish-speaking staff at recruiting events. Though the agency has not made any specific efforts to recruit working class white foster parents, the current media campaigns do reach a significant number of potential foster parents who are caucasian. When I inquired about the lack of caucasian foster parents in the agency (there are currently only two homes with caucasian foster parents) I was given two potential reasons: caucasian individuals generally choose to adopt rather than to be foster parents; and there were so few caucasian children in the agency that there was not a pressing need for caucasian foster parents. When I asked about recruiting within the city's gay community, I was told that while there were many potential caucasian (though not working class) foster families in the LGBTQ community, their lifestyle would be met with opposition by the agency's religious majority of foster parents. Thus, while the agency had attempted to reach the LGBTQ community once in the past, the efforts had not been continued.

Another important part of foster parent recruitment is the certification and subsequent training classes the foster parents are required to attend. Because of the lack of caucasian foster homes it is difficult to tell whether the agency makes any special consideration or efforts in working with these foster families. The agency does make efforts to be conscious and respectful of foster parents currently at the agency, including conducting the trainings in a manner that is respectful to cultural differences, making an effort to speak Spanish to bilingual foster parents, and serving food at the trainings that the foster parents will enjoy.

Quality The second major service the agency provides concerns placing foster children with appropriate foster homes. Placement is based upon many different factors such as the type of placement (short-term, shelter, long-term, etc.), language the foster child speaks, special needs or emotional state of the foster child, and most often, availability. Though in 1996 the U.S. Congress passed legislation that required states to eliminate racial matching as a factor in placing foster children (Multi-Ethnic Placement Act 1994 Amended 1996), it appears that the agency does sometimes consider ethnicity in the placement process. After reviewing the list of current placements, I found that ten of the 22 Latino foster children had been placed with Latino foster parents, 11 of the 15 Asian/Pacific Islander foster children had been placed with Asian/Pacific Islander foster parents, and 19 of the 24 African American foster children had been placed with African American foster parents. However, none of the 15 caucasian foster children had been placed with caucasian foster parents.

The vast majority of work done at the agency consists of case management services provided by ten full-time caseworkers. These include making home visits, writing quarterly reports and case notes, meeting with DHS employees and teachers, connecting clients with resources, and responding to emergencies. In providing foster parents and children with these services, the agency does make some attempts to be culturally competent.

Effectiveness Although the agency does not match clients with a caseworker of a similar ethnic or cultural background most of the time, they do make exceptions when the client is Spanish speaking. Many individual caseworkers also make efforts to provide clients with culturally competent services through connecting them with resources that reflect their cultural or ethnic backgrounds, including after-school programs, clubs, support groups, and community organizations. These efforts are predominantly made with foster children from historically under-represented ethnic minorities and not the agency's foster children from caucasian working class backgrounds. There was only one instance when I noticed a caseworker mentioning a client's whiteness in the context of providing services, and this was when therapy was recommended for a caucasian foster child who was getting teased at school for culturally identifying as African American. I am not aware of any special consideration or attention being given to cultural concerns of other caucasian children.

Efficiency The agency's efforts seem effective and efficient in placing children in certified foster homes, and providing ongoing case management services.

Personal Cultural Competencies

I initially chose working class whites as the population to study in this paper after recognizing my own biases and preconceptions toward them, especially regarding issues of racism and politics. However, after having the opportunity to immerse myself into their culture, I was able to identify some positive values and strengths within the population, as well as to better understand how some of their more conservative values might evolve. I was even more surprised at how much I empathized with the caucasian foster children in my agency after realizing the extent to which, in comparison with the agency's foster children from ethnic minority backgrounds, their cultural differences are ignored.

My thoughts about this issue are somewhat mixed, as I feel the primary responsibility of social workers should be to serve and advocate for disadvantaged and oppressed populations. However, I also feel that, as social workers, it is imperative that we are respectful of the cultural values and experiences of all our clients, even if they are members of the more dominant culture. Thus, as a social worker, I would utilize the following guidelines in serving clients who are of working class white backgrounds:

Engagement, Trust, and Relationship-building Given that independence and personal responsibility are core values among working class whites, they may be particularly hesitant about using social agencies for help. They also may have reservations about receiving services from social workers, as the mistreatment or invisibility they have experienced in the workforce may have caused resentment toward those they might perceive as more educated and/or professionally trained. Thus, I would make every effort to be welcoming and encouraging during an initial interaction, and especially careful not to use language or behavior that would indicate the slightest hint of condescension. Giving a firm handshake, making direct eye contact, and maintaining body language that reflects the stance of the client are ways in which I would communicate respect for clients from this background.

Assessment and Problem Definition Because of the initial reservations working class whites may have about receiving social services, during this stage I would show awareness and respect for the pride and independence of such clients. I would offer praise and support, emphasizing that it takes strength to open up about something that is challenging them. (Using the word "problem" could be seen as stigmatizing.)

Working class white clients may have suffered discrimination from more economically advantaged individuals, but it is extremely unlikely that they will acknowledge this as a contributing factor in their current need for services. They may instead communicate resentment toward more educated or affluent individuals, or toward populations whom society may have identified as oppressed or discriminated against, such as ethnic minorities. As a social worker, I would try to understand these feelings in the context of their experiences, and also make efforts not to show offense or disapproval of their position. This could prove to be especially challenging, given my background and political orientation, but nonetheless it is an important skill to learn in interacting with any client holding views which differ from my own.

Contracting and Goal Setting In this stage, I would utilize the working class white values of determination and an unwavering work ethic as strengths for contracting and setting goals. First, I would ask the client to share his or her experiences in facing challenges at work, and praise their achievements and ability to follow through. I would explain that goal setting is similar to accomplishing tasks at work, and ask them to identify a few goals that they would like to achieve. I would then help the client list and prioritize these goals, taking into consideration their own understanding of what is important as well as cultural issues. I would assist the client to state the goals in language that is comfortable and avoid using professional jargon.

Interventions I would again utilize some cultural strengths and values in the process of developing appropriate interventions to assist working class white clients. The first cultural value I might incorporate would be spirituality or religious faith. To determine whether this would be appropriate, I would ask a neutral question about a client's beliefs in the assessment stage. In my population immersion study, I found that religious working class whites are often very proud of their spiritual beliefs, and thus I would anticipate that they would be able to share this information comfortably with a social worker.

Some of the ways that I might incorporate these beliefs into an intervention would be through having prayer and involvement with a church community as an integral part of the service plan. Many religious organizations offer support groups, which might be an ideal setting for a client to meet and receive help from individuals with similar challenges and values.

In the process of organizing an intervention, I might also incorporate the working class white values of dedication to hard work and follow through. To do this, I would help the client organize the steps needed to achieve the goal into a checklist, which might be more manageable for the client. In developing this with a working class white client, I would ask them how they complete tasks at their job and assure them that the intervention will be structured in a similar way. I would try and draw parallels between completing a job and follow through on the elements of the intervention as an important part of achieving their desired outcome. I would provide encouragement, and utilize a strengths perspective by telling them that if they put the same effort into the intervention that they do their work, they will be successful in meeting their goal.

Evaluation and Termination Because the efforts and contributions of working class whites often are invisible to the rest of society, I would universally incorporate praise into the evaluation and termination stages when working with clients from this population. To do this, I would highlight the elements of the intervention that the client completed successfully and acknowledge their efforts. Given that working class whites are extremely independent and often quite reserved about asking for help, I would also praise them for having the courage to seek help and ask them if they would feel comfortable doing so in the future. I would ask them what they felt was most successful about the services and intervention and would encourage them to not hesitate in seeking help if they needed it again.

NASW Standards for Cultural Competence: Self-awareness

Of the ten standards for cultural competence outlined by the National Association of Social Workers (2001), the standard of self-awareness seems the most relevant for the population of working class whites. The standard of self-awareness postulates that social workers shall develop an understanding of their own personal and cultural beliefs as the first step in appreciating the importance of multicultural identities in the lives of people. I would also add that for social workers, self-awareness should include a consideration of how one's cultural and ideological values might affect their preconceptions about others.

Agency, Programs, and Services For my agency, this would translate into a willingness to examine values within the organization that might influence the way working class white clients are treated. Currently, working class white clients are often overlooked and considered "cultureless." Though the agency is cognizant that it is making efforts to provide culturally competent services to clients of historically oppressed populations, with greater self-awareness it might realize how issues of difference and discrimination can also be manifest when working with clients who appear to be from the dominant culture. Similarly, with greater self-awareness the agency might feel more comfortable about developing a program and services that recognize and that working class whites also have cultural values and beliefs and may experience discrimination from more economically advantaged individuals.

Personal Competencies Finally, the process of self-awareness has been an integral part of my study of working class white culture and will hopefully guide my subsequent interactions when I see members of this population as clients. While it initially took a degree of self-awareness to recognize my discomfort with working class whites, after I began the immersion process I truly became aware of how my own values and experiences limited my view of this population. As a liberal woman of Jewish descent, I overwhelmingly associated working class whites with racism, antisemitism, and conservative values, and thus felt a degree of hostility and discomfort toward them. As someone from an upper-middle-class background, I was completely ignorant of the struggles and invisibility working class white individuals experience.

While I felt a great deal of compassion for individuals from historically oppressed populations who were struggling economically, I failed to recognize that working class white people also face obstacles and discrimination. Lastly, through examining how my own experiences and privilege have shaped my spiritual, political, and educational values, I was able to gain a greater understanding of how the ideals of working class white individuals might similarly develop from their life experiences. While I may not always agree with all of these values, as a social worker it is imperative that I set aside judgment and make every effort to approach working class white clients with respect, compassion, and ideological neutrality, for their success in achieving their goals through agency service depends upon it.

REFERENCES

Erenreich, B. 2001. *Nickel and Dimed*. NY: Henry Holt and Company.

National Association of Social Workers (NASW). 2001. *NASW Standards for Cultural Competence in Social Work Practice*. Washington, D.C.: Author.

Shea, C. 2006. Who are you calling working class? *The Boston Globe*, February.

Sutherland, D. (producer), *Country Boys* [documentary]. Boston:WGBH.

Wikipedia. 2006. *Class in the Contemporary United States*. http://en.wikipedia.org/wiki/Class_in_the_Contemporary_United_States

Worksheet

1. There are many ways to define "diversity." Two of the most prevalent are: diversity as difference, in general, so that every group is a "diverse" group; and diversity as difference from some prevalent, or dominant, "norm." Caucasians in general are a "diverse" group using the first definition (which has been described in Part One as the "tossed salad.") Caucasians are generally excluded from the second definition, which includes members of groups that are not dominant in our society, and traditionally have been oppressed and discriminated against. Which of these definitions seems best in working with people as a social worker?

2. This author's project focuses on the intersection of two differences: race and socio-economic class. (a) Do you view working class caucasians as a separate, diverse group? The author has focused on religion and spirituality and the work ethic as two distinguishing values of this group. (b) What are some of the differences that you believe are important in distinguishing between working class whites and middle-class whites?

CHAPTER

9

Cultural Competence with Gender and Sexual Orientations

PROJECT

9

Culturally Competent Social Work Practice with Transgender Women

Diversity Project by Elissa Klein

My field placement is in a private, nonprofit mental health clinic that serves a low-income area with many bars, single room occupancy hotels, low-cost restaurants, and massage parlors. There are many homeless people, people with mental illness, sex workers, and people with substance abuse in the community. There are also many transgender people who live and work in this area, and I have chosen to focus my work on learning about this population so that I can serve them competently. I would like to stress that my experiences, and the knowledge I gained, do not reflect the experiences of the transgender population as a whole, as each person's experiences are unique, but will hopefully provide some helpful insights.

Trangender is a term that encompasses a wide variety of phenomena. A transgender person can be a person who simply cross-dresses, a person who has had surgery to transform his or her genitalia, and/or everything in between. For the purposes of this project, a transgender person is anybody who presents themselves, through dress and behavior, as a member of the gender into which they were not born.

KNOWLEDGE

History

Though people have been dressing as members of the other sex since time immemorial, it is only in the twentieth century that surgical and hormonal methods of transformation have been used. Hormones for both male and female transformation were introduced in the 1940s. Male-to-female surgery was probably performed as early as 1930 in Germany. Female-to-male surgery occurred even earlier, in 1917, in the United States. In the late 1960s universities began to open clinics that performed transsexual surgery. Whereas previously this surgery was only performed on intersexed individuals, these clinics began to perform genital surgery on those who wished to completely transform their sex (Brown 2005).

173

Transgender people, and especially trans-sexuals, have fought a number of legal battles in order to become recognized as their chosen sex. For instance, in 1976 Renee Richards, a male-to-female transsexual, was barred from entering a tennis tournament as a woman. Her subsequent legal battle established that transsexuals are to be legally recognized as their chosen sex after sex reassignment surgery. However, this legal right is not recognized for transgender people who have opted not to have genital surgery. Another arena in which this right does not apply is marriage. A transgender woman cannot marry a man because she is still viewed as a man in the eyes of the law for marriage purposes (Brown 2005).

The history of transgender people in the United States is also a history of friction with the feminist community. Transgender people have been fighting for recognition as an oppressed gender by the feminist community since the feminist movement began. Feminists have accused transgender people of mocking women and adopting those aspects of femininity, such as makeup and high heels, which are aspects of patriarchal oppression.

For the past 12 years, much of this friction between the transgender and feminist communities has centered around the Michigan Womyn's Music Festival. This is an annual women's only festival that takes place in the summer. In 1992 a transgender woman was kicked out of the festival after it was discovered that she was not a woman-born-woman. The next year, members of the transgender community set up "Camp Trans" outside the gates of the festival. For every year since then, trangender people and their supporters have gathered to protest the gender policy at the festival. Ironically, the festival organizers will permit a female-to-male transgender person as long as they have not had sex reassignment surgery. The organizers argue that they want the festival to be a safe space for women-born-women to gather with the knowledge of having shared the trials of being raised female in this society. The transgender community has countered that they

too are victims of patriarchal oppression and narrow gender expectations, as well as misogyny experienced through their acquired femaleness (Zeisler 2002). However, this battle over what it means to be a woman still rages.

Film: *Normal*

The movie, *Normal* is the story of Roy and Irma Applewood, a married couple in the Midwest with two children. After 25 years of marriage, Roy reveals to Irma that he plans to pursue a sex change operation. However, he wants the family to stay together. Irma is understandably shocked and confused and kicks him out of the house. We see Roy begin to acquire the trappings of being female, such as dresses and perfume. We also see him confront the fear and anger that his transformation stirs in his small community. However, he finds acceptance with his teenage daughter and his boss. Eventually, Irma too begins to accept Roy's decision and much of the movie is about her struggle to understand how her husband, who is becoming a woman, can be the same person with whom she fell in love.

My emotional reaction to this story was as confused as the characters' emotions within it. Like Irma, I felt anger at what seemed to initially be a very selfish decision on Roy's part. Being part of a family, and especially being a parent and spouse, requires that we give up some of our selfish desires for the sake of the unit. Roy simply made this monumental, life-altering decision and expected Irma and his children to live with it. On the other hand, I felt a great deal of admiration for Roy. The courage to self-actualize on such a radical level, within such a small community, and in such a socially unacceptable way, is a courage that very few people have. It speaks to the strength of his desire to be recognized as a woman that he was willing to take such a tremendous chance.

I also felt admiration for Irma. To continue to love a person through this kind of transformation, and to risk ostracism from the community alongside him, also demonstrates a great deal of courage. However, the strongest emotion that I had for all the characters was compassion. There was a great deal of pain for all of the characters in the story, pain that came from internal confusion about their own identities as well as pain inflicted on them from a community confused and frightened of a person who would so radically violate gender norms.

Biography: *Sexile*

Sexile, by Jaime Cortez, is a graphic story about the life of Adela, nee Juan Carlos, and her journey from young boy to woman. Adela's story begins as a young boy who knew that he was meant to be a girl. At one point Adela says that she remembers being 6 years old and excited to turn 10 since that was when she was sure her penis would fall off, and she'd become a girl. Adela's story is full of the ridicule she suffered as a child because the other boys at her all boys' school knew that she was different. She began cross-dressing in her late teenage years. In her early twenties, she got a job as a teacher, and came to work dressed as a woman. After a few months, she was fired, even though her class was the best performing in the school. She went to live with a gay friend, Rolando, who let her stay rent-free for two years. She did odd jobs to support herself.

Adela also shares her experience of the early days of AIDS. Rolando worked at a clinic in L.A. that treated a lot of gay men, and Adela remembers him coming home one day and telling her that she had to use a condom at every sexual encounter. She laughed in his face, because the most serious thing they had seen thus far was gonorrhea. "It was early 1981, and sexually transmitted diseases were a joke to the queer world. You got them, you went to the clinic, got meds and that was it. But Rolando had seen something hella serious. He saved my life," (Cortez 2004, 46).

Though Adela had not cross-dressed for some time, that changed when she discovered the underground Queen culture of L.A. The fashion shows with transgender women inspired her and she began "exploring what it meant to be a woman." To Adela, being a woman was about glamour, seduction, and "living with emotions in a new way." But it also meant "giving up my big, fat bag of male privileges, like feeling safe when you walk" (57). Her changed attitudes had repercussions in her friend relationships, for when she revealed to her gay male friends that she wanted to be known as a woman, they rejected her. She had believed that the gay community was open about sexuality, but discovered that they were almost as closed-minded as society at large.

Adela received some Mexican black-market hormones from a transgender friend. The transition from male to female was extremely dramatic for her, and is dramatically described. Not only did she develop real breasts, but a completely different emotional life. Adela describes no longer feeling aggressive in threatening situations, but having more clarity of thought. She describes feeling more compassion for those in pain around her. And she states, "It doesn't hurt to cry anymore. My heart is more tender, almost maternal," (60). Like many transgender people, Adela decided to keep her male genitalia.

At this point, Adela was having a hard time supporting herself. She started to observe other "trannies" on the streets of her neighborhood, and saw that most of them made a living in sex work. She decided to try it, advertising herself as a "she-male" in the free weeklies. Though she liked some things about the work, it was very hard on her emotionally and she turned to drugs and alcohol to numb herself. After two years of sex work, she decided to quit alcohol, manage her drug use better, and get out of sex work. Adela ends her story by saying, "All the in-between places are my home. This beautiful freak body is my home. And every day, I love it" (65).

This book affected me deeply. It made me laugh because Adela is so completely exuberant in the telling of her story. It is clear that there is a great deal of pain involved but she handles it with humor and grace. Once again, I am struck by her courage in living such a renegade existence. And I am full of admiration that she has maintained her joy in living.

Personal Interview

I interviewed a male-to-female transgender person named Ann. Ann does not remember a time when she was not a girl, at least to herself. As a child, she played with all girls and they accepted her as a girl as well. She came out to her family when she was 13, but she came out as a gay man rather than transgender woman because there was no framework for her to explain to them that she was really a woman. Much of our discussion focused around Ann's perceptions about the transgender community. Her definition of a transgender person is anyone who is born to a sex with one "bag of privileges" and decides to exchange it for the other bag of privilege, though she knows that the "female bag is much smaller." Ann explained to me what she sees as the challenges within the transgender community. She believes that transgender women have a hard time being happy with themselves, and sees this manifest itself in a great deal of plastic surgery. The surgery is also an expression of what Ann sees as endemic shallowness within the transgender community itself. Moreover, when many of the women start to transition, they begin to get attention from men, which they have always craved. This attention becomes difficult for them to manage and, when drugs are added to the mix, most transgender women become prostitutes. Although Ann has done sex work herself, she believes that not only is sex work bad for many people, but that it leads to transgender women becoming stereotyped as sex workers. This stereotype is expressed by the hyper-sexualization of transsexual people in society. As Ann explains it, one of the outcomes of the hyper-sexualization of transgender people, and the primary challenge that transgender women face, is constantly having to explain themselves to other people. Finally, Ann wishes that biological women and transgender women were better able to develop friendships because she believes that transgender women need more female role models.

One of the most interesting parts of our discussion was Ann's explanation of the hierarchies within the transgender community—which she says is very discriminatory, and also reflects the racism of society at large. However, an additional hierarchy within this community has to do with body type. Transgender women with bigger breasts look down on those with smaller breasts. Transgender women who have had sex change operations look down on those who have not. Among prostitutes, who typically have not had a sex-change, those with bigger penises look down on those with smaller penises. To Ann, the most upsetting thing about this situation is that it reflects male expectations. Because transgender women are competing with each other for men, their judgments of each other reflect their perception of what these men seek in a transgender woman.

Though there are a great many challenges within the transgender community, Ann also sees some strengths. First, she believes that transgender women are extremely compassionate and caring. As she explained it, transgender women attract "the worst kind of men—gang members, thieves, criminals, violent people." Even though these men are shunned by society, transgender women "take them in and show them love." Second, Ann believes that transgender women are extremely courageous in making the transition that they make and in living outside of society's boundaries.

Ann has seen a lot of changes in the transgender community over the past two decades. She states that girls who are coming out now are much less likely to become prostitutes than before, because there are other career options open to them. Moreover, transgender people are recognized as a social group by the government, and now have some legal rights.

My interview with Ann was inspiring. She manifests a confidence in herself that most people do not have, let alone people who have had to battle against so much prejudice in their daily lives. She has found a way of being a transgender woman that few seem to achieve: she is happy with herself and doesn't feel the need to pass or imitate a biological woman. She states, "You are a biological woman, and that is beautiful to me, but I am a woman too. I am not a biological woman, and so we are different. But I, and all transgender women, can have our own way of being a woman. We don't have to imitate you—we *can't* imitate you. But that's OK. I am myself and I am a beautiful woman."

Cultural Immersion: A "Trannie" Bar

During my interview with Ann, she told me about a bar known as a transgender hangout. Ann told me that she had not been there for some time because it is a place where sex workers hang out to pick up customers, which explained the expressions on the faces of the men circulating through the bar during my visit. I was the only biological woman in the bar, and I noticed a lot of double-takes in my direction, from both men and women in the bar. None of the men actually approached me, but their continuous stares made me quite uncomfortable. This discomfort was two-fold: first, because I was the only biological woman there, I felt as though I was encroaching upon somebody else's space. Nobody said anything to make me feel this way but it seemed clear from the stares I received that I was not welcome. As Ann had explained it before I went to the bar, much of this was probably because I was seen as competition for the men's attention.

The second reason that I felt uncomfortable was because I felt that the men presumed I was a sex worker. Though nobody approached me as a sex worker, there was a certain intangible feeling in the air that I was there to be looked over for purchase. The disturbing thing about this was that it was not a completely unfamiliar feeling to me. As a woman, being stared at in the street or hearing comments about my body is an all too common experience. In the streets I feel that I have the right to defend myself, and have no compunction about confronting men for this type of behavior. However, in this setting, I felt that I did not have that right, and that whatever these men said or thought was completely acceptable in that environment. This experience gave me a small glimpse into the hyper-sexualization that Ann had tried to describe.

Reflections

Over the course of my field placement, I have served a few transgender women in this community. Therefore, I was familiar with some of the issues I saw, read about, and listened to. However, the one thing that I had not experienced before this project, but that I felt throughout it, was admiration for the courage that transgender people demonstrate. Now that I have discovered this admiration, I am sure that it will affect my future work with transgender women.

I also fully realized the frustration that many transgender people feel at being constantly sexualized. As a woman, I feel sexualized much more than I would like to be; however, I am overtly sexualized only by some men on the street. Transgender women are sexualized by both men and women almost constantly. By this, I mean that the focus of attention is always on their sexual identity and the behaviors that are presumed to accompany it. I cannot imagine how frustrating it must be to never be recognized as a human being first and foremost, but to be considered always as a sexual object.

This project also affirmed for me how far society still has to go in addressing gender issues and gender differences. The type of anger and rejection that transgender people experience is indicative of a society that is structured around gender hierarchies to such an extent that a violation of gender roles arouses intense rage and confusion. It is viewed almost as blasphemy. It makes me wonder *why* gender is such a sacred cow. What is so threatening about a person who changes his or her gender? I have no answers to offer at this point but this is a question that I have found myself pondering, and one that I will continue to explore.

Applying the Knowledge Base: Agency, Program and Services, and Personal Competencies

FIELD WORK AGENCY: A PRIVATE SECTARIAN MENTAL HEALTH SERVICE AGENCY

Community My agency is the primary healthcare provider for much of the homeless population in the area, which is primarily African American. Because of its convenient inner-city location, people from all over the city come for free primary health care, mental health services, and HIV testing. Though the majority of our clients are African American, we also serve Latino, Asian, and caucasian populations. This neighborhood is also home to many transgender women.

Access There are large numbers of transgender people in my agency's community, who view the agency as a neighbor. There is good public transportation available for transgender clients coming from other areas of the city, as well as outreach services to the transgender community for HIV prevention. Many transgender women living in the agency's community tend to be sex workers. Outreach services are led by a transgender health specialist who is herself transgender.

Receptivity My agency has a long-standing reputation for being receptive to people of all sexualities and ethnicities. Transgender women feel comfortable when they come to my agency, and some have been employed there. In addition, there is a full-time transgender health specialist on staff. Though the agency's publicity literature does not mention transgender people specifically, the website does feature several transgender people and includes their testimonials.

Administration and Training There is minimal formal staff training in culturally sensitive practice. The only discussion of diversity and cultural competence takes place during the orientation, and the one I attended did not address cultural issues for transgender women specifically.

Staff Sensitivity The vast majority of the staff is highly sensitive to clients' needs, and respectful of clients' humanity. However, I have at times observed insensitive treatment toward homeless clients, many of whom suffer from severe mental illness. The clients were treated disrespectfully by a couple of employees in particular; however, these employees were quickly informed by their supervisor that they had been witnessed being disrespectful toward clients, and informed that such behavior would not be tolerated.

Funding Due to budget constraints, funding for HIV testing from the Department of Public Health has recently been completely cut. This will prove to have negative consequences for the transgender community, as many members of that community come to our agency for free, confidential testing. Additionally, my agency was one of the only sites that did the rapid HIV test, delivering results within 30 minutes of testing. I fear that this loss will have negative consequences for the transgender community: they will now have to travel elsewhere to get an HIV test, and go to an agency that may not be as receptive to transgender people. This could mean that fewer members of the community have regular HIV tests. Apart from this problem, my agency is able to be culturally responsive in its use of funds because much of the funding comes from private sources, who are familiar with, and supportive of, their inclusive philosophy.

My Program and Its Policies

Effort My agency makes a concerted and consistent effort to maintain an atmosphere in which people of all races, creeds, and genders are comfortable. Anytime a new project or program is started, staff members analyze it to determine whether or not it is culturally appropriate for the targeted population. Moreover, the staff seeks feedback from the targeted population about how the program could better serve their needs. This is true of the transgender population as well. The agency has had transgender women advise them on the two main programs in which transgender women seek help: recovery services and health services.

Quality The agency seeks to ensure that the quality of services is culturally appropriate for transgender women by constantly seeking feedback from the clients. While policies are generally inclusive of other worldviews, values, and belief systems, the agency is a part of a church, and there is a religious culture that could make some people feel uncomfortable. The church is nondenominational, and there is no evangelical mission attached to it; however, there is a way of talking that could make a non-Christian person uncomfortable. This is certainly not a formal policy, and it is not true of every program: the health clinic, for instance, does not share the same culture as some other programs in this respect.

Efficiency Though it is not uncommon to see transgender women being served in the health and mental health program, I do not think that their numbers in the community are reflected by their presence, especially in the health clinic. One reason for this might be that the transgender women in this neighborhood tend to do sex work, and there is another clinic nearby that specifically serves sex workers. At that clinic, it is often sex workers or former sex workers that provide the care, and it is possible that transgender women who are sex workers go there for healthcare rather than coming to my agency. I do not necessarily see this as a failure on the part of my agency or its programs. The transgender women who do receive their healthcare at my agency can have almost all of their healthcare needs met there. The one exception to this is that HIV-specific care is no longer provided.

Effectiveness My agency has a number of different programs, and I am unfamiliar with outreach efforts and effectiveness within all of them. However, I know that the health clinic and HIV services do specific outreach to the transgender community. This outreach is only somewhat effective, and might be improved if it took place at night as well as during the day, when many more transgender women are out and about. An impediment to evening outreach is that the neighborhood is barely safe during the day, and not safe at all at night. Though it is understandable that the agency would not want to put its staff at risk, the transgender community would be better served by doing outreach at night.

Personal Cultural Competencies

Engagement, Trust, and Relationship-building Transgender people use a number of its different services, including the medical clinic, mental health services, meals, recovery, and job training. The transgender people I have met seem rather comfortable about seeking help at my agency; however, I do not think that this is necessarily true for all social agencies. In general, I believe that transgender people are wary of seeking help within "the system," and are more likely to seek help among each other. When addressing members of the transgender community, one must always be careful to use the pronoun for the gender they have transitioned to unless instructed by them to do otherwise. It is also important to refer to transgender clients as Mr. or Ms. until they are comfortable with a more informal form of address. In general, transgender people seem to frequently be independent decision makers, though they are likely to consult with close friends. My transgender clients have responded well to guidance and suggestions but I am careful not direct them.

Assessment and Problem Definition In order to engage my client in the assessment process, I would ask her what her view of the problem is. I would also probably ask her what her friends might say about the problem and any possible solution, and if she thought their approach made sense, in order to understand the cultural context more deeply. One challenge that I have had in working with some transgender clients is that there seems to be a cultural norm and expectation that violence within relationships is normal. While this belief is by no means restricted to the transgender community, it may mean that a transgender woman does not identify an abusive relationship as particularly problematic, even though it may seem to me that it affects a number of other aspects of her life, such as employment and substance abuse.

I believe that the relationship of the dominant society to my transgender clients is one of oppression, disrespect, and violence. Many of the challenges for the transgender community come from the dominant society's negative views of them. This means that it is difficult for transgender people to get jobs in fields other than sex work. It means that they often have no place to live because people are hesitant to rent to them. Moreover, they are targeted for violence at an alarming rate. In assessing transgender clients, it is important to fully explore and understand the potential of violence and of substance abuse in their lives.

Contracting and Goal Setting Because the transgender community deals with a great deal of discrimination from society, I would make sure that my transgender client had complete personal control over goal setting and contracting. In other words, I would not be defining what is culturally appropriate at all but would instead let the client define what is appropriate individually. I would ask the client what issues she would like my assistance with, and tell her that there is a greater likelihood that she will accomplish her goals if we both agree to work on steps to accomplish them. However, I would probably not use the word "contract" as this could seem pushy and overly formal to transgender women.

Interventions Substance abuse/dependence are rather common in the transgender community. Therefore, an intervention to deal with these issues may be appropriate. However, whereas abstinence is commonly thought of as the appropriate remedy for substance abuse, abstinence is not necessarily appropriate or likely for many transgender women. This is true for several reasons, including a need to escape from current or past abuse and the necessity of substance use to cope with sex work. Therefore, a more culturally appropriate intervention for substance abuse/dependence with transgender women would take a harm reduction approach. I would engage my client in a discussion of when it is more safe or less safe to use drugs/alcohol and provide her with resources for needle exchange, needle cleaning kits, etc., if appropriate. Moreover, there are several organizations in the area that employ transgender drug/alcohol counselors and take a harm reduction, rather than an abstinence, approach. I would refer the client to one of these resources if she was interested in pursuing harm reduction goals.

Evaluation and Termination In my limited experience treating transgender women, I have seen that the focus of change for them has been internal. Violence, rejection by families, and oppression by society has resulted in very low self-esteem for many transgender women. Therefore, most positive change for them comes from learning to love and accept themselves without relying on outside validation (particularly as they often seek validation from men who are abusers). Transgender women are of necessity very independent. Though they may solicit input from friends in the transgender community, they individually determine whether an intervention has been helpful or successful.

I do not think that it is appropriate for me to extrapolate from my limited encounters with transgender women the norm regarding separation and ending a professional relationship. I do know that transgender women have people coming in and out of their lives regularly: family from whom they are estranged, friends they have lost to violence and drug addiction, or sex work clients. Therefore, it is no surprise to me that as I end work with my transgender client, she stops showing up for appointments. I know from seeing the work of transgender counselors in other areas, such as drug addiction, that it may be appropriate as the therapeutic relationship comes to an end to leave the office and have a more casual session or two in a park or a coffee shop.

Compliance with NASW Standards for Cultural Competence

Agency: The agency is lacking in several dimensions of the Standards for Cultural Competence laid out by the NASW (2001). As there is no training or education in cultural competence, the agency is not helping its employees to "seek to develop an understanding of their own personal, cultural values and beliefs," nor "develop specialized knowledge and understanding about the history, traditions, values... of major client groups they serve."

However, there are ways in which the agency is fulfilling these standards. For instance, the employees represent many diverse populations, and specifically include transgender women. In addition, by constantly seeking feedback from participants in its programs, the agency is helping to assure that its employees are "using appropriate methodological approaches, skills and techniques that reflect... understanding of the role of culture in the helping process," and "are aware of the effect of social policies and programs on diverse client populations," (NASW 2001).

Program and Services The health clinic shares some of the same problems as the agency in general, as it does not provide any training for cultural competence. However, the workforce is diverse, and includes a transgender woman as a health specialist. In addition, the health clinic employs a full-time Case Manager who is extremely knowledgeable about transgender services available throughout the area. He is able to make culturally appropriate referrals to diverse clients.

My Own Cultural Competence With regard to transgender women, I have acquired a rea-sonable level of cultural competence, however, there is much room for improvement. For instance, I have acted with respect for my transgender clients' self-determination, as stipulated by the NASW Code of Ethics, even when their decisions conflicted with my personal values and beliefs. This conflict was particularly salient in the area of sex work. However, by seeking an understanding of my clients' actions, I learned a great deal both about them and myself. This is in line with the NASW Standard regarding self-awareness.

Through this project, and through listening to my clients in an open way, I have developed a body of knowledge about the transgender community. Though this knowledge is not complete, I have established a foundation on which I can continue to build. Moreover, I have developed skills that enable me to ask questions of all my clients that will educate me about their cultures. Through ethnographic interviewing, I can continuously add to my understanding of the cultures of the clients I serve. In this way, I have begun to act upon the Standard regarding cross-cultural knowledge.

In regard to the Standard relating to appropriate methodology for different cultures, this seems to be a never-ending process of calibrating interventions to fit both the client's culture and their individual needs. In my practice thus far, it has become apparent with several clients that I needed to educate myself about more culturally appropriate interventions. Simply being aware of this fact is a step in the right direction. In most cases, the exigencies of time have dictated that I let the client lead me by the hand to show me what kind of help they needed. However, in the future I can seek out research related to specific groups that I will be working with to determine needs, increase sensitivity, and explore resources. For my transgender clients specifically, it was only toward the end of my work with them that I realized I had some knowledge of their culture that I could use in the helping process. Now that I have realized this, it will play a role in any future work with transgender clients.

I have learned a great deal about the services available to transgender women in the area. I have also realized how important this knowledge is if I am going to be a resource for my clients, and it is clear to me that I must make an effort to learn the resources available to clients in whatever agency I find myself in the future.

The Standard regarding empowerment and advocacy has been the most difficult to achieve, and continues to elude me. My work with my clients thus far has focused upon the therapeutic relationship. I have not yet attempted to effect change for my clients in the policy realm. These are skills that I hope to learn and exercise in the future. I am sure that I will have the opportunity over the course of my career, as many of the challenges that oppressed communities face are grounded in unjust policy.

I have not yet had the opportunity to exercise the Standard regarding a diverse workforce. During my placement, my supervisor was searching for another part-time social worker. Three of the four social workers in the mental health clinic, including myself, are white women, while many of the clients are people of color. I discussed this with my supervisor who was desperately hoping that people of color would apply for the position, but, unfortunately, none did.

Though it remains a problem that the mental health practitioners in my agency remain overwhelmingly white, there is some solace in the fact that the new therapist is a gay man, thus increasing the overall diversity of the mental health staff. If I am ever in the position to have the opportunity to hire a social worker, I would research ways to reach out to mental health practitioners of color.

Another Standard in which I fall short at this moment is regarding professional education; were this my full-time workplace, I would advocate for more education for employees. For my personal growth, I shall look in the future for educational opportunities to help advance my own cultural competence.

Finally, I have made some progress toward the Standard regarding cross-cultural leadership. As I have learned more about the transgender community, I have shared this information with my supervisor, who had never treated a transgender client before. I have also educated the Case Manager both about transgender culture and resources for transgender clients.

I feel at this point that I have only started down the path of gaining cultural competence. This process will last as long as my career, but now I know what guideposts to look for on the road.

REFERENCES

Anderson, J. (director). *Normal* [made-for-TV film]. United States: HBO Films.

Brown, K. 2005. *Trangender History*. www.transhistory.org

Cortez, J. 2004. *Sexile*. New York: Gay Men's Health Project.

National Association of Social Workers (NASW). 2001. *NASW Standards for Cultural Competence in Social Work Practice*. Washington, D.C.: Author.

Zeisler, A. 2002. MI Way or the Highway—The Michigan Womyn's Music Festival is at a crossroads over its admissions policy: A roundtable discussion. *Bitch Magazine: A Feminist Response to Pop Culture* no. 17, Summer, 37–39.

Worksheet

1. It is important for social workers to understand the legal rights of transgender people. From what you have learned here and from other sources, what are the rights of transgender people in terms of their gender identity in public places?

2. Sex reassignment surgery is an extremely complex and costly affair. Many transgender people choose not to have surgery and use hormones to address gender identity issues and personal comfort. Others, however, would like to have the surgery, but find that it is not a covered benefit under standard insurance policies. Advocates state that surgery to correct gender errors is as necessary as surgery to correct any other type of congenital problem. Do you believe that transgender people's sex reassignment surgery should be covered by private insurers and by medical assistance programs? Why, or why not?

Culturally Competent Social Work Practice with Transgender People

Diversity Project by Lisa Dazols

As a lesbian who struggled during childhood and adolescence with the coming out process, I had a long road to acceptance of my sexual orientation and identity within the queer community. Yet, my journey was quite easy compared to the transition process that transgender individuals face. In an attempt for myself to better understand the past, present, and future of this oppressed community, I conducted a population immersion study by gathering background information on the transgender population, reading the book *Stone Butch Blues*, viewing the film *Transamerica*, and attending a Transgender Job Fair at an LGBT center.

KNOWLEDGE ACQUISITION: CULTURAL IMMERSION

Background

Unlike homosexuality, which was removed as a mental disorder from the American Psychiatric Association (AMA) in 1973, Gender Identity Disorder (GID) still remains as a classified mental disorder. GID is diagnosed when an individual has a "strong and persistent cross-gender identification" and a "persistent discomfort with his or her sex" (American Psychiatric Association 1994, 246). The transgender community continually fights against this diagnosis and runs into fierce opposition. George A. Rekers, Ph.D., Research Director for Child and Adolescent Psychiatry, at the University of South Carolina School of Medicine, is the editor of the *Handbook of Child and Adolescent Sexual Problems* and advocates for treatment of GID today. His work with boys who have GID is geared to prevent "severe sexual problems of adulthood such as transsexualism and homosexuality." His treatment for these boys includes "videotape feedback, behavior shaping sessions, family son interaction programs, including athletic skill training." He speaks across the country and his book is widely available (Rekers 1995).

Advocating to remove Gender Identity Disorder from the AMA are many LGBT groups and medical teams including those from state hospital. The Transition Project at the state hospital defines the term "transgender" as an umbrella term referring to anyone whose behavior, thoughts, or traits differ from or transgress the societal expectations and stereotypes for their sex (e.g., boychicks, grrl, femme queens, two-spirit, drag king, cross-dressers, transsexuals, genderqueers, gender variant, butch, studs, etc.). The state hospital provides hormone treatment to male-to-female (MTF) and female-to-male (FTM) individuals, performs gender reassignment surgery, and organizes educational workshops for providers to improve health services to the transgender community. Rather than pathologizing the individual, they are helping transgender persons to safely transition and live well adjusted lives as they face many challenges.

The reality of hardships transgender individuals face is staggering, even in a progressive city. A 1997 Department of Public Health study interviewed 392 MTF women and 123 FTM men. Among the MTF women, 80 percent had a history of survival sex work, 35 percent were HIV positive, and 59 percent had been raped at least once. Among FTM men, 30 percent reported physical abuse from a sexual partner within the past 12 months. In both groups over 80 percent reported regular verbal abuse because of their gender identity and 32 percent had reported at least one suicide attempt (***Department of Public Health 1997). My internship at the AIDS Collaboration has allowed me to get to know many

MTF women who are HIV positive and bear witness to their stories of survival.

Novel: *Stone Butch Blues*

This novel, *Stone Butch Blues* (Feinberg 2006), follows the history of a young girl named Jess in the 1950s who identifies as a "he-she" because people often ask whether she is a boy or a girl. After her parents discover her trying on her father's suit, her parents send her to charm school, take her to a mental hospital, and then later abandon her. After Jess runs away from home, she finds community with other he-shes in gay bars in the 1960s and finds fulfillment in sexual encounters with femme lesbian lovers. Yet, she continues to be a victim of hate crimes including rape throughout her life. She lives in constant fear of physical attack from boys at school, police raids on gay bars, and harassment from strangers on the street. Jess decides to begin taking male hormones and have a breast reduction to pass as a man in order to survive. During the 1970s, right after the Stonewall movement, Jess reaps the benefit of fitting in as a man by ensuring a stable job, using bathrooms with ease, and avoiding verbal abuse. She even makes love to a straight woman without being discovered.

Despite having a beard and being called "Sir," she always feels trapped in her body. Jess asks, "But who was I now—woman or man? The question could never be answered as long as those were the only choices; it could never be answered if it had to be asked" (Feinberg 1993, 222). Jess decides to stop taking the male hormones and lives between genders, falling in love with Ruth in the 1980s, who understands her because of her similar struggle having been born a man and later identifying as a woman. They live a quiet and hidden life together as they support friends in the community who suffer from AIDS while joining in the community organizing efforts to create a more just working environment for transgender people.

A striking theme in this book is the way in which the he-shes come to identify as "stone butch." When Jess first runs away from home, she is taken in by an older he-she, Butch Al, and her femme girlfriend, Jaqueline. They worry about her becoming "stone," meaning so badly hurt that she is numb. As Jess survives more and more physical trauma via multiple hate crimes, she becomes increasingly "stone." She doesn't know how to let her lovers touch her or how to express her feelings for them. Due to her repeated victimization, Jess feels powerless, unable to protect herself and those she loves most. Her friend Ed, who endured various beatings by the police with Jess, reaches desperation and kills herself. Butch Al, the father figure who tried to prepare Jess for the road ahead by teaching her to be tough, ends up in a mental institution from extreme distress. Jess identifies with these he-shes who are stone butch like her, and their brotherhood gives Jess a will to survive despite all obstacles.

The he-shes were not always accepted by the gay community or by one another. When Jess begins taking hormones as she transitions to a man's body, her femme girlfriend leaves her. Jess feels that her girlfriend did not love her enough to stick by her through this transition. As a transitioning man, Jess also feels alienated from the feminist and lesbian movements. Jess later rejects her he-she friend Grant, who chooses another he-she as a lover, because Jess feels threatened by thinking of two "butches" in bed rather than a butch and a femme. The roles within the gay movement at the time were strict, not leaving room for the transgender community; and, the roles within the transgender community were strict, not allowing for diversity. As the book expands over four decades, we see not only the emergence of hormonal and surgical procedures in the transgender community, but we witness the gay and lesbian community grow into the more inclusive lesbian, gay, bisexual, and transgender (LGBT) community.

Film: *Transamerica*

The film *Transamerica* (Bastian and Tucker 2005) is the present day story of Bree, a self-identified, pre-operative, male-to-female transsexual, who is preparing for her final surgical operation to complete her transition. One week before her surgery, she receives a phone call from a prison in New York and learns that she fathered a son during a casual sexual experience in college. Bree's therapist convinces her to face her past and meet her son. Bree flies from Los Angeles to New York in order to get the boy out of jail. The boy, Toby, is released to her, but Bree is unable to reveal to him her true identity and leads him to believe that she is a Christian missionary. Bree has no intention of taking care of the boy and first drives Toby to his hometown to be with his stepfather. When Bree witnesses the stepfather physically abusing the boy, she allows Toby to get a free ride with her to L.A. Toby inadvertently sees Bree naked while peeing on the road trip and comes to accept her as a transsexual.

Bree then drives Toby to L.A., and along the way discovers the boy's history of drug use, prostitution, and incarceration. When their car and money is stolen, Bree and Toby end up at Bree's parents' house where Toby finally learns about his true father. The boy rejects Bree and runs away from her, and Bree returns home on her own to undergo her surgery. After becoming a full biological woman, she discovers an emptiness left by Toby's rejection and is filled with a desire to be close to him. The film ends with the possibility of a parental relationship when Toby locates Bree in L.A.

The most powerful theme in this film is the sense of shame that Bree carries within. The character of Bree is brave when encountering the world, but lives with little self-esteem or pride. Bree is ashamed of herself as a transsexual and does her best to live "stealth" so that nobody uncovers her gender transformation. She is embarrassed to have Toby meet a group of transsexuals with whom they stay while traveling. She has no friends in L.A., is not involved in the transgender community, and closes herself off to everyone with the exception of her therapist. She does not want to have any connection to her former life as Stanley, thereby cutting off any potential to love her son.

As Bree internalizes repeated verbal abuse, her sense of shame deepens. When Toby discovers that she is a transsexual, he calls her a "freak." Bree also receives disapproving remarks from a healthcare worker and others who learn of her identity along the trip. Most shocking is Bree's arrival in her parents' home. Her parents refuse to respect Bree and spew out degrading remarks that reveal their repugnance toward their child. Bree's mother refuses to accept Bree's decision and states, "I just miss my son." Bree's answer, "You never had a son," clearly shows that Bree never identified as a man. Bree considers her parents dead to her and their own shame costs them the loss of both a child and a grandchild.

Most fascinating is Bree's full physical transition that leads her to a healthy life as a woman. Bree frees herself from her own shame after her operation. She recognizes her own capacity to love as a parent. She also embraces her talents and desires to become a teacher. In the opening scene in which Bree is being interviewed by the health worker she jokes, "Funny how an operation can cure a mental disorder." When Bree's transformation is complete at the end of the film, she is able to fully embrace life.

Cultural Event: The Transgender Job Fair

The Transgender Job Fair, held at the LGBT Center, inspires hope for the future by empowering transgender people with job opportunities. According to newspaper reports, 75 percent of transgender people living in the city are unable to find a full-time job. 59 percent earn less than $15,333 and only 4 percent earn more than $61,200, the median income in the city. In other words, more than half of the transgender population lives in poverty and 96 percent earn below the medium income.

While it has been over a decade since the city expanded nondiscrimination laws to cover the transgender community, 59 percent of participants in the study stated that they experienced some form of employment discrimination. The most common problems occur with respect to changes in name or pronoun preference as well as controversy over which bathroom to use. While verbal and sexual harassment are common, few formal complaints are filed.

There were 20 companies and agencies present at the Transgender Job Fair, representing both the public and private sector. The state hospital as well as the county office participated, two public systems that offer sex reassignment surgery as part of their full health benefits. Other attending agencies included a handful of HIV nonprofits that are perceived as accepting of the LGBT community such as Benefits Resource Center and the sex positive shop Good Vibrations. Representing the private sector were Charles Schwab, Wells Fargo, and Ameriprise Financial Advisors. Most shocking to me, however, was seeing the recruiting booth of the San Francisco Police Department. After reading about the violence toward transgender people during police raids in *Stone Butch Blues*, I realized the significance of police recruiting the very enemy they despised in recent history.

Interview: Lilly

At the job fair, I was fortunate to interview a transgender MTF woman who I will call Lilly. Lilly walks tall and proud in her business suit as a six-foot-three, 27-year-old from Tennessee. Lilly came to the job fair looking for opportunity that she was unable to find in other settings. She attended college in Tennessee and left her home state immediately after graduation. Lilly has a strained relationship with her family, who has never accepted her as a woman. She considers herself lucky to have had role models due to being "young enough where I'd seen transsexuals on TV and in films. I knew that someday that would be me." She lived as a man in Tennessee through college because she knew that she would need to complete her education. She found some friends within the isolated gay community, but knew that she could only find true acceptance in a major urban center.

As soon as she graduated, Lilly moved West to begin her new life. She went to a public health clinic where she could access hormone therapy. She attempted to find several jobs, but because of her transitioning features she felt she was never welcome. She says, "I just wanted to hide. Even here I would get strange looks. I knew I couldn't walk into an office." Eventually, she was employed part-time by a gay couple who ran a small bed and breakfast, which barely enabled her to afford basic monthly expenses.

Lilly came to the Job Fair to "finally use my education." She was excited to find the opportunities that she was looking for. At the same time she pointed out to me, "Look at these booths. They are here recruiting us, but they do not look like us. Only one HIV agency has a trans employee sitting here. It is like being at a Latino Job Fair where nobody speaks a word of Spanish." Yet, Lilly recognized that it was a big step for the community and "a way out for my trans sisters. After all we don't have anything like this in Tennessee."

Reactions, Conclusions, and Synthesis

In conducting this population immersion study, I learned about my own reaction to the transgender community. I realized that the line between lesbian and transgender is not always clear cut. Growing up, I was always a tomboy who played sports with the boys at recess and who had action figures instead of dolls. I never wanted to wear a dress, or do anything "girly." Once in a while, I would be mistaken for a boy. Yet, after surviving the awkward stages of growing up and understanding myself better, I've always felt comfortable with my body as a woman.

The thin line between what is gay, lesbian, or transgender has hurt the transgender community. I recognize that in the gay and lesbian community there is a push toward wanting to be accepted, which sometimes excludes the extremes of the spectrum, the people feared most. While my family is extremely accepting of the lesbian community and my relationship with my girlfriend, I can't imagine that they would be as accepting if she were transitioning to a man, or if I were for that matter. When I was single, I never was open to dating someone who was transgender, either FTM or MTF. Just as Jess in *Stone Butch Blues* finds, when one of the partners is FTM transgender, it is difficult to be accepted by a lesbian partner because the partner's identity as a lesbian becomes threatened. This discomfort gives rise to fear in which one questions their own identity and risks loss from not belonging to their former community.

I caught myself in another uncomfortable moment when I was at the Transgender Job Fair and people were looking at me wondering how I fit in. In a polo shirt, jeans, and sneakers, I can sometimes look androgynous. Amongst the other transgender people at the fair, I was uncomfortable thinking that the recruiters questioned if I was a transitioning FTM or a transitioned MTF. I found that in being aware of my discomfort, I was able to realize how ridiculous I was being. As open minded as I believe myself to be, I realized during this immersion that I have a bit of internal transphobia myself.

Jess in *Stone Butch Blues*, Bree in *Transamerica*, and Lilly at the Transgender Job Fair are people who serve as examples for myself and for others to be more accepting of people who are different from ourselves. They are brave enough to think outside of their conventional roles and strong willed enough to fight for the dignified life they deserve. Now understanding the history of the movement, the present day struggles, and the glimpses of opportunity ahead for transgender people, I want to be part of the revolutionary movement that makes the world more respectful of them.

Applying the Knowledge Base: Agency, Program and Services, and Personal Cultural Competencies

I have been placed at the AIDS Collaboration in a major city with a transgender population that is higher than the national average, at least in part because hormone therapy, facial surgery, and sex reassignment surgery are all available through major hospitals and out-patient clinics. My agency provides a variety of services to the LGBT population with a focus on HIV-related problems such as harm reduction, practical needs including housing and employment, and counseling.

The Agency

Community The AIDS Collaboration is located in the neighborhood with the highest concentration of poverty in a major city. Homelessness, drug use, and prostitution are common along the streets outside the agency. As one of the leading AIDS organizations in the country, my agency attracts clients from all parts of the state for services. The majority of clients are of low and middle socioeconomic status.

Access The AIDS Collaboration is highly accessible to the HIV-positive transgender population. The district in which it is located has the highest concentration of male to female (MTF) AIDS cases (McFarland 2003). Other agencies that specialize in social services for the transgender community are also located in the neighborhood. The Transgender Law Clinic, which provides free legal services, and a medical clinic, which has a transgender primary care unit, are located within walking distance of my agency. Clients arrive at the agency through referral or by word of mouth, as there are currently no outreach programs that specifically target the transgender population.

Receptivity The AIDS Collaboration is welcoming to the transgender population, as the literature and reading materials in the lobby include services geared toward this community. Of the 86 agency employees, the large majority identify as gay, lesbian, or bisexual. In the two and a half years that I have worked at this agency, there has not been a transgender employee.

The agency has traditionally been dominated by white gay men, while in recent years more women and people of color have been hired. The AIDS Collaboration prides itself on being an Equal Opportunity Employer. On the bottom of every job posting it is written that the agency seeks applications from "people living w/HIV/AIDS & other disabilities, people of color, women, lesbians, gay men, bisexuals, transgender, and other diverse backgrounds." I believe that this would be an accepting place for a transgender employee.

At the same time, the agency has not actively recruited transgender employees. I wish that the AIDS Collaboration would have participated in the Transgender Job Fair that I attended at the LGBT Center, where there were other HIV agencies present. I also wish that the AIDS Collaboration's health insurance plans covered sexual transitioning costs for any transgender employee. My coworkers and I made phone calls to Aetna and Kaiser, the two options for health coverage at my agency, and neither plan covers the costs for an individual in the process of transitioning. A transgender employee would have to pay out of pocket for psychological counseling, hormone replacement therapy, and sexual reassignment surgery. These costs can amount to approximately $20,000.

Administration and Staff Training This year, all of the staff will attend a diversity education workshop. Hopefully, current information about the needs of transgender people will be discussed. Small efforts have been made for training in the HIV Services Department. The Director of HIV Services also sent a social worker to a training this year called the Transition Project. The training educates providers on how to be culturally competent with this population at high risk for HIV.

The training materials include a glossary of terms that transgender people use to identify themselves such as boychicks, grrl, femme queens, two-spirit, drag king, cross dressers, genderqueers, gender variant, butch, studs, etc. The training includes information on how agencies can use appropriate language, create a safe environment, provide staff training, increase outreach, and establish resources. In the past, client advocates have attended trainings on transgender health including topics such as hormone treatment, sex reassignment surgery, and mental health interventions.

To find out more about the AIDS Collaboration's services to the transgender population, I interviewed the HIV Services Department Director. She said that "there still needs to be more knowledge and sensitivity on our part to understand how to work with this population. I'll be the first to admit that I lack an understanding myself and get nervous as how to address or label people. We're just learning the definitions and what they all mean" (***HIV Services Department Director 2005).

Staff Sensitivity Traditionally, transgender people have often felt both hatred and discrimination from the gay community, who do not want to associate their struggles with those changing their gender. The transgender community has fought to be part of the gay movement and to educate the queer community. As the transgender population has now become more visible in part due to the alarming numbers of HIV infection, there should be a lot more energy directed to HIV services to this community.

The AIDS Collaboration is an agency that began services to the community by responding to the rise of HIV in the gay population, and has been traditionally directed by gay males, so that the culture of the agency seems to be very gay focused. However, from my direct observation, the staff is as respectful of differences between themselves and the transgender community as they are considerate of all diverse populations.

Of the staff of 13 social workers in the HIV Services Department, there are currently seven lesbians and one gay male. One of the lesbian social workers is currently dating an FTM transgender person, who has visited our office on several occasions during his transition. To show solidarity with their coworker, two other lesbian social workers have shared stories of their previous relationships with FTMs. In informal settings, there has been a lot of education about dating someone who is transgender and how to accompany partners through that process.

Sharing one another's experiences has helped us avoid "they" language when talking about the transgender community. While we previously addressed her girlfriend by her female name, we now ask about her boyfriend. As a staff, we all had to educate ourselves on how to use pronouns that fit a person's desired gender when talking about clients, partners, and friends.

"Our department seems to be different from the rest of the agency," notes the HIV Services Director. She asserts that other departments, which consist of more gay males, have some level of transphobia. "I have even heard jokes about trans people in our management meetings. Sad to say, the gay community can oftentimes be our worst offenders. Perhaps gay men are internally threatened. The T in LGBT often is an afterthought" (***HIV Services Department Director 2005).

Funding Our agency definitely could improve funding efforts to support the transgender community. Community programs at the AIDS Collaboration include special programs for the Latino community, the African American community, crystal meth users, and an HIV Prevention Project needle exchange. These groups represent the populations at highest risk for transmission of HIV in the area. While all four groups include transgender clients, there is no group specifically created for them. In fact, according to our agency's brochure, the African American program is for "same-gender loving men" and the crystal and meth program is for "gay and bisexual men." The word transgender is not mentioned in the brochure. Adding a weekly support group and clinical case management

program for the transgender community would fill a growing need in the city.

Programs and Services

Effort I think that our programs at the AIDS Collaboration can be more proactive to be culturally sensitive to the transgender population. One way to demonstrate our care and concern for the transgender community would be to change the bathrooms in our lobby so that the labels Men and Women do not require transgender people to define themselves by a gender or put themselves at risk. In a 2002 survey conducted by the city's Human Rights Commission, nearly 50 percent of respondents reported having been harassed or assaulted in a public bathroom (Transgender Law Clinic 2005). To help create a safer atmosphere for transgender clients and staff, universal gender inclusive restrooms are essential. Other agencies serving the transgender community, such as the LGBT Center and a Counseling Center have gender neutral bathrooms. As a leader in the HIV community, our agency should also make the effort to change.

When I asked the director of HIV Services's opinion of the topic, she stated that, as a woman, she had concerns for safety and cleanliness that prevented her from wanting to change the restrooms. She pointed out that the bathroom codes on the locks were made the same, so that when clients asked for the bathroom code, they would be given the same number and left to chose which bathroom to use. This was an improvement from the previous year, when the front desk assistants would have to assume the gender of a client and give them a corresponding code to either the men's or women's restroom.

The director was receptive to opening up the discussion to the department and receiving a letter and further information from me based on a pamphlet written by the Transgender Law Clinic. It would be helpful to conduct a pilot study of transgender clients, so that we could hear their input on this topic specifically, as well as seek their assistance in formulating and designing more culturally sensitive ways to welcome the transgender community.

Quality Quality control is met through a client satisfaction survey, which is administered each year, as well as through individual and group supervision of staff. Programs and services have been shown to offer equitable, respectful, and equal access to all clients. Our programs take into account variations between the transgender population and the dominant society. For example, our database and agency forms are all written in gender neutral language. Clients can register on the agency database with any name they choose and do not have to identify as female or male in the system. Programs are designed to be inclusive and to treat the transgender population with respect.

Effectiveness The number of transgender clients who use services in the HIV Services Department are proportional to the total population of people who have HIV. We have transgender clients in all of our advocacy programs: Intake, Housing, and Financial Benefits. Over a period of one year from April 1, 2005, through April 1, 2006, the department served almost 30 MTF transgender clients. These clients make up 2.59 percent of the total number of clients served in this department over 12 months. According to the *Quarterly AIDS Surveillance Report* (Hsu and Scheer 2006), 2.7 percent of all new HIV/AIDS cases in 2005 were among transgender individuals. In looking at cases from 1980 to 2006, the transgender population makes up 1.3 percent of the total HIV/AIDS long-term survivors in the city.

While these numbers are relatively insignificant, what is most alarming is the statistics on physical and mental health risks that transgender people suffer, which highlight a great need for concern for this group. It is made clear in a 1997 study by the city's Department of Public Health that of transgender MTF, 35 percent were HIV positive, 80 percent had a history of survival sex work, and 59 percent had been raped at least once. In looking at some statistical characteristics

taken of the transgender clients seen by our agency in one year, 75 percent have a history of serious mental health symptoms and 90 percent have a history of drug abuse. (***Department of Public Health 1997).

Although the numbers of people in the transgender community in the city with HIV reflect the numbers served by our agency, the question is whether or not the agency addresses all of the needs of transgender individuals, given the extremely high risks that this population faces. One unmet need in the community is comprehensive case management geared specifically toward transgender MTFs. While there are case management programs for individuals with HIV that transgender individuals utilize, none are specially designed for this group. The MTF population faces obstacles that other clients do not, such as accessing hormone treatment and therapy for sexual reassignment surgery. Given the multiple needs arising in this community due to an increased number of hate crimes, domestic violence, substance abuse, and suicide, transgender clients would benefit greatly from a specialized long-term clinical case management.

Efficiency The AIDS Collaboration currently does not do any outreach to the transgender community. As the HIV Services Director notes, "The key to improving services for this population is through ally building both on an agency and individual level" (HIV Services Department Director 2006). The HIV Services Department has made efforts to collect resource guides for transgender-specific programs to distribute to clients.

More effort should be made to do site visits to these resource agencies and to invite speakers from agencies such as the Transgender Law Clinic to meet with staff and increase awareness. The AIDS Collaboration has often been a leader in creating coalitions between agencies to provide comprehensive services. It is my hope that we can partner with other agencies to improve overall services to the MTF population to increase prevention so that fewer MTFs come to the agency with HIV-positive diagnoses.

Personal Cultural Competencies

Engagement, Trust, and Relationship-building There are few barriers to access for the transgender population to engage in services at the AIDS Collaboration. There are some communication barriers for non-English speaking MTF clients such as the Asian, Latino, and deaf MTF clients who have come to the agency in the past year. In these instances, translators are provided and social workers must be attuned to cultural differences. Appropriate forms of distance, eye contact, touch, and empathic response all vary from culture to culture. Ethnographic interviewing can be used to ask global questions as to how each individual's culture calls the problem, condition, or situation.

A beginning step in the intake process is to ask, "What name do you prefer to be called?" Many transgender people do not go by their birth name. It is also important not to assume the sexual orientation of a transgender person, as many can identify with different orientations, including heterosexual. Also it is important to use gender neutral language and appropriate pronouns for gender identity. A growing trend is for gender neutral pronouns such as "ze" instead of he or she and "zir" instead of his or her (Center for AIDS Prevention Studies 2006). Also, in asking about other people in a clients' life, it would be preferable to use words such as partner instead of asking if someone has a boyfriend or girlfriend. In the same light, it is preferable to ask if someone is a parent rather than a mother or father.

Assessment and Problem Definition Transgender people face enormous difficulties in being accepted by others. The transgender culture is not accepted by the dominant society, and transgender people are largely regarded as outside of society due to their differences. In making an assessment, it is necessary to take a client-centered approach and meet them where they are within their own identity and journey. In order to discover their chief "problem," motivational interviewing would be an effective way to align with a client and gather information for a clinical biopsychosocial assessment. Drawing out an eco-map of the client's surrounding world would also help the social worker map out both the supportive and stressful relationships in the client's life.

Contracting and Goal Setting Two culturally appropriate goals for clients in this population might be to fully transition to the other gender and to maintain HIV health. In order to support clients in developing, expressing, and setting their own goals, it is important to be empathetic, nonjudgmental, and supportive. Using a harm reduction approach, we should let clients design their own goals and praise them for any positive change in their lifestyle.

Once the goals have been determined, I would work with the clients to establish clear objectives that are both culturally and personally appropriate, and support the clients' goals, and develop a written contract. In weekly sessions, I would discuss how certain behaviors support certain desired objectives. Progress would be measured together as the overarching goal becomes within reach.

Interventions A social worker should have a good understanding of the social stigma and obstacles that transgender people face, and work with the strengths that each client presents. Narrative therapy would be an appropriate treatment for transgender clients because it suggests the creation of a personal story that could highlight identity development. The story could be reconstructed to highlight the individual's strengths, coping, and survival skills.

In addition, support groups can be beneficial for a transgender individual. Any transgender person who wants to undergo sexual reassignment surgery must go through individual counseling, but there is also a need for peer support and affirmation that could be met in a group. Because transgender individuals are often rejected by their families of origin and isolated by society in general, they often need to construct new families. It would be therapeutic to meet others who have successfully undergone the transitioning process, or are working through this process, and who live with similar risk factors, such as HIV.

Evaluation and Termination When the client and social worker have reached the specified goals within the services that are provided by the AIDS Collaboration, the point of termination is reached. Through individual supervision and group case conferences, evaluations of these decisions are made. Each year a survey gives clients a chance to evaluate the services and staff of the agency, and to describe their experiences.

The transgender population could measure success as either an internal change, which may not be visible, or as an external change, in which everything visible is completely altered, or possibly as both internal and external change. Some clients that come to the agency for service are at the beginning of their transition process, while others who come in have been transitioned for years. It is essential to understand that most come to our agency not for help in transitioning, but rather hoping to find assistance with practical needs such as housing, HIV medication, and financial benefits.

One difficulty that I have noticed in regard to termination with transgender clients is that there are few resources to which referrals can be made in confidence where clients' long-term needs will be met. The other agencies and the primary medical clinic serving this community are chaotic, understaffed, and serve primarily homeless populations with long lines in the waiting rooms. I wish that there were clinical case management programs and support groups designed for this population so that a smooth transition of services could be easily made to a referring agency. Collaboration between agencies is the key for successful termination of treatment.

Evaluation Using NASW Standards for Cultural Competence:

Standard #4 NASW (2001) provides Standards for Cultural Competence to guide social workers when working with diverse populations. The standard of Cross Cultural

Knowledge stood out to me when reflecting upon the transgender population. The NASW defines this Standard as: "Social workers shall have and continue to develop specialized knowledge and understanding about the history, traditions, values, family systems, and artistic expressions of major client groups served."

Agency This agency needs to train employees in transgender related topics, and should also participate in events such as the Transgender Job Fair in order to recruit transgender employees and create a more diverse work environment. Employee health benefits should strive to meet the medical needs of this community as well. The bathrooms in the agency should also be gender neutral to be as respectful as possible to this population. The agency should also make more attempts to align with other agencies that serve this population, in order to coordinate services and develop a support network that can more fully meet client needs.

Programs In the HIV Services Department, a focus study should be developed to determine the gaps in services this community needs, and the ways in which our programs and services could be more welcoming toward the high risk HIV-positive MTF population. A clinical case management program and a support group for transgender individuals with HIV should be considered as well.

Personal Competencies On an individual level, I have learned a great deal from this population immersion study. I recognized my own transphobia and misunderstanding of these individuals, with whom I have been working for some time. After taking the time to educate myself about their struggles, I will now be able to better empathize and work with these clients in a culturally competent manner. This study has also increased my own advocacy efforts in the agency, in recognizing that I can truly be an effective ally for change. After completing this project, I wrote a letter to the director of HIV Services to change our bathrooms in the building to be more welcoming to the transgender population.

REFERENCES

American Psychiatric Association. 1994. *Desk Reference to the Diagnostic Criteria from DSM-IV.* Washington, D.C.: Author.

Bastian, R. (producer), and D. Tucker (director). 2005. *Transamerica* [motion picture]. United States: Belladonna Productions LLC.

Center for AIDS Prevention Studies. 2006. *Transition Project: Skills Building for HIV Prevention Efforts in Transgender Communities* [brochure].

*** Department of Public Health. 1997. *The Transgender Community Health Project.*

Feinberg, L. 1993. *Stone Butch Blues: A Novel.* Ithaca: Firebrand Books.

*** HIV Services Department Director. 2006. The AIDS Collaboration ***

Hsu, L., and S. Scheer. 2006. *Quarterly AIDS Surveillance Report.* *** Department of Public Health, AIDS Office. http://www.dph.sf.ca.us/Reports/HlthAssess.htm

McFarland, W. 2003. *Atlas of HIV/AIDS in* *** *1981–2000.* *** Department of Public Health, AIDS Office, HIV/AIDS Statistics and Epidemiology Section, 132.

National Association of Social Workers (NASW). 2001. *NASW Standards for Cultural Competence in Social Work Practice.* Washington, D.C.: Author.

Rekers, G. 2002. *Gender Identity Disorder.* Leadership U. http://www.leaderu.com/jhs/rekers.html

Rekers, G., ed. 1995. *Handbook of Child and Adolescent Sexual Problems.* New Britain, CT: Lexington Books.

Transgender Law Clinic. 2005. *Peeing in Peace: A Resource Guide for Transgender Activists and Allies.*

Woodward, T. 2006. Transjobless. *The* *** *Guardian.* 40 (24): 13.

Worksheet

1. One persistent issue transgender people face is the use of public restrooms. While accommodations and cultural sensitivity apply to the use of names, pronouns, and dress, enabling people to individually determine whether to use the male or female restroom has proven to be a challenge for transgender people and activists. When one person's perceived right to make this decision impacts the perceived rights to safety and privacy of another person, the issue becomes more complex. How do you view this issue?

2. Currently, as the author notes, Gender Identity Disorder, the medical diagnosis for transgender people, is classified as a mental health disorder. The transgender community is fighting this designation and wants it removed from the accepted list of mental health disorders. What are some of the pros and cons you see in regard to this issue? Think about the Americans with Disabilities Act, health insurance, discrimination and oppression, empowerment, and advocacy.

11

Culturally Competent Social Work Practice with African-American Men on the Down Low

Diversity Project by William J. Beyer

The population I chose as the focus for this project faces discrimination from different groups within our society. This discrimination creates feelings of shame and anxiety among them: African American men on the down low. I was intrigued when I first heard of the African American men on the down low phenomenon. Like them, I am a racial minority and I am attracted to the same gender, but I am a different racial minority than African American and I claim a different sexual identity. Furthermore, I also hold a strong interest in the complex relationship between race and sexuality and aspire to spearhead programs that specifically assist lesbian, gay, bisexual, and transgender adolescents of color in the future. Thus, I used this project as an opportunity to learn about a major population that struggles with both race and sexuality in order to increase my awareness of relevant issues that I should be conscious of in order to provide sufficient services for all queer youths of color.

As an intern in a publicly sponsored AIDS Project, I work with program managers to monitor the quality of services offered to people living with the human immunodeficiency virus (HIV) and acquired immune deficiency syndrome (AIDS). Some consumers of these HIV/AIDS services are African American men on the down low.

This project will address the diverse facets of African American men on the down low through literature, a film, a weekly event affiliated with this population, and an interview with a self-identified man on the down low; all of these different sources of information illustrate the complexity behind African American men on the down low.

KNOWLEDGE ACQUISITION: POPULATION IMMERSION EXPERIENCE

Beyond the Down Low—Is There a History?

One of the major challenges in trying to become culturally competent with this population is to define what "down low" actually means. Keith Boykin, the author of *Beyond the Down Low* (2005), shares my inquiry: What does it mean to be on the down low? In his book, he writes about a few examples of individuals who may be considered to be on the down low. These include Raheem, a 24-year-old who exclusively has sex with men but wants to eventually settle down with a woman in the future; David, a 36-year-old married man with two kids who meets men at his gym to sleep with and identifies as heterosexual; and Jerry who is open about his long-term male lover to his wife and identifies as bisexual. All three of these case vignettes offer very different lifestyles, yet they are all considered men on the down low. Boykin argues that the "down low" is a term that has no stringent meaning and can be generalized to many different kinds of people.

Phill Wilson, the director of the Black AIDS Institute in Los Angeles, states what the down low means to him:

> Like many slang terms, DL means different things to different people. Some DL men identify as straight and have wives or girlfriends but secretly have sex with other men ... Some are closeted gay men. And then there are African-American brothers who openly have relationships with other men but reject

the label 'gay' or 'bisexual' because they equate those terms with white men. (Boykin 2005, 15)

It seems that there is no clear-cut definition for a man on the down low; however, the term revolves around African American men who have sexual relationships with men and strong reservations with identifying as gay publicly. For this project, I will be utilizing this general definition for men on the down low because, apparently, not all African American men on the down low behave the same way.

Unfortunately, because there is such an indistinct definition of men on the down low, there is no cogent data or statistics to confirm how many men on the down low actually exist in the United States. Furthermore, if the definition of the down low were hetero-sexual men who secretly have sex with men, these men would not be willing to admit that they are participating in these clandestine activities.

In his book, however, Boykin argues that the act of men secretly having sex with men has existed within African American history for decades (35). He states that they have always been there but they were never talked about because homosexuality was not to be discussed due to homophobia (30). The first mainstream media account of men on the down low was on February 7, 2001, in the *Los Angeles Times*, in which the article connected this population to the HIV/AIDS epidemic in the African American community and described them as men who cheat on their girlfriends and wives with men (Wikipedia 2005). This created a negative stereotype and stigma around this population, which made them a scapegoat for the spread of HIV/AIDS.

With the upsurge of the HIV/AIDS epidemic, black gay poets, writers, artists, and filmmakers told the public about the culture that predated the term "down low." However, by 1999 almost all the top black gay figures—Joe Beam, Melvin Dixon, Craig Harris, Essex Hemphill, and Assotto Saint—died of AIDS-related complications (Boykin 2005, 35). Fortunately, new gay black writers are emerging, writing stories, and creating films about

African Americans and sexuality that address the down low phenomenon. The following sections of my paper will address the works of African American writers and filmmakers who acknowledge the down low culture and attempt to educate the greater public about this unique population.

Book: *B-boy Blues*—A Trapped Syndrome or an Acceptable Way of Life?

The book I read for this project is entitled *B-boy Blues* by James Earl Hardy (1994). Although it is not a biography, it offers a realistic story of an African American man on the down low.

B-boy Blues is a love story between Mitchell Crawford, a 27-year-old African American gay man, and Raheim Rivers, an African American B-boy. In this book, B-boys are similar to men on the down low. They are very hyper-masculine men who maintain a heterosexual status among everyday society but still sleep with men (27). Hardy writes, "For many Black heterosexuals . . . there is no such thing as a homosexual, so most would faint if you were to even suggest that a B-boy could be gay" (27). Since homosexuality is still an unmentionable topic in most African American households and churches, many men who have sexual attractions toward other men remain tacit and supposedly heterosexual, and adopt the B-boy stance (28–29). These descriptions of a B-boy illustrate the constant inner struggle a man on the down low endures because of discrimination and homophobia from the African American community.

However, one of the characters in this book, a friend of Mitchell, refers to B-boys as trapped in a syndrome of self-acceptance. He thinks that they are denying their sexuality and yielding to the greater dominant mentality of society.

Raheim, the quintessential B-boy, on the other hand, revels in his hyper-masculinity while admonishing the dominant white gay culture. He believes that by claiming a gay identity, a person concedes to a white identity because most men in the visible gay community are white. It is interesting to note that although Raheim acts very heterosexual and lets strangers assume that he is, he is very open about his love for Mitchell. In addition, Raheim does not mind the company of very effeminate men because Mitchell is a feminine gay man in this book.

In terms of the B-boy identity, Mitchell thinks, "For African Americans, it has been a question of oppression; for homosexuals of all colors and strides, it has been repression" (114). In other words, while the dominant white group within society has oppressed the overall African American community, African American homosexuals have to repress their homosexual identity and behaviors from the African American community, which spawns the down low or B-boy identity. Needless to say, racism and homophobia play integral roles in the formulation of the down low community.

Film: *Tongues Untied*—Is Silence the Perfect Weapon?

Tongues Untied (Riggs 1991) is as much about racism as it is about homophobia within the African American down low community. Unlike Raheim in *B-boy Blues*, the characters depicted in this avant-garde film are not at all open about their sexuality. In fact, they struggle with it both internally and in public.

In the opening scene, there are images of very heterosexual scenes in public areas: masculine and strapping African American men playing basketball, men gazing at women as they walk by, and men giving each other high-fives.

The next scene involves a poem that depicts a merchant who denies an African American customer service because of the color of his skin. From the very beginning, this film, which targets the gay/bisexual/down low African American community, focuses on racism because racism is still a relevant issue for them. This issue echoes Raheim's beliefs, which reject the dominant gay white community because of the racism that exists within it.

In contrast to the public scenes that are introduced in the beginning of the film, a very private scene is shown later that portrays a masculine African American man engaged in interpretive dance, a very stereotypically feminine activity. Again, it contrasts the opening scene of African American men playing basketball. While the movie focuses on this dancer, a voice in the background repeatedly states, "Silence is my shield. Silence is my sword. Silence is the deadliest weapon." At the end of this scene, the man dancing is met by another African American man, and they embrace.

This profound scene offers a glimpse of the struggle that an African American man on the down low might experience. "Silence" is obviously a method most African American men use on the down low to cope with discrimination. Unfortunately, they compromise a part of their identity and have to maintain a secret lifestyle in order to avoid stigma and discrimination.

Lastly, there is an anecdotal scene of a man on the down low who recognizes another man on the down low from a gay club earlier that week. He states:

> I recognize him walking down Castro. But at the moment that we are supposed to look deep into each others' eyes, he studies the intricate, detailed architecture of a building and I check my white sneakers for any scuff marks. What is it that we see in each other that we avert our eyes that we turn away from each other not to see our collective anger and sadness? (*Tongues Untied* 1989)

This scene depicts the reservations that men on the down low have when seeing someone in public who is associated with the gay community. They are so concerned with hiding their attraction for men that they cannot even acknowledge someone they may have met or recognized at a gay-related event or location.

Cultural Event: The Lion That Roars— Do They Really Exist? Invisibility and Ambiguity Ensue

The event I attended is a weekly event for some African American men on the down low at a sports bar a coworker suggested called

The Lion That Roars. The AIDS Project, for which I am interning, does a special outreach to The Lion That Roars to promote safe sex practices. Therefore, two very valid and reliable sources were able to confirm that African American men on the down low do frequent this particular bar.

I was very apprehensive when I first walked in. I knew that I would stand out because of my difference in race and sexual identity. So, I prepared myself to be ostracized. From the outside, a person would not assume that this sports bar was a location that facilitated down low activity. As I walked inside, one of the first things I noticed was the plethora of sports memorabilia prominently displayed all over the walls. From framed jerseys to signed photographs of famous sports players to mounted baseball bats and balls, this was definitely a venue that catered to sports-minded individuals, who are usually thought to be heterosexual men.

The bar was very crowded and consisted of mostly African American men who appeared stereotypically heterosexual. There were a few women scattered around the bar who were also African American. I saw one Latino man and one white woman. I was the only Filipino American. In fact, nobody else in the bar looked even remotely Asian or Pacific Islander. Furthermore, no one else in the entire venue looked like a gay man or a lesbian. I think I was the only openly gay person in the entire place, which may have been obvious to some of the patrons. I did observe one man gazing at other men in the bar. However, I have no idea if this man was sexually interested in the men or if he was just interested in what they were doing or what they were talking about. Again, the conundrum of not wanting to be identified or perceived as gay among this population makes it difficult to identify a person from this population.

Additionally, the mere fact that I was not African American, almost instantaneously garnered a number of stares in my direction. I sat on a bar stool at a small table by the wall and during the hour I spent observing, no one ever approached me. Their stares made it

clear, though: I was different, and I did not belong. I am sure their stares demonstrated curiosity rather than hostility, because no one behaved in any overly aggressive manner toward me. However, if some of the men who were staring at me were in fact men on the down low, and they sensed that I was gay, they could have been staring at me because they were interested in me sexually or because they were threatened by my presence. That is to say, because I am an openly gay male in down low territory, I could threaten their perceived heterosexual status if I were to talk to them. Therefore, men on the down low might not feel comfortable in my presence because I could be sullying their efforts at maintaining a "straight" identity in public.

I did not react to these stares at all. I did not feel that I was in any dangerous situation, and I did not want to place myself in danger by reacting impetuously to stares from others. In retrospect, I am glad that I was able to walk through the doors and sit at a table at the The Lion That Roars because the experience illustrated what I had read about in *Beyond the Down Low* (Boykin 2005) and watched in *Tongues Untied* (Riggs 1991).

Two concepts that came out of this experience were *invisibility* and *ambiguity*. Without a doubt, men on the down low are a highly invisible population. There is nothing in their actions or clothes that indicate that they are from this population. They want to preserve their heterosexual identity among their heterosexual community, thereby maintaining their invisibility.

In addition, these men are ambiguous because they share characteristics that are both typically gay and straight. They like to behave and blend in with their heterosexual African American peers, but at the same time, have sex with men like gay men.

Interview: Niko—A Man on the Down Low. Or Is He?

Finding an African American man on the down low to interview posed a very complicated task. Obviously, I could not just approach a person and ask him if he is on the down low because if he were, he would most likely not admit it to me. Secondly, it would be offensive if I asked someone based on my stereotype of what an African American man on the down low looks like. So, as suggested by a colleague at my field placement, I placed an advertisement on a website (www.downelink.com) that some men on the down low utilize to meet other men for sex. Surprisingly, I received a response within five minutes.

I viewed Niko's online personal profile, which had no picture and stated "not sure" under his sexual orientation. My interview with him was conducted through an instant messenger program that allows individuals to communicate online through messages typed over the computer.

Niko had an interesting perspective as a member of the down low community. He stated that the only reason why he associated himself with the term is because his few gay friends label him as such. His definition of a person on the down low is a "guy's guy not really personifying the whole gay stereotype," but his friends think that a man on the down low is a gay man who hides his sexuality from others. Niko stated that he would rather hang out with men who "act straight" because feminine men are "odd." He described stereotypical gay men as immature and unappealing. Paradoxically, Niko attends exclusively gay events such as bars and clubs weekly, locations where very effeminate gay men have a large visible presence.

Niko is attracted to both men and women, but has only had long-term relationships with women. He mentioned that he attempted to have a relationship with a man once, but it did not prosper for undisclosed reasons. The only people who know he is attracted to men are his four gay male friends. Even when he is in a relationship with a woman, he does not inform her of his attraction for men. However, he disdains infidelity and does not cheat on anyone he dates, regardless of gender.

Divulging his attraction for men to his close friends and family members did not seem like an issue for him. He does not believe that he is hiding these feelings from them, but rather, he is not bringing it to their attention because his sexuality should not be a huge concern for them.

Not like the aforementioned African American men on the down low, Niko states that he is not a typical masculine, "hip hop thuggy" type of person. He describes himself as stylish and states that his style in clothes has triggered homophobic attitudes from some of his heterosexual friends and family members. However, he will still not reveal his attraction for other men to them.

Reflection and Synthesis

After reviewing my notes from the book, film, cultural event, and interview, I have realized that there is a continuum of different types of African American men on the down low. In *Beyond the Down Low* (2005) Boykin mentions reports of men on the down low who have very diverse lifestyles and sexual identities. Furthermore, Raheim from *B-boy Blues*, who may act hyper-masculine, is not ashamed to admit that he is attracted to men, unlike the men portrayed in *Tongues Untied* and Niko, my interviewee. However, Niko does not feel like he is hiding anything about his sexuality; he justifies not telling others about his attraction for men by stating that it is because his sexuality is not his defining characteristic. Moreover, the men on the down low featured in *Tongues Untied* (Riggs 1991) make a conscious effort to hide their attraction for other men and remain utterly silent, even amongst themselves. Therefore, a continuum of hiding one's attraction to the same sex would seem to exist among African American men on the down low.

I also noticed that men on the down low are not all typically hyper-masculine individuals; Niko stated that he is not very masculine and that looking masculine is not a priority when deciding on what clothes to wear because he is more concerned with style.

Lastly, the stereotype of all African American men on the down low being HIV/AIDS positive and cheaters who only have sex with men (as opposed to having a long-term relationship with them) has proven to be false by Niko, who is HIV/AIDS negative, has clearly stated that he does not cheat on anyone he dates, and has attempted to date a man before. Stereotypes, especially those that are negative, need to be demystified because they perpetuate negative preconceived notions of anyone associated with this population, which foster counterproductive social work practice.

In addition to deconstructing stereotypes, I was also able to identify particularly important issues for this population, which have greatly enhanced my understanding and will certainly assist me in helping African American men on the down low in my future career. Racism, homophobia, internalized homophobia, invisibility, and ambiguity are all issues that resonate with this population. I have to be cognizant of these concepts in order to develop and provide culturally congruent services to the African American down low population. Keeping these issues in mind while still being aware of the major individual differences within the population will facilitate and foster culturally competent practice as a social work professional specifically assisting queer youths of color.

Applying the Knowledge Base: Assessing Agency, Programs and Services, and Personal Cultural Competencies

My field placement, a county department of AIDS within the public sector, provides funding for several hospitals, agencies, and community-based organizations that provide HIV/AIDS services. Although my agency does not offer any direct services, we serve people living with HIV/AIDS by directly assisting those organizations that do. Furthermore, after the Department of AIDS has allocated the money to these contracted agencies, program managers monitor the services of these agencies to ensure that they are culturally competent, effective, and meeting the needs of people living with HIV/AIDS.

Agency

Community The mission of the Department of AIDS is to work in partnership with the community to prevent the spread of HIV/AIDS and to improve the quality of life for those living with and impacted by the disease (***County Public Health Department 2006). Although it is not clearly stated in the mission that the Department of AIDS is culturally competent and aware of diversity, a diverse clientele is served, including but not limited to the African American, Asian and Pacific Islander, Latino, caucasian, gay, transgender, men on the down low, and documented and undocumented immigrant communities.

Although the county's population is very diverse, a significant number of recipients of HIV/AIDS services are African American men who have sex with men (MSM), which includes men on the down low. In 2000, MSM accounted for a little less than half of all new AIDS cases and accounted for most of the newly diagnosed AIDS cases. Furthermore, most of the MSM cases live in the county's major urban center (***Department of AIDS 2002). It is almost impossible to discern how many of those MSM are men on the down low, but it is assumed that a significant number of those men do not identify as gay, and therefore, would fit the description of a man on the down low.

Access If a recipient of HIV/AIDS services has a complaint about an agency that is contracted with the Department of AIDS, the recipient might come to our office, which is conveniently located in the downtown area of the city, a city that is considered an emergency metropolitan area (EMA) for HIV/AIDS because there are so many residents who are infected with the disease. Most of the clients that receive HIV/AIDS services live in the city and do not have to travel far to visit the agency. Public transportation is readily available directly outside the agency.

As the city is a very diverse space, an African American man on the down low should not feel alienated or out of place when coming to the Department of AIDS, especially because it is a heteronormative environment and men on the down low prefer to behave in a typically heterosexual manner.

Also, for African American men on the down low who have physical disabilities, the building where the Department of AIDS is located is compliant with the 1990 Americans with Disabilities Act (ADA).

Receptivity The agency is very receptive to the needs of African American men on the down low who are living with HIV/AIDS. The staff reflects the client population: there is a representation of African American employees, Filipino employees, a self-identified gay male, and a self-identified bisexual male. It is unknown whether any of the employees at the Department of AIDS is a person living with HIV/AIDS or is on the down low.

The waiting room is very welcoming; there are magazines laid out on the table that cater to the African American and gay, lesbian, and bisexual communities. In addition, there are several pamphlets and informational guides about HIV/AIDS prevention and treatment that target men on the down low, African American men and women, Latino men and women, gay men, and transgender individuals. There are a number of pamphlets that are in Spanish or both Spanish and English.

Administration and Staff Training The Public Health Department offers free workshops on diversity at least once a year for all public health employees. These trainings address culturally sensitive methods for interacting with people of color, the LGBT community, people with disabilities, and people who have severe illnesses such as HIV/AIDS.

Planning council meetings are held to hear public comments, decide what services will be funded, and determine policies related to HIV/AIDS services, and many cultural topics come up regularly. For example, three monolingual Spanish speakers attended a planning council meeting with an interpreter to plea to the council that the monolingual Spanish speaking community is not receiving any HIV/AIDS care because not enough agencies in the area have translation services. As a result of the visit, the planning council expanded funds for translation services in all agencies contracted with the Department of AIDS. If an African American man on the down low were to do the same thing, then services that cater to a person from that population would receive the same receptiveness. However, African American men on the down low would probably be uncomfortable in an advocacy role. Overall, cultural competent practices are a popular topic because HIV/AIDS affects many minority groups so the Department of AIDS ensures that all of these groups are receiving the appropriate care and treatment.

Staff Sensitivity From direct observation of the staff, I have noticed that some staff members are in need of cultural competence and sensitivity training. Although all of these employees clearly have the ability to be culturally sensitive when interacting with a client, they seem to lose this when they interact with each other. The receptionist is homophobic, and one program manager who is not African American mimics stereotypically African American sayings in an effort to be funny. In addition, the racial minority employees tend to ostracize the one white person working in the office. In spite of this behavior among employees, when they encounter a client who is gay, transgender, or an African American man on the down low, they all offer to utilize their culturally sensitive and competent skills.

Few if any employees have attended a diversity training, although they are required to attend one after being hired; if they have attended, it has only been one time. In addition, there are policies that protect employees from discrimination and harassment based on gender, race, sexual orientation, etc. (***Department of AIDS Administration 2002). In conclusion, I personally believe that the Department of AIDS staff should be required to attend a cultural competence and sensitivity training, and that this requirement should be enforced. I have shared my opinions with my supervisor as well as the other employees. Some of them agree with me.

Funding The Department of AIDS receives funding from the federal government (Health Resources and Service Administration and Ryan White Comprehensive AIDS Resources Emergency Act), the state, and the local county government through the Public Health Department. These three sources of funding total over $11 million every fiscal year (***Department of AIDS Administration 2005). Though this may seem to be a large sum, it is actually not enough to provide services for HIV/AIDS-positive clients. Firstly, medication for people living with HIV/AIDS is very expensive, so a large sum of money is allocated for this purpose. Secondly, this is geographically a large county, and has a population of 1.5 million people (***Department of AIDS Administration 2004). Since the 1980s when the HIV/AIDS epidemic hit, there has been a cumulative total of over 6,500 AIDS cases in this county (***Department of AIDS 2005). The sheer number of people that need services overwhelms the allocated funding. Thirdly, the amount of dollars granted from the federal government has decreased over the years. Factors that may account for this include the quality of the grant proposal, the quality of data collection/needs assessment that contracted agencies conduct, and the politics of the administration that oversaw the renewal for HIV/AIDS funding.

Despite the lack in funding, the Department of AIDS tries its best to provide cultural variations of services. For example, the Department of AIDS extensively funds agencies that target men on the down low, also known as men who have sex with men (MSM), and intravenous drug users (IDU) who are usually from low-income backgrounds.

Programs and Services

Effort The Department of AIDS does make an effort to be sensitive and aware of cultural differences for recipients of HIV/AIDS services. In order for agencies to receive funding from our office, they must sign a nondiscrimination contract: marginalized populations such as men on the down low or racial minorities will not be denied services. Furthermore, program managers conducting site visits to ensure the quality of care evaluate the agency's effort to both increase diversity within the working environment and be culturally competent for different groups that may seek HIV/AIDS services.

Quality During the site visits, the program manager inquires whether contracted agencies have a staff that reflects the service population. The program manager encourages executive directors to increase diversity among staff, and to participate in cultural competence trainings that are sometimes offered at the Department of AIDS for contracted agencies.

Another method to ensure that African American men on the down low are being served appropriately is client satisfaction surveys, which program managers of the Department of AIDS also examine during site visits. If there are grievances from a particular group of clients, or if there are claims that the agency staff has acted in a discriminatory way, the Department of AIDS will investigate.

Furthermore, the Department of AIDS tries its best to reach out to minority groups through funding for services. Many of the programs that are funded for prevention target the African American men on the down low population, which include outreach teams that venture into down low territory and sensitivity trainings toward men on the down low.

Effectiveness Clients appear to effectively use services offered them. One contracted agency holds a weekly support group for HIV/AIDS-positive men who have sex with men, which includes men on the down low. A Case Manager for that agency stated that attendance is high every week and clients are taking full advantage of the emotional support, food services, and transportation services that are offered to people living with HIV/AIDS. A therapist from another contracted agency providing mental health services for men who have sex with men stated that they have a consistent full load of clients who come in for therapy sessions. It appears that most of the clients are satisfied with the services. If they are not, then they could come to the Department of AIDS or a planning council meeting to complain. That has not happened during my time with the Department of AIDS.

However, it is still unclear whether men on the down low are utilizing services in proportion to their numbers in the population at large. Without a doubt, there are men on the down low who do not want to receive services from an agency that provides HIV/AIDS services because HIV/AIDS is closely associated with the gay community, which is often viewed negatively. These men may not be receiving services through the contracted agencies.

Efficiency The Department of AIDS certainly attempts to reach out to the African American down low community. In order to get African American men on the down low interested in getting tested for HIV/AIDS and receiving services, the Department of AIDS has come up with novel and innovative ideas for outreach. The department is working with local community-based organizations that serve the African American down low community on a social marketing campaign to attract this population and encourage them to consider their HIV/AIDS status. There are tentative plans to have billboards promoting safe sex strategically placed in areas where men on the down low meet for sex. In addition, in the summer of 2006, a community event addressed HIV/AIDS topics and prevention in the African American community. The committee working on this project attempted to get Keith Boykin, the author of *Beyond the Down Low* (2005), as well as other black leaders to talk about the epidemic in a social context. By attracting men on the down low, this event was designed to urge them to think about their sexual practices and HIV/AIDS, and offered resources for health services. Also, many of the organizations contracted with the Department of AIDS specifically target the African American community, the LGBT community, and men on the down low.

Personal Cultural Competencies

Engagement, Trust, and Relationship-building
In general, African American men on the down low do not seek out HIV/AIDS services, as they do not want to be associated with the gay community. There is a resistance to accessing HIV/AIDS services through agencies associated with the LGBT community. Therefore, contracted agencies must make extensive and culturally sensitive outreach efforts in order to make HIV/AIDS services available to this population. One of the difficulties in outreach to this population for service providers is the difficulties associated with determining membership in the down low population. Most men on the down low will not admit to having sex with men and will refuse services if a service provider approaches them with an HIV test.

If a social worker has an African American client who may be secretly having sex with other men, the social worker must not make any assumptions about the client's sexual orientation or sexual identity. Instead, the social worker should explore the client's sexual practices without judgment and not define his behaviors with a sexual label (i.e., gay, straight, bisexual, etc.). Furthermore, the focus of the conversation should not be on the *identity*, but rather on the *behavior*. The social worker should assist the client to consider his actions and how they might positively and negatively affect the people around him. For example, if the client states that he is not using a condom when having sex with his wife and with these other men, the social worker should address how diseases are spread and the consequences of unprotected sex.

Also, a social worker should avoid discussing LGBT-related issues because men on the down low do not want to be associated with LGBT populations, preferring to claim a heterosexual identity and blend in with the rest of the dominant society. The social worker should not even suggest that the person on the down low is secretly sleeping with men. Once the client on the down low admits to the social worker that he is having sex with other men and the social worker reacts positively and states that he or she appreciates the disclosed information, the client and social worker can start to build a healthy and beneficial working relationship.

Assessment and Problem Definition Two tools that would be especially helpful with a person from this population are the ethnographic interviewing tool and an understanding of the cyclic effects of racism and sexism. The global questions for ethnographic interviewing described by James Leigh in *Communicating for Cultural Competence* (1998, 77–88) suggest ways in which the social worker can address the issues and concerns that the client is experiencing from his perspective. For men on the down low, this perspective is essential to understanding the challenges of a person who is experiencing inner struggles about identity, while being simultaneously faced with discrimination from the dominant society. This interviewing tool will help make the African American down low's perspective about problems and issues clear to the social worker.

The other tool that could be used in working with an African American man on the down low is an understanding of the cyclic effects of racism and sexism. Men on the down low experience racism, and simultaneously perpetuate sexist values by deliberately behaving in hyper-masculine ways. Assessment might assist the client and worker to understand the complex interplay between racism and sexism as each person experiences it. Considering the role that the external environment has had in shaping ideas and beliefs can assist the client on the down low to explore identity and social role issues in greater depth.

Contracting and Goal Setting Competent and empowering social work practice suggests that the worker must meet the client where she or he is. For contracting and goal setting, it is important to encourage the client to take the lead in framing and developing a plan of intervention. Addressing identity issues, HIV/AIDS testing, and other concerns that relate to being on the down low should be done in the language and with the time frame that the client determines. Rushing to address these sensitive issues may destroy trust and the initial relationship, and the client may even terminate contact with the social worker.

It is also essential to recognize that being on the down low may, or may not be, a central issue for the client that needs to be addressed during the course of services. It would be culturally insensitive to assume that the reason the client has come for services is primarily related to his identity and feelings about being on the down low. Goals should also consider the client's cultural background and values.

Interventions Interventions for men on the down low should be culturally appropriate. Because men on the down low are secretive, interventions that do not impact their public identities, or reveal their status, should be implemented first. Both the client and the service provider should work together to decide the most beneficial and appropriate types of interventions.

If this appears appropriate to the client's situation and needs, the social worker might refer an African American man on the down low to a support group for African American men on the down low. Engaging with this support network can be helpful in working through some of the issues that are often faced by men on the down low. However, the social worker should be sensitive to privacy and secrecy issues when offering these services.

Evaluation and Termination Failure or success must be interpreted by the client, and is, of course, based on the achievement of the goals which the client has set. The same behaviors can constitute success or failure for different clients. For some clients, coping with the issue that brought the client to the agency for services, while maintaining privacy and secrecy about being on the down low, means success; for others, it means failure to confront identity issues and to be open with personal relationships. For some clients, being tested for HIV/AIDS through a clinic means success; for others, achieving the goal of being tested while avoiding any exposure to others constitutes success. For some, maintaining a heterosexual identity means success; for others, resolving the inner confusion and conflict means success. Because the social worker also makes judgements and assumptions about what constitutes success and failure, it is important to ensure that the client's criteria for success, rather than the social worker's, are paramount.

It is also important to understand that not all clients will want to make a commitment to inner change, or perceive that as a desirable goal. For men on the down low, the elimination of symptoms may also constitute success.

It is impossible to know what the termination process would be like for an African American man on the down low because there is a lot of diversity within this population. However, I would suggest that the social worker process the termination with the client and review what the client has learned from their sessions. Also, the social worker should not be offended if an African American man on the down low does not express any gratitude or appreciation for the services, because African American men tend to behave in stereotypically hyper-masculine ways, which often translates as a lack of expressed emotions.

Evaluation Using NASW's Standards for Cultural Competence: Standard #4: Cross-Cultural Skills

The Agency The Department of AIDS does have a strong commitment to utilizing cross-cultural skills in its work with clients. Although it often does not seem to utilize these skills in its interactions among its staff, it certainly utilizes the skills with clients such as African American men on the down low. The county tries its best to support vulnerable groups that the HIV/AIDS epidemic has hit hardest: most of those groups are associated with the LGBT population and racial minorities. Although African American men on the down low resist association with the LGBT community, outreach efforts and sensitivity clearly include this population.

Programs Cross-cultural skills are definitely used through programs of community-based organizations that are contracted with the Department of AIDS. Programs that target and support African American men on the down low include support groups, outreach at venues where men on the down low meet for sex, and trainings that address the sensitive issues that African American men on the down low experience. Therefore, the individuals providing these services learn the skills and techniques needed to effectively assist this population with coping with HIV/AIDS.

Personal Competence With the knowledge I am gaining in my graduate social work program, and the skills I am learning at the Department of AIDS, I have developed my own set of cross-cultural skills to assist clients from many different backgrounds and cultures, including African American men on the down low. Although I feel confident that I can be culturally aware and sensitive to the needs of an African American man on the down low, I am still cognizant of the fact that being culturally competent is a process that takes years to learn. Therefore, I continue to strive for the knowledge and skill that will assist me in becoming a competent professional who is able to help others from diverse and vulnerable groups.

REFERENCES

Boykin, K. 2005. *Beyond the Down Low*. New York: Carroll & Graf Publishers.

*** County Health Department website, 2006.

*** Department of AIDS Administration. 2002. Employee manual.

*** Department of AIDS Administration. 2005. Total budget listing FY 2005–2006.

*** Department of AIDS Administration Official Website. 2004.

*** Department of AIDS. 2002. AIDS in *** County-The epidemic from 1980 to 2000.

*** Department of AIDS. 2005. HIV/AIDS Epidemiology Annual Report.

Hardy, J.E. 1994. *B-boy Blues*. Los Angeles: Alyson Publications Inc.

Leigh, J. 1998. *Communicating for Cultural Competence*. Prospect Heights, IL: Waveland Press.

Riggs, M.T. (director). 1991. *Tongues Untied*. [documentary]. United States: MRT Productions.

Wikipedia 2006. http://en.wikipedia.org/wiki/Down_low

Worksheet

1. As the author notes, the effects of racism and sexism, and the complex ways in which the two can be related for members of this population, are essential issues to explore in order to gain an understanding of African American men on the down low. What are some of the commonalities between racism and sexism? What are some of the differences? How do you see the two interfacing in African American men on the down low?

2. Because some African American men on the down low are married, their behavior can also impact their wives. What are some of the possible effects on these women? If you were developing a program at your family services agency for these wives, what kinds of outreach might be effective in reaching this population?

10 Cultural Competence with People with Disabilities

Culturally Competent Social Work Practice with Deaf People

Diversity Project by Allison Reid-Cunningham

My field placement is an out-patient hospital clinic that serves children and families who have experienced trauma. I have always been interested in deafness and in D/deaf culture, but I have not been aware of a single deaf or hard-of-hearing client or family coming for services at my agency. Because hard-of-hearing and deaf children may also have experienced trauma, I wanted to explore my agency's interaction with the deaf community, and cultural competence issues in relation to that community. I have elected to explore deafness and D/deaf culture in order to better understand possible issues in accessing and utilizing agency services for this community.

People who have profound hearing loss are considered to be deaf,[1] while to those who have some hearing, and are able to use it for communication purposes may be called "hard of hearing" (National Association of the Deaf,

NAD 2006). Most people use the terms "deaf," "Deaf," or "hard of hearing" to identify themselves (NAD 2006). The labels "deaf-mute" and "deaf-dumb" are antiquated and demeaning, and the phrase "hearing impaired" may offend D/deaf people who do not consider themselves "impaired" (Kisor 1990; NAD 2006). Many factors may contribute to the development of deafness, including genetics, diseases, infections, fevers, noise exposure, head trauma, prenatal drugs/alcohol exposure, aging, and medications (Lazorisak and Donohue 2004, 7; Padden and Humphries 2005; NAD 2006). There is considerable speculation with regard to the cause and degree of hearing loss, age at onset, educational background, race and ethnicity, socioeconomic standing, sexual orientation, family of origin, communication methods, identity affiliations, community loyalty, and feelings about hearing loss (Padden

---

[1]When capitalized, "Deaf" refers to members of Deaf Culture, while "deaf" refers to the physical condition of not hearing, or people who do not hear and do not identify with Deaf Culture. The term "d/Deaf" indicates groups of both deaf and Deaf people, or people of unknown Deaf cultural affiliation.

and Humphries 2005; Paris and Drolsbaugh 2001; NAD 2006). These differences may influence the level of connectedness that individuals feel toward the hearing and D/deaf communities.

Approximately .1 percent of the world's population is deaf, but there is considerable regional variance (Gallaudet 2006a). The U.S. Census does not ask specifically about deafness, so there is no precise measure of the number of D/deaf and hard-of-hearing Americans, but there are some estimates. There are approximately 1,000,000 Americans who are functionally deaf and 10,000,000 who are hard of hearing (Gallaudet 2006b). It is estimated that there are 45,000 to 50,000 Americans who are both deaf and blind (Mitchell 2005). Although the majority of the deaf population are older adults, Gallaudet University (2006d) reports that approximately 968,000 American children age 3 to 17 are deaf. An estimated 90,948 Californians are deaf and 1,078,325 are hard of hearing (Gallaudet 2006c).

KNOWLEDGE OF POPULATION: POPULATION IMMERSION EXPERIENCE

History

Timeline In order to understand the history of deafness, deaf people, and D/deaf culture, it is helpful to be aware of a timeline that extends from ancient times to the present day. This timeline highlights some of the major events in the development of D/deaf culture as it exists in the United States today.

Selected Deaf History[2]

427–322 B.C.: Plato and Aristotle condemn deaf people as being incapable of learning.

476–1453 A.D.: Deaf people barred from churches because they cannot hear the word of God.

1620: Juan Pablo de Bonet publishes the first manual alphabet for the deaf.

1755: Abbe Charles Michael de L'Epee in France establishes the first free school for the deaf.

1727–1790: Samuel Heinicke establishes the Oral method and vehemently opposes sign language.

1817: Laurent Clerc and Thomas H. Gallaudet establish the first school for the deaf in the United States.

1820: New York and Pennsylvania Institutions for the Deaf and Dumb open.

1865: The National Deaf-Mute College (later Gallaudet University) grants college degrees.

1868: California School for the Deaf established in Berkeley (the first school for deaf in California).

1872: Alexander Graham Bell opens school for educators of deaf in Boston, promoting oral methods.

1880: National Association of the Deaf (NAD) is founded.

1887: First Deaf women admitted to the National Deaf-Mute College.

1898: Miller Reese Hutchinson invents first hearing aid.

1902: Thomas Edison produces a film of a deaf woman signing "The Star Spangled Banner."

1904: Helen Keller, deaf and blind, graduates (cum laude) from Radcliffe.

1941–5: World War II. Deaf Americans readily employed in factories; deaf in Nazi areas were persecuted and exterminated along with others.

1951: World Federation of the Deaf founded in Rome, Italy.

1960s: Telephone Teletypes (TTY)/Telecommunication Device for the Deaf (TDD) proliferated.

[2]ASL 2006, Cohen 1994, Gannon (1980), Kisor 1990, Lazorisak and Donahue 2004, Padden and Humphries 2005, Ruben 2005.

1967: National Theater of the Deaf is established.

1971: First Captioned Television Commercial broadcast in Boston, Massachusetts.

1985: Cochlear implants approved for clinical trials on people over 18.

1986: Deaf actress Marlee Matlin wins an Oscar for *Children of a Lesser God*.

1988: I. King Jordan named first Deaf President of Gallaudet University after student body protests.

1990: Americans with Disabilities Act passed by Congress, prohibits discrimination on the basis of disability.

1990: U.S.-produced television sets require a decoder to provide closed captioning.

1992: Americans with Disabilities Act implemented.

1995: Heather Whitmore, an orally educated deaf woman, is crowned Miss America.

2000: National Association of the Deaf takes moderate stance on cochlear implants for children.

Sign Languages Sign languages have been called the natural languages of deaf people (Lazorisak and Donohue 2004). Sign languages use visual and spatial strategies to communicate nuanced ideas. They are fully developed linguistic systems with syntax, grammar, accents, and regional variations (Goldin-Meadow and Mylander 1998; Paris and Drolsbaugh 2001; Weisberg and Aronson 2000). Sign languages are not mimed, broken, or gestured forms of spoken languages. Signs represent concepts, not individual words in spoken languages (Goldin-Meadow and Mylander 1998).[3] Sign languages follow unique syntax, natural to native users, and quite different from spoken languages.

There are many sign language systems, and all people who sign cannot communicate with each other, just like hearing people cannot communicate with each other if they speak different languages. Some examples include British, Kenyan, Irish, French, Armenian, South African, Chinese, Cuban, and American Sign Languages.

American Sign Language (ASL) is the most commonly used sign language worldwide. It is the third most commonly used language in the United States, following English and Spanish (Lazorisak and Donohue 2004; Padden and Humphries 2005; NAD 2006). One-half million Deaf people in the United States and Canada communicate using ASL (ASL 2006; Lazorisak and Donohue 2004).

Deaf Culture The National Association of Social Workers (NASW 2001) describes culture as implying an "integrated pattern of human behavior," including thoughts, communications, actions, customs, beliefs, values, and institutions," that are shared and passed down within a group (9). The traditional conceptual framework for deafness is to consider it a deficit, but there is a cultural framework in which deafness is not a disability. It is a way of interfacing with the world through a visual culture and language (ASL 2006; Breivik 2005; Padden and Humphries 2005).

Many D/deaf people feel grateful to be part of a Deaf Culture and they do not consider themselves disabled at all (Bauman 2005; Padden and Humphries 2005; Paris and Drolsbaugh 2001; Weisberg and Aronson 2000). Some Deaf people say that hearing people are "deaf impaired," and to be called "hearing" can be an insult (Padden and Humphries 2005). Not all deaf people support Deaf Culture, and the idea of Deafness as a culture has created controversy in the D/deaf and hearing communities (ASL 2006).

During the 1970s and 1980s, American Sign Language (ASL) received public recognition, and "the idea of a language and a culture promised a great deal" for deaf people (Padden and Humphries 2005, 131; Breivik 2005). This was a pivotal moment in cementing the foundation for Deaf culture, because "the realization that sign languages were

---

[3]Signed English (SE) uses standard English grammar with one sign per word. SE may be perceived as an attempt to assimilate Deaf culture, but it may make signing more accessible to hearing people.

equal to, yet uniquely interesting among, human languages brought to D/deaf people a sense of vindication and pride" (Padden and Humphries 2005, 157).

The idea of Deaf culture brought about a new way for D/deaf people to be defined. In the past, deaf people had been defined by the degree of hearing loss, and whether they could hear at birth, but now there is a cultural framework that may be useful in thinking about one's identity as a D/deaf person (Padden and Humphries 2005). Deaf culture is proliferated through the use of a common language, common learning and life experiences, community contacts with D/deaf people, D/deaf clubs, schools, or societies, and shared experiences of oppression and marginalization as a minority group in society (Lazorisak and Donohue 2004; Padden and Humphries 2005).

Autobiographies and Other Literature: *What's That Pig Outdoors, A Loss for Words, Train Go Sorry, Deaf Child Crossing, Deaf Espirit,* and *Deaf Culture: Our Way*

In my quest for books by and about D/deaf people, I went to a Deaf community center in the East Bay called DCARA (Deaf Counseling Advocacy and Referral Agency). I panicked when someone signed *hello,* realizing that I really need to learn how to say, "I only sign a little." I communicated by rough signs and mouthing the words, as well as writing down the names of some books. I felt more uncomfortable than I anticipated at the community center, because I felt like an outsider. I found a lot of books written by hearing people about Deaf people, and very few books by Deaf people about themselves. Padden and Humphries (2005) refer to this as the "tradition of writing about Deaf people as *objects* of description, but not as *masters* of their own description" (8). I wanted to avoid depending on hearing people's accounts of Deaf life.

First, I read *A Loss for Words,* Lou Ann Walker's story of growing up a hearing child with Deaf parents who depended on her too much at an early age. I quickly moved on to *Train Go Sorry,* Leah Hager Cohen's memoir

of growing up among D/deaf children at the famous Lexington School for the Deaf; later she would become Deaf too. Her insights into the D/deaf community and the miscommunications between hearing and D/deaf people were helpful to me in preparing for the cultural immersion experience, but I was still searching for a first-person Deaf narrative. I read *Deaf Child Crossing,* Marlee Matlin's novel loosely based on her childhood experiences. It was compelling, but it was aimed at a young adult audience, and failed to address the complicated identity issues I hoped to explore.

I came across two books that provided a smattering of Deaf voices, in the form of anecdotes, poems, and short essays: *Deaf Esprit;* (Paris and Drolsbaugh 2001) and *Deaf Culture: Our Way* (Holcomb et al. 1994). These collections introduced me to the diversity within the D/deaf community, and showed me that there was considerably more variety within it than I had imagined. *Deaf Culture: Our Way* described situations that could plague any D/deaf American, and which would probably never happen to a hearing person (such as getting stuck in an elevator with no TTY). The book is full of misunderstandings, mishaps, and missed opportunities, told with humor and lightheartedness. *Deaf Esprit* gave me insight into the level of importance or prominence that deafness plays in individuals' lives, and helped me to explore issues of identity and community. Reading these two books gave me more of a sense for the people and subgroups that make up D/deaf communities.

I discovered Henry Kisor's autobiography *What's That Pig Outdoors?* (1990), and I read it voraciously. Kisor lost his hearing to meningitis and encephalitis at the age of three. Early on, he thought that everyone was like him: they could not hear and they read lips to communicate. Later, he thought of deafness as a minor human characteristic that varies between people (like freckles), and he used oral communication with no signing. His mother "refuse[d] to accept the reality that her child [was] deaf" and he grew up believing that "the limitations of the deaf in general did not apply" to him (Kisor 1990, 127). Kisor "refused to associate with the deaf" because he believed they "behaved peculiarly, were too clannish, and depended too much on others for help" (127). He avoided "deafisms," such as sign language, and he asserted that people who depend solely on sign language for communication are "condemned to a narrow, limited world" (205). He explained, "deafness is not part of how I define myself . . . I was Henry Kisor, book editor and literary critic, husband and father, son and brother. 'Deaf man' brought up the caboose of that train" (212–213). I never found a book detailing the experience of someone who identifies with Deaf Culture, but Kisor's perspective on being deaf demonstrates that even without the cultural framework, deafness does not have to be considered a disability.

Film: *Sound and Fury*

The documentary *Sound and Fury* (Weisburg and Aronson 2000) follows the Artinian family as its D/deaf and hearing members consider cochlear implants, surgically implanted electronic devices designed to bring a sense of sound to deaf people. Hearing aids merely amplify sound, so some hearing ability is necessary in order to use them, but cochlear implants bypass the outer and middle ear to present auditory signals directly to the inner ear (NAD 2006). There is an internal component that is surgically implanted, and an external component without which the person can no longer hear. Worldwide, about 60,000 people have cochlear implants, including some 13,000 adults and 10,000 children and youth in the United States (NAD 2006). With costs ranging from $40,000 to $60,000, the procedure is expensive and controversial (NAD 2006).

Peter Artinian, Jr. is proud to be Deaf. He values the Deaf culture, and he speaks of the spiritual and cultural connection that Deaf people share. He married a Deaf woman. When his three children were born Deaf, he thought, "Great, they're just like me!" For many families, Deafness is a source of pride, a way to share their language, culture, and experiences (Bauman 2005). When

his five-year-old daughter began asking about cochlear implants so she could hear birds, music, telephones, and lions, the adults were stunned, because they loved their D/deaf family and they felt she was rejecting them. Little Heather signed, "I want a cochlear implant now . . . Hearing people don't sign. I want to communicate."

Whether deafness is a culture of which to be proud, or a disability to overcome is a heated daily struggle for the Artinian family. Hearing grandfather, Peter Artinian Sr., tells his Deaf son, "It is not intended for people to have a handicap." Peter Jr. signs furiously, "You think deafness is a handicap. But I don't think deafness is a handicap. That's from my heart. I just can't hear." His father does not sign to him except to finger spell the word "cripple" in reference to his son's family. His mother uses signed English as she speaks, "If you were born today . . . tomorrow you'd go get a cochlear." She advocates for implanting the deaf grandchildren. Peter Jr. signs, "I never knew you didn't accept deafness until now."

Peter's hearing brother Chris and sister-in-law Mari have twin baby boys, one of whom is deaf. Mari's parents are both deaf, and as a child, Mari interpreted and advocated for her parents (similar to the experiences Walker describes in *A Loss for Words*). Mari "rebelled against" her parents, and tried to get away from D/deaf culture, but then she had a deaf child. Mari said that a part of her died when she learned of her son's hearing loss because she knows what he is missing. She felt that the cochlear implant would not remove his deafness, but he would be able to function better in the hearing world. Mari's parents had been thrilled to have a deaf grandson; her father happily signed, "It's the first time we have a deaf person in our family" and her mother added, "God blessed him!" They were appalled and offended when Mari and Chris decided to have a cochlear implant for their grandson.

The National Association of the Deaf (2000) asserts that people with cochlear implants are still deaf, but many D/deaf people view cochlear implants as a way of eradicating deafness. At a Deaf gathering in the movie, an elder asks the group, "Do we think the implant can kill Deaf culture?" and amidst much vigorous agreement, he signs "Y-E-S!" with a flourish. Some advocates of cochlear implants call them a cure or a step in the process of a cure for deafness, but some D/deaf people wonder, "What if there are no D/deaf people in the future?" Like many D/deaf parents, Peter Jr. and his wife were worried that a cochlear implant would change their daughter's identity as a D/deaf person. As one D/deaf elder signed, "Once someone is implanted, they will migrate from the D/deaf world to the hearing world."

The cochlear implant doctor in the film reassures the hearing parents that after surgery, children "relate to hearing people, not to deaf people." The parents of an implanted child reported proudly, "She views herself as a hearing person." The mother further remarked, "I don't think she realizes she's deaf. She thinks she's just like everybody else." Statements such as these were encouraging to the hearing parents and horrifying to the Deaf parents. Ultimately, Peter and Nita decide not to have the surgery for their daughter, and move to a Deaf community out of state.

Cultural Event: A Coffee Social

As the ASL coffee social approaches, I feel more and more nervous. I practice my signs every day. My fingerspelling is painfully slow, but I am trying my best. Hopefully people will understand that I mean well. I am afraid that I will forget the basic signs, or I will make a mistake and say something stupid or offensive. ASL is so beautiful, and I am feeling daunted by the task of signing with people at the coffee social. My anxiety increased after watching *Sound and Fury*, because there was a lot of complicated signing, and I only grasped shreds of the content.

One of the things I have learned about Deaf culture is that it is incredibly important to maintain eye contact during conversations. I have a tendency to break eye contact and stare off in the distance, or to be easily distracted in conversation, so I have been practicing with my friend (a hearing person who does not sign). He simply maintains eye contact while I haltingly sign, spell, and mouth the phrases, *"Hello! Nice to meet you. My name is R-U-B-Y. What is your name? I am a social work student at Berkeley. I am a hearing person, but I can sign a little. I want to communicate . . ."* I practice over and over again. I am slowly becoming more confident.

Of course I know I will never be considered a member of Deaf culture as a hearing person, but I hope to be accepted as a person with whom friendship and connection are possible (Walker 1986; Padden and Humphries 2005). I wonder how I will be perceived, with my self-taught signs and shy nature to boot. I remind myself that the coffee social is "open to all signers," and that the organizer was friendly and welcoming in her email. It is important to be brave and stretch myself to use a form of communication that is new to me, in order to better understand the other's experience, even though (and perhaps especially because) I am scared.

Immersion Experience. Walking into the coffee shop reminded me of a junior high school dance, with the room split down the middle, and two clearly delineated groups occupying their respective walls. Half the room had their hands flying with animated facial expressions, and the other half were anxiously staring, eyes darting, sipping their coffee on the other side of the room. I must admit there was a powerful urge to sit with the hearing people, pull out a book, and pretend I didn't come here to make new friends. I slowly perused the coffee and tea selection, buying myself a bit of time to scope out where I might sit. Armed with my tea, and reviewing the fingerspelling of my name in my head (it would be bad to mess that up right off the bat), I made my way to an empty seat. I signed, *Seat?*, and was politely informed that it was taken. About to let my shyness get the best of me, I breathed a sigh of relief as a nice Deaf gentleman pointed to a free seat across the table from him.

He asked me my name, and I was thrilled because I had actually understood what he said and I knew how to sign the answer. We had a lovely, if halting, conversation about a variety of topics. I understand more than I thought I would, and there was nothing I wanted to say that I couldn't figure out a way to express. I need to get better at reading other people's fingerspelling, because he had to spell so slowly it was embarrassing (maybe for both of us?). The people at the table showed me how to sign "joke," and then the gentleman told me a long story-joke about a Deaf man in the "NYC mafia" (this was the first finger spelled phrase that I understood). I caught most of the story, but I missed the punch line. After he had repeated it twice, I still didn't get it (the punch line was a long word finger spelled), so I pretended to understand. I have been feeling guilty about this and trying to figure out what the punch line could have been. I felt badly being insincere, but I was so embarrassed by my lack of understanding that I allowed myself to hide behind pretending. I gained perspective on what it is like to be a linguistic minority trying to communicate, and feeling like you need to give the impression that you understand.

The gentleman was very helpful, slowed down his signs for me, and did not show any frustration (if he had any). His signs were clear, crisp, and he would repeat himself if he noticed the crinkle in my brow broadcasting my confusion. He told me that he works in a hospital, reading EKGs and monitoring people who have heart procedures. When I recognized the sign for "hospital," I became very excited, because this was the first real point of connection. I signed, "Me too I work at a hospital!" We talked about the hospitals where we work, and I got to use the phrase I had been practicing: "I do therapy with children and families in the hospital." I feel such a kinship with other hospital folks, and it was so nice for me (and I think for him, too) that we had something we could both relate to that helped bridge the gaps between us.

After talking for a while with the gentleman, he introduced me to his friend, who is either in his "class" or his "community" (I could not remember the exact meaning of the sign he used). We talked briefly, but I could understand precious little of what he said. His hands seemed sloppy, and he often would start to finger spell or sign something, then shake his open hand towards the floor (meaning "oops, start over"). This made it difficult to understand him, and he did not seem to have as much patience with my need for repetition, so I nodded and smiled a lot, hoping I wasn't agreeing with anything terrible.

It was good for me to have the first experience with the gentleman who was relatively easy to understand, and then to converse with someone who required more effort on my part in order to communicate. When several people, including the men I had been conversing with, got up to leave, I thought I'd better do the same. They asked if they would see me again next month. I was so thrilled that they wanted me back and that I had understood their signs, and I signed back, "yes." I felt so happy leaving that coffeeshop, because I had opened the door to a whole community of new friends by learning ASL in order to communicate with them.

Interview

As part of my search for someone to interview, I used the California Relay Service, which provides free translation so that D/deaf and hearing people can communicate on the telephone (Deaf and Disabled Telecommunications Program, DDTP 2006). The operator types what the hearing person says, and then reads aloud what the D/deaf person types in to their TTY, so it is a slow form of communication. I was so nervous that I hung up the first two times I tried to make a call. My face flushed as the operator connected the call, and I felt a familiar relief when I realized I had reached an answering machine. My heart started to race and my face felt hot as I embarrassingly left my message. When I put down the receiver, my hands were shaking, and I wondered if this is similar to the way that D/deaf people feel when they are trying to communicate with hearing people.

I interviewed the Executive Director of an agency that provides a hotline and other services to d/Deaf women who have experienced domestic violence or sexual assault. We had planned to use a video relay service as an interpreter, but when I got there, we found we could communicate well with both of us signing and speaking, so we ended up communicating directly. I felt good about this, and the woman said that she liked this because she and I could look at each other, instead of looking at the screen.

Born deaf in a hearing family, she always felt different. She attended mainstream schools, and she learned to sign and be proud of being Deaf when she was in college. Her Deaf identity is not separate from her general personal identity, and D/deafness is not a disability to her or to her agency.

We discussed the film *Sound and Fury*, and she said it was a perfect example of how the medical model and the cultural model of d/Deafness collide. Her organization serves all d/Deaf people, and she said it is important not to alienate children who have been implanted. They are not accepted by Deaf culture, so they are not getting the support that Deaf culture provides.

She said the most important thing for hearing social workers to think about when working with d/Deaf clients is to remember to use an interpreter. Too often, social workers assume that the d/Deaf person can understand well enough, or the need for an interpreter is simply forgotten. It is essential that the worker take responsibility for securing an interpreter. It should not be considered the d/Deaf person's responsibility. Additionally, it is crucial that social workers be aware that there are many different sign languages and the d/Deaf person may not use ASL.

She said that most d/Deaf people, including herself, would prefer to receive services from a d/Deaf provider. She would at least prefer to work with someone who signs. However, some d/Deaf people prefer to work with a professional who is outside the d/Deaf community, because it is a small and tight-knit community, and people may wish to maintain privacy and confidentiality.

Integrating the Experiences

The immersion experiences and the process of learning about deafness and Deaf culture have been very enriching for me. When I started out the project, I assumed that a deaf person's primary identity would be their deaf or Deaf identity. I was familiar with Deaf people like the Artinians, for whom Deaf culture is a source of pride, identity, and community, but I had no idea that there were people like Henry Kisor, who only consider themselves incidentally deaf. For some, D/deafness is the most important thing in their lives, but for others, it is just a small variation between people.

For me, the immersion experience was both enhanced and confounded by the language component. Most of my anxiety about the immersion surrounded my lack of mastery of the language, and it was only after having such a positive experience communicating in ASL at the coffee social that I was able to let myself relax a bit. I thought once or twice during the process that I wished I'd picked a culture that uses English, because at least there wouldn't be the language barrier between us. But I realized that to some extent, all cultures have their own language and their own way of communicating, and there is always some kind of gap to bridge.

Sign languages are unique and gorgeously expressive forms of communication, and I now understand some of what D/deaf people mean when they say hearing people are "Deaf impaired."

Applying the Knowledge Base: Agency, Service and Program, and Personal Competencies

My agency is a small psychotherapy clinic for young children and their caregivers, situated at a large, urban public hospital. Children who have experienced a significant trauma, such as death of a parent, domestic violence, community violence, or abuse are eligible for services. The agency is funded through research grants, so services are free. Recently, the director received a phone call from a D/deaf advocacy group, wondering whether we were able to serve D/deaf clients. She responded that unfortunately, because of the language barrier, we were not equipped to work with that population. My enthusiasm about serving this community has led the agency to assess the possibility of expanding services to D/deaf families.

The Agency

Community The population the agency serves includes all of a major population area, but most clients live in the area's largest city. It is estimated that over 17,000 city residents have severe hearing loss (Deaf and Hard of Hearing Community Coalition of***, DHHCC*** 2001). There are certainly D/deaf and hard of hearing people living in the hospital's neighborhood and catchment area.

Access Issues of access to the clinic need to be addressed. There is literally no way for D/deaf clients to get in the front door. There is no receptionist, so clients ring a doorbell, alerting any available staff to let them in and lead them to the waiting area. The clinic is located in a locked wing of the hospital, and clients are "buzzed in," so the sound of the buzzer alerts the client when the door is unlocked. A simple solution to this problem would be to install a light that would illuminate to announce the unlocked door.

Overall, the hospital has made accommodations to become more accessible to D/deaf patrons, but there are some persistent practical issues. For example, there is a TTY/TDD number to reach the hospital; however it is not listed on the hospital's main web page along with the telephone number for the hospital. I called the main number to ask if there was a TTY/TDD number, and the operator said, "Umm . . . I think we used to have something like that. . . . That's for talking to deaf people with that machine-thing, right?" I said yes, and spitefully quipped, "So what if I were D/deaf and had an emergency?" She said she would transfer me to the emergency room, and promptly did so. The ER nurse gave me the TTY/TDD number.

There is an ASL interpreter on call 24 hours per day for the emergency room. I have seen signs around the hospital announcing the availability of interpreters and the patient's right to have one present. The ER nurse declined offering an estimate of the average wait time before the interpreter arrives, but I understand that it can be hours (DHHCC*** 2001). Some patients have complained that the hospital often uses off-site interpreters who communicate via video relay service. This can lead to misunderstandings because the interpreter is not physically present in the room. While it is positive that interpreters are available to assist D/deaf patients at the hospital, there are some concerns with the system.

Some of the physical structures of the hospital are accessible, but others need work. The fire alarms have both a siren and a flashing light that would alert D/deaf and hard-of-hearing people of an evacuation. When there is a more minor announcement, such as "Code Blue" (medical emergency) or "Code Pink" (infant abduction), the announcement is solely oral, and D/deaf employees or patients would not know what was happening unless someone translated for them.

Many hospital patrons commute via public transportation, which seems to be accessible to D/deaf people. For those who drive, the parking structure could incorporate a light or sign for the gate in addition to the talking ticket machine, which would improve the experience of D/deaf patrons who park there. Structures are in place to make the hospital more accessible for D/deaf patrons, but the systems are not functioning at the optimal level.

Receptivity and Sensitivity If the agency served D/deaf clients, significant changes would be required in terms of staffing, waiting room protocols, and staff training in language and cultural competence. I believe that the staff would be sensitive to the needs of D/deaf clients if services to that population were incorporated in the clinic, because they are very sensitive to the populations we currently serve. Staff have been excited to learn more and to expand services to a previously overlooked population. The current lack of sensitivity to the D/deaf community results from oversight, not from bigotry or incompetence. The D/deaf community was not originally part of the plan, in terms of who would be served by the clinic, because no one involved had expertise in this area.

There are no staff members who are D/deaf or hard of hearing. The former office manager knew ASL because his brother is Deaf, but he never had the opportunity to use his skills at work. I believe a few staff know how to finger spell, but, at present, my own limited experience with ASL represents the highest level of competency among the agency's staff. If the clinic were to invite D/deaf clients, it would be essential to employ social workers fluent in ASL to conduct therapy sessions. Other staff should become familiar with at least the basic phrases they would need to communicate in the waiting area with D/deaf clients, such as asking the person to wait here and telling the D/deaf person they will call the social worker.

The entrance and the waiting room do not seem particularly welcoming to D/deaf individuals. There are posters and pictures of multicultural children and their parents, but no images of people signing or other D/deaf-referencing images. The waiting area is not clearly delineated from the hallway, and there are no signs, which could make it more difficult for D/deaf people to orient themselves. Because staff do not know ASL and could not necessarily explain to the clients where they should wait, this could cause a problem, as the hospital wing is shared with another program.

Administration and Staff Training The potential needs of the D/deaf community have not been on the agency administrators' radar until recently. There is no mention of D/deafness in any of the agency trainings, although there is an extensive coverage of diversity topics, including language barriers and disabilities. Trainings for current staff would be an important part of the proposed expansion.

Ideally, the D/deaf community should have a role in developing the training program.

Funding Budget restrictions may create a roadblock for the expansion of services to the D/deaf community because of training, equipment, and new staffing costs. The agency is very careful with its grant-based funds, and there may be other projects that receive higher priority. A careful cost-benefit analysis will undoubtedly be weighed and considered as the agency contemplates making this change.

Agency Programs and Services

Effort The agency has made little effort thus far to begin serving deaf clients. As the agency considers expanding its services to include this population, it will be important to include members of the D/deaf community in the process of designing and implementing a culturally sensitive program. Members of the deaf advocacy group who initiated the call to the agency about services might be both helpful and interested in involvement with this project, and would be an excellent community resource. As they are familiar with services and supports in the D/deaf community, they may be able to assist the agency to develop the necessary community network

Quality, Effectiveness, and Efficiency The quality, effectiveness, and efficiency of services for D/deaf clients are nonexistent at this time. There is no outreach to the deaf community. The agency is cautiously considering expansion of services, and it will be crucial to reassess the agency's effort, quality, effectiveness, and efficiency once the agency begins to serve the D/deaf community.

Personal Cultural Competencies

Engagement, Trust, and Relationship-building I do not think that the process of engaging a D/deaf client would be all that different from engaging any other client: by being real with them, respecting them, and asking their opinions, I build trust. It is difficult to characterize a population, because there is so much diversity within each group. That being said, it seems that there is a sense within the D/deaf communities of not wanting to appear needy or incapable of doing for one self. In this way, help-seeking attempts may be less obvious coming from D/deaf clients than from their hearing counterparts. However, many D/deaf clients' help-seeking behaviors will not vary from the help-seeking behavior of hearing people.

In delivering services or providing outreach to the D/deaf and hard-of-hearing communities, it will be critical not to assume that the client cannot do something because he or she is D/deaf. It is widely stated in the D/deaf communities that a D/deaf person can do everything except hear. With D/deaf clients, as with any group considered by others to be "disadvantaged" or "disabled," it is essential to honor the client as an individual, and to respect the dignity of her/his personhood. Because they are often patronized by the establishment, their families, and others, it is critical not to treat D/deaf clients like children. Because many D/deaf people, especially older adults deafened at birth, may have been labeled mentally retarded or incapable of running their own life, a strengths focus may be particularly appreciated.

Social workers should not assume that clients need help from the social worker, or from their families, and should provide whatever assistance is requested in a nonthreatening and nonshaming way. While taking into account the need for empowerment and self-efficacy in the lives of D/deaf clients, the clients' families may be used to taking care of her or him, and may expect to be involved in the treatment. The social worker may work with the client to determine a comfortable role for the family in her/his life and/or in the treatment, if appropriate.

When expressing empathy to a D/deaf client, a hearing social worker should avoid acting as though she or he knows what it means to be D/deaf, or how hard or easy it may be for the client. This is considered very offensive, and may impede the social worker's efforts to continue building the relationship. As with all clients, the social worker should regard the client as the expert on her/himself,

while building bridges toward understanding and common experience.

In creating a relationship based on trust, empathy, and mutual respect, it is helpful for the social worker to take on the norms and mannerisms of D/deaf culture to the degree that is practical, appropriate, and genuine. For example, using signs to the degree that is possible (even if an interpreter is present, it is usually welcomed if the hearing social worker makes an effort to communicate in the D/deaf person's language). One easy place to start is to learn to sign a short greeting (such as hello or good morning). Additionally, it would be helpful at a basic level to learn the client's name-sign, so that the client can be addressed in her/his own language.

In the D/deaf community, the appropriate social distance seems to be determined primarily by the level of intimacy between people, as in many other cultures. That being said, D/deaf people do tend to stand relatively close to each other, while leaving enough space to see the signer's hands. It is important to face the person to whom you are speaking, whether she or he reads lips or signs, and it is essential to maintain eye contact unless there is a reason to break away. The listener should look at the signer's face and the signing area in front of the torso, not focusing directly on the signer's hands.

Eye contact is incredibly important within D/deaf communities, because it forms a solid bond, as well as focusing the speaker and the listener's attention on the communication. If a social worker is using an interpreter, it is essential that he/she look at the deaf person, not the interpreter. This is a way of establishing contact and trust with the client, and demonstrating that the focus of the worker's attention is the client and not the interpreter.

It is difficult to anticipate how an entire population will respond to touch, because of individual differences, but touch presents a particular set of issues and possibilities when it relates to D/deaf people. Touching or tapping a D/deaf person is a way to get her/his attention if she/he cannot see you, but it would be important to discuss with each client how she/he would like to be approached. Effective strategies other than touch include banging on a table or stomping on the floor, which sends vibrations that the D/deaf person can feel, or walking around the person so that she/he can see you. It is very important in the early stages of relationship-building to discuss what constitutes appropriate touch for the client, before assuming that it is acceptable to tap her or him.

Ethnographic interviewing is a powerful tool for learning about a culture, and for understanding the broader context of the client's concerns. Naturalism, the basis of ethnographic interviewing, assumes that one can only "capture the character" of human behavior through "first-hand contact, not through inferences derived from outside the culture" (Leigh 1998, 17). The interviewee is considered a cultural guide, and ethnographic interviewing is a good way to discover "where the client is," and to explore points of connection (18). Although ethnographic interviewing can be an excellent resource in learning about culture, the social worker should be careful not to assume that she/he "understands" D/deaf culture after interviewing one person, or even a few people, using ethnographic skills. It is essential to remember that one person's experience may be related to the larger cultural experience, but that each person is unique. Each individual's experience within the culture may be significantly different from other D/deaf people.

Assessment and Problem Definition In assessing D/deaf clients, one important tool will be the ability to communicate with the client, something that is taken for granted in many practice contexts because there is a shared language. If the social worker does not have ASL fluency, she/he will need to be comfortable and skilled at using an interpreter to communicate with the client. The ideal situation would be that the social worker bridge the language gap directly, which will lead to more accurate and expedient assessment of D/deaf clients. Other than the language component, I would not change how I assess the person because he/she is D/deaf, because it does not seem to me that accommodation is necessary. If any assessment was not compatible with the

client (related to D/deafness or not), I would try to restructure the process to make it more relevant to the client's experience.

The strengths assessment is an excellent tool, because it focuses on exploring clients' personal and environmental strengths. Building on these, social worker and client are able to build focused, appropriate, and achievable goals and interventions. For example, a client may have limited communication possibilities in an employment setting or in a college classroom. This may impact access to resources or socialization. However, the strengths perspective encourages the client to explore resources in the environment for socialization, support, and communication that are accessible.

Because I have not worked directly with D/deaf clients, I will refer to Henry Kisor's description of his experiences with a mental health professional. Kisor went to a clinic because he wanted speech therapy to curb the decline in speaking skills he had noticed. The clinic required a battery of psychological tests and a counseling session to determine qualification for speech therapy services. Kisor grudgingly agreed to both the testing and the counseling session, though he noted that he had not "experienced an emotional crisis that was a direct result of [his] deafness" in years (1990, 125). The clinician who worked with him was very concerned that Kisor was "denying his deafness" by associating with hearing people and avoiding D/deaf people (126). She suggested that he "learn something about deafness," and she made many culturally incompetent assessments. For example, when Kisor described a picture as a mother shushing the children's noisy footsteps so that he could study, the clinician interpreted this as a denial of his deafness, because obviously he could not hear the children's footsteps. Kisor said he could feel the vibrations made by the noisy children and was aware that they bothered him, though he could not hear them.

When Kisor resolutely refused to take advice during the speech therapy sessions, the clinician became more obstinate, and finally Kisor stopped attending speech therapy. This example illustrates how a clinician can drive a client away by clinging to her/his own conceptions or assumptions about the client or the client's cultural group. For me it provides a classic example of what *not* to do. Had the clinician taken a strengths perspective, she might not have lost the opportunity to be of service to this client, and she might have learned something from Kisor about deafness, instead of acting like it should be the other way around.

This example also illustrates an important element in the relationship between D/deaf people and the mainstream culture: many hearing people assume that D/deaf people are disadvantaged, less intelligent, and less capable than hearing people. This is infuriating for D/deaf people, many of whom believe that D/deaf people are smarter, or that there is no difference in intelligence between D/deaf and hearing people. The hearing culture is inaccessible to D/deaf people at times and in certain ways, which may be frustrating and difficult for D/deaf people. Hearing people have the luxury of not even noticing that some people are excluded from participating fully in our society. Even Henry Kisor, who describes himself as "culturally hearing," also admits to feeling like an outsider at times, because the hearing culture lacks acceptance of his deafness.

Hearing people may be confused by the D/deaf community's perceptions of hearing people's attempts to "help" D/deaf people. Many D/deaf people worry about "cures" that could potentially eradicate deafness worldwide. Some scientists and doctors rely on a medical model in which deafness is a deficit, and they espouse cochlear implants and genetic testing, believing that these could lead the way toward "curing" deafness. To the D/deaf community, this kind of talk reeks of eugenics, not of progress. For many D/deaf people, deafness is not a condition that needs curing; hearing people's ignorance about deafness is!

When a hearing social worker is working with a D/deaf client, it is crucial not to assume that the D/deaf person is more needy, because she or he is D/deaf. Also, the social worker should avoid imposing the values of her/his culture, especially as they relate to hearing, on to her/his D/deaf client. Instead, the worker should try to understand the client's world from her/his perspective, and to learn about the experience of D/deafness from the client's viewpoint. Rather than sitting in judgment like Kisor's clinician, and pompously telling the client to learn more about deafness from the hearing perspective, the social worker should seek to learn and understand.

Contracting and Goal Setting There are no global changes to the contracting or goal-setting process that I see as applicable to any and all D/deaf clients. However, I do believe in making personal adjustments to protocols if needed for individual clients. I believe that D/deaf people could participate in a normal goal-setting process with a social worker, with no changes based solely on their deafness.

As with all clients, it is essential to develop goals that are culturally congruent and relevant to the reason that the client sought services. Using a client-centered approach to contracting and goal setting is effective with D/deaf clients as it is with hearing clients.

Interventions As with contracting and goal setting, the interventions developed to address the client's concerns should be culturally congruent. It is essential that goals and interventions focus on the *client's* perception of needs and concerns, and that deafness not be automatically considered the central issue to be addressed. It may be that the client wants to address issues concerning D/deafness, but more likely will be seeking help with issues not related directly to hearing. Family problems, employment issues, and personal concerns predominate for this population, as they do for others.

One of the areas in which a social worker might be helpful is in the expansion of choices for the client. It is possible that cultural and/or language barriers have limited the client's access to a full range of resources and opportunities, and the social worker may be able to assist the client in availing her/himself of them. Additionally, the worker may be aware of services within and outside the D/deaf community. Collaborative exploration of client abilities, connections, opportunities, and resources based on the strengths perspective may assist in client empowerment and self-advocacy.

Social workers should also be aware of the oppression and discrimination that people who are D/deaf may experience. Utilizing both the strengths perspective and the empowerment perspective can help clients to advocate for themselves, form or join advocacy groups, and build coalitions. In some instances, social workers can also serve as advocates for clients, and/or refer clients for legal services in support of their rights.

Evaluation and Termination Each client has her/his own way of determining success or failure, and those individual differences in evaluation and termination must be handled with each client. I do not think that there is anything about being D/deaf that defines how success or failure is determined, so the focus may vary. The client and worker should decide together what constitutes success. Timing and strategies for termination are considered collaboratively, in accordance with the value of client self-determination.

However, in working with D/deaf clients, there could be differences in the way that the social worker structures the termination process to provide culturally competent closure. It is the norm in D/deaf culture to take a long time saying goodbye. Friendships are very important in the D/deaf communities because they provide solace from the disconnection and isolation that many D/deaf people feel in their daily lives. The ending of a meeting or a relationship can feel like a terrible loss, and goodbyes are often drawn out as long as possible. Because goodbyes tend to be long and highly meaningful, it might be a good idea to present the idea of termination earlier to D/deaf clients than to hearing clients, for whom long goodbyes are not the norm. This way, there is more time for the process of saying goodbye.

Resources There is a strong network of support services for D/deaf people in most settings. These can include: interpreters and referral agencies for interpreters, vocational counseling, training and assistance with job placement, ASL/ESL language and skills development classes, social and support organizations for LGBT D/deaf people, special programs for D/deaf seniors, HIV education and support services, recreational activities and summer camp programs for children and adults, independent living skills programs, library services, speech and hearing testing and services, counseling and support services, hearing dog programs, and newsletters. Educational facilities from elementary school through high school are available. Gallaudet University in Washington, D.C., was founded to provide quality college and advanced education for D/deaf people.

Applying NASW Standards for Cultural Competence

While my agency is interested in serving the D/deaf community, it is not currently meeting cultural competence standards. Both my field placement agency and I are working to develop competence, in order to begin to serve the D/deaf and hard-of-hearing communities.

NASW mandates that social workers use "appropriate methodological approaches, skills, and techniques that reflect the workers' understanding of the role of culture" in the process (NASW 2001). The agency is only beginning to consider the role that D/deafness could play in the therapeutic relationship, in access to the clinic, and in attitudes toward service provision.

My personal cross-cultural skills have vastly improved through this immersion process, but I still do not consider myself to be culturally competent enough to work without an interpreter. With the assistance of a professional interpreter, I feel confident that I could be a sensitive and effective clinician for members of the D/deaf and hard-of-hearing communities.

To me, the most important tool in working with D/deaf clients is ASL fluency. If the client and social worker can communicate without a mediator, the helping process will be facilitated greatly; it will be less frustrating for both client and worker, and less chaotic. There will be less lost in translation. Additionally, when one learns the language of a culture, one learns about the culture in an intimate way and new insights are gained. Because I believe language fluency is the most important piece of cultural competency with the D/deaf population, I have focused on the standard of language diversity in this analysis.

NASW mandates that social workers "seek to provide or advocate for the provision of information, referrals, and services in the language appropriate to the client" (2001). It is essential to be able to communicate with D/deaf clients in order to serve them. NASW states that this language diversity standard may be met through the provision of interpreters. However, the agency generally finds the use of interpreters cumbersome, and refers clients who cannot be served in a language spoken by agency workers. Thus, the agency has not met the standard of language diversity.

One of the important ways that I have increased my cultural competency is to gain a basic familiarity with ASL. My skill level is improving, and while it is not at a level of competence to practice directly with clients, I am working on it. Although I still have a lot to learn, I conquered many of my fears of communicating directly through the immersion process. The set of skills that I have developed through this process, from the ASL to the information I have learned about cultural norms within the D/deaf communities, will help me immensely in my future work with this population. I do not feel that I have achieved full cultural competence, because I know that this is impossible to attain. But I have made progress toward that goal and I have become a more culturally competent clinician, aware of the needs of the D/deaf community and able to be of service.

REFERENCES

ASL Info.com. 2006. *Deafculture*. http://www.aslinfo.com/deafculture2.cfm

Bauman, H. D. 2005. Designing deaf babies and the question of disability. *Journal of Deaf Studies and Deaf Education*, 10 (3): 311–5.

Breivik, J. K. 2005. Vulnerable but strong: deaf people challenge established understandings of deafness. *Scandinavian Journal of Public Health, Supplement*, 66: 18–23.

Deaf and Disabled Telecommunications Program (DDTP). 2006. California relay service. http://www.ddtp.org/california_relay_service/Default.asp

Deaf and Hard of Hearing Community Coalition of *** (DHHCC***). 2001. *Needs assessment of the deaf and hard of hearing community of San Francisco*. http://72.14.203.104/search?q=cache:EBLuqzclfNMJ:www.uccd.org/needsassessment1.doc+san+francisco+deaf+population&hl=en&gl=us&ct=clnk&cd=4&client=safari

Cohen, L. H. 1994. *Train go sorry: Inside a Deaf world*. New York: Vintage Books.

Gallaudet University Library. 2006a. *Deaf statistics: other countries*. http://library.gallaudet.edu/dr/faq-statistics-deaf-other.html

Gallaudet University Library. 2006b. *Statistics: Deaf-blind in the U.S.* http://library.gallaudet.edu/dr/faq-stats-deaf-blind.html

Gallaudet University Library. 2006c. *Statistics: Deaf population of individual U.S. states, territories and localities*. http://library.gallaudet.edu/dr/faq-statistics-deaf-us.html

Gallaudet University Library. 2006d. *Statistics: Deaf population of the United States*. http://library.gallaudet.edu/dr/faq-statistics-deaf-us.html

Holcomb, R. K., S. K. Holcomb, and T. K. Holcomb. 1994. *Deaf Culture: Our Way*. San Diego, California: Dawn Sign Press.

Kisor, H. 1990. *What's that pig outdoors? A memoir of deafness*. New York: Penguin Books.

Lazorisak, C., and D. Donohue. 2004. *The Complete Idiot's Guide to Conversational Sign Language*. New York: The Penguin Group.

Leigh, J. W. 1998. *Communicating for cultural competence*. Boston: Allyn & Bacon.

Goldin-Meadow, S., and C. Mylander. 1998. Spontaneous sign systems created by deaf children in two cultures. *Nature* 391: 279–281.

Matlin, M. 2004. *Deaf Child Crossing*. New York: Aladdin Publishing.

Mitchell, R. E. 2005. How many deaf people are there in the United States? Estimates from the survey of income and program participation. *Journal of Deaf Studies and Deaf Education*, 11 (1): 112–9.

National Association of the Deaf. 2006. *American sign language*. http://www.nad.org/site/pp.asp?c=foINKQMBF&b=99566

National Association of Social Workers (NASW). 2001. *NASW Standards for Cultural Competence in Social Work Practice*. Washington D.C.: Author.

Padden, C. and T. Humphries. 2005. *Inside Deaf Culture*. Cambridge, Massachusetts: Harvard University Press.

Paris, D. G. and M. Drolsbaugh, eds. 2001. *Deaf Espirit: Inspiration, Humor and Wisdom from the Deaf Community*. Salem, Oregon: AGO Gifts and Publications.

Ruben, R. J. 2005. Sign language: its history and contribution to the understanding of the biological nature of language. *Acta Otolaryngologica*, 125 (5): 464–7.

San Francisco Public Library. 2006. Deaf services center. http://sfpl.lib.ca.us/librarylocations/accessservices/deafservices.htm

University of California Center on Deafness. 2006a. *Deaf services network directory for northern California*. http://www.uccd.org/dsn.html

University of California Center on Deafness (UCCD). 2006b. Client services. http://www.uccd.org/clientservices.html

Walker, L. A. 1986. *A Loss for Words: A Story of Deafness in a Family*. New York: Harper & Row.

Weisberg, R. (producer) and J. Aronson (director). 2000. *Sound and Fury* [motion picture]. United States: Aronson Film Associates.

Worksheet

1. The writer believes that language fluency is an essential ingredient of cultural competence, and social workers seeking to become culturally competent in working with a population should be able to communicate with clients directly in the language of that population. This position goes beyond NASW Standards for Cultural Competence in Social Work, which state that language competency requirements may be met through the effective use of interpreters. (a) What are some of the positives and negatives of learning a language in order to provide culturally competent services? (b) What has been your experience in working with interpreters or in working with clients in another language?

2. The Americans with Disabilities Act prohibits discrimination on the basis of disability in all public services and venues. In the past, this agency has referred deaf clients for services elsewhere, rather than providing services that it felt might not be culturally competent, and where social workers would not be able to communicate directly with clients without the use of an interpreter.

Using the ADA website, research the provisions of the Act. How would they be applied to the past position of the agency in terms of providing services to clients who could not be served directly because of language barriers? Assuming that other appropriate resources for services exist, are they required to provide services using an interpreter, or may they routinely refer clients elsewhere? Would the requirements differ if there were no other appropriate services available?

Culturally Competent Social Work Practice with Mental Health Services Consumers

Diversity Project by Megan Moore

My field work placement this year is in a county outpatient mental health clinic. It serves residents with mental health needs throughout the county, but primarily people residing in the city in which the clinic is located. As a future social worker with a focus and interest in community mental health, I chose mental health consumers as the population in which to immerse myself. I looked to the mental health consumer movement to gain a perspective on history, care, and health from the consumer's viewpoint. I attended a mental health consumer meeting at a self-help center, and I had the opportunity to speak with several mental health consumers about their experiences with their illness as well as their experience with the mental health care system. I listened to a consumer's presentation that provided insight into the current thinking of the leaders of the consumer movement. Additionally, I read an autobiographical story about a woman with bipolar disorder called *An Unquiet Mind: A Memoir of Moods and Madness* by Kay Redfield Jamison (1995), and watched the film *Man Facing Southeast* (Subiela 1986).

KNOWLEDGE OF POPULATION

History: The Mental Health and Consumer Movement in the United States

Prior to the American Revolution, the mentally ill received care locally in townships, poorhouses, and workhouses (Segal 2005). After the Revolution, Benjamin Rush opened the first psychiatric hospital, and in 1844, the American Psychiatric Association was founded (Andreasen and Black 2001).

From 1830 to the 1950s, asylums flourished in the United States. Many horrific treatments or "heroic cures" were inflicted on the patients at these hospitals, including lobotomy, electroshock, and insulin shock (Segal 2005).

Around the turn of the twentieth century, Freud began to explore the possibility of explaining mental illness by means of his developmental theories and a method of clinical observation known as psychoanalysis (Andreasen and Black 2001). The height of psychoanalysis' influence on mental health care was in the 1950s in the United States, but its lingering effect continues to be prevalent today in the use of the medical model to provide mental health services.

The advent of new legislation, increasing costs of caring for patients in hospital settings, new medications, and changing perspectives on people with mental illness led to the development of community care during the era of the 1950s to 1980 (Segal 2005). The years 1980 to the present are marked by an even greater push toward community care, and the emergence of the mental health consumer movement. The passage of the Americans with Disabilities Act in 1990, with its inclusion of mental illness as a disability, provided legal grounds for increasing empowerment and further encouraged consumer movement advocates.

In September 1983, the California Network of Mental Health Clients was formed as the first mental health client-run state organization in the country (California Network 2005). Catalyzed by the deinstitutionalization movement in the 1970s and 1980s this group of former patients in institutions began to meet together to discuss their negative experiences and talk about how treatment could be improved (California Network 2005). Eventually, the group organized and sought funding from the government in order to realize their ideas of self help centers, client-centered services, and effective lobbying techniques (California Network 2005). The self-help center that I visited is one of the California Network services that mental health consumers run and attend.

Autobiography: *An Unquiet Mind: A Memoir of Moods and Madness*

Kay Redfield Jamison, a prominent psychiatrist, wrote *An Unquiet Mind: A Memoir of Moods and Madness* in order to explore her own experience with bipolar disorder, commonly known as manic-depressive illness. One quote that touched me follows, and I think summarizes her internal struggle to take medication and give up the exuberant highs to avoid the devastating lows of her illness:

> People go mad in idiosyncratic ways. Perhaps it was not surprising that, as a meteorologist's daughter, I found myself in that glorious illusion of high summer days, gliding, flying, now and again lurching through cloudbanks . . . past stars and across fields of ice crystals. Even now, I can see in my mind's rather peculiar eye an extraordinary shattering and shifting of light; inconstant but ravishing colors laid out across miles of circling rings; and the almost imperceptible, somehow surprisingly pallid moons of this Catherine wheel of a planet. I remember singing "Fly me to the moons" as I swept past those of Saturn, and thinking myself terribly funny. I saw and experienced that which had been only dreams, or fitful fragments of aspiration. Was it real? Well, of course not, not in any meaningful sense of the word real. But did it stay with me? Absolutely. Long after my psychosis cleared, and the medications took hold, it became part of what one remembers forever, surrounded by an almost Proustian melancholy. Long since that extended voyage of my mind and soul, Saturn and its icy rings took on an elegiac beauty, and I don't see Saturn's image now without feeling an acute sadness at its being so far away.

While this book gave me insight into one woman's amazing story, I realized that many clients never get a similar opportunity to verbalize their experiences. Using a Life Course approach provides the client with a therapeutic opportunity to tell her/his story, and provides a context within which I can develop a client-centered approach to treatment.

Film: *Man Facing Southeast* (Subiela 1986)

The film *Man Facing Southeast* is set in a Buenos Aires psychiatric hospital. A man, Rantes, appears in the hospital, claiming to be an alien from another planet, and is labeled as paranoid and delusional. Rantes treats the patients at the hospital with respect; like people, not patients. He illustrates how the label mental illness is given to those who do not share the same perceptions of the world as those in the dominant culture. Rantes tragically declines and eventually dies as a result of the treatments inflicted upon him.

This movie illustrated that clients who carry the label mentally ill, are perceived in a way that anything they say is heard in the context of their illness. The possibility that there is truth to a seemingly bizarre story is not entertained, even though the same clinician or doctor might view the same story differently if relayed by someone considered "mentally healthy."

Man Facing Southeast vividly reminded me of the clinicians' immense responsibility to clients as well as the power differentials between consumers and clinicians. The goal is to then give the power to the client by treating each client as a worthy person, one who knows what treatment will work best. The client is the "educated" one, the "expert" when it comes to her/his life.

Population-Specific Event: A Community Mental Health Consumer Meeting

I went to the consumer operated and attended self-help center to attend a community meeting regarding the use of Proposition 63 funds, allocated by the state of California for the provision of mental health services in the community. The facilitator of the group welcomed me and immediately said, "You must have a college degree." I quickly felt like an intruder in this environment that was built specifically to provide a safe place for clients to participate unjudged by the professional mental health community.

The facilitator, in a caring and effective way, was asking consumers in attendance questions that had been put together by the larger California Network of Mental Health Consumers. The responses from each county were going to be compiled into a large document that would eventually be presented to the legislature in Sacramento. The questions shared a major theme: What/who helps you cope when your symptoms begin to come back? What services do you like/dislike? What services would you like to have? No one thought forced treatment was helpful, and each said, in some form, that the people she or he knows well and trusts are most helpful when she or he is in crisis.

All of this made sense to me, and if I were to answer these questions about my own life, I think I would have similar answers. At the end of the meeting, the facilitator said, "We want to be thought of as people, not in-patients and out-patients." I related this to the concept of naming, and the meaning that words or labels have to different groups. The clinic where I work is called "the out-patient clinic." This is a very loaded name. I became cognizant of how degrading and depersonalizing these terms were when the facilitator made the comment.

It was amazing to see the variety of activities the consumers organize and participate in at the center. This made me consider that just as my work at the clinic is only one small aspect of my entire life, the consumers' treatment at the clinic where I see them is only one tiny part of their lives and their histories. As I listened to them at the meeting, they conveyed a sense of independence, intelligence, and a distinct empowerment that I have not seen expressed at the clinic, despite the fact that these are the very same consumers that visit the clinic.

As I thought about this experience, I became aware of the disconnect between the clinic and the self-help center. The self-help program is located ten minutes from the clinic. When clients come to the clinic, they know they are not going to talk with their familiar peers, but rather they are going to "be seen" by the doctor or therapist. This incongruity between what consumers in the movement say they want, and what the clinic provides, stands out clearly in my mind as one of the biggest barriers to successful treatment at county clinics. As they stated in the meeting, consumers do not always feel valued or treated as equals in a nonjudgmental way at my setting, the clinic. Despite this, they treated me as a valued, respected person at their community meeting. I learned a great deal from the experience of being the minority in the group. I also learned about the group's sincere feelings about the mental health system and how they are treated within it.

Personal Interviews

I had the opportunity to informally interview several members of the mental health consumer group and also to listen to one consumer present her story. The consumers remember horrific procedures, forced treatments, and unwilling incarcerations in psychiatric hospitals. These terrifying memories led them to both begin, and affiliate with, the consumer movement.

I asked one consumer what she saw as possible alternatives to forced treatment in instances where someone's life might be in danger. She explained that she envisioned a place where people could go that was away from the stresses in their life—a place where they could relax, eat, sleep, and commune with others until they felt ready to re-enter the stressful world we have created. We talked about this and how it might work, and I was impressed with how much she had thought about the idea. Of course, she said, at this safe haven, there would only be consumers, no clinicians or doctors who were not also consumers.

This struck me because I am a clinician who is not also a consumer, and this theme was repeated in many of the interviews. I thought about how this would work, and I also thought about what this means to me as a person who has built both education and ideas about the future on the premise that I can effectively serve mental health consumers, despite the fact that I am not one myself. It boils down to the question: can one truly understand the pain and difficulties of another unless she or he has also experienced similar pain and difficulties? I would answer that question with a strong no.

I also thought about the implications of a consumer-only mental health system, and I see many reasons why this approach might work. Consumers would have automatic respect from other consumers in the movement and trust them more easily. Trust, and confidence that the treatment can be successful are two of the highest determinants of successful treatment. So, theoretically, if these were already in place, the rate of success could increase markedly. However, to cut out those who do not directly suffer from the symptoms although they are professionally trained is to cut out many people who care, and those who have the energy and experience through their interactions with loved ones to collaborate on treatment. I hope to continue to pursue a culturally competent practice that is inclusive of consumers' needs as a way to bridge the gap between consumer and clinician.

Conclusions

The immersion experience was an intense one. Not only must I strive to accomplish competence in regards to serving a diverse population in terms of race, ethnicity, gender,

class, and sexual orientation, but I must also explore and talk with clients about their identity as a mental health consumer. This will be an ongoing task for all of my professional career. Every interaction with a consumer, every immersion experience in my life must be one that helps me examine my own power and privilege as a middle class, mentally healthy, worker.

Reading the book and watching the film about mental illness were helpful learning experiences because I am used to learning material in that format. The experience of attending the consumer meeting as the minority clinician, and interviewing several consumers was challenging and even more powerful as a learning tool for me, as it forced me to be put in the position of many clients— the one on the outside. It also gave the consumers a chance to tell me their opinions and their stories. I was literally in their house. I was not the "expert"; they were the experts, and they were the teachers.

This was especially meaningful as I thought about my practice, about how I name things, and about my role in empowering or disempowering clients. I must continue to examine these things in my life and work. Providing culturally competent, empathic services to clients is my priority, and I know the consumers help me toward that goal if I remain open and honest. I have to take the time to really listen.

Applying the Knowledge Base: Agency, Services and Policies, and Personal Competencies

The Field Work Agency: County Mental Health Out-patient Clinic

Community The county is large, consisting of 411,925 individuals over 909.6 square miles. The ethnic makeup according to the 2000 Census is as follows: 49.2 percent white, 17.6 percent Hispanic, 13 percent Asian and Pacific Islander, 14.5 percent African American,

1 percent American Indian, 4.7 percent two + races reported.

Access The clinic is located in a remote area of the county, in a business park, surrounded by factories and industrial warehouses. The route of access for many clients is public transportation, and many must travel long distances to reach the facility. The agency is not considered a neighbor by the clients, because it is so isolated from where they live. Because most of the county services are located at the same site, it is hoped that residents can access them as needed with minimal difficulties. The clinic's hallways and doorways are wide, accommodating wheelchairs, and it has accessible restrooms.

Receptivity The waiting room, although plainly decorated, welcomes clients with magazines, literature on events in the community, mental health groups, educational pamphlets on different mental health diagnoses, and a snack machine. Reading material includes members of the consumer movement and culturally competent educational material.

The administrative staff that registers clients for appointments is friendly, respectful, and efficient. Staff members know many of the clients by name and attempt to accommodate each person, do not keep clients waiting unnecessarily, and often take the time to ask a client how she or he is doing and really listen. Administrative and clinical staff include several bilingual Spanish speakers, and interpreters are also available in person with proper notice and planning on the clinician's part.

There are no consumers on staff at the clinic. The county funds consumer-run self-help centers, such as the one I visited, off-site, providing a space for clients to run groups, organize, and hold community events, staffed by paid and volunteer consumers. It is of note that the self-help centers are located separately from the clinic, where most consumers receive their standard mental health treatment.

The consumers in the movement would like to see a more integrated system of care. The clinicians at the clinic support the consumer self-help centers, but are resistant to the idea of integrating them into the traditional services due to a fundamental difference in the two approaches to care. The consumer movement believes in consumer empowerment and responsibility to achieve health, a basic recovery model of care. The clinicians adhere to a medical model. This disconnect in approaches can lead to hostile discourse, but in general the two groups attempt to work together at a comfortable physical distance. Proposition 63 funding prospects have both groups involved in planning.

Administration and Staff Training The county does encourage ongoing training of staff on issues related to cultural competence. There are meetings and trainings offered periodically, but staff finds it difficult to attend due to large caseloads. I am not aware of any trainings that address members of the consumer movement's specific needs, values, and goals.

Staff Sensitivity Despite the differences in approaches, staff at the agency is generally respectful of diversity, sensitive to special client needs, and generally nonjudgmental. However, the language used at the clinic to discuss consumers often refers to them by their status as out-patient or in-patient, or by their category of disorder, such as borderline. During my visit to the self-help center, a consumer said to the group that it was time the consumers were seen as people, not in-patients or out-patients.

Funding Only 10 percent of the county's budget is allocated to healthcare, and only a portion of that is devoted to mental health. There is a paid position for a cultural competence liaison in the county, but the person has other duties as well. There is also county funding for the consumer-run self-help centers, but it is insufficient to meet all consumer needs. There are some cultural variations in programs and services, and there is hope that Proposition 63 money will help culturally competent services to grow.

Agency Services and Policies

Effort The agency's services and programs do reflect a consistent effort to be sensitive to cultural differences, and to the specific needs of mental health consumers. While I was an intern, I assisted the administration in distributing evaluations to clients. Hundreds of evaluations were collected and will be used to help design culturally sensitive policies and programs and modify current ones.

Quality The county employs a cultural competence liaison, whose responsibility is to ensure that the quality of services provided is culturally competent for employees and consumers. The county does complete periodic surveys and also has a system in place so that clients can provide suggestions and complaints on an ongoing basis. The clinic is required to assess all clients that come through the door, so it does support equitable, respectful, and equal access to all clients.

Agency services are designed to follow a basic medical model of mental illness, and consumer-run services are provided at another location. It appears that the policymakers want to support varied viewpoints, but are unsure how to do that under one roof. Separate services make it difficult for clinicians to address the cultural variations between mental health consumers and the dominant society's view of mental illness. There is a disconnect here that needs to be addressed at a policy level.

Effectiveness In general, the agency's programs appear to be effective. Consumers are utilizing the services, despite the inaccessibility of the clinic. From my informal assessment, interviews, and discussions with clients, consumers from the consumer movement seem to accept and utilize the programs at the clinic. Clients do point out that there are no consumers represented on the clinic's staff. Other unmet needs include a telephone line that clients can call in case of an emergency, with a nonjudgmental and helpful person on the other end. Consumers expressed a need for a facility or house where clients can go as an alternative to hospitalization, ideally a place with consumer-staff, a warm environment, no locked doors, no security guards—a peaceful retreat.

Efficiency The self-help center is funded by the county and serves as an alternative service delivery system to support clients. The consumers who run the center do outreach to the community. The agency tries to meet the multifaceted needs of the consumers by providing many community resources and links to self-help groups. There are many resources available to clinicians for referral. Because the county is relatively rural, the community resources are linked to one another in order to maximize services. It is a priority of the county to maintain these community connections.

Personal Cultural Competencies

Engagement, Trust, and Relationship-building In general, the consumers in the consumer movement are wary of using social agencies to address their problems and needs. The historical abuse and mistreatment of people with mental illness has created distrust of formal agency care. Although hesitant, many consumers seek formal mental health services when their resources in the community are exhausted. To be culturally competent in engagement, trust, and relationship-building it is important to recognize that seeking help at the clinic is a difficult, humbling experience for many consumers.

In order to engage and build trusting relationships, it is important to recognize each client's cultural differences and communication styles. I try to be empathic, listen carefully, and follow the person's lead in terms of eye contact, distance, and style of address. I utilize ethnographic interviewing regularly. I ask clients to tell me about their experiences, what brought them to see me, how they have dealt with similar problems in the past, and how their community deals with problems like this. I ask about family involvement and their personal involvement with community resources, including the self-help centers. Using the technique of ethnographic interviewing provides a way to discover individual and community strengths, talk about them, and determine how these can play a role in the client's service plan.

I also assess my own reactions to the client. I try to ask myself how my own biases, feelings, and cultural norms affect the relationship. Once aware, I accept the ethical and personal obligation to attempt to remedy any negative effects my personal identity may have on a client by consciously striving to be nonjudgmental, validating, and accepting. I also ask clients how they feel about working with me; what concerns they have; and what I can do to make them comfortable. I have learned that, if these problems are present, confronting them within myself and then talking with clients about their feelings is the best way to maintain cultural competence and to avoid the client dropping out of treatment altogether.

Assessment and Problem Definition In the assessment and problem definition phase of the process, I use a variety of tools and techniques to engage the client. Initially, I begin with global questions from the ethnographic interviewing model to gain a picture of how the client views the problem, and how it affects her or his life. A very important aspect of culturally competent consumer mental health care is to ask clients to explain what has led them to seek services, and to use this to guide discussion. It is crucial not to challenge their interpretation by using different terminology and descriptors, or by defining their issues in my own terms. This will disengage the client and disempower her or him in the treatment process.

Additionally, there are limitations to clinical assessment tools like the DSM-IV, and these limitations should always be taken into account when working in mental health. Labels are powerful, and cultural competence means understanding what a label means within each client's cultural norms.

Consumers might identify the problem as a somatic one, an episode, or as a personal crisis that may or may not be defined as a mental illness. The culture of mental health consumers is marginalized in dominant society. Consumers experience discrimination, disempowerment, and the negative effects of stigma in their daily lives. To address this in the assessment and problem definition phase, I find it useful to employ the strengths assessment model and the life course perspective. I realize that I see a client at one point in the course of her/his complicated, rich, interesting life, and it is important to listen to and

incorporate a more holistic view of the person into the assessment and problem definition phase. Additionally, I find the strengths assessment and life course perspective helpful for the clients to begin to understand their issues and resources.

Contracting and Goal Setting I think the key to defining some culturally sensitive goals with mental health consumers is to realize that they are not passive actors in their lives. They are active, complex people who have possibly had many disempowering experiences. I have noticed that if people feel safe and recognize that they have choices, the contracting and goal setting is client-centered and effective.

Another essential of competence is the ability to adjust, adapt, and be flexible. In contracting and goal setting, true empowerment means that the client can feel comfortable changing her/his mind about appropriate personal goals. To be culturally sensitive, I strive to adapt with my clients, recognizing that if the client is not invested, my efforts are futile. I try to support their goals for themselves and provide honest feedback about strengths and possible obstacles that will need to be overcome to reach them.

Interventions In order to provide culturally competent interventions, I must first understand the person within her/his environment, and the issues and concerns in the individual context. One very important aspect of interventions with mental health consumers is the level of family involvement. The consumer movement has been both supported and thwarted by the help of nonconsumer family advocates. Although family members can be viewed as a legitimate voice because they are considered competent, consumers can then be left with no clearly defined role in "their own" movement. Interventions that empower consumers toward advocacy can both enhance self-esteem and provide the sense of self-control that is so important.

Some competent interventions for clients new to the system might include connecting them to the self-help center, and offering an array of services for them to choose from, including appropriate groups, individual therapy, psychiatric medication evaluation, and consultation with the nurse. It is important to provide options, yet not overwhelm the client. For clients who are not new, interventions might include previously successful strategies, reconnecting them to the self-help center, and providing new options for treatment if available. If a client is in crisis and has a crisis plan in place, then I would revert to this plan and work with her or him.

Most importantly, in any intervention I carry out with a client, I stress mutual respect, appropriate boundaries, empathy, and her/his autonomy. The client is the expert in her/his life, and I see myself as an advocate, a resource link, and an agent to assist a client in fulfilling the social roles that she or he wants to fulfill. I think this is valuable to the success of any intervention, whether long term or crisis.

Evaluation and Termination Evaluation and termination is a difficult process. The way I have begun to look at evaluation of my services is to accept where clients are in their recovery, whether or not it is where I think they could be. The clinicians at the clinic say that a client cannot fail in treatment, only the therapist can fail by providing treatment that is not client-centered enough. I think this is a philosophy congruent with how the consumer movement evaluates services. Each part of the recovery process is crucial to the client's progress. Each step represents inner changes that may or may not be immediately visible. The outcome of the intervention may not be known until many years have passed. The social worker may never know the outcome of a particular intervention, so the client definitely determines success.

For the clients in the consumer movement, termination can be a long process. Often, consumers struggle with symptoms of a disorder for many years, with many highs and lows. Termination with a particular clinician may be difficult, but can be eased by maintaining a connection with the "system" in other ways. Many clients keep their connection to the self-help center after treatment at the clinic is finished. As a social worker, it is important for me to be aware of these cultural norms within the population. It is also important to validate clients' possible frustration around the need to stay connected to formal services for medication evaluation. It is important to recognize the unique needs of each individual in terms of time, manner, and degree of termination.

I try to actively engage clients in the closure process, and stress the importance of follow-up and contingency plans when appropriate. I think it is also important to summarize what happened during treatment, and how the client feels about it, and to validate the work the client accomplished and point out strengths. I provide honest feedback about areas of continued improvement and reframe the feedback to provide encouragement and hope for success in the future. I try to build on what she or he has accomplished and encourage her or him to use her/his strengths to continue her/his recovery process.

Evaluation: NASW Standards for Cultural Competence

Standard 8 addresses Professional Education. It states, "Social workers shall advocate for and participate in educational and training programs that help advance cultural competence within the profession" (NASW 2004).

In evaluating County Mental Health as an agency, the agency's guidelines include a requirement that professional social workers maintain their continuing education requirements. The agency also encourages advancing understandings of cultural competence.

On a program and service level, however, one clinician reported that, because of growing case loads, the hiring freeze, and filling positions when people leave, oftentimes clinicians do not have time to attend educational training on such things as cultural competence. The clinical staff has done a lot of advocating around this issue, and they feel they have made some important headway in remedying the problem. Unfortunately, funding is a systemic problem that requires attention at all levels. Social workers have a professional and ethical duty to fulfill these NASW requirements, but they also need the real support of the agency to do so.

Because I am a student, my time was much less structured. I was able to attend educational training on issues that dealt with cultural competence and participate in some wonderful discussions about this topic. I also participated in the diversity class, which aims directly at meeting this social work competency standard. I definitely had the opportu-

nity to work on this competency during school and at my field placement. I also realize, however, that as a social worker in the future I may have to do some serious advocating in order to fulfill the NASW social worker competencies. I hope that funding and policy practices will begin to better support this type of training for social workers in mental health. I am grateful for the training I have received, and I hope to continue on my journey toward culturally competent social work practice.

REFERENCES

Andreasen, N., and D. Black. 2001. *Introductory Textbook of Psychiatry*. 3d ed. Washington, D.C.: American Psychiatric Publishing.

California Network of Mental Health Clients. 2005. *About the California Network of Mental Health Clients*. Sacramento, CA. http://www.cnmhc.org

Jamison, K. 1995. *An Unquiet Mind: A Memoir of Moods and Madness*. New York: Vintage Books.

National Association of Social Workers (NASW). 2001. *NASW Standards for Cultural Competence in Social Work Practice*. Washington, D.C.: Author.

Segal, S. P. 2005. *Historical Perspectives on Mental Health Policy*. Social Welfare 222 course lecture.

Subiela, E. (director). 1986. *Man Facing Southeast (Hombre mirando al sudeste)*. Argentina: Anchor Bay Entertainment.

Worksheet

1. California's Proposition 63 provides funds to enhance mental health services. In the case presented, various needs were identified by consumers, social workers, other clinicians, and the author as important to enhancing mental health services. What methods or structures would you utilize to determine how funds should be allocated, and which identified needs should be given priority?

2. Empowerment and advocacy clearly support the consumer movement in mental health services. Within this framework, the author of this case is struggling to determine her role as a professionally trained social worker. How would you define a culturally competent professional role within the context of the consumer movement?

11 Cultural Competence with Age Groups

PROJECT 14

Culturally Competent Social Work Practice with Elderly People

Diversity Project by Christina Pollard

As the social work intern in the emergency room of a major urban hospital that serves members of its Health Maintenance Plan, I see a wide variety of patients. My hospital's medical social work policy states that the emergency room social worker will attempt to meet with all patients over the age of 75 who enter the emergency room in order to assess their safety and support at home. I see at least ten elderly patients each day I am in the field, and many others may be admitted or discharged before I am able to meet with them and perform an assessment. Some come to the emergency room with minor complaints, while others have had serious falls, life-threatening emergencies, or are coming from a nursing home because of failing health. Needs vary markedly, and may include nursing home placement, arrangement of transportation to return home, reports to Adult Protective Services for abuse or neglect, counseling and support, or simply a packet with information about resources for help at home and the medical social work

office phone number to contact if needed. Ultimately, this can be an extremely challenging and gratifying group of patients to work with. My daily work with this population has led to my interest in learning more about elderly people.

KNOWLEDGE OF POPULATION

History of the Elderly in the United States

Unlike specific groups of cultural immigrants who may have arrived in the United States at different times, from different places, and faced different obstacles, there has always been an elderly population in the United States. As centuries have passed and the country has changed, the very definition of elderly has also changed. While one may have been considered "elderly" at 50 or 60 in the early 1900s, many Americans now live well beyond 75 years. Eventually, if one lives long enough, regardless of class, or race, or cultural affiliation, or any other variables, one will reach the phase in life when she/he is considered "elderly." Many elderly citizens face similar challenges, but there are also often significant differences. A poor elderly person may have many more difficulties surviving than a wealthy one, while an African American elderly person may have had drastically different life experiences than a Caucasian elderly person, or from a monolingual Chinese immigrant. Among the hospital patients with whom I have worked, some are entirely independent, while others require massive amounts of support. Some elderly patients have a large support network, while others have nobody at all. They are white, black, brown, yellow, and every shade in between. Some are straight, others are homosexual or bisexual. While this population is specific by age, an enormous amount of diversity exists within it.

The Life Course perspective helps to illuminate the history of this population, for the history of the United States and the world in the past 90 years has been the history of most of the elderly patients in the emergency department. Many have witnessed at least one World War and all subsequent wars. Some have been strongly affected by the Great Depression, while others barely remember it. All have lived through the Cold War, the Civil Rights movement, and other major historical events in the United States. They have witnessed immense advances in the medical and technological fields. In the past 50 years alone, cancer treatments, heart surgery, dialysis, organ transplantation, and other surgical advances have changed the face of medicine.

As this population has aged, life expectancy in the United States has increased markedly, now at an all time high of 77.2 years (United National Center for Health Statistics 2005). The United States Census 2000 found that of the 293,655,404 residents in the United States, 34,992,000 were over age 65. The Census Bureau also estimates that in 2003 there were 35,919,000 residents of the United States over age 65, a nearly one million person increase in three years (U.S. Census 2004). Clearly, this population is growing

and will continue to do so as the baby boomer population ages. As my field placement is in the healthcare setting, it seems appropriate to consider critical health legislation that impacts elderly members of the United States.

Perhaps one of the most significant programs for elders in the United States has been the introduction of Medicare. President Theodore Roosevelt first proposed a failed national health insurance plan in 1912, and later President Franklin D. Roosevelt considered implementing national health insurance along with Social Security, but was blocked by political opposition. Even Harry S. Truman's advocacy of such a program was blocked by fears that national health care was "creeping socialism" (Weitz 2004). Finally, widespread concern for health coverage for vulnerable members of the population caused Congress to enact both Medicare and Medicaid programs in 1965 (Weitz 2004). Since then, Medicare has insured more United States residents than any other insurance program. While a full discussion of the Medicare program is outside the scope of this project, it is important to know that Medicare provides some health insurance coverage for many persons over the age of 65, and is expected to serve 77 million, or more than one of five Americans, by the year 2030 (Lee and Estes 2003). The elders my hospital serves have chosen to enroll as members of a special Senior Plan within a broader national HMO. Many watch the current Medicare debate with great interest, as they can remember what it was like before the program existed, and they hold strong convictions that this program is vital, and should remain in place.

Book Selection: *Tuesdays With Morrie*

To learn more about the aging experience, I wanted to stay away from a book that would feel like a textbook, and chose something that would speak to me on a different level. *Tuesdays With Morrie* (Albom 1997) was an excellent choice. The book gives the reader a real sense of aging and the different phases a person may pass through as she/he prepares for the end of her/his life. The most inspiring thing about this book is all the knowledge that Morrie, an elderly man who is dying throughout the course of the book, has to share with Mitch, his former student. I chose this book because I had heard that it reflected the great wisdom and insight elderly people have to share with younger generations. I did not want to read a book that *told* me what elderly people were like or what they struggled with, but rather *demonstrated* these things. The book shares conversations between the author, Mitch, and Morrie, his 78-year-old former college professor, who is dying from Lou Gehrig's disease, and includes Mitch's reflections on the taped conversations between the two men that took place every week while Morrie approached his death.

The reader comes through this book not only with a sense of what the dying process can mean to an individual, but also with a profound awareness of the immense amount of knowledge, insight, and experience that elderly people have. Very often, members of younger generations may not realize all that elderly people have experienced. They may look at elderly people and think "they just can't understand, they're too old," without stopping to think that they have already been the same age as younger people, and may have some great insights to share. At one point in the book, Mitch asks Morrie if he envies him for his youth. Morrie says it is "impossible" for him not to envy young people. He goes on to share that he believes a person must accept his age at that moment, and that he has already experienced Mitch's age, and he is a part of every other age up to his own. Morrie questions how he can be envious of Mitch's age when he has already lived through it. Morrie also says: "As you grow, you learn more. If you stayed as ignorant as you were at twenty-two, you'd always be twenty-two. Aging is not just decay, you know. It's growth. Its more than the negative that you're going to die, it's the positive that you understand you're going to die, and that you live a better life because of it" (120). This book really demonstrated how much

strength, dignity, and resolve can contribute to a peaceful death.

One thing I kept in mind while reading this book was that Morrie's views on life and dying are unique, and that each person will approach the end of life differently. Morrie also has had the added benefit of having lived a very comfortable life as a professor at Brandeis University. I think the most useful aspect of this book for the purpose of this project was to reflect on the wealth of insight, knowledge, personal pains, and triumphs of one man in his late seventies. It sounds very cliché, but this book is a fantastic reminder that each person has a story to tell, and that each elderly patient I work with is not just "some old person," but rather someone whose years of life experience and insight should be respected and recognized.

Film Selection: *Complaints of a Dutiful Daughter*

Doris, an elderly woman with Alzheimer's disease, and her daughter Deborah, her caregiver, are the principal characters in the moving film *Complaints of a Dutiful Daughter* (Hoffman 1994). The movie begins with Deborah's attempt to create home-movie memories of her ailing mother. During the course of the film, the relationship between mother and daughter is transformed, as Deborah assumes her new position as her mother's caregiver. This transformation, or reversal of roles, was not a surprise to me at all, as I have witnessed a similar shift in roles between my mother and grandmother over the past ten years. What was amazing for me to witness, however, was the process of Doris's deterioration over the course of the film. The elderly people in my life are entirely oriented and aware, so I had never experienced dementia on a personal level until my experiences in the emergency room.

Of course not all of the patients I meet in the emergency room have severe dementia or Alzheimer's. But when I meet such patients in the emergency room, my interactions with them are so brief, and I am exposed to their mental state for a such a short amount of time that I am unable to gain a full understanding of what it is like to be, or to live with, such patients. This film enabled me to look into what the life of an Alzheimer's patient can be like, day in and day out. From major confusion in conversation, to difficulty performing daily tasks, Doris's condition worsens throughout the film. It was difficult to watch the mother's slow decline and her daughter's struggle with her role as a witness to this powerful and ravaging disease that was stripping away the vibrant and capable woman she used to know.

It was also difficult to witness Deborah's great emotional stress. This film really helped me understand the painful, difficult issues and insights that family members must confront when a loved one has dementia or Alzheimer's disease. Deborah oftentimes appears to be frustrated and fall into despair, yet she remains lovingly devoted to her mother. While the film certainly has moments of humor, it is a stirring account of one family's journey through Alzheimer's disease. This film was an excellent look into the world of Alzheimer's patients and their family members, and demonstrates both triumphs and immense challenges that each must confront each day.

Event: Elderly Member Dementia/Alzheimer's Support Group

After viewing Complaints of a Dutiful Daughter, I knew that I wanted to understand more about the elderly population from the perspective of the caregivers. When I attended this group, I was not surrounded by the population that is the focus of this project, but, rather, by those who spend long stretches of time caring for elders with Alzheimer's disease and dementia. During the two sessions I spent with this drop-in support group, I was able to learn a great deal about the population through their moving stories.

Many caregivers at the meetings felt torn between devoting their lives to their ailing parents, and living their own lives with their families. Several spoke about placing their loved ones in a nursing facility, but said they felt guilty even having such ideas. Many

seemed to be greatly distressed. They wanted to have their "own lives," but they felt bound to their parents because it was their "duty" to care for them in old age. It was a very difficult and emotionally draining situation for the caregivers. Some spoke of how their parents seemed more like "little children," and needed to be watched constantly so that they didn't wander away from the home. Many had special locks at home to keep their parents from wandering away. Caregivers also spoke of how angry and frustrated their elderly parents were at times, because they wanted to be independent and live in their own homes and perform their own activities without supervision. A recurring theme was that many elderly people with dementia simply do not understand the extent of their debilitation and try to continue to be independent. Caregivers shared with me the sadness and depression that many of their parents experienced, their frequent isolation, and their minimal interaction with anyone outside the family. Some families used adult day care, which seemed to be an immense help for both patient and caregiver.

In reviewing my notes from these sessions, I am able to identify some major themes that have been helpful in my work with this population. Many caretakers expressed isolation as a concern for both themselves and their parent. They felt they could not have a social life because they are tied to their parents, who are so dependent on them, and they also worried that their parents do not have enough social interaction. Others talked at length about depression and hopelessness, which once again seemed to affect both elders and caregivers.

Although I expressed great empathy, I got the sense from many that they did not think I could grasp the intensity of their experience, which made it very difficult for me to be at the meetings. One woman said to me, "I hope you never have to go through this with your parents, honey, but you just never know who it's going to hit." There was a general feeling that I was far too young to understand this situation or relate to the caregiver's experiences. Though this may be true, I was a little put off by the assumption that my young age, 22, does not allow me to understand the challenges this group faces. I have a 91-year-old grandmother who, while she does not suffer from dementia or Alzheimer's disease, does require an immense amount of support. At the same time, I know that I cannot fully appreciate the experience of being a full-time caregiver for a parent. In some ways, the meetings made me very fearful for my parents, now in their mid-fifties, and their future. More than anything, I am just afraid that they will become ill or suffer from dementia, but I know if this happens I want to help take care of them.

Interview

I interviewed "Mary," a 78-year-old African American. Mary lives alone and has four children and ten grandchildren who all live either nearby or in neighboring cities. Mary was born in Oakland in the mid-twenties, right before the Great Depression, but does not remember much of her childhood. Her father worked in the naval yards, and her mother stayed home with her and her five brothers and sisters. Mary was a middle child, and she remembers playing a lot with her siblings as she was growing up. She spoke at length about "The Wars," and expressed regret that the United States is involved in war yet again. Neither her father nor her brothers served in the war, but she does remember distant younger cousins who fought in the Vietnam War and died. "I can't see why they can't seem to learn that violence is not the way. I've seen so many boys die in these wars over the years. And for what? What are they dying for?"

Mary also shared her insights into the Civil Rights movement and the Black Panthers, and mentioned several times that she witnessed protests, and had feared that her children might take part in the movement and be arrested. She also found great hope in the Civil Rights movement, and became quite distressed when she spoke of the assassination of Dr. King. Ultimately, she feels very grateful for the movement. "I remember," she said,

"where the city I grew up in was called 'the most racist city in the United States.' Can you believe it? That little old city? Now I have a grandbaby who lives there and does just fine. There's been changes around here, so many changes. There is still a long ways to go in this world, but things are different. It used to be a way that you couldn't even imagine, thank God." It was amazing to reflect on the fact that she knew the city where I grew up long before my parents even lived there, and that she has seen the world pass through so many stages that I will never experience.

I asked Mary about her experience as an elderly member of society, and how her life had changed in the past ten years. The most noticeable thing, she told me, was that her husband had passed away five years ago. In the past ten years, several of her close friends have also died. She said: "Each year, there's a few less of us around. It's sad, and it's lonely. I'm losing my friends—the people I've been through life with." Her support networks were mainly her children and grandchildren, who make a point to call or come by her home every day. She said: "I'm proud of them you know. They look after me. I have some friends whose kids don't even stop by but once a week. Now that's a shame! It used to be that you took care of your own, but it seems like more and more of us older folks are being left alone. We aren't valued like we used to be. Families are so busy they think they don't have time for us. Don't they realize they wouldn't be where they are without us?" Mary was clearly upset by this topic, and expressed her displeasure several times during the interview regarding how society does not highly value the elderly and often pushes them to the side. She is greatly troubled that more families do not "take care of their own."

Mary also spoke at length about how it feels to be a senior and the different resources and programs that are available. She says she used a senior center for socialization until recently, when she became weaker and unable to walk the five blocks to the center. She can no longer drive, which she describes as the "worst thing" because she can't "just get out where I want to be when I want to be there." She reports that it was a decline in her vision that led to her being unable to drive. Mary also talks about the declining health of her friends quite frequently.

At one point she grew very quiet and looked off into the distance. She looked at me and said, "You know, a few weeks ago I had a friend come to the hospital and she never came back. I hope that doesn't happen to me. I don't want to die in a damn hospital." Aside from having friends who have died, Mary also has several friends who have entered nursing homes because of dementia. She said, "It's like they're there right in front of you, but they don't know what's going on. Linda was always happy, so she's still happy. But she can't even remember her kids, and she certainly doesn't remember me. It's scary to see it, because I never thought it could happen to her. I never want to be like that. I'm so afraid of becoming like that some day." Mary expressed her fears of becoming a burden on her family as well.

When I reflect on my interview with Mary, I can identify some very important themes: she faces more and more isolation as her friends pass away and become less able to socialize with her because neither of them can leave the home with much ease; she relies on her family members for support, and while she is glad they are there for her, she does have fears of being too much of a burden; she has fears about death, but knows that she will be confronting it soon; she is also aware that she has had a full and rich life, and has many wonderful and insightful stories to share.

Final Thoughts

While I used the support group as a place for an immersion experience, I also regard my daily experiences in the emergency department as an immersion in the elderly population. I often hear patients speak of how nobody cares, and feel a little bit of guilt and sadness every time I hear this. A few days ago, I was interviewing an elderly couple, and we made a joke about an outdated sign on the wall. The husband looked at me and said,

"Well, we must be considered pretty outdated for as long as we've had to wait here!" I knew that he honestly felt neglected and unimportant because of his age, but I didn't know what to say. He went on to say, "You young people, you don't really have time for us, do you?" I tried to assure him that he was important to our hospital and that the medical staff had been very busy all day long and would be in to see him soon. However, I was aware that privately some part of me couldn't help wondering if his experience would be different if he was thirty years younger and more of the medical staff could identify with him. Because of the nature of emergency room social work, most of my interactions with patients are time limited. During my interview with Mary, I could see that in a situation where there was time to talk, the amount of information that could be shared was truly amazing. The things Mary shared included some very difficult and stressful situations that I heard many loved ones discuss in the support group meetings I attended, in the film and book I used for this project, and in the everyday conversations of clients I serve in the emergency room. I am distressed by the sense of loneliness, isolation, and despair that I feel in this population. *Tuesdays With Morrie* (Albom 1997) is the only part of this project that was not entirely depressing to take in, even though it too was tinged with the sadness of death, disease, and final goodbyes.

As a 22-year-old social worker, I know that many elderly patients may feel that I cannot understand their situation in life. While I certainly cannot claim to know what it is like to live in the United States as an elderly person, this project has given me the opportunity to reflect upon the many challenges this population faces. I think that after completing it, I will be less likely to give a little sigh when I take down the long list of elderly patients I need to see that day, and instead try a little harder to convey the respect and understanding that this population deserves, do my best to identify the challenges clients may be experiencing, and link them to the appropriate resources.

Applying the Knowledge Base: Agency, Services and Policies, and Personal Competencies

THE FIELD WORK AGENCY: URBAN HMO HOSPITAL'S EMERGENCY ROOM

The Agency

Community The hospital serves a very large community and is located at an intersection of three neighborhoods: the downtown business center; a working class predominantly African American community; and a wealthier neighborhood with many Caucasian residents. Patients come from all of these neighborhoods as well as nearby urban centers, and the ethnic composition is extremely diverse. A hospital social worker is likely to encounter patients from a wide variety of cultural groups, and most likely to encounter patients over the age of 65, as is the case in the emergency room where I am placed.

Access Patients reach the hospital by a variety of modes of transportation. Those in acute medical distress often arrive by ambulance and are taken to the emergency department. Others are brought by family members, arrive via public transportation, are referred by physicians from clinics, or walk. Patients cross a variety of geographic and ethnic boundaries when they come to the hospital, as most of the patients do not live in the immediate area. While the emergency department does not provide outreach services to the community, the HMO itself advertises on billboards and in the media. However, most plan members join the group through employee benefits. The hospital and surrounding clinics are all accessible to wheelchairs with the appropriate ramps and hallway and door widths. Translation services and TDD assistance for blind patients are also offered by the hospital to ease access to resources for patients with disabilities.

Receptivity The vast majority of patients served are members of the elderly population.

Nurses, physicians, physical therapists, social workers, and many other professionals that the hospital employs are very familiar with working with elderly patients. While staff in the hospital is certainly trained in working with the elderly population, very few are actually members of this population. Many elderly patients may be cared for by medical residents and other staff who are quite young, some under the age of 25. It is rare to see physicians over the age of 60 in the hospital. The only group of staff members consistently over the age of 75 are the volunteers, who staff the gift shop and information desks, and generally do not have much direct contact with patients.

The hospital does have support groups, literature, and services available for the elderly population. The literature, posters, and signs often depict a mix of young and old members of different ethnicities, so elderly patients can likely identify with some of the literature. Most of the literature, however, is not in large print. This may make reading more difficult for some elderly patients who have difficulty with their vision.

Administration and Staff Training I have been told that social work staff members receive some training in working with elderly patients, particularly around the more complex and sensitive areas of patients with dementia, depression, and end-of-life decisions. However, it seems to be generally assumed that social workers in the hospital will inherently know how to work with the unique issues the elderly population faces.

Some training and discussion is held around issues that are commonly dealt with in work with elders during weekly staff meetings. The meetings I attended often included guest speakers from either outside agencies or services within the system that can be resources to this population. As an intern, I participated in several meetings that included education about adult day health care, Alzheimer's support groups, nursing home financing, home health services, and a variety of other services available to elderly patients. Attendance at these meetings is not compulsory; however, many members of the social work staff may miss them.

Staff Sensitivity Elderly patients may often feel isolated in the hospital, particularly in the emergency room. Staff members are likely to make comments within earshot of patients about "old people," and they often behave in a patronizing manner toward elderly clients. Many patients feel as if they do not receive the respect they deserve. The vast majority of nursing and medical staff in the emergency room is under the age of 50, so those patients over 75 are unlikely to ever interact with practitioners they feel can relate to the challenges they face as they age.

The younger staff very often use "they" language when referring to the elderly population, and speak to the patients in a very casual manner. This style of communication may leave elderly patients feeling as if the staff does not respect or value them. Some even make inappropriate comments regarding patients' ages. In an extreme case, a nurse was overheard exclaiming, "She's 91 years old for God's sake! Why did they bring her in? She's going to die soon anyway. Go to the light, go to the light!" Unfortunately, these sorts of jokes are not uncommon in the emergency room. They clearly reflect a lack of sensitivity to the end-of-life issues that many elderly patients grapple with.

Funding

In comparison to smaller, community-based health maintenance organizations, this national HMO has an enormous amount of funds at its disposal. The hospital is a non-profit organization, but the physicians that work in the hospital and clinics are a part of a separate, for-profit system. The main source of funds is member purchases of health plan memberships. This large amount of money and many other sources of revenue are more than enough to fund programs that are culturally sensitive to the elderly population; however, different programs and populations compete for adequate funding, and training in sensitive and culturally competent work with the elderly population has not been a priority in spite of their preponderance in the patient population the hospital serves. In general, however, the hospital does provide competent services to the community.

The Program and Policies

Effort While I have certainly witnessed an effort to be sensitive to the needs of the elderly population in my work at the hospital, the actual policies and procedures of the social work department do not specify any sort of consistent effort social workers should make to ensure there is a voice for this population. Elderly patients are rarely, if ever, consulted to formulate or design policies and programs. In fact, the main role of the hospital social worker is to work with patients in the face of policies and programs that many social workers find quite inadequate and unfair.

Social workers are often called upon to assist with discharge plans even when patients do not feel they are ready or safe to return home, and they may have to inform a patient that she/he is not entitled to certain benefits that she/he thinks she/he should be. There seems to be a distinct disconnect between the social worker's role as agent of the hospital who renders service with hospital policy, and the social worker's role as a patient advocate who serves the patients' best interests.

Quality HMO and hospital policy require that all plan members be treated equally and receive services regardless of age. The organization requires respectful treatment of all members, including members of the elderly population. Because the organization is so large and serves such a wide variety of populations—from birth to death, those with or without developmental, cognitive, or other disabilities, Asian, African American, Caucasian, Indian, and many other ethnicities, religious identities, and sexual orientations—the policies and procedures do not specify how employees should treat one group in particular. Rather, it is clearly stated and emphasized that *all* patients, regardless of any distinguishing characteristic, should be treated in the same manner and with respect and dignity.

The hospital makes efforts to include staff representatives of different religious denominations through the chaplaincy service, and there are translation services available to those members who do not speak English. There do not seem to be specific provisions in place for the elderly population; however, elderly patients are often also members of other diverse populations that the hospital makes special attempts to serve.

Effectiveness The hospital and emergency department serve more elderly patients than any other group. This is representative of the enrollment of patients in the health plan at this time, and also reflects the increasing medical needs that patients encounter as they age. Most of the elderly patients in the emergency department utilize the services appropriately; however it is generally not these patients who are most often referred to the social worker.

More frequently, a social worker will receive a referral for an elderly patient who has been labeled as a "frequent flier," a patient who is admitted to the emergency room frequently, and with some sort of vague complaint that the nurses and physicians believe is a social issue more than a medical one. The hospital has several services available to frequent flier patients. The two most commonly used include home healthcare and high risk case management.

Unfortunately, home health is an overburdened service that cannot meet all referrals in a timely manner, while high risk case management appears to be an underutilized service. When patients are successfully enrolled in these programs, they have significantly fewer visits to the emergency depart-

ment because of the support and community linkages they receive at home, and the programs are effective.

While most necessary social services are not provided directly in the emergency department, patients can receive a wide variety of referrals to community agencies or health plan services for elderly patients through the emergency room. Social workers also assist in arranging transportation home and assessing the patient's safety at home prior to discharge. Overwhelmingly, however, patients feel they are pushed out of the emergency department or hospital and back into the community far too soon. This issue seems to be occurring in hospitals nationwide and is not unique to this hospital.

The most common request that patients have is for a caretaker in the home to assist in custodial, everyday activities of daily living (ADLs) such as bathing, dressing, and preparing meals. This is not an included plan benefit for members at any age, and patients are often very upset that they must privately pay agencies to receive these services. The social work department is effective in making outside referrals for such support, but cannot guarantee that the patient will receive such services at home.

While this health plan policy issue does not affect the effectiveness of in-hospital treatment of elderly patients, it does have a major impact on health services to elderly clients as a whole who are plan members.

Efficiency It is difficult to measure the efficiency of social work in the emergency department because of the unique needs of the elderly population in this setting. As a medical service, this department is extremely effective and efficient, and the patients are either stabilized and discharged or admitted to the hospital for more care. As far as social services are concerned, it is my belief that social workers are only marginally able to address the psychosocial needs of elderly patients in the emergency department, due to time constraints, and thus do not utilize their professional skills in an efficient or effective manner.

The health plan's designated role for social workers is primarily as discharge planners. The social worker is often too busy arranging transportation, ordering durable medical equipment, or arranging admission to a skilled nursing facility to perform an indepth psychosocial assessment of a patient. Thus, the important psychosocial interventions are not explored because the social worker has so many other tasks and must focus her/his time with the patient on developing a discharge plan.

Social workers in the emergency department do have an extensive list of outside agencies that may provide support and assistance to elderly patients, and most patients who enter the emergency department who express need for such resources receive them. While the department is certainly efficient in distributing resources, very little follow up exists to make sure patients' support increases at home. Unfortunately, it is not until an elderly patient is identified as a frequent flier that she/he receives more in-home services.

It might be more efficient use of professional time to arrange for social workers to work with paraprofessionals. After a social work needs assessment, a paraprofessional can follow up on making calls to arrange transportation, durable medical equipment, and other concrete services the patient requires. This would free up professional social work time to address clients' psychosocial needs and increase both the effective provision of services and the efficient use of professional skills.

Personal Cultural Competencies

The elderly population is an incredibly diverse group. While members of this population all have their age in common, they differ greatly across race, class, gender, sexual orientation, religion, and many other qualities. Often, in my interactions with elderly patients, I had to work hard to decipher when behavior or beliefs stemmed from a part of a patient's identity that was separate from her/his identity as an elderly person. Individuals clearly carry with them many identities, and the

experiences of a 78-year-old African American male of the upper class are quite different than those of a 78-year-old monolingual immigrant from China who relies on her daughter for support.

The elderly patients I have encountered during my year of work have been so diverse that I have hesitated to speak about them as a group, implying that they are all alike, when the differences and unique circumstances among them have been so great. This said, and while recognizing that at times a patient's ethnicity and cultural notions of the problem as well as the patient's mental state (i.e., dementia, Alzheimer's) influence my interaction with her/him more than her/his status as an elderly person, I will attempt to focus this portion of the assessment on the characteristics that seem to be most common among the elderly population I served in the emergency department.

Engagement, Trust, and Relationship-building

As a group, elderly patients seem to be reluctant to use social agencies outside a health plan. There seems to be a prevalent belief that the health plan should provide comprehensive services for all patient needs, and not just medical ones. Consequently, most patients are shocked to hear that they will not be provided with some sort of assistance at home with ADLs (activities of daily living), and become especially upset to hear that transportation home from the emergency department is not a plan benefit.

In such situations, the social worker must often position her/himself as the patient's ally, and express her/his empathy for the patient's frustrations with these service limitations. If the social worker simply "lays down the law," and states the plan's policies, she/he is much more likely to face resistance from the patient and end up in a situation in which the patient refuses to leave the emergency department.

Elderly patients are often eager to engage with the social worker. They expect respect from the worker, and most expect a handshake with the initial introduction to the worker. The worker should first address the patient as Mr., Ms., or Mrs., unless the patient indicates a preference for another form of address.

A patient's expectations of the interview vary greatly depending on her/his mental and medical status at the time of the interview. Many wish to give as much information as possible, but quite frequently defer to their adult children or other friends and family in the room. At times, the social worker may have to ask that the patient answer questions directly in order to gain insight into the patient's view of the concern rather than the family member's. When asked directly, most elderly patients will answer questions without hesitation.

If still married, elderly patients overwhelmingly state the need to check with a spouse/partner before making a major decision. Others may say they need to ask other family members. As a group, elderly patients seem to value the input of individuals they feel close to, and will often consult them before making major decisions. That said, elderly patients become very upset if they feel that anyone is attempting to make decisions without their input. When family members assume that the elder does not need to be consulted in the decision-making process, the elder is often very offended.

It is always best practice when first meeting an elderly patient to begin the interview by addressing her/him and later asking the patient for permission to speak with family members or friends who may be able to share information. Most patients will agree to this and appreciate that the worker has come to them first for information.

Assessment and Problem Definition Several tools are useful in assessing elderly patients in the emergency department. The hospital requires that the social worker use a discharge planning tool, which prompts the worker to ask several questions regarding the patient's medical conditions, support at home, transportation plan, and advance directive status. As an intern, I had the luxury of spending more time with patients that were presented with more complex psychosocial needs, or patients who appeared to have a questionable mental status. In those interventions I often used a Mini Mental Status exam or the Geri-atric Depression Scale (short form) and any other useful assessment tools to develop my assessment of the patient.

While many staff members and family members of patients would identify the patient living on her/his own as a major problem and concern, the patient rarely agreed that this was a problem. Instead, patients would state that "falling at home" or "getting around" were problems. They rarely attributed living alone as an issue of concern, and as the social worker I had to be very careful to respect the patient's conception of her/his living situation and provide gentle confrontation about her/his living situation when necessary.

Contracting and Goal Setting The most culturally appropriate goals for this population are ones that include support for maintaining independence. More than any other concern, elderly patients express great fear and anxiety about losing independence and having to leave home. If it was very clear that a patient was simply unsafe at home on her/his own, I would never jump immediately to the option of a nursing home, as patients would react very negatively to this suggestion. I worked with the patient to set the goal of safety and good health, as most elderly patients were uncomfortable in the hospital and eager to return home. The patient and I would discuss her/his living situation, and I would emphasize the importance of safety at home to decrease the patient's risk of injury and illness in the future because of falls at home or her/his inability to care for her/himself. The patients were often very agreeable to these goals because they did not include any sort of decrease in independence and instead focused on helping them live healthier and safer lives.

The next step of this process often included walking the patient through the different options available to her/him to make her/him safer at home. The first option we discussed was help in the home, which the patient could receive from private agencies or from In Home Supportive Services if she/he had Medicaid coverage. The next suggestion was often an assisted living situation, which is quite different from a nursing home. If the patient had family in the area willing to have the patient move into their home, we discussed this option as well as other community-based resources. Finally, I would discuss a custodial nursing home with the patient. Patients often felt empowered by having a range of options to choose from, and expanding choice was a powerful tool in working with this population.

Major decisions such as admission to a nursing home were rarely made in the emergency department. Instead, I often found myself laying the groundwork for future conversations between the patient and the hospital floor social workers. I would discuss the different options available to the patient so that when the floor social worker spoke to her/him about the possibility of nursing home placement or hiring help in the home, the topic would not be completely new and thus less overwhelming. The floor social worker would also receive my notes on the patient so she/he would be aware of the wishes and concerns the patient expressed and any sort of resistance she/he was likely to encounter in her/his work with the patient.

Interventions While I performed many assessments in the emergency department, concrete interventions were less common. When an elderly patient was admitted to the department as a result of abuse, neglect, or self neglect, I immediately made an Adult Protective Services referral to ensure the patient's safety and to involve an agency with a wide array of available resources.

Overwhelmingly, the patients preferred to receive support from their family members or do things on their own, but these were often the least viable options. I provided elderly patients with resource packets that included information on advance directives, agencies offering support in the home, assisted living, custodial care, and community agencies such as Meals on Wheels that offer services to elderly patients at home. I often made referrals to senior support groups as well as support groups for caregivers of patients with dementia.

If patients fit into the frequent flier category, I made referrals to high risk case management in the hopes that this department could help the patient manage her/his healthcare at home. Almost all elderly patients preferred interventions that would help them maintain independence and enable them to live at home on their own, so I attempted to do this whenever possible. There were also many interventions such as empathic listening, emotional support, education, and bereavement counseling for the patients. While these interventions did not result in an outside referral, they were an integral part of the patient's experience in the emergency department. In the frantic atmosphere of the emergency department, it is usually the social worker that represents a caring and compassionate human connection and can take the time to listen to a patient's story.

Evaluation and Termination In general, elderly patients understand success or failure in dealing with their problems in terms of their ability to maintain independence. This does not necessarily mean that the only acceptable or successful solution to the problems they are facing is to remain living independently, but it does mean that they maintain the control and independent decision-making power over their lives. For some clients, however, success is measured in terms of absolute independence and any intervention that includes help or assistance in the home is regarded as a failure. For most, the ultimate failure is admission to a nursing home or assisted living facility.

At times, especially in my work with patients living with severe dementia or Alzheimer's disease, I could not rely on the patient's opinion regarding the helpfulness of my intervention. Many of these patients often believed they could live independently even if they had been nursing home residents for years. When this was the case, I would politely listen to the patient's story and also work closely with family members or conservators who had the patient's best interests in mind. I often relied on their opinions about the helpfulness of my interventions.

Interactions with elderly patients in the emergency department are very brief. At best, a patient may interact with me for 30 minutes and then see me a few more times as I pass by to check in with the patient. I rarely saw patients more than once and did not have the opportunity to form close relationships with them. Termination was not difficult for me or the patients in the emergency department because of the brief nature of my encounters with them.

Patients were often much more preoccupied with their medical emergency than dealing with issues of support at home, or other issues I would address as a social worker. They were often overwhelmed by the wide array of specialists they were seeing, and were sometimes sent home or up to the hospital floors before I had a chance to say goodbye. This lack of continuity with patients and lack of relationship building in the emergency department is certainly one of the most frustrating aspects of emergency department social work.

Evaluation through NASW Standards of Cultural Competence

NASW (2001) sets forth standards for cultural competence and diversity among social workers. Section 1.05, part B states: "Social workers should have a knowledge base of their clients' cultures and be able to demonstrate competence in the provision of services that are sensitive to clients' cultures and to differences among people and cultural groups." When assessing the hospital, the emergency department, policies and programs, and my cultural competence against this standard, I am generally encouraged by what I see, with a few notable exceptions.

The hospital requires equal treatment of all patients, regardless of age. The majority of patients the hospital serves are over the age of 75, and they receive kind, caring, and competent service each day. Great diversity exists among the elderly population, and the hospital and emergency department strive to accommodate members of all populations.

The practitioners across the hospital and in the emergency department in particular are all knowledgeable in working with members of the elderly population and competent in work with members of this population who have different levels of physical and mental capabilities. The hospital and the emergency department have a wide variety of resources and referrals that are appropriate for elderly patients.

Doctors, nurses, and other professionals all strive to provide patients with culturally congruent care, but they may often fall short. Some are extremely callous about issues of aging, and many infantilize patients in their interactions with them. This sort of behavior cannot be ignored, and stands as the most obvious and disturbing failure of the hospital and the emergency department staff. Ageist and often discriminatory statements would seem to demonstrate that many of the emergency room staff do not value or respect their elderly clients, nor their lives as older members of our communities. Comments made within earshot of elderly patients further degrade and victimize them, and there seemed to be little effort directed at limiting or containing, let alone addressing, the issues that were raised by such comments and stereotypical attitudes. It seemed as though despite the fact that nondiscriminatory policies existed on paper, there was little follow-up to ensure that members of the staff adhered to them in respect to the elderly population.

In terms of my personal cultural competence in work with elderly patients, I have seen an immense improvement throughout the year. I feel that I have met this standard the NASW set forth in my work with patients. I have learned about the most common beliefs, fears, anxieties, and needs of the elderly population and what services they may need and use the most. I pay close attention to the unique struggles that this group faces and attempt to work with them as a partner, respecting their independence and dignity in finding a solution that is acceptable in their culture.

REFERENCES

Albom, M. 1997. *Tuesdays with Morrie: An Old Man, a Young Man and Life's Greatest Lessons*. New York: Doubleday.

Hoffman, D. (producer, writer, director). 1994. *Complaints of a Dutiful Daughter* [documentary]. New York: D/D Production.

Lee, P., and C. Estes, eds. 2003. *The Nation's Health*. 3d ed. Boston: Jones & Bartlett Publishers.

National Association of Social Workers (NASW). 2001. *NASW Standards for Cultural Competence in Social Work Practice*. Washington, D.C.: Author.

U. S. Census. 2004. USA Statistics in Brief—Population By Sex, Age, and Region. http:/www.census.gov/statab/www/pop.html

Weitz, R. 2004. *The Sociology of Health, Illness, and Health Care*. New York: Thomson Wadsworth.

Worksheet

1. Demographic changes in the age of the population of the United States that are expected to occur as the Baby Boomers age present many challenges to policymakers. One issue that has received a great deal of publicity is the future of the Social Security program. Originally designed as supplemental income to a much less long-lived population, Social Security today is the sole source of support for a substantial portion of the elderly, who are enjoying longer and healthier lifespans. Ideas for addressing the expected shortfall proliferate, and include eliminating Social Security payments for the wealthy, raising the cap on annual contributions, delaying the eligibility until later in life, terminating the program, and changing to a pay-as-you-go system. What do you believe to be an equitable and reasonable way to address the issues with Social Security?

2. Hospital acute care services are designed to treat all patients equally in terms of the amount of care received, days of hospital stay, and conditions of service. For example, the expected length of stay in the hospital for a hernia repair will be the same for a 26-year-old athlete and a 74-year-old elder. However, "justice as equal treatment" fails to address the longer healing times and weaker conditions of many elderly patients in the hospital. (a) How might length of stay issues be addressed to take into consideration the needs of individual patients? (b) How would this be reflected in insurance policies and premiums, Medicare, and Medicaid?

Culturally Competent Social Work Practice with Adolescents

Diversity Project by Erica Tom

My field work placement is with an agency that serves foster youth and youth on probation, and services are provided primarily in the public schools. As my career goal is to work with adolescents, I hope to increase my knowledge of current adolescent issues and concerns through immersing myself in this culture.

KNOWLEDGE OF POPULATION

History and Background

Adolescence was seen to be a unique developmental period beginning only in the early 1900s (DeHart, Sroufe, and Cooper 2000). Biologically, adolescence begins with the onset of puberty (Ashford, LeCroy, and Lortie 1999). Adolescence is described as a period of dramatic physical, cognitive, emotional, and social change that starts approximately around age 12 and extends to age 17 or even age 19 (DeHart, Sroufe, and Cooper 2000). There is not a specific age when adolescence begins or ends. Adolescence as defined by Ashford, LeCroy and Lortie (1999) can begin around ages 10 to 12 and end around ages 21 and 22. However, those from the upper-middle class and upper class may extend their adolescence into their late twenties or early thirties by attending graduate or professional school and then receiving additional advice and financial support from their parents as they start their own families, careers, or businesses (Kendall 2002, 92).

According to Kendall (2002), in industrial societies, such as the United States, the adolescent or teenage years represent a buffer between childhood and adulthood. There is no specific rite of passage into adulthood (Kendall 2002). During adolescence, many young people spend a lot of their time thinking, planning, or being educated for future roles they hope or are expected to occupy in society (Kendall 2002). However, some adolescents may have to take on adult responsibilities such as caring for their own children, siblings, or family members.

Biographies

Picture the Girl: Young Women Speak Their Minds (Shehyn 2000), presents thirty-six teenage girls from a variety of backgrounds speaking about the things that are most important to them, such as: friends, body image or physical appearance, motherhood, sexuality, and peer pressure. They also speak about their relationship with their families and their life experiences.

Real Teens: Diary of a Junior Year (1999) presented a more in-depth look into the lives of eight youths attending the same high school. It is part of a 6-volume series of journal entries by teens about their life experiences. Examples of teen handwriting lend another dimension of "reality" to these "real teens", whose entries are authentic experiences collected by Scholastic, Inc. (Anonymous 1999). Represented were four teenage males and four teenage females: Marybeth, Billy, Teresa, Jake, Katie, Edward, Emma, and Kevin. The book contains excerpts from each teen's diary, clearly illustrating both the similarities and the differences in the teens' experiences. Some teens wrote about beginning to think about college and planning for it, while others made no mention of college planning. The teens all wrote about cliques at their school, and some wrote about their feelings about not fitting in. Romantic relationships were mentioned often: they wrote about their boyfriends or girlfriends if they had one, or people that they were interested in dating, and/or about the relationships of their friends. There was also mention of sex, and their mixed feelings surrounding it. Some of them had had sex with their partners, while others were still waiting for the right person. There was mention of underage drinking, raves (large parties typically with dancing and drug use), and their own or their friends' drug use.

Although Marybeth is athletic, plays basketball and runs track, she is concerned about her weight and image, and some days thinks she is fatter than others. She loves hanging out with her friends and thinks her parents, brother, and sister are "cool" as well. She is 16 and wants to get her tongue pierced but her mom won't allow it. She doesn't always get along with her family, but she says in the end they always pull through. She says, "People say we are supposed to enjoy the teenage years because they are the best days with no worries and no real problems," but she disagrees (16). She loves high school, but it is "tough" and she thinks it is harder being a girl. She feels like other girls are questioning themselves as well: about their looks, weight, or how well others like them. She looks at herself in the mirror all the time but feels kind of disgusted by what she sees (Ibid).

Billy gets good grades, but feels that being smart is not good enough and feels he needs to do something that stands out, like playing sports (2). He is really excited about football, and practiced over the summer. He also talks about his relationship with his girlfriend Blair, a freshman at his school, and how his older brother told him to keep his options open especially when it's just the beginning of the relationship (14). His relationship with his parents is "totally up and down" (2). In his diary, he writes about his older brother, their relationship, his brother's accomplishments, his parents' constant comparison of him to his brother, and how he wishes he were more like his brother (15).

Teresa has many interests including loving to write, read, dance, sing, act, play field hockey, listen to all kinds of music, and being with friends and family. She loves reading magazines and horoscopes. She knows she's smart and gets really good grades, but she has a problem, because, she believes, "everyone sees (me) as this airhead." She would love to get all As but she acknowledges her weak subjects: AP history and physics. She is very insecure at times. She wants to go on a diet and is concerned about her weight and appearance. Her parents are divorced and she lives with her mom and older brother even though they don't get along. Her dad lives in the next town and she sees him frequently (3–4).

Jake describes himself as "ladies think (I'm) cute sometimes" (4). He mentions a girl he talked to over the summer, but he felt unsure of himself, so he asked his best friend Kevin for advice. He talks about how good of a friend Kevin is. Jake is shy but loves to dance and is always on the go. He loves raving, riding a Jet Ski, playing pool, and fixing up his new car. His dad is really ill and he says things are terrible at home but he tries to help out as much as he can. His family is always arguing and he wishes it weren't like that. He likes to make his mom and sister laugh.

Katie is very active in different groups. Among other things, she is involved in the community club and student council, on the tennis team, and is a peer ministry leader of her church (4–5). She wants to do really well in school this year, and her schedule is hectic, but she handles the stress with her sense of humor. She feels she has the ability to get along with everyone. The most important thing to her is her family, and they are very close. She shares a special bond, with her mother, to whom she feels she can tell "everything" (4–5).

Edward loves listening to music, watching TV, and playing Nintendo (5). He's a yearbook editor, sometimes runs track, and is in the community club even though he is beginning to hate it. He is doing well in school. He describes his parents as big kids, with his dad being a real comedian and his mom as stupid-funny like himself. He has an older brother that is away at college (Ibid).

Emma is the ice-hockey team manager and is in the community club and student council. She loves hanging out, but makes plans at the last minute, usually with Marybeth. The most important thing to her is her friends. She bought new clothes to prepare for her first day as a junior. Her parents are always busy running around doing many different things, so she and her sister babysit their little brother often, which "can be a drag, but whatever" (6). She likes having a boyfriend but hates being left out. She says, "it seems like everyone has a boyfriend or a girlfriend to talk to except me." (7)

Kevin is very active and goes from one thing to another—wave running, clubbing, swimming—mainly any sport, but mostly "just chilling (hanging out) with friends." (7) However, he gets bored easily. His dad has been married twice so there is "a lotta freakin' people here to deal with and we argue like all the time," but he does really love them all (Ibid). He was really close to his sister, who died eight years ago when he was 8, and he is still mad and constantly thinks about it. He is also concerned about his appearance and called his friend Jake to talk about the new clothes they were going to wear for the first day of school. He likes dressing and doing stuff his way without anyone telling him what to do. He is very excited and looking forward to driving. In his diary he keeps track of the number of days until he will get to drive. He also wants to find a girlfriend this school year (8).

The teens seem to share much in common, but also have unique and different family constellations, interests, goals, and concerns. As an example, it is helpful to explore their feelings about one particular circumstance that will affect them all: the beginning of their junior year at school.

Kevin and Jake are not looking forward to the homework and waking up early (8–9). Katie is "terrified about school": in the past someone was always there to help with homework or listen to her and take care of her, but now she realizes she has to take care of herself (11). Edward doesn't know why everyone makes a big deal out of it being their junior year because he feels it is going to be just like other years. He is also most excited about seeing his friends again: school is the only place where he sees everyone in one place at one

time. His parents are already talking about college, and he feels pressured to do well and feels he has a lot to figure out for himself (12). Billy also likes seeing all his friends at school because "he didn't get to see them much over the summer" (14). However, he knows they won't be in any of the same classes. Emma is glad to be back in school because her "summer was really boring." (15) She and her sister were busy watching their little brother so she couldn't get a summer job or go out during the day. All her friends had summer jobs. She's excited that it's her junior year—"the most important year of high school" (Ibid).

It is clear that, though the event (starting junior year) is the same, each teen's reactions are grounded in her or his own personal experiences, hopes, expectations, social relationships, and family circumstances. Similar differences can be traced by exploring other teen issues, such as dating, sex, driving, or family relationships.

Film: *Mean Girls*

The experiences of 16-year-old Cady Heron, the new girl in school, gives viewers a special window into both the new school and the new-friend-making experiences in adolescence. Cady had lived in Africa with her researcher parents until recently, and was home schooled. Her first day at school didn't go well. She got in trouble for various things in her classes, and she said this was the first time that adults didn't seem to trust her and yelled at her. At lunchtime, she had difficulty finding a place to sit in the cafeteria. No one wanted her to sit at her/his table, so she ate her lunch in a bathroom stall.

Her second day went a bit better. She made friends with two classmates, Janis and Damian. Damian is gay, and Janis joked that he was too gay to function. Cady didn't know where her class was, so asked them for help. They brought her to the schoolyard instead of class, and, although she knew it was wrong to skip class, she decided to stay because they said they were her friends. They helped her to map out the cafeteria seating arrangements.

The cafeteria was divided by cliques: there were the plastics (the most popular girls), the jocks, the nerds, etc.

The leader of the plastics, Regina, the Queen Bee, and her followers, Karen and Gretchen, invited Cady to sit at their table. They talked, and later asked if Cady was interested in any of the guys at the school. Cady shared that she was interested in Aaron, who was Regina's ex, and the plastics told her exes were off limits. They taught Cady the rules of their clique: no wearing sweatpants on Mondays and only wearing a ponytail once a week. They allowed her to join their group and gave her a makeover. Cady began wearing more makeup, and dressing like the plastics. The plastics were very preoccupied with their physical appearance, looking in the mirror and talking about which part of their body they didn't like and wanted to change. When Regina said she wanted to lose three pounds, Cady offered to help, tricking Regina by giving her Swedish candy bars that were supposedly going to help Regina lose weight, but actually made her gain weight.

Cady was very smart, and was taking twelfth grade math. She was invited to join Mathlete, the school math club that competed in the state championships. However, both the plastics and Janis and Damian told her that it was social suicide to join. Though Cady was getting very high grades in math, she pretended to not understand math and repeatedly asked Aaron, whom she was still interested in, for help. When she said she needed a tutor, he offered to tutor her. There were also scenes of underage drinking and house parties when the parents were not home.

Personal Reactions to the Book and Film

The book provided a glimpse into the lives of different teens. There were many similarities: concerns about appearance, especially the girls; concerns about doing well in school; and relationship issues of finding or maintaining a romantic relationship. They all talked about cliques at their school. Ashford, LeCroy, and Lortie (1999) define a clique as small interaction-based groups in which (adolescents) spend a great deal of time and develop close relationships (339). From watching movies, TV shows, reading books, talking with others, and personal experience, I am aware that cliques are very important. Both the book and movie were in school settings, underscoring the important role school plays in the lives of adolescents, as it is the center of both social and academic life.

During adolescence, young people are often concerned about their physical appearance and how others see and think of them (Ashford, LeCroy, and Lortie 1999). Adolescent girls generally have a poorer body image and tend to think of themselves as being too heavy (DeHart, Sroufe, and Cooper 2000). The girls in both the book and movie seemed to support this perception. Physical appearance is a common theme not just in school settings but in adult women's lives as well. U.S. society values thinness, and there is a proliferation of services and products aimed to help women lose weight and become thin. Adolescent girls' concerns are magnified and reflected in the media and are thus strongly reinforced, clearly reflecting pervailing values and body image concerns.

There were also some issues with parents in both the book and movie. Adolescence is a time when adolescents come into conflict with parents who attempt to restrict their freedom (Kendall 2002). Many youths want to express themselves through dress or appearance, but some parents regard that as a sign of rebellion and perhaps deviation from the norm. As an example, Marybeth, 16, in *Real Teens* (1999), wants to get her tongue pierced, but her mom wouldn't allow it. In *Picture the Girl*, (Sheyhen 2000), one of the young women talked about wanting to dye her hair purple but her father wouldn't allow it, because he felt it would reflect poorly on him. There were also parents in the book that pressured their children to do well in school.

A great deal of peer pressure and peer influence affects adolescents. During adolescence, peers are important, and young people need to spend time with them. According to Ashford, LeCroy, and Lortie (1999), peer interaction is a critical source for personal and social competence development, because through peer interaction, youth learn about sexual relations, compassion, leadership, conflict, mutual problem solving, etc. In the movie *Mean Girls* (2004), Cady felt peer pressure when her friends told her it was social suicide to join the Mathlete, even though she was interested in math. Peer acceptance is important to adolescents, as is sitting in at school, and both of these can limit activities and opportunities for teens.

Both books and movie mentioned underage drinking, and the book also mentioned drug usage. Some adolescents are also sexually active or are thinking about sexual relations. These are current concerns of parents, school staff, and administrators, and school curriculum has been developed to address them.

Teen pregnancy rates have been on the decline. However, in 2000 there were 5,846,000 females aged 15 to 17 in the United States and there were 281,900 pregnancies for this age group (Alan Guttmacher Institute 2004). The prior year, 1999, there were 5,811,000 females aged 15 to 17 and there were 293,570 pregnancies (Alan Guttmacher Institute 2004). There are also concerns about STDs (sexually transmitted diseases) or STIs (sexually transmitted infections). In certain high schools in urban areas, youth have access to confidential and free condoms. It is a positive step that youth are being educated about sex and birth control methods at school, where they spend most of their time, so that they can protect themselves from unwanted pregnancies and diseases.

Cultural Immersion Experience

Arcade Center and Shopping Mall There were about thirty teenagers and pre teens at the arcade center. The majority were male, with about three females. I observed them playing arcade games, such as car racing and other games involving shooting and fighting oppo-

nents. I stood by the side or behind the games and watched the teens intently staring at the screen and playing the games. I also participated sitting next to some of the teens and playing racing car games with them. The teenagers wore casual attire—jeans, t-shirts or sweatshirts, and tennis shoes, and a few had baseball caps. I wore casual attire as well—jeans, a sweatshirt, and tennis shoes. When I sat down to play the racing car game, I asked the teen next to me if people were waiting. He said there was a line but it was OK, I could stay and play, so I stayed and played a game with him. He told me to select any track and any car as it didn't matter because he didn't play well. I responded that I didn't know how to play either. We raced and he won. Afterwards, I told him it was a good game, and thanked him for letting me play. The teens were very involved with their gaming and did not seem to pay attention to their surroundings while they played.

At the mall, teenage girls were mostly with other girls; there were also teens with their mothers or teenage guys. The girls asked each other for opinions on what to wear, what would look good on them, and if they should make a purchase or not. Teenage guys also gave their opinions and helped the girls carry their belongings. Some teens were shopping with their mothers. Mothers told daughters what they felt looked good, and what they were willing to purchase.

Personal Reactions to the Cultural Immersion Experience I was aware that there was an age difference between myself and the teens playing arcade games and some of the teen girls that were shopping. I am not sure if they were aware of the age difference. I did not really feel that I stood out in these settings. The teens did not make me feel uneasy or out of place. They were very much involved in their gaming or shopping with their friends or moms. Observing them brought back memories of being an adolescent, just a few years ago. I too, like the teen girls, enjoyed shopping with female friends or with my mom. I also asked for their opinions on what was nice and what I should purchase. However, unlike the teen males, I did not spend much time at the arcade. I have a younger brother and male cousins that are very interested in gaming, and I noticed that most teen males are interested in gaming.

Personal Interview

First Generation American Recent High School Graduate I interviewed an 18-year-old who had just completed high school about his high school experiences, his family, and his friends. He was comfortable with my questions and with my interest in learning about teenagers, and also provided insights into the experiences of a first-generation American, and some of the additional challenges this presents. His own words, I think, describe his experience best, and I include them here:

Fitting in "High school was filled with worries about not fitting in and being cool. It felt like I didn't have enough brand name clothing like the other kids. I didn't have much trendy clothes at all, because my parents never bought them for me. They said it was too expensive.

"To be cool, you have to talk to and hang out with cooler looking kids. Whoever you talk to defines your group. For me, I liked games and my friends weren't cool looking, so I wasn't one of the cool kids. I did talk to one of the popular cool kids; he was very nice and we'd talk in class sometimes.

"I felt pressure to fit in from the whole high school community. There was pressure to wear the right brands of clothes, shoes, have the cool haircut, and use the right slang words. I tried to buy cool clothes. I remember my first major name brand item was this blue fleece GAP vest. It was expensive and not being used to spending that much, I thought it was overpriced for the material. I bought other name brand items: Nike tennis shoes, jackets, and sweatshirts."

Relationship with Parents "There was pressure from my parents to do well in school. My parents always compared me to my cousin,

saying how come she had better grades and asking why I couldn't be more like her. As an only child and the first American-born, I felt added pressure to go to college. From an early age, my parents stressed the importance of education. They made me feel guilty, saying things about when they were my age they didn't have as much as I do and weren't as lucky, and how I'd be the first to go to college."

Schoolwork and Grades "My parents wanted me to do well, but when you do, kids at school call you names like nerdy. I tried my best to fit in at school by conforming to the style and manners of the other kids. I didn't try my absolute best academically, so that the kids wouldn't call me a nerd.

"My grades were OK; I got a few Cs but mostly Bs in my classes. Classes were easy so I didn't even try at all. I didn't really do homework or study. Not that I didn't care, but I just didn't feel like it. Of course, my parents didn't like it, and I'd get scolded. I was scared whenever it was time for report cards. Although my parents don't know much English, they looked at the letter grades and were able to figure out if I was doing well or not at school.

"I didn't cut class until senior year. As a senior, I didn't think my grades mattered anymore. Plus, I had a car and was in journalism. Being in journalism allowed me the freedom to walk around campus without being afraid of getting in trouble or being caught. I'd cut class to go with friends to eat during lunch time, since our period was only 50 minutes long."

Smoking and Drinking "None of my friends drank or smoked, but this one guy I knew did. Since my friends didn't smoke or drink, I didn't feel any pressure to do so. This one guy I knew, he smoked marijuana saying it helped him to concentrate. There were other kids from school that would smoke under the bleachers. I also didn't hear about my friends having sex in high school. I did have this one cool guy friend from middle school; he was one of the popular kids but not super popular. He had some way to meet girls outside of school, so he dated this one girl from another school. He was sleeping with her, got her pregnant, and she dropped out of school, I heard."

Dating and Social Life "My parents were annoying. I didn't go out much and stayed at home all the time. My parents wouldn't let me go out and didn't like my friends coming over. My parents would ask what time I'd be home whenever I went out. In senior year, when I had a car, I went out more during the day. I would make up things and tell my parents that I needed to stay after school when I didn't need to, and go out instead.

"I didn't have an official curfew, but my parents would call me on my cell to check on where I was and yell at me to come home. There was this one time, I was at my friend's house, whom my parents knew, a block away and my parents still told me to come home when it was like 9 or 10 p.m.

"My parents don't understand. I feel like they didn't know what they were talking about and guess I just had to live with it. The times they grew up in were different from mine. They think that if I go out late, it'll be very dangerous. I've been out quite late, but nothing remotely dangerous has happened to me. All my friends have never been in any dangerous situations either. My parents' response was 'Well, you don't know the unexpected and stop arguing with us.'

"I did have a girlfriend in senior year, but didn't tell my parents. I didn't tell them because I don't think they'd like it and would not approve. I think they wouldn't like dating in general and the girl, because she was of a different ethnicity. I was worried about what they'd think and didn't want to be bothered with that. When I'd go out with my girlfriend, I'd tell my parents I was going out with some other guy friends. I don't think they knew that I was dating her. For prom, I just told my parents that there was a dance at school, I needed a partner and I found one. They were OK with it and I went to prom."

Conclusion

An open mind, willingness to learn, active listening, awareness of oneself, and acknowl-

edgment of lack of knowledge are important in working with teens. I know that it is vital to be aware, that although I have been a teenager once, my experiences will not necessarily reflect all or any of the experiences of my adolescent clients. Each individual, and each generation, has a unique set of experiences. As a social worker, it is important to recognize that clients' experiences are unique, and they know themselves and their situation best. Clients can and should be the cultural guides in helping social workers understand their unique background and experiences. In the ethnographic model the client or person being interviewed becomes the social worker's cultural guide (Leigh 1998) and teaches the social worker about her/his experiences. Ethnographic interviewing is a method of interviewing that sets forth ways of gathering information from the client in a nonthreatening way (Leigh 1998), and can be used to encourage teens to share their experiences and worldview with the social worker.

There have been common themes throughout this project that illustrate issues that are important to a teen: school involvement, peer influence, relationships with families (especially parents), peer relations, romantic relations, sexual relations, drug and alcohol use, etc. It is important for social workers to be aware of the different influences on teens and the various stages of adolescence.

Peer groups are of particular importance during adolescence. According to Kendall (2002), peer groups function as agents of socialization by contributing to our sense of belonging and our feelings of self-worth. Most youth want to be accepted by their peers, but often that requires conformity to particular norms, attitudes, speech patterns, dress codes, etc. However, conforming to the demands of peers and peer pressure frequently places youth at odds with their parents.

It is important to look at the youth's support system, experiences, and outside influences to get a beginning glimpse of the variety of issues that today's adolescents face.

Applying the Knowledge Base: Agency, Policies and Program, and Personal Competencies

THE FIELD WORK AGENCY: FOSTER YOUTH SERVICES AGENCY IN A PUBLIC SCHOOL SETTING

My field work agency's program is a part of a group of special programs that the school district provides to address foster children's needs in the school setting, and services are available in both middle and high schools to all foster youth who are living in group homes. While there is a central office location, clients are served within their school settings, and social workers travel to the schools as needed. Clients may also be seen in their group homes.

Community The diversity of the city is reflected in the diversity of the client population that my agency serves. All cultures and ethnicities, all races, all religions, all languages, all sexual orientations, all levels of ability are served, with the restrictions being that clients must be in group foster homes or on probation and in middle or high school.

Access The agency office has ramps, wide hallways to accommodate wheelchairs, and handicapped-accessible restrooms. There are several public transportation lines nearby. However, as interns meet with clients at their schools, or at their group homes, they are rarely seen in the office setting. Interns travel by public transportation or their personal vehicles to various schools across the city.

Clients can be self-referred, or referred by counselors, group home staff, schools, social workers, probation officers, and/or other service providers. The program's outreach services are focused primarily on service providers. However, at the first meeting interns encourage clients to tell their friends (other foster or probation youth) about the program and the services that are available. Supervisors and interns also provide outreach at group homes by providing program information to the youth.

The agency is very receptive to the needs of youth; it houses various programs such as health monitoring, nutrition, and after-school programs. No teenagers are hired as staff, but the program has a diverse workforce, with staff representative of teen population characteristics such as: gender, sex, race, ethnicity, language, and sexual orientation. During my internship, all of the interns were female MSW students of various ethnicities, representing a number of area MSW programs. The office is located across the street from one of the local high schools. During the students' lunch, and after school, they assemble in front of the office building to socialize or wait to be picked up.

The agency's entrance and waiting room welcomes clients with agency literature, information pamphlets, posters, magazines, and other materials written for and by teens. For example, on bulletin boards and tables in the waiting area, there are magazines written by local youth, and information relating to youth health concerns such as smoking and nutrition. The staff is bi-lingual and the interns are bi-lingual as well.

Administration and Staff Training The program has on going bi-monthly staff meetings and professional development meetings, which clerical support staff, school staff, other agency staff, and interns are invited to attend. There are also workshops throughout the year on a variety of issues such as: LGBT (Lesbian, Gay, Bisexual, Transgender) youth issues; Asperger's and ADHD; marijuana and drug use, and other issues teens face.

Staff Sensitivity From my direct observation, agency staff is very respectful of differences and nonjudgmental. I am unaware of any stereotypes or "they" language when staff speak about teens. Staff members and interns are respectful of clients and of each other. Interns use informal expressions with their clients, the working relationship is on a first name basis, and interns do not use jargon that teens do not understand.

Funding The Department of Education funds the agency and programs to address the needs of foster youth and probation youth in group home care. The program's supervisor oversees four MSW students (who receive a stipend) and a clerical support staff. Each intern has a maximum of three to four clients at one time. Because some of my clients went AWOL (absent without leave), transitioned to Job Corps, or returned home, by the end of my internship I had worked with a total of seven clients. There are a large number of foster youth and probation youth residing in group homes who cannot be served due to staff and funding limitations. Also, because funding stipulates that services can only be provided to foster youth and probation youth residing in group homes, foster youth living with kin or probation youth residing at home are not eligible to receive services.

Program and Policies

Effort The program in which I am interning is focused on middle- and high-school aged (primarily teens) foster and probation youth. There is a Steering Committee that oversees the program representing teachers and school administrators, Family and Juvenile Court representatives, Department of Human Services, probation officers, the attorney's office, former foster youth, group home providers, and various community-based organizations. This broad group demonstrates the program's effort to include representation of all who might contribute insights and help the program provide appropriate services. It is especially important to note that former foster youth who have been through the program are included.

Quality Feedback is elicited from clients as they terminate services and has supported other indications that the services are meeting the needs of the clients.

Effectiveness Although funding and staffing limit the number of potential clients, outreach efforts are continual, and I have personally provided outreach to my clients' probation officers, social workers, and school staff, informing them of available services and the referral process. Termination feedback from my clients demonstrates that they feel that the services (educational support, counseling or "advice," case management, referral to programs, assistance with completing job or school applications, accompaniment to court, etc.) were helpful and sufficient. The teens did not feel they had any unmet needs or that services were insufficient.

Efficiency In order to maximize the services available to clients, the program collaborates with various community-based organizations, especially the Independent Living Skills Program, where a majority of our clients receive some form of service, including workshops, college preparation, tutoring, or other service. Interns have also referred clients to YMCA, teen clinics, high school wellness centers, after school programs, the Mayor's Youth Employment Education Program, and an educational case management program. These programs facilitate meeting client's comprehensive needs, and good communication prevents the overlap or duplication of services so that each program's services are utilized appropriately.

Personal Cultural Competencies

Engagement, Trust, and Relationship-building Engagement of clients also involves respect, a nonjudgmental attitude, patience, a display of genuine concern, and empathy.

In general, teens may feel that they do not need help with issues they face, that no one understands them, that they can solve their own problems, or that they do not have any problems. For example, a probation youth that I worked with did not feel he had problems stopping his marijuana use, although his probation officer felt the opposite; he felt therapy and drug counseling was not helpful, and he felt he could stop smoking on his own when he wanted. However, it is important to recognize that each youth is different. For example, another probation youth that I worked with felt that her drug counseling and individual and family therapy sessions were beneficial. She wanted to continue with them in addition to anger management when she left the group home.

Culturally appropriate forms of address for teens are informal, clients and workers can be on a first name basis, and eye contact does not appear to make most youth uncomfortable. At my first session with my teen clients, I introduce myself by first name and asked how they would like to be addressed. My clients have asked me to call them by their first names, their middle names, or a shortened form of their first names. It is important to respect clients' rights to "name" themselves and use the name they prefer.

It is not generally advisable to touch the youth, for it is easily misinterpreted in a variety of ways and may also be an invasion of privacy. However, at the last meeting with clients, some have thanked me and held their hands out for a goodbye/thank you handshake, which I accepted.

The dominant society sometimes seems to present conflicting values to teens. For example, anyone aged 18 and older can smoke cigarettes legally and anyone aged 21 and older may consume alcohol legally. However, it is a crime for teenagers to engage in these activities, which are quite normal in the dominant society. Advertisements that glorify such activities exacerbate the conflict.

Assessment and Problem Definition Some teens expect to be guided (depending on age, personality, or preference), while others appreciate options (which sometimes may not have been their past experiences). However, society seems to feel that youth should be told what to do, and wants them to consult with family on major decisions; in group home living situations, that is not always possible. All clients are unique, and I have utilized ethnographic interviewing with my clients to learn about their individual and cultural experi-

ences. For example, I have asked clients to tell me about themselves (likes, dislikes, short- and long-term goals, etc.) and their families (rules, expectations, childhood, relationships, etc.).

Specific tools that have been effective and applicable in assessing my clients' needs and resources include the ecomap and genogram. These assessment tools are interactive, interesting, informative, and engaging to the clients, most of whom have never done these type of assessment activities. The clients I worked with enjoyed these activities and were given a copy to keep. It allowed both of us a visual representation of their family structure, support structure, and some stressors.

Contracting and Goal Setting The program offers opportunities and incentives for goal setting and goal achievement. Clients are able to receive up to $100 worth of gift cards for completing their educational goals. My clients and I together decide upon and set educational goals (one goal at a time), and together decide on an achievable time frame and other details. Also, clients can choose which type of gift card incentive they would like. If necessary, clients and I reassess progress and barriers and then determine and agree on extensions or modifications. It is important to be flexible and supportive in helping clients achieve their goals. I have attempted to involve their service providers, so they may provide support and encouragement, by informing them of the clients' goals, progress, and achievements.

Interventions Appropriate interventions for my teen clients have included assistance with job applications and high school or college applications; referrals for tutoring, mentoring and after school programs; counseling regarding any issues the youth would like to discuss; collaboration with their various service providers; and facilitation of communication between service providers. Appropriate local resources include: Planned Parenthood, high school wellness centers, the Independent Living Skills Program and other similar programs, financial aid resources, tutor and mentoring, SAT preparation, Youth Connection (an advocacy, empowerment, and involvement program for current and former foster youth), and others.

Evaluation and Termination In general, it seems that teens understand success or failure in immediate terms, and often have difficulties seeing the larger picture. As social workers, we need to help teens see that perhaps not achieving their goals or wants at this moment is a minor obstacle that can be overcome, and may itself be a learning process and a stepping stone toward greater success, because we do not always succeed on the first try.

Thus, I believe it is important to encourage our youth and foster hope. Although teens may regard immediate change and the elimination of the problem or issue as a measure of success, I view progress as an accomplishment and understand that change is a process. During termination, I acknowledge the client's strengths and achievements, and encourage her or him to continue to progress.

Supervisor and interns have weekly meetings to evaluate clients' progress, assess interventions, and consider alternatives if the current interventions are not working. It is important to ask clients each week if they would like to discuss something in particular or any specific information. At termination, clients should be asked for their feedback regarding both the program and the services they received.

For foster youth in particular, separation and relationship endings may feel like a loss or abandonment, especially because they typically have had frequent physical moves that have disrupted placements, schools, and friends. Also, they may have had family members, friends, or service providers leave them. At termination, it is important to inform clients of the option to continue receiving services. I offer to make a referral if they are interested. It is important to inform clients at the beginning about the length of the working relationship and remind them before termination and offer follow up services or resources so that clients do not feel abandoned.

NASW Standards of Cultural Competence: Agency, Program, and Personal Competencies

NASW Standards for Cultural Competence in Social Work Practice includes the following ten standards: ethics and values; self-awareness; cross-cultural knowledge; cross-cultural skill; service delivery; empowerment and advocacy; diverse workforce; professional education; language diversity; and cross-cultural leadership. (National Association of Social Workers: NASW Standards for Cultural Competence in Social Work Practice, Washington, D.C.: Author). In this section, I briefly highlight what I believe to be very important competencies and mention a few standards in assessing my field work agency and program as well as my own cultural competence.

A Personal Cultural Competence Standard 2. Self-awareness states that "social workers shall seek to develop an understanding of their own personal, cultural values and beliefs as one way of appreciating the importance of multicultural identities" (Ibid). The school program allows me to reflect and examine my background and identity to increase my awareness of personal assumptions, values, and biases. Class discussions, videos, and assignments allow me to value and celebrate differences. Attending professional development meetings has allowed me as well to reflect and examine my feelings and values regarding issues surrounding teens such as: marijuana use, teen pregnancy, tobacco use, etc. Weekly supervision meetings with my field work instructor also allow me to reflect on my experiences, feelings, and values in regards to my clients and their confronting issues.

Cultural Competence of Program, Agency, and Personal Cultural Competencies Standard 5. Service delivery states that "social workers shall be knowledgeable about and skillful in the use of services available in the community and broader society and be able to make appropriate referrals for their diverse clients." The program has a variety of trainings led by staff or outside agencies that bring in community and societal resources that are applicable to youth and teens. The program has a resource file that is continually updated with resources of which we were previously unaware. Supervisors and interns add to this resource file when they come across services that may be beneficial to the youth we serve. During my internship I have found several community resources through word of mouth or the Internet and have shared them with my supervisor, other interns, and included them in the resource file. At home, I also have a personal collection of community and societal resources that I may be able to use or refer to future clients. My collection of resources include: domestic violence shelters and assistance programs, low or no cost legal services, transitional services, immigrant and refugee social services programs, and an adolescent provider's guide from my supervisor.

Standard 8. Professional education states that "social workers shall advocate for and participate in educational and training programs that help advance cultural competence within the profession." The program's learning support consultants are school social workers, who facilitate professional development meetings and provide training for all staff on a variety of issues such as: conflict resolution, bullying, ADHD, and Asperger's. Our program's supervisor possesses an MSW degree and provides training for group homes and also facilitates professional development meetings. As an undergraduate in social welfare and a graduate student, I have performed community outreach for the Asian Women's Shelter and also made presentations on domestic violence and resources to students and service providers.

REFERENCES

Alan Guttmacher Institute. 2004. U.S. Teenage Pregnancy Statistics With Comparative Statistics For Women Aged 20-24. http://www.guttmacher.org/pubs/teen_stats.html

Anonymous. 1999. *Real Teens: Diary of a Junior Year*. NY: Scholastic Inc. Petersen Publishing Company, LLC.

Ashford, J. B., C. W. LeCroy, and K. L. Lortie. 2001. *Human Behavior in the Social Environment: A Multidimensional Perspective*. 2nd Ed. Belmont, CA: Brooks/Cole.

DeHart, G. B., L. A. Sroufe, and R. G. Cooper. 2000. Child Development: Its Nature and Course. Boston: McGraw-Hill.

Kendall, D. 2002. *Sociology in Our Times: The Essentials*. Belmont, CA: Wadsworth-Thomson Learning Inc.

Leigh, J. W. 1998. *Communicating for Cultural Competence*. Boston: Allyn & Bacon.

National Association of Social Workers. 2001. NASW Standards for Cultural Competence in Social Work Practice, Washington, D.C.: Author.

Shehyn, A. 2000. *Picture the Girl: Young Women Speak Their Minds*. NY: Hyperion.

Waters, M. (director). 2004. *Mean Girls* [motion picture]. United States: Paramount Pictures.

Worksheet

1. Foster youth graduate from the system when they turn age 18. There are a number of programs that assist teens to prepare for independence and responsibility with housing, education, employment, and other needs. Foster parents may also stay in touch with children they have cared for once they leave the system.

   Imagine you have received a substantial government grant to develop a program of support services for former foster youth *after* they have graduated. From what you have learned about teens, and about foster care, what kind of program and services would you design that would be culturally appropriate and yet meet some of the needs of the special group of teens?

2. Despite the many programs that schools have developed to address scapegoating since Columbine, the problem continues to affect students across the country. From your understanding of some of the challenges and concerns teens face, what are some of the factors that may account for the persistence of this behavior? What could be done to alleviate the problem?

Culturally Competent Social Work Practice with Homeless People

Diversity Project by Michelle Scheurich

"I want to be a lawyer." The man talking to me doesn't have the money to attend law school, so he spends his time in the law library, reading and thinking. He thinks that education should be free and available to all; paying tuition is "giving in to the institution." I think that some of his statements are delusional but I cannot make this judgment from our five-minute conversation. Whatever may come in his future, he speaks to me in the present of hope and dignity.

I have been working in soup kitchens on a weekly basis for five years. Every time I stand in the serving line or walk through the dining room, I have a chance to talk to the variety of people who come to eat the free meal I am serving. And I do talk to them. I ask them about their lives, their education, and their plans for the future. Many of them are homeless, some are not. Some are physically sick, some are mentally ill, and some of them are younger than I am. The transient nature of homelessness makes it difficult to study and describe.

My field work placement is in a county adult mental health clinic. The agency's catchment area includes well over 3,000 homeless people, and there are a number of homeless encampments located near the agency. Because of my interest in working with this special population, I have chosen to focus on homeless people for my project in cultural competence.

KNOWLEDGE OF POPULATION

Definitions

Homelessness is an important problem in our local and national community, and, for this reason, many have attempted to define and document homelessness. The McKinney Act states that a person is homeless if she or he "lacks a fixed, regular and adequate nighttime residence" (42 U.S.C. [sec] 11301) (US Department of Housing and Urban Development, The McKinney-Vento Homeless Assistance Act 1987). For children and youth, this can include people who are sharing inadequate or overcrowded housing due to financial hardship. The myriad of possible accommodations makes it difficult to identify the number of people who are homeless at a given moment or over a period of time. People sleep in their cars, in campgrounds, and in caves, making it especially difficult for researchers and demographers.

Prevalence and Demographics

Despite these difficulties, national estimates suggest that 3.5 million people, over a third of them children, experience homelessness each year.[1] This is approximately 1 percent of the population of the United States. Homelessness appears to have increased over time, based on the increase in shelter beds per population in various cities around the country. Children under 18 account for 39 percent of the homeless; estimates of homeless people over the age of 55 range from 2.5 percent to 19.4 percent.[2] The small percentage of homeless people over the age of 55 illustrates a life expectancy shortened by inadequate medical care and nutrition.

Although people of any age, gender, and ethnicity may be homeless, certain trends exist. Single homeless people are more likely to be male than female. Roughly half the homeless population is black, one-third white, one-sixth Latino, and a small proportion are Native American and Asian American.[3] Forty percent are veterans, 23 percent suffer from a mental illness, 30 percent suffer from an addiction, and 17 percent are employed. Of the women and children who are homeless, half are escaping domestic violence problems.

Causes

According to the 2000 Census, 11.3 percent of people in the United States are living in poverty; 39 percent of these have incomes that are less than half of the poverty level, and 40 percent of them are children (US Census Bureau [2000] American Fact Finder). These numbers are due to declines in both incomes and levels of assistance. Combined with a decrease in affordable housing, they lead to an increase in homelessness.[4] The 17 percent employment rate of homeless people illustrates a shortage of affordable housing in the United States. A minimum wage worker would have to work 89 hours a week to afford a two-bedroom apartment at 30 percent of her/his income.

Reading Homelessness

shelter In *shelter*, Bobby Burns uses a 40-day stay in a Tucson, Arizona, homeless shelter to reframe his life. He has a degree in education and has worked as a schoolteacher and a naval cook. He is an alcoholic, like the rest of his family, and he drinks until he loses his job and girlfriend in Phoenix. During his stay in the shelter, he stops drinking and begins to teach again. He relapses once he moves out into his own apartment, but finds ultimate relief in a house of recovering addicts.

Bobby discovers that he is treated differently when he is without an address. He seems to wait longer at the vocational rehabilitation center and the hospital. The medical personnel are rude to him and discount his wishes and opinion. He is embarrassed to share his situation with new colleagues and friends. His accounts illustrate how difficult a lack of car, house, and money makes daily activities. To get to work, he must spend two hours on two different buses each way. He must have his mail delivered to the vocational rehabilitation office; the office is not always open and the manager will not always release the mail. Bobby's clothes are stolen at the shelter, often just when he needs to wear them to work or church. What he hates most about living in the shelter is the lack of privacy. He is forced to share his life and his space with anyone else that needs the service. Although he sometimes resents this intrusion on his privacy, it exposes him to people with

[1] www.nationalhomeless.org.numbers/html
[2] www.nationalhomeless.org/who.html
[3] www.nationalhomeless.org/who.html
[4] www.nationalhomeless.org/causes.html

illnesses, physical and mental, in varying degrees of recovery, and he later uses this knowledge in his own recovery.[5]

Tell Them Who I Am Members of the homeless population are often visibly marked as belonging to this master status. Their homelessness or poverty usurps other personal characteristics, traits, and accomplishments that are valuable to their self-worth. In *Tell Them Who I Am*, women who live in shelters and on the streets are presented as people, not as a "population." Their message is clear: "homeless" is an adjective and not a noun.

The women in this book are battling many forces that keep them out of homes and out of work. Some of them are substance users. They spend what little money they receive from public assistance or from small jobs on their substance of choice. Some of them have children to support and cannot afford housing on their minimum wage jobs. Affordable housing is an issue for women without children as well. Unskilled laborers do not make enough money to support themselves without public assistance. Some of the women are mentally ill and cannot work at all. Many of them have conflicting attitudes toward the shelters: they resent the lack of privacy, but appreciate the social support that the shelters provide.[6] All of the women have a name and story, both of which are tenderly documented in this group biography.

The Mole People Jennifer Toth's book depicts a group of people with a very interesting way of life. "Mole people" is a derogatory term for people who live underneath a city, for lack of more acceptable housing alternatives. This book focuses on the people who live beneath New York City, in abandoned subway tunnels and between water mains. According to the author, approximately 5,000 people are living beneath Manhattan alone.

The author spent several years meeting, interviewing, and following the people in her book. The thousands of people living under the city, she found, seem to fall into groups. Some are employed above ground but sleep in tunnels or caves at night. Some remain underground for weeks at a time. The different underground communities have diverse requirements and expectations. Substance abusers and people with mental illnesses tend not to belong to a closely-knit community. The ways that people live underground seem to mirror the ways that people live aboveground: to suit their needs and habits.

The tunnel dwellers are very aware of their relationship to the "world above" and to the ways they are perceived. Many characteristics have been ascribed to people living underground over the centuries; for the most part, they have been considered less than human.[7] While those in the figurative underground are criminals, those in the literal underground are considered animals, and those in the underclass are viewed as living below an acceptable standard. The people chronicled in this book are very much people: they are artists, scholars, homemakers, and human beings.

Viewing Homelessness

The Fisher King In this film, Robin Williams plays Parry, a man who has a psychotic break, loses his job, and becomes homeless after his wife is murdered. He joins forces with Jack Lucas, a radio deejay played by Jeff Bridges, who inadvertently contributed to Parry's wife's murder. Jack unknowingly convinced a psychotic caller to kill himself and several restaurant patrons, among them Parry's wife. When he realizes this, Jack becomes depressed and alcoholic.

After three years of this, Jack walks to the river to kill himself. He is disheveled and dirty, and a gang in the park mistakes him for a homeless person; they light his clothes on fire. Parry is nearby and rescues Jack from himself and his torturers. In *The Fisher King*, no one is far from the bottom. The only thing keeping Jack from living on the streets is the patience and resources of his girlfriend.

[5]Burns, Bobby
[6]Liebow, Elliot
[7]Toth, Jennifer

In this movie, the randomness of fate is stressed. Both characters lose their footing after experiencing trauma. Only the kindness of others keeps Jack from losing his housing, and ultimately his life. This widely distributed and highly regarded film seems to drive home the point that there is always a story behind the homeless faces you see on the street.

Pharaoh's Streets A young filmmaker chronicled the lives of several homeless Los Angelenos during the year 2000. Unfortunately, I was unable to view this film in its entirety due to its limited distribution. The clip available online contains a statement by the main character and several other people.[8] He focuses primarily on a man who makes his living off of recycling. He spends the day gathering cans and bottles. This gives him enough income to provide food and clothing, but shelter is often a gamble. "The recycler" does just that; he says that he does not drink or use drugs, but that he has been arrested several times for having a shopping cart.

One woman says that "they won't touch me, they won't kiss me." Initially, she seems to be talking about human contact as a result of her homelessness. However, she is referring to her treatment as a person with AIDS. When she tells friends who are homeless her HIV status, they still love her; she does not find this to be the case with people who are not homeless.

A man becomes enraged by the way that money is used in his neighborhood. "They don't have enough money to feed us, but they can pay someone $18 an hour to make us get up and take our blankets." He questions the use of funds for punishment rather than for assistance or prevention.

The questions this film raises are important ones. How can we prevent homelessness? Who is worthy of services? What makes someone untouchable?

Field Research: A Cultural Event

All over the country, at all times of the day, various government and nonprofit organizations are cooking and serving food to those who cannot afford to buy food at market rates. People, homeless and poor, come to eat together and prepare for, or relax from, their day. The people who eat these free meals are as diverse as the people described in the books and movies above, but they have one common factor: they cannot afford to pay for them.

While living in Los Angeles, I helped to cook and serve dinner every Thursday night through an organization called Feed Hollywood. A church donated their facilities for this purpose, and volunteers ran the organization. Now that I am in school, I help to cook and serve breakfast on Tuesday mornings with the Dorothy Day House. The Veteran's Building donates their kitchen, and we serve the meal in a church multipurpose room. Both of these meals sites serve roughly 100 people.

We serve more meals at the end of the month; that is the most established trend I have found over the years. As welfare checks and paychecks run low, more people need to subsidize their food budgets with free meals. At the end of the month, there are more people in line who are not homeless, but who have found the soup kitchen necessary.

I am a marked outsider at these events. Although I often eat the meal as well as serve it, I don't have to ask anyone for more bread or juice, because I am a provider. Many people who come through the line display shame at asking for food. I notice this especially when the patrons are close to my age; they hang their head and speak in a whisper if they say anything at all. Some mitigate this discomfort by helping with the meal: when they help to cook, carry, or serve, they are no longer asking for a "handout." The shame of the people served makes me uncomfortable as well. I try many things to make our interactions more positive: I eat the meal we are serving, I look people in the eye, and I try to call them by name. I muster up my best nonverbal communication skills to let everyone know that I am not judging them. I think this is helpful.

Many of our patrons are regulars. They know us and one another, and we all greet each other as acquaintances. A meal is a great

[8]www.dartmouth.edu

social gathering, and often these meals are no different. Gossip is exchanged, help is given, and body and soul are refreshed. There are a limited number of free meals being served in each community on a given day, so these meals serve as a gathering point for those in the neighborhood who cannot afford to eat, many of them homeless.

Interview with a Member of the Population

Although I have had many conversations about realities of being homeless, a recent one comes to mind. "I'd much rather sleep in the park in Berkeley during the winter than in New York City." The man who made this comment grew up in Massachusetts and moved to Manhattan after high school to "see the city." Unable to sustain employment that afforded him an apartment, he remained on the island because of the excitement. "I don't know how I survived," he said in amusement. I am also incredulous: he lived homeless in Manhattan for ten years before coming to California.

Another young woman came to Los Angeles for the weather. When living outside is a necessity, "it's better to live where there's no snow." She said this one night during the pouring rain; she had already tried to get into the local shelters but they were full for the night. Resigned to spending the night in a doorway, she asked me for a plastic bag to serve as a raincoat. "At least it's not freezing outside."

Like the prospective lawyer I described in the beginning of this section, many of the people I have talked to have plans for continuing their education. I met a woman in Los Angeles who was attending community college for free because of her Native American heritage. She told me night after night how much she loved her English class, and the plans she had to become a public speaker some day.

Synthesis and Reflection

There are very few generalizations to be made about the homeless community. It seems inappropriate to call it a community at all; it is rather many communities, all over the country, full of a myriad of people. For many it is a transitional state, something to look back on or to use for motivation in the future. For most it is a consequence. People lose their housing because healthcare is often inadequate and unaffordable, because cheap, decent housing is scarce, and because minimum wage does not make a living wage. System failure is as much a factor in homelessness as is choice and chance.

Applying the Knowledge Base: Agency, Services and Policies, and Personal Competencies

THE FIELD WORK AGENCY: COUNTY ADULT MENTAL HEALTH CLINIC

My field work agency serves the mental health needs of a section of a large, urban county. As noted earlier, there are over 3,000 homeless people in my agency's catchment area.

Access There are several homeless encampments close to the agency. Additionally, one of the county homeless shelters is less than a mile away. For homeless people who choose to live in a shelter or camp, the agency is accessible by foot. The agency is also accessible by several bus lines; case managers and psychiatrists have free and reduced-price bus tickets available for clients. Occasionally, bicycles are donated to the agency and are given to clients in need of transportation.

Receptivity The agency is located in a consumer-friendly building. On the first floor, the Consumer Affairs Office runs a library and self-help agency. Additionally, they serve a free lunch every weekday to anyone who wants one. The availability of a free meal makes the building more receptive to homeless people, as this is generally a concern of people with little to no income. A county vocational center is also located on the first floor of the building, addressing another concern—employment. Many people in this homeless population are "transitionally" homeless, and employment would help them secure desired housing.

The agency's waiting room has many brochures concerning consumer rights and substance abuse recovery. These brochures do not specifically address the issue of homelessness, but are often concerned with corollary issues. For example, the brochures explain that the agency can help with applying for benefits and finding housing. Other brochures describe the process of recovery, and list places that individuals can go for help. The county estimates that 10 to 50 percent of the homeless population has a problem with drugs and alcohol, so this is a relevant issue for this population.

Administration and Staff Training The county offers diversity-related trainings on a monthly basis that are available to both staff and consumer providers. The trainings relate to general cultural competency skills and working with specific populations. However, the specific populations are restricted to ethnic groups; low-income or homeless people are not included as a culturally diverse population in the county literature. Issues of cultural diversity are also addressed on a weekly basis in team meetings. A team of psychiatrists, nurse, and social workers meets to discuss progress and solicit suggestions for cases. Access to services and financial issues are often discussed within the context of cultural diversity at these meetings.

Staff Sensitivity Staff persons at the agency are moderately sensitive to issues of cultural diversity. Among the social workers, client behaviors are occasionally stereotyped. Many of the staff members seem somewhat "jaded" after having worked with a "difficult" population for many years. They make despairing/disparaging comments about the likely outcome of a case on a regular basis. These comments are generally reserved for dually diagnosed clients, or people who they think have borderline personality disorder. I cannot recall any staff members being disrespectful about clients because of ethnic/racial/socioeconomic differences.

Funding The agency is adequately funded to serve homeless clients. Case managers are able to assist clients with applying for benefits and finding housing. All staff members are able to give their clients free or reduced-price tickets for public transportation. The agency has ten county cars available so that staff can give clients rides to appointments/meetings. Staff members can also apply for emergency funds to cover food/clothing/shelter needs for clients, which are pressing needs for homeless clients.

Agency Programs and Policies

Effort The county health department of which my agency is a part includes in its mission increasing access to and reducing disparities in healthcare for all citizens of the county. This inclusive language refers especially to homeless individuals, because they are considered among the more fragile populations of the county. While the county makes an effort to be sensitive to cultural differences, low-income/homelessness is not always recognized as a cultural issue. However, the county health department includes the Homeless Continuum of Care among its advisory groups. Consumers are always encouraged to deliver informal feedback to their service provider or to use the formal complaint/comment form.

In addition, the agency strives to hire workers from diverse cultural backgrounds to meet the special needs of clients and to offer culturally competent services. However, there were no homeless people on the staff of the agency in any capacity.

Quality According to county policy, the agency is committed to serving fragile populations with mental health needs. Clients must be eligible for medical assistance to receive services from the agency; a homeless person's low-income would qualify her or him for these services. Thus, a homeless individual should receive the same quality of care afforded anyone who receives services at the agency. The director of our agency supports a strength-based model of case-management. This model is client centered and driven; clients are supposed to receive only services that they want and think are individually appropriate.

Effectiveness According to the 2003–2004 Cultural Competence Plan, 67 percent of the homeless population in the county is in need of mental health services. In the year preceding this report, 2,000 homeless people accessed drug or alcohol services (out of the 14,000 estimated to be homeless at some time in the year). No figures are given for those accessing mental health services. Although these figures may not be fully comprehensive, they do seem to indicate that homeless people are underutilizing available health and mental health services in the county.

The bulk of case management at the agency is centered on the client's access to food, clothing, and shelter. Thus, it is very rare for a client to be living on the streets while under the care of a case manager or psychiatrist. It is not rare, however, for people to be living in shelters or transitional housing. One of my clients was very dissatisfied with the options available to her through our agency when she became suddenly homeless. While the county has two shelters near our agency, couples are not allowed to stay together in either of them. She felt that the shelters were dangerous, and were the least appealing housing alternative. On a long-term basis, the agency is able to help clients apply for benefits and find jobs to increase their incomes, but the shelters are the only option short term.

Many of our clients take advantage of the free lunch available on the floor below our agency. Case managers may refer clients to food distribution centers and soup kitchens. The majority of clients receiving case management are on SSI or SSDI and living in supported housing. Social workers spend a lot of time making sure that their clients have housing.

Efficiency Although very few of the agency's clients are homeless, staff members are effective in meeting the needs of these clients. I recall a client who preferred being homeless to living in supported housing; her case manager was supportive of this decision. The case manager remained the client's money manager, and made sure that the client was adequately fed and clothed at all times. The client slept in shelters, on the street, and at friends' houses. The agency is in the same building as a free lunch program run by consumers, as mentioned earlier. This program is known in the homeless community and serves as ancillary outreach for our agency. The agency is also linked to several programs in the community serving homeless individuals, including churches, the Salvation Army, and shelters.

Personal Cultural Competencies

Engagement, Trust, and Relationship-building The homeless population can be roughly divided into two sub-categories: transitional and chronic. Transitionally homeless people have lost stable housing due to a change in income, illness, or environment, while chronically homeless people are either always homeless or cycle rapidly in and out of homelessness. A homeless person has had a myriad of life experiences that will affect how she or he views "the system." Someone who has always gotten help from others in the past and who becomes unemployed will have little hesitation using a social agency to address this need. A person who does not see social agencies as positive forces will be more reluctant to make use of services.

A person who is chronically homeless, especially one who chooses to remain on the streets, may mistrust social agencies. She/he may feel it is not worth the trouble, and that society always lets her/him down. An example of this is Billie Boggs, aka Joyce Brown, a woman from New York City who made news in 1987 when she sued the city for unjustly hospitalizing her. She felt that she had a right to live where she chose, and that she should not be discriminated against because she was mentally ill and chose to live on the street (Involuntary Medication 1989).

It is important to remember that anyone can be homeless. During an initial assessment in a clinical setting, the clinician should ask where the client lives. If the client responds that she or he is homeless, follow up questions should be sensitive. The clinician must understand the client's thoughts regarding her or his living situation and what, if anything, she or he would like to do about it. It may also be necessary to ask follow up questions if the client gives an ambiguous answer, or one that leads the clinician to believe that the client may not have a permanent residence.

The majority of homeless people are single. Chronically homeless people especially may lack traditional family groups and support. Therefore, it is important during the interview to discover what constitutes family to the client. A clinician can ask the clients with whom they spend their time and who gives them emotional support.

Assessment and Problem Definition Homeless people face a great deal of discrimination from the dominant society, and homelessness is generally a well-marked category. Depending on the person's situation, homelessness can be identified by clothing, accoutrements, and/or smell, as homelessness renders regular maintenance of good hygiene very challenging. People assume that "they" are lazy, crazy, or addicted to drugs. One of my clients found herself without a home just before I left my field work agency. When I suggested that she go to a shelter for temporary housing, she said that she "didn't want to be around those people." She, like many others, views homeless people in a very negative light; however, many homeless people are just as she is, transitionally homeless. It is important to keep any negative associations a practitioner might have from coloring his or her relationship with a homeless person.

Assessment should explore support networks and resources, and also include a mental status evaluation. The client's needs in relation to food, shelter, and housing are primary, and these may need to be addressed before any other issues are considered. People who are homeless also often have difficulties accessing healthcare, and a referral for a general health evaluation may be helpful. If employment is a reasonable option for the client, motivation and interests should be explored. Because people who are homeless often feel a sense of disempowerment, it is very important to assist the client to define needs and concerns and to work within a client-centered practice modality.

Contracting and Goal Setting It can generally be assumed that most homeless people who approach our agency for help would like to find stable housing. However, the clinician must check that this is a goal for the client before proceeding with arrangements. It would be appropriate to work toward a goal of stable food, clothing, and shelter. To this end, a client may wish to apply for disability benefits or to seek a job. Homeless people do not generally have use of a permanent telephone; therefore, it would be appropriate to set up a regular appointment time with the clinician and establish a means with which the client can contact the clinician if necessary.

As with problem definition, it is essential that the client define goals and develop some of the strategies toward meeting those goals. The role of the worker should include assisting the client to explore options and resources, as the worker may know of many resources of which the client is unaware. Major goals should be broken down into smaller component parts, so that clients have the experience of meeting their goals and can develop self-confidence.

Interventions The agency is linked to several sources of income and housing in the county. We are able to help the client apply for benefits and work with vocational rehabilitation for job searching. Additionally, as case managers, we can link clients to independent and supportive living arrangements. As described above, it is culturally appropriate to work toward providing food, clothing, and shelter in the manner that the client wishes. After this is secured, interventions concerning employment, education, and interpersonal relationships can be implemented.

Once the client's basic needs are met, it is important for the client to be assisted to explore additional goals and objectives, and to develop intervention plans. Intervention plans may require strong support from the worker, and regular contact is helpful in maintaining motivation and offering support.

Evaluation and Termination It is difficult to ascertain the most appropriate ways of evaluating and terminating with homeless people; they are a heterogeneous group. However, it is important that a clinician be certain a client will continue to provide the necessities of living for her or himself. It is also important to remember that the cause of homelessness does not always rest in the individual; the lack of affordable housing makes this an ongoing and sometimes insurmountable problem.

Because this population is very fragile and vulnerable, it may be important to maintain some contact with the client on a long-term basis. Even very infrequent contacts provide support and a sense of continuity. If this is not possible, clients should always be provided with a way back into the system to use in times of need.

NASW Standards and Evaluation of Agency, Programs and Policies, and Personal Competencies

According to Standard 4—Cross-Cultural Skills—of the NASW Standards for Cultural Competence, social workers shall use appropriate methodological approaches, skills, and techniques that reflect the workers' understanding of the role of culture in the helping process. This standard incorporates the benefits of several other standards. A social worker can use all of her/his tools of language, assessment, and advocacy to practice in a culturally competent manner.

Agency The agency's client population reflects the rich diversity of the surrounding county. As an intern, I was required to attend monthly seminars on a number of topics,

including diversity. The diversity trainings I attended focused on African Americans and Latinos. Staff members at the agency are encouraged to attend cultural competency trainings as well; these trainings are geared toward working with specific populations and general cross-cultural work.

At the agency, case managers tended to have very similar goals for most of their clients. They had prefabricated goal sheets referring to improving the client's quality of life. Most of the clients were assumed to have similar goals: participate in education/employment, find stable housing, and improve their social network. Because of this lack of variability, culturally competent goals may not be for all members of the homeless population. A one-size-fits-all set of goals may be inappropriate for clients whose unique experiences would suggest other, more cogent, goals.

Policies and Programs The county has a Cultural Advisory Board, which informs and shapes various programs and services. This advisory board contains councils on various racial, ethnic, socioeconomic, and uniquely abled groups. They help the county and its agencies to better provide services to members of these groups.

At the agency, we were encouraged to take advantage of specialized programs and services targeted toward certain groups of people. Finding the best fit with a day program or board and care home was a high priority for the case manager, who solicited input from the client.

Team meetings were utilized on a weekly basis to give staff an opportunity to reflect on cases. I witnessed several occasions when potential cultural miscommunications were aired and resolved at team meetings. The agency seeks to recruit and retain workers from diverse cultural backgrounds to improve the cross-cultural communication of its staff.

Personal Competencies I have had the good fortune to work with clients from backgrounds very different from my own. In my limited experience, I have had clients from a variety of countries and cultures, who spoke varying degrees of English and came from diverse socioeconomic backgrounds. I always try to encourage the discussion of differences with my clients and am not averse to hearing criticism about my interactions.

During school and in my life experiences, I have learned and practiced a variety of interview techniques. I am able to alter these techniques depending on the culture of the client with whom I am speaking. Unfortunately, I do not speak any language other than English well enough to conduct an interview in that language. I fault myself for this; I believe that possessing the ability to speak multiple languages is an essential tool for cross-cultural communication. I am slowly building up my vocabulary and hope to be at least bi-lingual at some point in the future.

I try to recognize the impact that culture has on my interactions with clients. Often, the biggest cultural divide to cross with clients is that of socioeconomic status. Clients

always perceive their social workers to be middle class professionals, and thus may think that their workers cannot understand certain aspects of their lives. I try to overcome this by supporting my clients' worldview and values, and by creating a welcoming environment in which they can discuss their problems (or triumphs).

Informal support systems are very important to me when working with a client to resolve her or his problems. I find extended family, churches, and friends to be invaluable in helping to secure clients' access to necessities and to strengthen social ties.

Lastly, I frequently take advantage of supervision to assess my own cultural biases in communication. My supervisor helps me to reflect on how my own culture can affect the way I "think the world should work." I try to keep these biases out of my work with clients so that their world can be their own.

REFERENCES

***County Cultural Competence Plan, 2003–2004

Burns, B. 1998. *Shelter*. Tucson: University of Arizona Press.

Gilliam, T. Director, D. Hill, and L. Obst, Producers 1991. *The Fisher King*. Tristar.

Liebow, E. 1993. *Tell them who I am*. NY: Free Press.

National Association of Social Workers (2001). NASW Standards for Cultural Competence in Social Work Practice. Washington, D.C.:Author.

National Coalition for the Homeless. *How many people experience homelessness?* http://www.nationalhomeless .org/publications/facts/How_Many.pdf

National Coalition for the Homeless. *Who is homeless?* http://www.nationalhomeless.org/publications/ facts/Whois.pdf

Rothe-Kushel, J. (producer and director) 2000. *Pharaoh's Streets*. Jethro Films.

Toth, J. 1993. *The mole people: life in the tunnels beneath New York City*. Chicago: Chicago Review Press.

U.S. Census Bureau. 2000. American Fact Finder. http://factfinder.census.gov/home

U.S. Department of Housing & Urban Development. The McKinney-Vento Homeless Assistence Act. 1987. http://hud.gov/office/cpd/homeless/rulesandregs/laws/

Worksheet

1. In late 2005 in the city of San Francisco, there was a substantial homeless population living under the ramps of the freeway in one area of the city. Although homelessness could be a cause for removal and possibly arrest, it was decided to allow the homeless encampment to continue with no intervention from the local police department. If reasonably stable and permanent homeless encampments are permitted (a) who should monitor or police them? (b) Should their location be designated and approved by city government? (c) What services should be offered to residents? (d) What alternatives could be provided to people who adamantly assert their right not to sleep in shelters?

2. Various agencies provide outreach services to homeless populations. Outreach includes offering shelter or other housing, emergency and nonemergency health services, needle exchange, food, clothing, and the attempt to meet other needs. People who accept any services may be considered "clients" of the program or agency that provided them. Once a person becomes a client, actions may ethically be taken to support the best interest of that person.

   However, some people refuse all services, and so cannot formally be considered clients. What, if any, ethical obligation could be considered above the standard of supporting self-determination?

17 *Culturally Competent Social Work Practice with Incarcerated Women*

Diversity Project by Victoria Fleming

INTRODUCTION

My field work placement is with a public agency that provides legal services to incarcerated women. My goal in this study is to understand, through the narrative of incarcerated women, the context of their lives and their communities, and to examine the cultural competence of the services they receive during the time they are in jail.

In my first year of social-work education, the notion of asking the question, "Why here, and why now?" has compelled me to become introspective and to examine my own decisions and directions for meaning and implications. I have been drawn to the study of women for over ten years now and to the study of incarcerated women for the past few years. My interest in this group is stimulated by the persistence of humanity under the insidious and inescapable ravages of poverty, racism, and sexism that intertwine to form the invisible cells of incarceration.

KNOWLEDGE

Demographics and Background

For the purposes of demographic information, I will draw upon state and national statistics for women prisoners. The numbers of women in jail increased sharply in the 1970s, and this rise continues. Dan Baum (1997), in his book, *Smoke and Mirrors*, postulates that women, especially women of color, have been targeted more intensely as a means to both stimulate prison industry growth and subvert the growth of healthy families of color. The Bureau of Justice Statistics Report for 2003 names California and Texas as the largest prison systems in the nation. In California in 2003, 124,179 prisoners were admitted, while only 119,683 were released (U.S. Dept of Justice). These general statistics paint a background picture of rising jail population trends in California and help to inform the understanding of factors impacting incarcerated women. For example, the increase in female incarceration outstrips the numbers for males; this calls for a discussion on changes in criminal justice and women's roles in criminal activity.

Women's involvement with the criminal justice system has increased at an alarming rate since the 1960s, and many of these women are repeat offenders. Researchers have been approaching the topic of recidivism by assessing various characteristics of criminals and the crimes they commit in an effort to predict future outcomes. Such research has been met with very limited success (Klein and Caggiano 1986). The profile of female offenders and the types of crimes they commit has changed little over the past four decades even as incarceration rates continue to skyrocket.

Profile of Female Offenders

The study of women prisoners was largely neglected prior to the 1960s; in fact, federally funded reports on prison populations did not include women until efforts were made by women's groups to change this (Feinman 1994). A 1977 study of women prisoner characteristics found that female prisoners were mainly young women under 35, with the highest prevalence between the ages of 22 and 25. More than 50 percent were black and on welfare; less than 20 percent were married; and over 75 percent were mothers. Fewer than 60 percent held high school diplomas (Feinman 1994; Glick and Neto 1977).

Twenty-two years later, the portrait of female offenders looks strikingly similar, with African Americans represented at 48 percent, the median age at 33 years, and 17 percent married. One major change, however, is a sharp reduction in offenders holding high school diplomas—39 percent. Additionally, more than half of the women had been arrested in the past and a third had been incarcerated as juveniles (Bureau of Justice Statistics 1999; Chesney-Lind and Pasko 2004). From the 1960s through the 1980s, the profile of the average female offender did not change significantly. Crimes continue to be drug and property-related, with violence generally reserved for abusive partners (Feinman 1994; Chesney-Lind and Pasko 2004).

According to an American Correctional Association (1990) analysis of the women surveyed, 55 percent had been arrested between two and nine times, with a rate of 39 percent for property crimes and 22 percent for violence. Of particular relevance to this research is that less than half, 45.8 percent, had been incarcerated only once. Additionally, one-quarter of all female prisoners in California are recidivists incarcerated for either drug possession or petty theft (Bloom, Chesney-Lind, and Owen 1994).

Increasing Arrest and Incarceration of Women

It is important to remember that recidivism rates are in part a function of each jurisdiction's incarceration policies (Klein and Caggiano 1986). Local statutes and prosecutorial discretion change the rate at which criminals are apprehended and brought to justice. Langan (1991) links the increase in incarceration without an apparent change in criminal behavior to the implementation of mandatory minimum sentences that strongly increases the likelihood of a prison sentence following an arrest (Chesney-Lind and Pasko 2004). Bush-Baskette (1999) found that, "sentencing guidelines that disallow the use of drug addiction and family responsibilities as mitigating circumstances subject Black females to prison and long sentences under criminal justice supervision, as they do White females" (222).

For additional statistics on incarceration please see Appendix A.

Biography: *Random Family*

Incarceration does not exist in a vacuum of prison or jail. Prisoners are people who have families, histories, and are part of a larger political and personal landscape. Author Adrian Nicole LeBlanc (2003) begins with a court trial of a teenage kingpin and branches out to grasp the complexities of urban poverty that interact with the prison as an institution.

Halfway through the book, when protagonist Jessica is arrested on Rico laws for conspiracy, the reader is already close to her, with good insight into her strengths, weaknesses, and family connections. Instead of beginning the story at the point of her incarceration, LeBlanc thoughtfully began at an earlier point, allowing the reader the unusual opportunity of seeing Jessica not as a criminal but a person who comes to be in the criminal justice system.

Similar themes run through Jessica's life and community as in the film I viewed, *Voices From Within*; (Epperlein, K. 1996) these include an intensified need to be needed and a willingness, if not a resignation, to accepting abuse in the pursuit of this. Through Jessica's commitment to different people in her life, we see that the relational capacity of women is a force not to be ignored. In speaking about her book during a radio interview, LeBlanc noted that it would not be possible to tell the stories of her female characters without including their male counterparts, because of the importance that women place on these relationships.

While Jessica is in prison, she does not limit her identity to her status as a federal prisoner. Instead, she continues to cultivate relationships with fellow inmates and guards. During her time in prison, she gives birth to twin boys fathered by a night-watch guard. She also writes long letters to her children, her brother, and even her ex-boyfriend whose drug dealing landed her in prison, and in the hospital, many times prior to her incarceration. The tenacity with which female prisoners cultivate their connections with others while living for years behind bars shows that one's humanity cannot be removed by an institution, unless one willingly hands it over. Over the course of my experiences in this cultural immersion study, I have found that female prisoners are unlikely to hand their humanity over to anyone.

Film: *Voices From Within*

The film I watched for this population immersion study was made by a dance and voice instructor who held classes in a federal prison in California and focuses on the experiences of a few female prisoners who participated in her class. The women shared their views and experiences of incarceration, and synthesized these into a musical-style production for inmates and volunteers. Though the women all had very different personal backgrounds and reasons for being in prison, the most salient theme that ran through their stories was the unbearable pain of being separated from their children. The women all found it particularly upsetting that, though they could see their children, they were unable to touch them because of the glass that separated them. Images of children's faces pressed up to glass and hands of mothers matched up with children's on either side movingly portrayed the humanity and love that prisons actively destroy.

Other themes that ran through this documentary included personal space and privacy. The women made up a song based upon a response to a child's inquiry: "Mama, what's it like living in prison?" "It's like living in a bathroom with someone you never knew." The women noted that they had no privacy, even when they used the bathroom. One of the most striking things about this documentary is the vitality and human strength that the women are able to express under the inhumane conditions of prison. The women express their humanity through the context of relationships, and through this referencing and expanding on family relationships in the outside world, women are able to slow down the rate at which they

become institutionalized. One song that they wrote included a chorus that rejoiced in their mothers as their favorite women in the whole world.

The strength of family relationships in the context of prison is not to be underestimated. Women who were able to keep closer contact with their children, partners, and parents seemed to have stronger senses of purpose and vitality. One woman had a grown child whom she hadn't seen since he was an infant. When she was taken into custody she arranged for family to care for him in Mexico. When he was an adult, the family decided to move near where she was incarcerated, so that they could develop their relationship. The family became focused on her release from prison and petitioned the parole board. After months of waiting for the hearing, the response from the board was to try again in 15 years. After this transnational relocation and heartbreaking verdict, mother and son were still invested and tied to their relationship and its promise.

Personal Interview: An Ex-prisoner's Experiences

As an ex-prisoner, Irma expressed that she felt continually dogged by her former misdeeds. She has raised five children, pursued graduate degrees, held a job, owned a home, and feels that she has paid her debt to society. She feels that the criminal justice system targets women and people of color, and this phenomenon stems from racism and power struggles. As a group, Irma perceives women prisoners' experience of poverty as their primary problem. Connected with poverty and concurrent with it, she states, are psychological and social damage from racism, addiction, domestic violence, lack of education, and limited opportunities.

Irma expressed her belief that the situation in which many women prisoners find themselves is supported by factors that serve to produce and sustain a damaging cycle. Her suggestions take on a social justice perspective, and are aimed at ameliorating social service inadequacies at all levels of society. Irma also commented that women prisoners are in a lot of pain. During her time in prison, Irma was able to cultivate her bodywork skills and be of service to her fellow inmates by working as a chiropractor. Her current work with female prisoners includes voice and movement lessons, along with information about pressure points and other mind–body connections.

Cultural Immersion: My Experiences in the Prison

During the days that I spent counseling women in prison, I became attuned to the culture of incarceration. As a civilian walking into the jail, I was met with glares from guards, who had to tone down their abuse of inmates in the presence of outsiders. From the women prisoners, I felt an incredible and overwhelming pull to provide care and attention. There was never enough counseling or basic human connection to mitigate the void this unnatural setting created. The nature of the institution, from the architecture down to the smallest rules of conduct is designed in a way that strips any person of a sense of individuality and humanity.

Simply taking a few steps in the wrong direction ensures an abusive reprimand. Failure to heed an order in a timely manner will send the inmate to the upstairs unit, which handles and monitors solitary confinement. When I enter the jail, I see a circle of single cells with faces and hands pressed against any openings, and eyes begging for contact. The stifling of the prisoners' humanity makes my heart ache with rage and sorrow.

On the lower level of the jail, inmates are "free" to move around and socialize with one another. The air smells of squalor, body odor, and angst. Inmates are not provided with toiletries unless someone from the "outside" puts money in their "books." Non-prescription medications are provided at inflated costs, which means that, on any given day, this prison's inmates are experiencing headaches, menstrual cramps, and flu without proper treatment. In order to see a medical practitioner, a prisoner must fill out a written request (though many of the women are illiterate), ask to approach the guard to give him the form, and hope that he passes it on. On more than one occasion, I saw serious medical conditions left untreated, including HIV/AIDS, broken bones, and mental illness.

I witnessed the humiliation that the guards used in a seemingly deliberate attempt to whittle away the self-esteem and spirit of the women on the units I visited. The women had to shower behind glass doors that were in open view to everyone on the unit. Inside the bathroom, a scanty metal partition did little to provide any privacy. Ironically, I observed that the guards who were most obviously involved in exploiting and manipulating inmates through denigration were demographically closest to them in terms of ethnicity and socio-economic background. Power-hungry guards seemed themselves to lose the humanity and dignity they were trying to strip from the inmates. Looking into the guards' eyes, I saw a coldness and emotional detachment that reminded me of the empty faces of past wartime criminals.

The prison itself is an industry built upon the forced participation of inmates in charter school programs that allow the county to collect school funds. Daily, women were shuffled into classrooms and indescriminately given materials and information completely inappropriate to their needs. Absence was not tolerated: each time an inmate stepped into a classroom, the county could bill the state for that pupil for that day.

Inmates did gather willingly for group events, such as song, dance, and discussion groups that my agency held in the evenings. Regularly, guards would "forget" that we were scheduled to provide opportunities for recreation and self-expression, and we would not be allotted the necessary space. When the groups did meet, however, it was very rewarding to see the prisoners become human once again, their collective spirit transcending the immediate boundaries that suffocated them, enabling them to have dignity and to express both their motherhood and sexuality. These were transient moments only, however, in the routine of the inmates' daily lives.

Reflections

Through my contacts with female prisoners, I heard more than once that, in relation to the poverty and violence that they regularly face in their communities, jail is a better option: jail provides free food and a dry place to sleep. In jail, there are no bills to pay.

The idea that jail could conceivably be viewed as a step up from freedom is particularly relevant to this group, in that the conditions of poverty can be so damaging that the prospect of trading one's freedom for room and board is worth considering. In short, when approaching the female prison population, an awareness of the difficulties of life on the outside is particularly important.

This population is different from that of many other potential focus populations for the study and acquisition of cultural competence in that incarcerated people are not born into jails, although I am certain that some might argue this point. This group is also special in that it is a group identification that is largely ego-dystonic and unwanted. In other words, "prisoner" is an un-chosen identity. Given a choice, most would choose not to be in this group, although as noted some see it as better than street life. This conundrum once again highlights an intractable portrait of oppression composed upon a canvas of poverty.

Applying the Knowledge Base: Agency, Service and Program, and Personal Competencies

FIELD WORK AGENCY: AGENCY PROVIDING FREE LEGAL SERVICES TO INDIGENT CLIENTS

My field work agency provides free legal service to people in an urban center, and serves incarcerated and non-incarcerated clients and families. All of the agency's clients are involved with the justice system, and many are referred to my agency by their attorneys for services.

Agency

Agency's Community The agency is located in a major urban center and serves indigent clients who need legal services. There is a wide socio-economic gap between service providers, who are educated, middle class professionals, and the clients they serve. Many service providers are Caucasian, but a sizeable proportion are men and women of color. The agency's clients are all without financial resources, many have less than a high school education, and almost all are African American or Latino.

Access Lawyers usually meet their clients in their holding cells in the county jail and during their court appearances in the courtroom. Most clients are visited in jail, as they are unable to post bail. For those who are lucky enough to post bail, our office is located close to public transportation.

There are two ways in which clients reach social welfare services. First, lawyers can recommend social services for clients, and make a referral to our department. The social worker would then visit the client and assess her both for agency services and for referral to appropriate outside resources. Social services that are provided are both on an individual and a group level, and include evening events that support and encourage relationship-building and community-building among the women.

Second, the agency provides outreach to clients who are in jail. Through daily visits to the jail, social workers are able to talk with women and establish a relationship. Needs and goals can be addressed through these relationships, and clients can also be assisted in dealing with challenges they experience within the prison setting.

Many clients view the agency as an ally where few exist. Some clients feel that it does not perform its duties adequately. On the whole, most clients view the agency as a valued neighbor.

The agency does not provide a program of general community outreach, as services are offered to clients only after their arrest. At times, the agency has supported some additional social services, such as services for children of incarcerated parents, and treatment for substance abusers and mentally ill people in lieu of incarceration. The agency complies with laws requiring access for handicapped people. There are wheelchair-accessible doors and elevators.

Receptivity Agency literature does not include information for female prisoners specifically. The literature covers larger themes of social justice and civil rights that apply to all clients generally. However, the agency is receptive to female prisoners, and there are staff members who are former prisoners. The décor is drab, like most under-funded government agencies.

There are attorneys on staff who are bilingual and field cases in which the client is monolingual. The office is required by law to provide necessary translation services. Though there is a considerable attempt to provide adequate language service, there are language barriers that may result from the disparity in education between clients and public defenders, and also from the legal jargon used by judges, prosecutors, and public defenders. I have witnessed clients go through court proceedings with their public defenders telling them how to answer the judge's questions because they do not understand them. I am not sure that the clients are ever given full explanations of what exactly is going on in lay terms. Services would be strengthened if an agency-wide effort to assure that clients understand the details of their own court proceeding as made. However, underfunding severely limits the amount of time that can be given to each client.

Administration and Staff Training This agency does not have ongoing training in culturally sensitive and competent practices for incarcerated women. As required by law,

trainings on sexual harassment are conducted, which include issues related to women. There are no other trainings of any sort related to diversity or specific groups of clients.

Staff Sensitivity From my direct observation, the staff is respectful of differences, sensitive to special client need and generally nonjudgmental. My experience with the attorneys at my agency is that they initially come with idealism and empathy. They are an eclectic group, and there are a few who are truly examples of cultural competence and empathy. However, they are overworked, and at times some are inconsiderate and disrespectful in the ways they refer to their clients. I think that given the intensity of the job, the socio-economic differences quickly make for an "us" and "them" dynamic, stereotypes and "they" language, and possible underlying themes of sexism, racism, and classism. It is this gap between the legal culture and the client culture that the social workers in my agency work to fill.

Attorneys often use formality and expressions consonant with a client's culture. Attorneys refer to their clients in court by their last names, and this connotes a respect for the individuals they defend. I have not had the opportunity to observe client–attorney meetings out of court, as my work focuses on direct social services.

Funding My agency does not have adequate funds to serve female prisoners in a culturally sensitive manner. As mentioned above, I believe that one of the reasons that the agency's lawyers become insensitive is that they are overworked, and become resentful and disdainful of their clients. Another contributing factor for insensitivity is that under-funding leaves attorneys not only with high caseloads but also with insufficient clerical support, and appropriate cultural competency trainings.

Funding limitations do not allow for cultural variations in program services. Aside from the independent social services funded through grants, the clients are given fairly identical services. It might be possible for grant funding to be used to implement programs and trainings to address issues of cultural sensitivity and competency.

Program and Policies

Effort The agency's philosophy espouses cultural sensitivity. Standards for codes of conduct are in accordance with the law. Individual public defenders consult with their clients to tailor defense strategy to their client, but, on an agency level, there is no consultation with clients for service delivery. The agency makes no effort to consult with or include female prisoners or any prisoners for that matter on designing culturally sensitive policies and programs.

Quality There are no policies or programs to ensure that the quality of services provided are culturally competent. In fact, the only quality control that the agency uses is a measure of the percentage of clients that each individual public defender is able to have acquitted. The agency not only supports, but requires, equitable, respectful, and equal access for all clients. However, there are no policies aimed at being inclusive of other worldviews, values, or belief systems. The only service offered is legal defense to indigent clients. The program does take into account that the socioeconomic status of their clients is one major factor that sets them apart from mainstream society, along with their involvement in the criminal justice system.

The primary service my agency offers is legal defense to indigent clients. Thus, the social services we provide must take a backseat to the legal aspects of the agency. This has become problematic at times, because the legal and social work professions espouse different ethical codes. One of the major issues this has created is that, from time to time, social workers at my agency were pressed not to fulfill their requirements as mandated reporters of abuse. The lawyers felt compelled to protect their clients' confidentiality, even if it meant that the safety of others would be in jeopardy. This perspective runs contrary to the Code of Ethics for Social Workers and placed the agency's social workers in a tenuous position. In the end, it

became clear that social workers could not maintain their professional ethical (and legal) responsibilities while operating under the auspices of an organization providing primarily legal services. The program with which I was involved was terminated by the "host" agency because of this unresolvable ethical impasse.

Effectiveness My population is not willingly seeking out the services of the agency, but rather is forced to use them or be jailed. From an informal assessment, clients from my population feel that the quality and quantity of the programs and services available to them is generally sufficient. This however, is a highly individual judgement, is very subjective, and is generally related to the disposition of the court case.

There are significant unmet needs around diversity and cultural sensitivity. Adequate training and paraprofessional support to engage in their work from a truly culturally competent position is not provided. The agency is narrowly focused on assuring that their clients receive a minimum sentence; beyond this, the agency is overburdened with cases, and underfunding and concerns around cultural competency are not recognized.

Efficiency The effectiveness of the agency's legal services in reaching and meeting the needs of the female prisoner's culture varies according to the random match between the individual attorney and the individual client. The agency as a whole makes no effort to address this issue. The agency does set up linkages with existing community institutions, especially around discharge services and substance abuse facilities when clients are released from jail. The agency would benefit from increasing linkages with other community organizations to serve their clients during the court proceedings and while serving jail time. The agency uses alternative service delivery only when two clients are being tried for the same crime. When this happens, they contract out services for one of the clients to prevent a conflict of interest. This example has little to do with the issue of cultural competency, but is relevant to female prisoners in that it is usually their cases that are contracted out, while their male partners receive agency services because they generally are the primary defendants. I am not sure of the implications of this method of service delivery, but I am curious about the quality of services that men and women receive in comparison to one another in situations like this.

Personal Cultural Competencies

Engagement, Trust, and Relationship-building Female prisoners often have a history of tragic encounters with social agencies. Many of these women have been through the foster care system, grown up on insufficient welfare payments, and had Child Protective Services remove their children from their homes. I think my population in general is wary of social services, but does use them as a last resort. Additionally, female prisoners often view legal services as a different category than social services. Interestingly, female prisoners see the police as a harmful social service agency, and legal service providers as protecting them from the police.

Female prisoners are not one generic cultural group, but a group marked by a common circumstance; thus, culturally appropriate forms of address, distance, eye contact, and touch will differ on an individual basis. It is important to remember the extreme distress that an incarcerated person experiences, be open, but let the client set the pace for the interaction. Female prisoners are variable in the ways that they are acculturated, and the decision-making process used with a lawyer or social worker will depend on their individual preferences and family group norms.

I would utilize ethnographic interviewing to learn about my clients' individual and cultural group experiences by asking them to be my guide and to explain what it is like to be a member of their ethnic or cultural group. I would follow up with more specific inquiries to see if they would be willing to guide me through their experiences as a member of the female prison population. During the ethnographic interview process, I would encourage my client to control the direction of the conversation. I would try to watch for body language, and be sensitive to the distress or anxiety that the ethnographic interview may produce for the client.

It is important to recognize that people who are incarcerated feel disempowered and devalued. For this reason, it is essential to treat clients with dignity and respect, to listen and to empathize, and to maximize choices and options.

Assessment and Problem Definition Using an assessment questionnaire that consulting colleagues and former clients compiled would probably be an effective and relevant means for identifying a client's needs and resources. However there was no specific assessment tool developed for social workers at my agency. I would engage my client in the assessment process after engaging in routine pleasantries by asking them if they would be willing to help with the process of identifying what may be possible to achieve within the clinical relationship, and some of their goals. I would then support the client in directing the conversation and encourage them to guide the interaction.

My clients generally identify problems grounded in cultural norms, beliefs, and expectations within the context of their family and group situation. When I ask my clients to explain how they came to be where they are, they almost always explain this within the context of their families and social groups. They rarely see themselves as individuals acting alone.

While issues of racism, sexism, and poverty are often interwoven with their stories, they are almost never viewed in terms of the broader social context. While I feel that the dominant society exploits my clients, who are undereducated and generally underserved, I do not try to impose this view on them. I have found that they very rarely share my understanding, and I try to respect and honor their perspective.

Contracting and Goal Setting The culturally appropriate goals that my client and I would define together would be based upon the client's culture and orientation to their current circumstances. Female prisoners are not a "cultural group," in the traditional sense except in terms of gender, so cultural appropriateness will have to be addressed on an individual level and is not relevant to female prisoners as a whole. There is, though, a "culture" in prisions which may influence goal setting and expectations.

Engaging a client while in prison is a very different experience from engaging a client in other clinical settings, because the power differential is so physically obvious, and the depth of distress and need is so intense. Clients in jail are often much more willing to engage, and be engaged by, social workers. In my experience, clients were anxious to meet with me to express their goals. Contracting with people in jail is more challenging because women behind bars have fewer material and social resources to support them in making personal changes. Contracting needs to be done mindfully with attention toward the powerlessness of the client in the situation.

Interventions Although there are programs, such as shelter services, vocational rehabilitation, and substance abuse treatment for women who are released from prison, there are very few services that cater to the needs of women in jail. There is a Sister's Program in one holding unit that provides education and life-skills for inmates. Interventions appropriate to women in jail must be client focused and individualized. Service providers should be aware of the time constraints of the jail sentence and plan with their client to use the time most effectively.

Evaluation and Termination Most female prisoners view success as getting out of jail, and many view failure as returning to jail. Some women want to change their lives in significant ways, while others consider going to jail a temporary pause in action. Client goals and measures of success or failure are very individual issues and may be measured differently by each client. It is important to understand the client's measures, rather than impose expectations and evaluate success and failure according to the worker's measures.

The release date from jail determines the termination and separation process for female prisoners. The content of the ending is unique to each relationship, and the social worker should consider the individual's background, and the nature, and duration of the relationship. One important thing to be aware of in planning to end the relationship is to check in with the client in weekly increments as their release date approaches. This is a time when the relationship may become of greater significance to the client as she prepares to leave jail.

Evaluation by NASW Cultural Competence Standards

Agency, Services, and Programs As has been presented in this case study, this agency does not meet the NASW standards for cultural competence. However, I think it is crucial to remember that nonsocial work professionals naturally have different professional cultures, and cannot be fairly judged by the code of a profession other than their own. Many individual practitioners and staff members at the agency are culturally competent in their work with women prisoners, while many others are not. As a whole, however, the agency seems generally unaware of the importance of cultural competence. However, due to the funding limitations that affect all services rendered, choices must be made and priorities set; within these limitations, the provision of services to all must come before the provision of sensitive and culturally competent services to some.

My Cultural Competence Through this course of study, I have deepened my appreciation for the importance of cultural sensitivity and diversity. I think it's easy to avoid in-depth consideration of this topic and get too comfortable with personal worldviews and beliefs. This opportunity to reflect on my cultural competence is a reminder that true achievement of this ideal is not the completion of a course or an assignment, but the incorporation of considerations of dignity and humanity into my everyday interactions with my environment. This idea of continued reflection is embedded in the NASW standards for cultural competence. I feel that I have gained a basic level of appreciation for the strengths that exist in all populations. I also feel that through this cultural immersion project I was able to gain a respect for the value of meaningful inquiry in relation to specific cultural groups, and a respect for the strengths of my clients, who face innumerable challenges both within and outside prison. I look forward to applying the skills and techniques that I have acquired to help my future clients.

APPENDIX A

Statistics (Bureau of Justice Statistics Report for 2003)

- Black women were nearly 2.5 times more likely than Hispanic women and over 4.5 times more likely than white women to be imprisoned. This applies across all age groups.

- Since 1995, the annual growth rate in the number of women prisoners has averaged 5.2 percent while the male average is 3.4 percent.
- In a period of only one year, July 2002 to June 2003, the number of women state and federal prisoners grew by 5 percent while the male population rose 2.7 percent.
- California, Texas, Florida, and the Federal system imprison four out of every ten women prisoners.
- There are 61 women prisoners per 100,000 women in the United States compared to 914 males per 100,000, but this number continues to grow smaller.
- California's imprisonment rate rose 14 percent between 1995 and 2003.
- 455 out of every 100,000 California residents is imprisoned.

REFERENCES

American Correctional Association. 1990. *The female offender: What does the future hold?* Arlington, VA: Kirby Lithographic Co.

Baum, D. 1997. *Smoke and Mirrors: The war on drugs and the politics of failure.* Bay Back Books.

Bloom, B., M. Chesney-Lind, and B. Owen. 1994. *Women in prison in California: Hidden victims of the war on drugs.* San Francisco: Center on Juvenile and Criminal Justice.

Bush-Baskette, S. 1999. "'The War on Drugs' a war against women?" In Cook, S. and Davies, S. (Eds). *Harsh Punishment: International Experiences of Women's Imprisonment.* Boston: Northeastern University Press.

Bureau of Justice Statistics, 1999. *Women offenders.* Washington, D.C.: Department of Justice.

Chesney-Lind, M., and L. Pasko. 2004. *The female offender: Girls, women and crime* (2nd Ed.). Thousand Oaks, CA: Sage Publications.

Epperlein, K. Producer and director. 1996. *Voices From Within.* Harriman, NY: New Day Films

Feinman, C. 1994. *Women in the criminal justice system.* Westport, CT: Praeger.

Glick, R., and V. Neto. 1977. *National study of women's correctional programs.* Washington, D.C.: National Institute of Law Enforcement and Criminal Justice.

Klein, S. P., and M. N. Caggiano. 1986. *The prevalence, predictability, and policy implications of recidivism.* Santa Monica, CA: Rand.

LeBlanc, A. N. 2003. *Random family: Love, drugs, trouble, and coming of age in the Bronx.* NY: Scribner.

Langan, P. A., 1991, March 29. America's soaring prison population. *Science,* 251. 1569.

Maltz, M. D., 1984. *Recidivism: Quantitative studies in social relations.* Chicago, IL: Academic Press, INC.

Worksheet

1. One of the issues that severely impacts incarcerated women, and which was addressed movingly here, is the effect of incarceration on mothers and children, and on the mother–child relationship. Women's prisons can be located far from cities and neighborhoods of origin, and visitation is often limited due to inaccessibility. Where there is access, the separation of prisoners from visitors allows minimal, if any, direct physical contact between mother and child.

    This problem potentially affects the children's development in many ways, and can serve as a negative factor in rehabilitation of the mother as well. How could this be addressed in a way that supports the mother–child relationship?

2. The author notes that although there are a number of services that address the needs of women once they are released from prison, there are few if any available to them while they are in prison.

   If a service for women who are incarcerated could be developed, do you think it is more helpful to focus on helping the women to make a good adjustment to life in prison, on education, and rehabilitation, or on planning for life after prison?

Culturally Competent Social Work Practice with Veterans of the Vietnam War

Diversity Project by Nancy O'Neil

INTRODUCTION

The population I have chosen for this project is men who served in combat during the Vietnam War. My field placement is a counseling center that serves all military veterans (men and women), and also serves women who have sexual trauma from the military. The veterans are from many different cultural and religious backgrounds, and also represent different social classes and groups. They include people in every field, from writers to lawyers to carpenters to business owners, teachers to plumbers and mailmen, and also people who are unemployed and/or are receiving SSDI. They have strong opinions of the military and the government, and discuss their worldviews frequently when they are together.

Since their experience in Vietnam, many veterans have developed a strong mistrust for the government and politics, and heated discussions often occur over how the military should operate. The Iraq War has been the focus of heated discussion against the current administration, and most if not all Vietnam veterans disagree with the war and feel sorry for the soldiers fighting and dying as soldiers did in Vietnam. Even though I might agree with them on how our administration is pursuing the war and have similar opinions about Vietnam, I will never know what it is like to be in their positions, and I have never known combat, or seen the death and terror that these men have experienced. Learning more about their experiences will be very helpful to me in working with these veterans.

KNOWLEDGE

History of Vietnam War

Fearing the spread of communism, President John F. Kennedy committed the people of the United States to the defense of the fledgling democratic government of South Vietnam. During the ten years of America's commitment to the Vietnam War, 55,000 servicemen were killed or listed as missing; three men served as President; and many American people waged their own war at home against the United States government's involvement in Vietnam.

In 1965 President Lyndon B. Johnson ordered the first of many sustained bombing missions over North Vietnam, known as Operation Rolling Thunder. In March of that year, the first U.S. combat troops were sent to Vietnam. As these men fought in the jungles of Vietnam, a different kind of war was taking place at home—Americans who opposed the war desperately struggled to resist the policies of the government. Lacking a credible plan for winning the war, and facing strong popular opposition, the government eventually withdrew its troops from Vietnam. In early 1973 under the Nixon administration, the Paris Peace Agreement ended open hostilities between the United States and North Vietnam (Military Advantage 2006).

There are many books written about Vietnam and the men's experiences, including *Semper FI Vietnam* (Murphy 1997), *Vietnam: The Necessary War* (Lind 1999), *We Were Soldiers Once* (Galloway 1992), and *Born on the Fourth of July* (Kovic 1979), which was later made into a film by the same name. Books and films about the war continue to be read and watched by the general public, testifying to the powerful effect of that experience on everyone in this country. Now that we are engaged in a war in Iraq, which many say is similar to the Vietnam experience, there is a resurgence of interest in the books and films about Vietnam.

There were also many songs written and played on the themes of the war, including: "War," "Soldier Boy," "We Gotta Get Out of This Place," "Who'll Stop the Rain?," "My Girl," "Light My Fire," "Sky Pilot," "Seems Like a Mighty Long Time," "Blowin' in the

Wind," "On the Road Again," "Black is Black," "Sitting on the Dock of the Bay," "Leaving on a Jet Plane," "Walking on a Thin Line," and "Homeward Bound." These songs were played both at home and in Vietnam, and some vets say that when they hear them, they have intrusive thoughts, or flashbacks. Since undertaking this project and learning more about the war, whenever I hear these songs or see these books, I think about all the men with whom I have spoken and counseled about their war experiences. These songs now hold a different meaning for me, although they represent a time when I was just a young girl and knew little of the war. These songs now represent the men that I have been fortunate to meet and possibly help in their struggles to readjust. Songs are a powerful medium, and whenever I hear the Doors, they will always take me back to the experiences of men in combat.

Autobiography:
Born on the Fourth of July

Ron Kovic's book, *Born on the Fourth of July* (1979), stands out for me perhaps the most strongly, as his story is very consistent with the experiences of the Vietnam vets with whom I have been working. He takes the reader on a journey through his experiences of being born on the Fourth of July, the most patriotic day of the year, to his experiences in Vietnam as a Marine, and, most importantly, to his experiences recovering from those experiences. Ron was raised on the films of John Wayne and Audie Murphy, which glamorized war. When he was in high school, a Marine recruiter came by and sold him and his classmates on the importance of serving in the Vietnam War. He went immediately from high school into the Marines, and, after a period of training, he was shipped to Vietnam.

In Vietnam, Ron's missions often engaged the enemy. During one particular mission, he worried that he was confused, and may have accidentally shot and killed another Marine. His superiors, to whom he reported the experience, insisted he was mistaken, and did not want to pursue his admission. Several

weeks later, during combat, Ron was shot in the spine and paralyzed from the chest down. This ended his tour of duty, and he was sent back to the United States for convalescence. Like many vets returning from Vietnam, Ron did not receive a hero's welcome, but rather was treated with neglect in the veterans hospital. There, as he eloquently writes, he learned that just because you give your body to your country, that country does not necessarily recognize your sacrifice.

Returning home to his family, he began the transition from combat to civilian life in a wheelchair. No one wanted to hear about his experiences in Vietnam, and Ron felt as though no one cared about what was happening to the young men who were being killed, or were still fighting. Ron began drinking alcohol to try and quiet the memories, feelings, nightmares, anger, and intrusive thoughts that he was constantly experiencing. When Ron's family finally had had enough of his drinking and constant anger, they kicked him out of the house, and he was left on his own and in a wheelchair to try and pull his life together. He eventually began speaking out against the war in which he had fought. On July 15, 1976, he pulled his wheelchair into the lights of Madison Square Garden to address the Democratic Party and nominate Jimmy Carter for the presidency.

Ron's book takes readers on his journey from the idealism of youth, through the degradation and defeat of manhood as a vet in a wheelchair, to finally becoming a voice for the Vietnam veterans who did not have a voice. He felt the treatment they received from both the public and the government was despicable, and that as soldiers, they should have been treated like any other veterans. This book seems to resonate with the experiences of many veterans with whom I have spoken. They share their stories of anger, hurt, and frustration at the treatment they received upon coming home from a war that was so traumatic to the country. I have read several books by soldiers from Vietnam, but Ron's book was especially meaningful in the way that it presented the idealism young men have about war.

**Films: *Born on the Fourth of July,
Platoon, Apocalypse Now, Full Metal
Jacket, Hamburger Hill, The Deer
Hunter, Good Morning, Vietnam, We
Were Soldiers***

There are many films that represent the men
who fought in Vietnam. The veterans I work
with recommended especially *Born on the
Fourth of July, Platoon, Apocalypse Now, Full
Metal Jacket, Hamburger Hill, The Deer
Hunter, Good Morning, Vietnam*, and *We Were
Soldiers*. One thing I found interesting was
that the vets always recommended films that
had to do with their own branch of the military. The Army veterans recommended
Hamburger Hill and *We Were Soldiers*, the
Marines recommended *Platoon* and *Apocalypse
Now*, while the Air Force vets recommended
Good Morning, Vietnam. I watched all of these
films again, though I had seen some of them
before. Seeing them in this new context
allowed me a glimpse of the world they had
experienced, and the traumas from which
they are still recovering.

Platoon was probably the most powerful
film for me, as it illustrated the experiences of
both the new soldiers entering the war, and
the soldiers who were getting ready to leave.
In the film, the new soldiers were called
names, and were picked on by the older soldiers, which is consistent with what the veterans at the center have shared with me. The
soldiers in the film that had been in Vietnam
for a while were cynical, angry, and often used
drugs to escape their memories of combat.
Most of the veterans I have spoken with state
that drugs and alcohol were a major problem
in Vietnam. If you didn't have a drug/alcohol
problem before you went, you surely had one
when you came home.

All these films show soldiers drinking or
using drugs to cope, or escape from, the difficult conditions of the war. Vets continued to
use these forms of escape upon returning
home to an unsympathetic public, creating an
ongoing readjustment problem.

These movies are difficult to watch, and
they make me feel angry and resentful at the
treatment the soldiers received, and con-

cerned about the possibility of the Iraq War
veterans coming home to a similar reception.

**Cultural Event: Two Support Groups
for Veterans**

I attended two male combat support groups for
four weeks to get a better understanding of the
veterans' experiences. At first, the men were
guarded and visibly uncomfortable with my
presence. After a few weeks, they seemed to let
their guard down, and spoke more freely as
evidenced by their language and subject content. I was uncomfortable about being in these
settings, as I have no experience with Vietnam
veterans, and I did not want to intrude on their
support group. I validated their statements of
discomfort with my presence, and encouraged
their feedback, which made them more comfortable with my presence.

The two groups were different in their
make up. The first group had approximately
13 men, ranging in age from 53 to 62. All
branches of the military were represented,
and the men were Caucasian, African American, Filipino, and Latino. I noted that they
did not discuss ethnicity issues at all: the conversations were centered upon their experiences in Vietnam, and how this bound them
as "brothers." They did discuss their feelings
about their war enemies, the North Vietnamese. Many seemed to have reconciled
their feelings about the North Vietnamese
soldiers, and stated they, too, were fighting as
their government ordered. There were a few
who expressed hatred towards their enemies,
and seemed not to have moved past these
feelings. A common topic was their past use of
drugs and alcohol as a means of coping. Out
of the 13 men, eight were in a 12-step recovery program, and had been for many years.

The second group's veterans seemed
quite different. They had not been together
as long as the other group, but they also
shared their experiences of their tours in
Vietnam. The nine participants included
African Americans, one Korean, one Caucasian, and one Native American. This group
discussed ethnicity and racism in the military,
and noted that it still occurs today. The
Korean vet said he has found acceptance in

this group through his Marine combat experiences. The group seemed less guarded in my presence than the first group, but two veterans stated that a "white woman from Pleasant Hill" wouldn't understand them as veterans, and as men of color. I validated their feelings and encouraged them to share them.

These men also discussed their past use of drugs and alcohol, and one of the members was in 12-step recovery. Both their use of language, and their content seemed to indicate that they were not uncomfortable with my presence.

I feel fortunate to have had the opportunity to listen and interact with these men, as they have opened my eyes to experiences I had never really considered. Their willingness to discuss the traumatic events they experienced, and the ways in which their combat experience has affected their lives forever, was truly inspiring. These men showed me that no matter what your culture or ethnicity, you can pull together to find the solution.

Interviews: Two Vietnam Veterans

I interviewed two Vietnam veterans for this part of my project. The first man is a 58-year-old retired Marine, who served in Vietnam from 1968 to 1969. He stated that he joined the Marines at age 18, as the recruiter told him he would be fighting for American safety and justice. He felt the recruiter sold him a "bill of goods." He trained for six months at Ft. Benning, Georgia, then transferred to Vietnam, arriving in Saigon. He still vividly remembers his arrival, and watching all the planes and helicopters going in and out of the base. He saw other soldiers that looked scared and new like him, but he also saw many others who were going home that, he said, looked like "the walking dead." He said they had a look about them that told a thousand horror stories. He remembers being scared, and thinking immediately that he had made a big mistake by joining. Being new to his unit, he was hassled about being a "newby" and "fresh meat." During his 13-month tour, there were many experiences that have left him haunted for life. One especially poignant experience was being out on patrol when the

Vietcong ambushed them, and everything became "crazy." The squad commander ordered him, and two other members of this squad, to guard the ridge. One of the squad members was shot and severely wounded at the ridge. The squadron commander ordered them to evacuate and, as they were bringing their wounded "brother" back, they were ordered to leave him. When the veteran told the commander "We never leave a man behind," the commander shot and killed the wounded soldier and told the other two Marines that if they didn't obey him the next two bullets were for them. The veteran said from that point on, he figured he would never come out alive. This experience was the turning point for this veteran, and he began using heroin to escape the horrors of war and its memories. This addiction continued for many years. Upon returning home, he was spit upon by protestors at the airport, and the taxicab driver kicked him out of his cab when he found out he had served in Vietnam. He said he felt anger at both the government and the people in the United States who turned their backs on the veterans when they most needed help. He eventually got clean and sober in 1990, but not before losing his job, his family and social relationships, and accumulating legal problems. To this day this veteran has nightmares, flashbacks, intrusive thoughts, anger, fear, and lack of trust. He works on these in 12-steps support groups and private therapy for his diagnosed PTSD. This veteran's story is like many other stories I have heard, and I feel angry and hurt that these men were treated with such disregard in both Vietnam and when they returned home.

The second veteran I interviewed was an Army door gunner, who served in Vietnam from 1970 to 1971. He began by telling me that the life of a door gunner in combat was estimated to be three seconds. His story is at first similar to those of the other veterans: he was trained and then sent to Vietnam. He feels he became addicted to the adrenaline from combat: he got a high from combat that was impossible to duplicate. Door gunners, he said, felt special from knowing that life could end any second; that was part of the adrenaline rush. He stated that he killed so many people, that he never counted them, and that he saw them only as part of the task at hand.

Upon his return to the United States, he had a difficult time adjusting to the "regular Army," where he was required to complete his service commitment of 18 months. He found himself becoming very angry with the commanding officers, who had never seen any combat, yet were "spouting" their professional opinion on war. He found it so difficult to adjust that he went AWOL for one year, until they finally caught up with him, and put him in jail for two months. He was finally discharged, as the Army didn't think he could be rehabilitated. He wandered around the country for a while before settling down, and has had a very difficult time adjusting to civilian life. He also struggles with PTSD and all the symptoms that cause dysfunction in his life. He works developing race car engines, and this gives him the adrenaline rush he has been looking for since his wartime experiences.

Conclusion

This project was a deeper journey into the lives of Vietnam veterans who, at a young age, believed that they were protecting our country from Communism. What these young men found instead was a lifetime of horrible memories and symptoms that inhibit a quality of life others take for granted. Vietnam is a culture unto itself: it has created a "band of brothers," all veterans, who when together, help one another. I am grateful for the opportunity to speak and work with these men, and I know this experience has changed my perspective on their plight.

For people in the military, perhaps more than for others, the policies and actions of our government have a strong, very personal, and direct impact. For them, it is not a theoretical discussion of the merits of two political systems, or a determination of whether to support or protest government policies. Rather, those policies and actions have an immediate physical, emotional, and spiritual effect. Yet, the commitment inherent in joining the military requires soldiers to go where they are sent and do what they are asked to do without question or choice. It is a difficult commitment, and yet one that demonstrates the very best idealism and patriotism that our nation can be offered.

Hopefully, we have learned some lessons from the veterans of the Vietnam War. We will honor the bravery, commitment, and idealism of our soldiers, provide them with the services they need and respect they deserve, and never again return them to a nation that seemed so unappreciative of these very qualities.

Applying the Knowledge: Assessing Agency, Program and Services, and Personal Cultural Competencies

As I had noted earlier, my field placement this year is with a Veteran's Counseling Center that serves veterans in a major, diversely populated urban area. Many of the clients we serve are African American, white, Latino, or Filipino, and they are veterans who have served during times of combat. There is a wide age range among the clients as well.

The Agency
Agency's Community The community surrounding the center offers many churches, community centers, a YMCA, and several schools including two high schools. There is a hospital less than a mile from the center, which also includes behavioral mental health services for substance abuse and psychiatric units. There are several shopping centers within a short walk from the center, as well as numerous eating establishments representing many ethnic cuisines.

Access Many modes of access to service are available to clients. Public transportation by rail is a ten-minute walk from the center, and, if clients are unable to walk that distance, a staff member or center volunteer will pick them up and drop them back off when their session is completed. There's a bus route that stops a block away as well. However, the center is near a major freeway off-ramp, and most clients drive and park in the parking lot in front of the building. Many of the clients are dropped off by family or friends for their sessions, and several clients have the person who drove them wait in the reception area, as it is very inviting and there is always someone to talk to. There is coffee, snacks, and plenty of reading material available for their convenience to help make their wait more comfortable.

The center is easily identified from the outside, as it has both U.S. and military branch flags flying. It has been viewed not so much as a neighbor, but as a friend by the community we serve. Many vets just come and visit with us, use the computer, read the literature, watch videos, or read a book from the library we provide. There is a long ramp leading to the entrance, as many of the vets have disabilities, and a handicap accessible restroom is available. The hallways and rooms in the center are large and wide to allow easy access to all visitors.

The center offers outreach services to the general community as well. There are special events where assistance is offered to the homeless, in an effort to reach out to homeless vets who might be suffering from mental illness and financial disadvantages. There are ceremonies to welcome home the Iraqi vets, and counseling services are offered if needed. The staff and volunteers also visit homeless shelters in the community to offer services. The staff also facilitates combat support groups in local communities around the center specifically for Vietnam and Iraqi veterans.

Receptivity Not only is the staff receptive to my client population, but most have deliberately chosen to work at the center, as they have a connection to the services being offered. My field instructor is a Vietnam veteran, as is the team leader. The office manager is a 20-year retired Army veteran, and the marriage and family therapist served in

the Air Force for 15 years. There is a tendency to employ former military personnel, or Vietnam veterans, as they understand the needs and demands of this population of clients. A volunteer group known as the Blue Star Mothers offers receptionist services.

Entering the center is somewhat like walking into a military museum, as mementos and uniforms in cases are displayed throughout the center. The reception area is warm and inviting, with military-themed posters and pictures, such as the Vietnam Wall, World War II battle scenes, and even the women nurses of World War II. They are powerful images, and most clients and visitors find themselves lost in memories. At the entrance there are flyers, pamphlets, and magazines offering both older and current articles. There is also a military library on the premises, with videos and books from all the wars. As most of the client population speaks English, most, if not all, of the materials are in English. Many center clients also offer to share their experiences in using veterans' services to new vets to orient them to available programs.

Staff Sensitivity The staff is not only sensitive to the needs of the Vietnam vets: they are emotionally and professionally invested in offering quality services to the clients and their families. Staff members are very culturally diverse, not only by their own individual ethnicity, but also by that of their families, several of which are bi- and multiracial. Because there is so much diversity, judgment of others is rare, and both staff and clients share many cultural differences.

The staff is well-versed in the military jargon of my population, and use this appropriately when addressing the clients. Depending on the circumstances and needs, they can be informal, using the same language as the clients, or very professional when the situations warrant. The clients appear very comforted with knowing the staff are former military and know what it is like to be in their shoes.

Administration and Training One of the best features of the vet center is the ongoing education programs. Our center is not far from the National PTSD Training Center, where all counselors are sent for a week-long intensive training to become better clinicians. PTSD is the major problem affecting the clients of the center, and the training is very helpful in understanding this disorder and how it affects individuals and their families.

Training through educational programs and clinics is also available at the center, and staff is also trained by working directly with the population currently utilizing the center. This amazing process offers staff an opportunity to see how the Iraqi and Vietnam veterans are working together, despite their service in different wars: men and women from all different cultural backgrounds and ages are relating to each other through commonality of experiences, rather than race or ethnicity. Monthly in-house training and clinical feedback are also offered, and, in summer, a three-day conference is held to educate staff on new trends in clinical and cultural care for the veterans and their families.

Funding All services provided at the center are funded directly from the government; no monies change hands. Counseling, group, and educational services are offered free of charge to clients who qualify. The only qualifications for services are that clients have served in the military during combat eras, such as 1965 to 1975, 1990 to 1992, and 2003 to the present. Veterans don't necessarily have to have been in combat, but just to have served during these timeframes to qualify for services.

There is no maximum amount of counseling sessions or group therapy, as the government covers all services. Funding allows for cultural diversity, as it represents all qualified military personnel and their families who seek services. The government also funds homeless and community outreach in an effort to get deserved services to vets at no monetary cost to them.

Agency Programs and Services

Effort The center devotes much effort toward developing programs that are culturally sensitive to the population. There are several support groups that are offered to men or women

only, Iraqi vets only, Vietnam vets only, and there are two African American Vietnam vet groups held weekly. Support group facilitators are aware of and sensitive to these diversities. I do not believe that my client population is directly involved in developing policies that are culturally sensitive to their Vietnam experiences, and there are many government policies and protocols in place that are not easily adaptable. However, during the service process, Vietnam veterans are able to facilitate any needed changes to increase sensitivity and better serve their needs.

The center has a mission statement on display in the lobby that reads:

> Vet Centers Serve Veterans and their families by providing a continuum of quality care that adds Value for Veterans, families and communities Care Includes professional readjustment Counseling, community education, outreach to Special populations, the brokering of service with Community agencies, and provides a key access Link between Veteran and other services in the U.S. Department of Veterans Affairs

I think that this mission statement reflects the views and effort the staff put toward providing sensitive and culturally competent services to Vietnam vets. But what is more interesting is the motto that is also framed and next to the mission statement, which is reflective of the center's views:

> "We are dealing with Veterans, not procedures, with their problems, not ours."
> General Omar Bradley, May 2, 1947
> Director of the Veterans Administration
> The adopted "motto" of this Vet Center

Even though the government has many procedures and manuals it would like the centers to follow, this center also has a simple and clear motto, helping all Veterans, including my population, and their families in need.

Quality The programs at the center are focused around offering appropriate mental health services to the men and women of the armed forces. Because this culture is recognized as unique, the center makes a point of ensuring the quality of its services. Surveys are sent out to each client and his/her family, inviting responses and comments on the services provided.

A *very* sensitive topic among the Vietnam veterans my agency serves is that of politics. In the process groups the agency offers, there are a few guidelines designed to reduce personal discomfort. These guidelines include limiting discussion of both religion and politics, as these hot topics can cause extreme agitation amongst the veterans. At this time, the daily news on the war in Iraq is serving as a trigger for the Vietnam veterans with PTSD. There is awareness that efforts must be made to keep the topics in group away from current politics and the government's role in events, while encouraging the expression of the feelings that arise as a result of U.S. involvement in Iraq and Afghanistan.

While outside society can discuss these issues more impersonally, the Vietnam veterans find themselves struggling with symptoms of anger, anxiety, depression, hyper-vigilance, isolation, and lack of trust when the current military involvement is discussed.

Effectiveness The catchment area surrounding the center is culturally diverse, and includes a homeless population that often utilizes services, even if only for computer access. The number of vets living in the area is large, in comparison to the numbers who utilize the center's services. Outreach is offered, but many of the homeless vets do not want help with their housing and mental health conditions. It is disappointing to realize how few military utilize the services we offer, but there seems to be a stigma attached to reaching out for assistance. It is possible that alternative outreach approaches need to be developed to reach more broadly into the Vietnam vet community.

Most Vietnam vets who do utilize the services report that the center has "saved their lives" as they find that the group support and the education offered have provided them with the means to survive.

One of the services not offered at our center that would be important to Vietnam

vets, based on my experiences in learning about this population, is education and support groups around substance abuse. Many Vietnam veterans have substance abuse problems as well as PTSD, but have no access to a program that addresses the complex interactions between these two issues. When I began my internship, I tried to educate the staff about substance abuse treatment, as I have been in this field for many years. I began to be assigned vets with recognized substance abuse problems, and I also taught classes on a disease concept approach to substance abuse. I have been able to introduce other support groups at the center, including Alcoholics and Narcotics Anonymous, and Al-Anon for families. The center staff and its clients have been open to these new treatment supplements and have printed an article about my services in the monthly center publication.

Efficiency The center has developed effective linkages to homeless shelters in the community, and to other housing resources. A large veteran's hospital provides clients who need these services with comprehensive medical and psychiatric services, mental health outpatient programs, housing, and financial benefits for the military. We also link our services to community agencies, primarily government agencies.

Personal Cultural Competencies

Engagement, Trust, and Relationship-Building It is important to recognize at the outset that Vietnam veterans are not very trusting in general, but seem to distrust the government above all else. Because the center is funded through the government and is, in effect, a government agency, it is often difficult for the vets to sort out the intricacies of this relationship and its potential effect on them. I believe this distrust may have a major effect on the numbers of veterans who seek and utilize our agency's services: they either have had a bad experience with services elsewhere, or they simply do not trust the government. Most Vietnam vets feel the government lied to them about what they were getting into in Vietnam, and that it is lying now about Iraq. Trust issues are also key symptoms of PTSD, a condition that the majority of Vietnam vets must spend their lives coping with.

If the veterans and their families do seek services, building trust is an essential step. Maintaining eye contact helps some vets and family members feel that you care and are listening, and it lets them know they are also worth helping. However, it is essential to be very sensitive with eye contact: some Vietnam vets do not like social workers to look them in the eye, as we represent authority figures to them, and many vets have difficulties with authority.

Most Vietnam vets, regardless of culture, race, or ethnicity, express a need for distance, both physical and emotional. They sit as far away as possible from others, including social workers and other center staff. One can gauge the level of comfort and trust by observing the distance the vet keeps between himself and others. With time, sometimes many months or years, they will move a little closer. In a combat support group that I co-facilitate, I changed the room configuration by putting the chairs in a circle so that people were a little closer together than they had been in this large room where everyone sat at least three chairs apart. This group of men had been meeting once a week for several years and knew each other well. Nonetheless, their discomfort with the change was painfully obvious, and one member did not come back the following week, instead calling to say he could not attend because of the change in configuration, and asking if the chair arrangement could be changed back.

In order to help a client feel more comfortable, the initial stage of relationship also involves a tour of the center, including the museum and library, introduction to other staff members, and to other vets. During this process, it is important to observe any reactions and interactions with others.

Assessment and Problem Definition The assessment process encourages the social

worker to use ethnographic interviewing, and progresses in chronological order through childhood and the military experiences. It is helpful to encourage the vets to share rich, descriptive accounts of her or his time in service. During this description, it is essential to watch body language and to look for any indications of distress, such as startled responses, intrusive thoughts, anger, trust issues, and accounts of problems in working with others.

Listening is one of the greatest tools a social worker can use to work with this population. Most Vietnam vets just want to be heard, to share what happened to them, and how this has affected their lives. It is especially important to validate their experiences as they are shared in the assessment process: most vets feel they were not validated when they returned from war. Attentive listening and empathic responding will encourage the client to continue to share experiences with the worker.

It is also important to understand the nature and extent of the support systems veterans have, as well as the community support systems for both themselves and their families. Using an eco-map can be helpful to both social worker and vet in visualizing all of the relationships and supports available. The eco-map can also include any veteran's services the client is utilizing, such as vet centers, educational groups, and hospitals.

A part of this assessment should also involve exploring any unhealthy supports clients are using to cope, such as substance abuse. Vietnam veterans also have triggers that tend to cause emotional and behavioral difficulties, including holidays such as July Fourth, Memorial Day, and military birthdays such as Marines Day. Vietnam vets identify their problems as related primarily to their past experiences in the military and feel that their military experiences, and the lack of support they experienced from the government and the general population, has caused the difficulties they are experiencing. They may describe in detail how their beliefs and idealism have changed over the years, and how their expectations about life have dwindled due to lack of support from the government. Many African American Vietnam vets share their painful experiences upon return to the United States, not only soldiers who fought in a war that was generally protested, but also as second hand citizens due to the color of their skin.

Contracting and Goal Setting Appropriate goals for Vietnam vets at the center might include joining some of the culturally diverse support groups in order to enable them to express how their experiences and vet culture have affected them. The support and feedback from the group facilitator and the other members would serve to validate the vet's experiences and perhaps help him to feel less isolated and distant.

It is also essential for the group facilitator to help the group members develop a contract for how the group is to be run, and a set of group rules that members agree to observe. These rules should include: respect for others in group, no name calling or ethnic blaming, listening while others are speaking without interruption, and strict limitation of the discussion of religion, as this is a population who tends to be very sensitive to discussions about organized religion. These guidelines can support the group's structure, fulfil its purpose of validating and providing a forum for discussion, ensure balance, and encourage respect for each member.

Interventions In addition to providing support groups, individual counseling, and avenues for education, recreation, and socialization within the center, clients can be referred to local community churches if they are interested in pursuing a religious or spiritual avenue. Clients can also be referred to 12-step recovery programs, and meeting schedules for Alcoholics Anonymous and Narcotics Anonymous are kept at the center. Families can be referred to Al-Anon for support.

Vietnam veterans often use illegal substances, a form of self-medication for their PTSD and other mental problems, and interventions for outside substance abuse support include detox centers, hospitals, and support groups.

Evaluation and Termination Vietnam veterans initially have a tendency to think in terms of all or nothing, which applies to the understanding of success or failure. However, through education, medication, and therapy, they can begin to recognize their symptoms and see how they affect behavior. Medical intervention to deal with symptoms is often the next step, accompanied by group and individual therapy to allow them to process their feeling and experiences and begin to desensitize.

When vets begin to see that their symptoms have reduced, they begin to think and speak in terms of acceptance (not success). The focus is definitely on the diminution of symptoms as they begin to understand that they will always have PTSD, but can learn to recognize and manage their symptoms. The vet, the social worker, family members, and other staff may all participate in evaluating the success of the intervention process.

Vietnam veterans generally spend several weeks to months processing separation and loss issues in individual and group therapy. They learn to trust each other, bound together by the culture of the war and its aftermath. The vets discuss separation and loss on many levels, including leaving home and loved ones, leaving their units, grieving dead comrades and dead ideals, losing innocence and trust, ending relationships, retiring, ending their military careers, and losing the person that they might have wanted to become. These scars are deep, and take years/lifetime to address.

NASW Standards

There are ten Standards of Cultural Competence defined by NASW to guide social workers. The eighth Standard applies to my agency, its programs and services, and my own goals of cultural competence. It states:

> Professional Education—social workers shall advocate for and participate in educational training programs that help advance cultural competence within the profession.

The agency is focused on education and training for all staff. Each employee and intern attends the national PTSD training clinic for one week of intensive training. The training clinic provides classroom education in ways to better serve our populations (Iraqi and Vietnam veterans). The training also offers a day of cultural competence training, which includes both interaction and participant observation. Methods and skills are taught that have the potential for more effective outcomes in working with veteran populations. The vet center also sends all staff/interns for a four-day training session each summer. This training is mandatory and teaches methods to better serve our population through cultural understanding.

My center offers a one-hour session upon return to the agency, so that training participants can share what was learned, and discuss its application to practice. This is a wonderful opportunity to learn from colleagues and is supported as an integral part of improving programs and services throughout the center.

The training and support that I have received has helped me understand the culture and experiences of the Vietnam vet population, and has increased my cultural competence by teaching me ways in which to interact more effectively. Part of the training involved sharing and learning what other social workers working with veterans were doing to offer culturally competent services. This expanded my grasp of concepts and skills. The supervision that I have been offered is culturally sensitive as well, as I have had the experience of having a Vietnam vet as my field instructor. As a white female, who is not a Veteran, I was quite uncomfortable in working with this population at first, and I truly valued the knowledge and support that was provided to me.

This immersion project and the training I have received at my agency have given me a much deeper understanding of, and appreciation for, the population of Vietnam veterans. I know that I have been able to communicate effectively and establish a meaningful relationship, as my support group of Vietnam vets invited me out for dinner to celebrate the completion of this project, and assured me that I understood "where they were coming from," and that they could talk to me "like I was one of them!"

REFERENCES

Cimino, M. (director). 1978. *Deer Hunter* [Motion Picture]. Hollywood, CA: Universal Studios.

Coppola, F. F. (director). 1979. *Apocalypse Now* [Motion Picture]. Hollywood, CA: Omni Zoetrope.

Galloway J. 1992. *We Were Soldiers Once*. NY: Harpertorch.

Irvin, J. (director). 1987. *Hamburger Hill* [Motion Picture]. Hollywood, CA: Artisan Studios.

Kovic, R. 1979. *Born on the Fourth of July*. NY: Simon & Schuster, Inc.

Kubrick, S. (director). 1987. *Full Metal Jacket* [Motion Picture]. Hollywood, CA: Warner Brothers.

Levinson, B. (director). 1987. *Good morning, Vietnam* [Motion Picture]. Hollywood, CA: Buena Vista Pictures.

Lind, M. 1999. *Vietnam: The Necessary War*. NY: Touchstone.

Military Advantage. 2006. Military Movie Source. http://www.military.com

Murphy, E. 1997. *Semper FI Vietnam*. NY: Random House, Inc.

National Association of Social Workers (2001) NASW Standards for Cultural Competence in Social Work Practice. Washington, D.C. Author

Stone, O. (director). 1986. *Platoon* [Motion Picture]. Hollywood, CA: MGM Studios.

Stone, O. (director). 1986. *Born on the Fourth of July* [Motion Picture]. Hollywood, CA: MGM Studios.

Wallace, R. (director). 2002. *We Were Soldiers* [Motion Picture]. Hollywood, CA: Warner Brothers.

Worksheet

1. The writer alludes to a significant population of homeless Vietnam veterans, many of whom are addicted to substances and/or are mentally ill. While it is important to acknowledge the principles of self-determination and autonomy, it is also important to consider whether the government has any special obligations to this population, and whether the support services and programs currently available for them are adequate and appropriate. (a) What do you believe to be the obligation of the government to these veterans? (b) What kinds of services not currently provided do you think would be beneficial?

2. There is a sense in which social workers represent their agencies and operate as agents of them. The Veteran's Administration is a government agency affiliated with the military. If you do not support current government policies regarding military actions, can you appropriately take a position as a social worker with the Veteran's Administration? Why or why not? If you believe that you could take such a position, would you feel that you should be able to express your political beliefs in the agency setting? With colleagues? With clients?

   This would apply similarly to any agency with whose policies or positions you did not agree—whether these are about the war, abortion, termination of life support, religious service participation as a condition of agency service, homosexuality, sexual relations outside of marriage, birth control, conditions for foreign aid, single parenthood, confidentiality and HIV, substance abuse, parental rights, undocumented immigrants, etc.

Culturally Competent Social Work Practice with Alcoholics

Diversity Project by Lawrence Smith

INTRODUCTION

My field work placement is with an agency that serves homeless individuals and families. Many of the agency's clients have a history of substance abuse. In order to become culturally competent in working with these clients, I have decided to focus my research on a specific sub-population within the community of addiction—current and former members of Alcoholics Anonymous, or AA. In my work in human services, I have found that many of my clients who suffer from addictions have at one time or another been part of a 12-step program. Twelve-step groups are modeled after the original group founded in 1935 by Dr. Robert Smith ("Dr. Bob") and Bill Wilson ("Bill").

KNOWLEDGE OF POPULATION

History of the 12-Step Movement Both Bill and Dr. Bob had suffered from alcoholism for many years. After overcoming a severe relapse into addiction, Bill had an epiphany, after which he decided that the only way to save himself from his own demons would be to save another alcoholic. After frantically searching for someone to share his newfound vision, he found Dr. Bob. Dr. Bob was not only a medical doctor, but also an alcoholic and skeptic (of everything in life). When Bill called Dr. Bob on that historical day, their initial conversation lasted for hours and opened the door for the development of a new movement—a movement that has lasted several decades.

Since its founding in the 1930s, AA has helped thousands of people overcome dependency on alcohol. The program's format is a model for other addiction recovery programs, like Narcotics Anonymous and Overeaters Anonymous. The 12 steps were designed with the intention of helping alcoholics first to admit that they had a drinking problem, then to change their behavior. (Kurtz, E. 1972)

This approach works for many people. The spiritual dimension of AA is an essential part of the program, and meetings end with a devotional to a higher power. In addition, members are encouraged to review their prior mistakes in order to gain insight and prevent a relapse. An example of this process is AA's fourth step, which involves doing a "searching and fearless moral inventory of yourself" and learning from your mistakes new ways of dealing with problems. The goal is to teach participants ways in which to gain a better understanding of who they are.

AA offers a nonjudgmental atmosphere in which alcoholics can discuss the issues affecting their lives and their recovery from alcohol addiction. AA encourages complete abstinence. Meetings last an hour to an hour and a half, and are free of charge. (Donations of a maximum of $2 are requested at each meeting, however.) The only requirement for joining any of these groups is a desire to stop drinking.

Currently, it is estimated that there are more than 15 million alcoholics in the United States, and AA groups function in 134 countries worldwide. Groups can focus on meeting the needs of various demographics based on gender, lifestyle (groups limited to women or gay men for example), and vary in format from workshops to large gatherings of over 100 people. It is suggested that neophytes in the first 90 days of the program attend as many meetings as possible and attend regularly.

The Big Book (officially titled *Alcoholics Anonymous*) serves as the definitive guidebook to the history and the program of AA. It includes the basic beliefs of the organization, as well as several stories of people who overcame alcoholism by embracing the Alcoholics Anonymous way to recovery.

The 12-steps are based on a philosophy for recovery Bob and Dr. Bill developed. These follow a specific order:

The Twelve Steps of Alcoholics Anonymous*

1. We admit that we are powerless over alcohol—that our lives have become unmanageable.

2. We believe that a Power greater than ourselves can restore us to sanity.

3. We make a decision to turn our will and our lives over to the care of God as we understand Him.

4. We make a searching and fearless moral inventory of ourselves.

5. We admit to God, to ourselves, and to another human being the exact nature of our wrongs.

6. We are entirely ready to have God remove all these defects of character.

7. We humbly ask Him to remove our shortcomings.

8. We make a list of all persons we have harmed, and are willing to make amends to them all.

9. We make direct amends to such people wherever possible, except when to do so would injure them or others.

10. We continue to take personal inventory, and when we are wrong promptly admit it.

11. Through prayer and meditation, we seek to improve our conscious contact with God, as we understand Him, praying only for knowledge of His will for us and the power to carry that out.

12. Having had a spiritual awakening as the result of these Steps, we try to carry this message to alcoholics, and to practice these principles in all our affairs.

The 12 steps are a foundational part of every AA meeting and are integrated into the daily lives of people who are participating in the program. (Alcoholics Anonymous 2006)

Biographies: The Big Book In order to gain a better understanding of alcoholism, recovery, and the Alcoholics Anonymous movement, I decided to read what is considered by some to be the manual and definitive text of AA—the Big Book. Written in 1938 during the beginning years of the fellowship, the Big Book (official title of the book is *Alcoholics Anonymous*) was written by the two original founders of AA and a committee of several other members of the fellowship.

This book is a fascinating read, to say the least. It is organized in two sections. Section One of the Big Book explains the 12-step program in detail, giving the reader a very clear and precise understanding of what the program is and how to implement it in one's personal life. (Smith, B. and B. Wilson 1938)

Section Two contains a series of personal biographical accounts of AA members who have successfully used the program and worked the steps in order to regain control of their lives and free themselves from the chains of alcoholism. While each story is unique, the themes of recovery, regaining control over one's life, the importance of AA, the mentors who assist people in the process of recovery, and the rediscovery of meaning in relationships and activities are common to them all. At the end of the book there is an appendix section, which includes other interesting facts about AA such as a list of over 20 other publications the fellowship has produced; a statement of individual medical community and religious community member views of the effectiveness of AA (in the United States); and information on how to get in contact with local AA chapters. (Smith, B., and Wilson, B. 1938).

Personally, I found the book to be very religious and spiritual in nature. One of the central themes and core beliefs is that in order to truly recover from alcohol dependency, one must believe in a source or power greater

*Reprinted with permission of Alcoholics Anonymous World Service, Inc. (AAWS).

than one's self, God. As a future mental health professional and social worker, I would find it very difficult to refer a client in need of treatment for alcohol abuse to a program with such overt religious overtones. Although the deity referred to in the pages of the Big Book is a universal being, it is apparent after reading the text that the spiritual leanings of the writers are rooted in the Judeo-Christian experience. Where, I wonder, does that leave potential clients who are of other faiths such as Buddhism or Islam, or who are atheist?

In spite of my reservations about the relationship between religion and the methods advocated in the recovery process, I do feel that any professional in human services who has even a remote chance of coming into contact with clients who are currently dealing with, or in the past have dealt with, substance abuse issues needs to read this book and become familiar with the process it so eloquently demonstrates. AA's approach to recovery has been the most effective one for many years and continues to be an excellent resource today despite the development of other models, such as harm reduction.

The philosophy and recovery process developed by AA is the foundation for many similar groups, such as Narcotics Anonymous, Gamblers Anonymous, and Overeaters Anonymous, and it continues to dominate recovery group philosophy and process in the twenty-first century.

Film: Once We Were Warriors This is an excellent film about the ravages of alcoholism and its negative impact on communities and family systems is set in the slums of Auckland, New Zealand, where the walls are covered with graffiti, and the streets are filled with garbage.

Jake has been married to Beth for 18 years. Because of his lower cultural and social status in their society (Jake is a descendant of slaves), Beth had been forced to choose between him and her Maori tribe. He has never forgotten how much shame his background has caused himself and his family. Since his marriage to Beth in early adult-

hood, he has dealt with his frustrations by getting into fights at the local bar and drinking heavily. (Duff, A. 1995)

Beth continues to do the best that she can to maintain the sanity of her household and their five children, despite the difficult conditions in which they live, and the circumstances they face. She has a strong relationship with her daughter Grace, who is 13 years old. Grace would like her mother to leave her father because he has become increasingly abusive.

During the film, Jake loses another job, and spends more time at the bar with his friends, who are also out of work. The bar seems to draw every bad element in their community. The late evening parties, filled with cheap food, cheap liquor, and loud music serve as an oasis in a sea of despair. In this environment, alcohol seems to be just as important to one's physical health as water or vitamins. (Ibid)

I was really shocked by this very powerful story—not only because of the graphic depiction of the lives of poor, marginalized people in New Zealand, but because of how eerily similar it is to the lives of poor and disenfranchised people in the United States. I can remember hordes of unemployed men— young adults, 30-year-olds, and almost-senior citizens—all out of work. These desperate circumstances seem to breed an atmosphere of hopelessness and violence in the communities of Oakland where I grew up. I had always assumed then that this was a local occurrence. Even after graduating from college I never would have imagined that such conditions could exist the same way in foreign countries. How naïve I was!

Cultural Immersion: A Recovery Meeting I was fortunate enough to attend a recovery meeting facillitated by a marriage and family therapist who has been leading such groups for the last 20-plus years. I chose this particular group for a number of reasons: the group is only open to agency clients living in the family shelter and is mandatory for all adult residents who have had issues around drugs and alcohol. Thus, it is especially relevant as a learning experience in services that can assist clients in my agency context. Another unique feature of this group is that the group leader is also in recovery, with more than 20 years clean, and is a believer and advocate of the AA organization. Each member of this group also attended AA meetings weekly.

The group consisted of 20 members, and, on any given week, at least a dozen members attend this required session. On the day I visited, there were 10 people in attendance, three heterosexual couples (not married, but residing together) and four single heads of household (three women, one man). Each person seemed to exist in a limbo of recovery/sobriety, with the possibility of slipping over the edge at any time because of life stressors. I was surprised at the candor of each participant. Alcohol addiction is such a personal and intimate aspect of one's life, not only for the alcoholic, but for the people who love and care about them.

Perhaps because of the nature of this particular group (all of the members were, or had been, chronically homeless), the effects of the alcohol abuse were very obvious. One of the group members, who was only in her mid twenties, appeared to have aged well beyond her chronological age. No one in the group had held a steady job recently, and only one member had had a successful career—she was a computer operator at a Fortune 500 company.

As suggested by the facilitator, the group talked about their victories over poverty (one person has received a large SSI settlement from the federal government) and their personal accomplishments for the week (several people had successfully completed a homework assignment from the therapist—find time for yourself to relax). As an MSW student, I expected some kind of empirically based, data driven, best practices model of how to run a therapeutic recovery group. Instead, I think what I experienced was a very humanistic and compassionate vision of how a therapeutic group can be run.

Personal Interview I decided to interview a person I met at church, who is in recovery and utilizes AA as a method for dealing with her addiction. Kate is a 45-year-old white woman who has been using alcohol since the age of 15. She is a single parent of two teenage children, a boy and a girl. She was willing to participate in a self-test that I gave her, which was developed by a group called Sober 24, a support system for people dealing with alcoholism (Self help therapy groups 2005), and to talk with me about her drinking history.

Kate believes that many outsiders are unaware of the fact that alcoholism is a disease. According to her, once infected, the individual is never cured or freed from her or his addiction. It remains an issue for all of a person's life.

Raised in an Irish family that embraced alcohol as part of their cultural heritage, alcoholism was never shunned in her family. Kate started drinking heavily during her youth. Later, Kate considered herself a functional alcoholic, able to support her drinking financially. While her excessive drinking never created difficulties with the law, it did affect her work and personal responsibilities. Kate often arrived late to work meetings, or important functions, such as church activities and services. She didn't feel a need to avoid social events that did not involve alcohol: Kate simply imbibed prior to the event. "No biggie, drunk is drunk, no matter how, when, or where."

Because she did not experience any of the serious side affects of alcoholism, such as blackouts or memory loss, her drinking was easier for her to rationalize and accept. She sometimes thought about quitting and becoming sober, but never seriously tried. Kate did, however, say that she reflected on what she was missing in life while drinking, and that she felt somewhat isolated.

Together, we worked on Sober 24's assessment and found that it revealed that Kate should have had professional help for her alcoholism. She agreed to seek this help. I was very pleased to have been able to find a good tool which allowed me to ask some relevant questions to help Kate understand herself and determine that she did indeed need help with her alcoholism.

Because I have at times been placed in a similar situation in other contexts, I especially did not want Kate to feel as though what she was saying in this interview was representative of all people who are either alcoholics, AA members, or both. I did try to reassure her that she represented only herself, and I think I was able to get a sense of her perspective and the attitudes she had about her addiction in a sensitive manner. This allowed me to approach the other sections of this project with more clarity.

Conclusions Alcoholism is a terrible disease with a history of destroying lives. It is not a new phenomenon. It has been part of our culture since its earliest beginnings. One of the keys to helping those who have suffered from the negative psychosocial impact of alcohol abuse is to find a straightforward way to deal with the problem. For millions of Americans, Alcoholics Anonymous has served such a function.

I have always been in awe about the thoughtfulness, dedication, and determination of recovering alcoholics who participate in AA. I am impressed with the organization and the philosophy of the organization. People are given guidelines like the 12-step process and resources like the Big Book to use

in their recovery, a well thought out and comprehensive program. I do have some misgivings about AA however.

I am especially concerned about how the AA movement frowns upon any type of medical or clinical professionals as a main source for treatment of this disease. I have always heard from AA members that only an alcoholic knows what it is like to be in that state, to suffer with that disease. This is very disturbing to me for several reasons: I see alcoholism as a disease, not just maladaptive behavior, and as a clinical issue, which both mental health clinicians and medical doctors can be trained to address.

As a society, we would never say only cancer patients should treat or do research on the disease of cancer, nor would we say only mentally ill therapists and mental health professionals can contribute to the development of cures and treatment modalities for mental illness. That type of perspective in the fields of mental health or medicine would seem ridiculous at best. Nevertheless, in the field of alcohol addiction treatment, 12-step programs have a virtual monopoly.

AA does enjoy a distinct advantage over other types of treatment philosophies in this country—it has the highest rate of success.

Applying the Knowledge Base: Agency, Program and Services, and Personal Practice Competence

My field work agency is a nonprofit dedicated to the elimination of homelessness in a suburban county. The agency annually provides a place of residence for approximately 2,000 people, which include an estimated 200 children. The agency offers transitional and long-term housing and support services for single adults without children, single adults with mental health disabilities, couples with children, and single parents. Within the agency are several different programs including: Family Services (couples with children and single parents), Adult Services (single

adults), Mental Health Services (individuals with mental health disabilities), and Into Housing (couples with children and single parents, and individuals with mental health disabilities). My internship was in the Family Services program.

Demographic information about my agency's catchment area includes: A population of around 60,000, of which 79.6 percent are White, 3.0 percent are African-American, 6.8 percent are Asian, and 23.3 percent are Hispanic, Latino, or other race. The median age is 38.5 (U.S. Census 2000).

Agency

Access The agency is located in a predominately white community, with a sizable Hispanic population. The neighborhood within that community is unique because of its very diverse population. It is dominated by bungalow style and Victorian houses along with a few apartment buildings and duplexes. A major freeway and public transportation are nearby, and the neighborhood has a middle class, blue collar feel to it. One staff member told me that back in the 1960s the residents were hardworking blue and white collar workers of modest means and background. As real estate values increased, many residents held on to their homes, and profited well from the changes.

My clients come from an emergency housing facility that my agency also administers, which is located in an area with a high concentration of low-income people and predominantly Hispanic immigrants in an industrial mixed zoning area. I noted that my clients did not seem comfortable coming to my agency's location for services and would often offer excuses when asked or invited to the agency.

Receptivity My agency is the most open and welcoming agency that I have ever been involved in as a volunteer, worker, intern, or client. While there is a clear zero tolerance policy in regards to substance use (in addition to all forms of violence), the agency's leadership has a keen aversion to doing any sort of testing for substance use, even when there is clear evidence that a client has violated the zero tolerance rules. Line staff are encouraged to engage clients immediately upon learning that a relapse has occurred and to refer them to a local detoxification center, in- or outpatient services, or to reentering the program in which they had been participating.

At least a third of the line staff and management are members of the local population. The agency tries very hard to recruit a diverse and progressive work force. During the interview process, potential employees learn about the client populations they will be serving, and their first and secondary presenting problems. It is emphasized to both employees and clients that, while the agency is not an alcohol treatment program, it works very hard to provide direct services to address the needs of clients who are dealing with alcoholism. If the scope of the problem is too much for the agency to handle, clients are referred to outside sources of help. Referrals to other programs and participation become part of the contract that is established between the client and the agency.

The agency is so committed to the right of the client to exercise self-determination that when clients first come to the agency they are asked to self-identify any life circumstances or problems that have led to their homelessness. Some clients initially state that they do not have a problem with alcohol. It is only after their family advocate engages them and builds a sense of trust that they are willing to be more open about their problems.

The quarterly agency newsletter features several articles on present or past program participants who are either making significant progress while in the program, or who have gone on to make substantial changes in their lives for the better. A high percentage of the clients that I observed in the last three newsletters had issues with alcoholism. Each article featured the details of the lives of clients before, during, and after the crisis that led to their involvement with my agency.

Although there is no formal waiting room at this facility, actually a three-story Victorian house, there are several bulletin boards in the hallway on the first floor, which is easily accessible to everyone. Any information staff deems useful for the clients/residents who are experiencing homelessness and/or some of the secondary issues often associated with homelessness, such as a need for recovery, life skills training, and parenting classes, is posted on the boards on a regular basis.

Administration and Staff Training The agency provides many trainings about alcoholism. My program has weekly staff meetings with guest speakers, and specialists provide workshops on a variety of subjects. I have taken part in several of these meetings, which were dedicated exclusively to the issues that alcoholics face in their recovery. These workshops repeat at least annually.

Once a month all line staff, managers, and the executive leadership team (clinical director, vice president, COO) participate in an all staff meeting: a three-hour meeting where the staff comes together to have lunch, socialize, and receive training. The population of alcoholics has been covered on several occasions this year alone. One of the trainings was an introduction to the concept of harm reduction, while another featured information about Al-Anon, an organization for alcoholics' families and friends.

Staff Sensitivity The staff is very sympathetic to the needs of alcoholics. It realizes that many of the clients either are having, or have had problems with alcohol. Through staff trainings, the hiring of members of the alcoholic population, and the policy for zero tolerance, the agency has made a great investment in making sure that all of its staff is aware of the needs of this particular population.

Funding The agency maximizes its resources excellently and forms partnerships with the community. Because of this, the agency is able to provide services to alcoholics and people in recovery at a minimal cost. The agency offers several substance/relapse prevention group meetings on a weekly basis at all of its residential locations. A specialist in the field runs each relapse prevention group, and is committed to volunteering to run the groups on an annual contract. The agency also utilizes alcohol and drug counselor interns. The agency requires all residents who have substance abuse issues to attend at least three weekly meetings outside of the agency in addition to the agency-based meeting. The majority of the meetings clients attend in recovery are 12-step meetings. None of these mandated services cost the agency directly. Occasionally, a family advocate might have to provide day care service for the relapse prevention meeting or drop a client off at an AA meeting.

Agency Program and Its Policies

Effort Although the agency has an annual budget of approximately $4 million, I was surprised to learn that the clients knew exactly who the executive leaders were. Some clients have even called to complain about services, received assistance from agency executives, and, amazingly, had their concerns addressed, in many cases actually resolved! Whenever a change to a program or services is considered, it is a common practice for this agency to survey line staff, clients, and program alumni, in addition to management. Clients are routinely surveyed about the quality of services and given opportunities to contribute to the agency's mission of eliminating homelessness. Client focus groups are organized to get feedback on a variety of topics concerning the current and future plans of the agency. Dealing with alcohol-related issues is a critical part of the agency's daily work.

Agency Policies and Programs

The agency has a number of policies and programs that apply directly to the alcoholic population. One of the policies with the greatest impact on them is the zero tolerance policy, which terminates all services to any client who abuses substances, including alcohol, while receiving services. This policy has been effective in getting clients to consider the options and alternatives: it is swiftly and impartially administered!

Quality The agency uses effective communication as one of its primary forms of evaluating and monitoring programs to ensure that they are culturally competent. Top management along with program directors and assistants work very hard at keeping the lines of communication open and flowing between staff and management, staff and clients, and clients and management. The newsletter, which is very descriptive, is one of the tools used, and a collegial atmosphere is encouraged at various support groups and meetings for clients as well as staff and management meetings.

The messages from the top of the organizational chart are always positive, thus setting an example for clients and staff to follow. Executive and middle management are well known to staff members and program participants. The Executive Director regularly visits my program. When policies, programs, or procedures grow outdated or otherwise become useless, the staff is able to make adjustments as soon as possible.

The agency strives to get people back on their feet by having them set and complete goals and claim victory over defeat. Less than a week after clients arrive, they are connected with a family or individual advocate with whom they can begin to devise an action plan. Action plans could include goals such as obtaining employment or another form of substantial monthly income, participating in drug and/or alcohol treatment, completing a credit history review, or conducting a housing search. Obtaining a sustainable monthly income is one of the keys to success in order to deal with the main presenting issue of clients—homelessness. Because of this emphasis of the program, clients are required to save a substantial portion of their income toward moving cost.

Effectiveness Many of the clients feel that they have to attend too many meetings. Some have been very resistant and feel that because the agency is neither a drug nor an alcohol rehabilitation facility, and is not connected to law enforcement, it has no right to police their recovery. However, the agency's approach has been effective with many of its clients, as indicated by the newsletter and agency statistics.

Efficiency To enter the program, clients must call and be placed on the waiting list. Emergency housing is offered on a first come, first served basis. Clients' and families' first contact is by telephone, and they are told to call back each day until a space opens up. They are also informed about eligibility criteria and where to go for a required free tuberculosis test. When a space is available, they are invited to make an intake appointment. At the intake appointment, their eligibility for services is determined, their needs are assessed, the various programs are explained to them, and the intake worker makes a decision on the family's eligibility for admission to the program.

I think the agency is both efficient and fair in its practices, and all of the major alcohol treatment agencies within the county have referred clients to our agency.

Personal Cultural Competencies

Clients from this population have traditionally relied on the 12-step model as the primary way of dealing with alcohol abuse. AA historically takes a stance against any type of treatment models run by professionals. Individual members of the alcoholic population are starting to explore alternative treatment models from groups following alternative models, such as the harm reduction model, physical health model (well being and healthy lifestyle classes, yoga), and the spirituality models (church-based spirituality meetings) of addiction treatment and recovery. Social service agencies over the last few decades have started to address the issues of substance abuse among their clients even if this is not the primary or even secondary mission of their organization. Because of this, more alcoholics are receiving some sort of treatment service from non-12-step groups, including social service agencies and other nonprofits.

These alternative models enable the professional, together with the client, to select the model that best seems to meet the client's needs as well as the agency's requirements. Professionals thus are now expected to have familiarity with all of the models, and to be engaged more directly in recovery efforts than during the earlier periods, when this effort was primarily delegated to AA. Practice skills that address the specific needs and characteristics of this population must be developed by each social work professional.

In considering the social work processes, both agency policy and the special qualities and problems of this population must be incorporated into a culturally sensitive model of service. From the earliest steps in relationship-building to the conditions of termination, the effect of agency policy must be considered carefully in working with clients.

Engagement, Trust, and Relationship-building: As mentioned earlier, the agency has a zero tolerance policy concerning drugs and alcohol. No alcoholic beverages of any kind are allowed on the premises. Any drug or alcohol use during one's residence, or one's affiliation with the agency as a client, is grounds for dismissal from the program. During the initial assessment for services, each client is asked whether or not he/she currently has, or in the past has had, a problem with alcoholism or drug abuse. If the client answers yes to either question, he/she will be required to participate in some sort of treatment like AA, in addition to the mandatory recovery group that meets at the facility.

Because participation in these programs is mandatory for recovering alcoholics and former drug addicts, the traditional social work practice steps concerning the process of engagement, trust, and relationship-building are often affected. The choices are quite stark, and immediate, and are not subject to negotiation and discussion. If a client refuses to participate in the required recovery program, the consequences are definitive: expulsion from the agency's programs. This generally means a return to homelessness.

In this sense, for my population, there is a degree of similarity between my agency's program and any other mandated service. As with other mandated services, a choice still remains, and this needs to be fully discussed and clarified for the client. However, the options are circumscribed and no new ones can be negotiated. The alternatives, which with other mandated services may be jail or participation, or separation from children or participation, in this case is housing or participation.

Assessment and Problem Definition Several assessment tools are utilized in order to identify whether a new client has issues with alcohol abuse during the early stages of the agency's work with clients. Because of the potential for relapse, ongoing assessments are important in working with this population and should include both self-reporting and observation by the social work practitioner for signs and symptoms of relapse.

The case plan for all of my agency's clients is centered on acquiring permanent housing. Clients are assessed for secondary presenting problems, which may interfere with achieving the first goal. Once these other problems have been identified (drug addiction, unemployment, mental health, etc.), they become part of the contract and must be reviewed for progress on a weekly basis. Each weekly meeting with the family advocate includes a review of the previous week's goals, adjustments to be made, and the setting of new goals. Clients are encouraged to talk about how they feel that week and how their relationships with other service providers are going.

Contracting and Interventions As noted above, the overall goal for each client at my agency is long-term housing. However, the contract may involve many secondary goals, and may also be broken down into a number of smaller steps. These are evaluated and adjusted weekly, so that the client's contract remains current and relevant.

I learned some culturally competent interventions from observing the work of other staff members during my internship. When a staff person believed that the client had a relapse (thus violating both the case plan and zero tolerance policy of the agency), the advocate immediately met with the client to voice concerns. If the client denied that she or he has or had been intoxicated, the client could be asked to take the appropriate test or be asked to take a night out to sleep it off and/or think about the consequences of his/her actions. Depending on the client's reactions, his/her advocate may allow him/her to stay in the program after attending a substance abuse detoxification center for several days, engaging with an out-patient alcoholism program, or some other appropriate measure. If there is a record of prior program violations, clients may also be asked to leave the program. While these measures may seem harsh, they are part of the culture of alcoholic treatment. One group dealing with these issues states:

> Since alcoholics almost universally deny that they have a problem, a treatment strategy called "interventions" is often

necessary. A professional alcohol counselor calls a surprise meeting which the alcoholic, their family, their closest friends, and sometimes-even coworkers attend. This group then "confronts" the alcoholic about their behavior.
(Selfhelp Therapy Group)

Evaluation and Termination There has been a paradigm shift of sorts in work with alcoholics in recent years. Ten years ago, relapse would have been seen as a very negative outcome—something to be avoided. Hardcore Alcoholics Anonymous members and practitioners took a dim view of those who strayed from the path of sobriety. They were chastised severely, seen as weak, and berated for making such a grave mistake. Today things have changed to a degree.

With some human service agencies' shift from considering the 12-step model as the only avenue for alcoholics, people suffering from the addiction of alcohol today have more models available. Groups such as the Harm Reduction Coalition have developed a new model for dealing with a variety of addictions, including alcohol abuse (Harm Reduction Coalition 2005). Below is a description of their philosophy:

Drug use is illegal in the United States and is not socially sanctioned. In the present political climate any help for drug users and other marginalized communities in the United States will remain controversial.

Materials and information on this website are presented to promote the reduction of harms related to drug use, and to promote public awareness of personal and community health options for people who use drugs. Materials and information on this website provide detailed discussion of ways in which drugs are used, and ways in which drug users understand their drug use. If you are offended by such materials and information, please leave this website. (Harm Reduction Coalition 2005).

In the past, a client's perspective regarding success and failure during her/his journey of recovery was grounded in the connection to a 12-step program. Based on my experiences at my most recent field placement, I noticed that some people relapse for only a day, but really feel as though they failed, while other clients may be out of the program for several months, then reenter the agency without guilt or self-condemnation.

In my experience with this population, the focus has been both on diminution and/or elimination of symptoms, and on inner change. Many people tend to take a very spiritual, almost mystical view about life. "God is always on time," or "Good things come to those who wait" are some of the common phrases and/or themes that I encounter when talking with members of this population about their recovery.

As a family advocate, I do not feel that there is a particular way that was preferable in terminating with alcoholic clients. Using Miley's Generalist Social Work Practice (Miley, O'Melia and DuBois p. 432–457) as a guide, I followed the five steps for closure when it became time to end our relationship, paying particular attention to ensuring that follow-up resources were available to my clients.

One of my clients was successful in finding long-term transitional housing, which made preparing for our eventual termination at the end of my internship less complicated than if things had remained unresolved. At every meeting (there were a total of approximately 28, one-hour formal meetings, not including the numerous informal minute meetings during dinner), we reviewed the status of the housing search, and the move-in costs. We had several false positives, where it seemed as though the client had secured housing, but the leasing agent picked another applicant. The client's readiness for transition was addressed on a weekly basis. When housing was secured, my client was ready and well-prepared for termination and the transition.

Overall, the entire case management process from start to finish is very professional at my agency, and termination of services is seen as a victory by both clients and workers. The agency initially gives clients four months to find housing, but as long as they are making progress, they can receive up to four extensions, which allows a client to stay for up to 16 months. The majority of clients, whether alcoholics or not, leave the agency in a much better position than they had been in when they were accepted into the programs offered.

Evaluation Using the NASW Standards for Cultural Competence

NASW Standards	Agency	Program	Self
Standard 1. Ethics and Values	The agency works in a nonbiased manner servicing all of their clients as long as they abide by the regulations of the program.	Aligned with Agency	I work as a professional, without judgments.
Standard 2. Self-Awareness	Invites guest speakers to come in and share their experiences as a member of the population.	N/A	I acknowledge my own feelings about alcoholism, but I do not share my opinions with clients.
Standard 3. Cross-Cultural Knowledge	Provides regular staff training about alcoholism.	Aligned with Agency	Attend trainings regarding specialized populations.
Standard 4. Cross-Cultural Skills	Agency provides training.	Aligned with Agency	Have learned some culture-specific skills for working with my population.
Standard 5. Service Delivery	Agency yearly evaluates policies on services provided to their clients.	Aligned with Agency	Advocate on clients' behalf for housing services and needed resources.
Standard 6. Empowerment and Advocacy	Maintains an extensive list of community based resources.	Aligned with Agency	I frequently use agency resources in addition to other referrals for my clients.
Standard 7. Diverse Workforce	Agency hires a diverse staff including members who were formerly alcoholics.	Aligned with Agency	N/A
Standard 8. Professional Education	Agency provides monthly on site staff development.	Aligned with Agency	I participated in agency staff development activities.

continued

| Standard 9. Language Diversity | Appropriate materials are printed in three different languages. | Aligned with Agency | When necessary, I use interpreters to assist in case management and referral process. |
| Standard 10. Cross-Cultural Leadership | Agency requires interdepartmental communication. | Aligned with Agency | I use my case notes and other observation to convey necessary information to outside resource agencies. |

REFERENCES

Alcoholics Anonymous. 1984. *Pass it on: The Story of Bill Wilson and how the A.A. Message reached the world.* NY: Alcoholics Anonymous World Services.

Alcoholics Anonymous. 2001. *The Story of how many thousands of men and women have recovered from Alcoholism* (5th Ed.). NY: Alcoholics Anonymous World Services

Alcoholics Anonymous. 2006. *The Big Book Online* (4th Ed.). http://www.aa.org/bigbookonline/

Duff, A. 1995. *Once We Were Warriors* (documentary). NY: Vintage International

Harm Reduction Coalition. 2005 www.harmreduction.org

hooks, b. 2000. *Class Matters*. NY: Routledge.

Kurtz, E. 1972. *Not-God : A History of Alcoholics Anonymous*. Center City MN: Hazelden Educational Services.

Leigh, J. W. 1998. *Communicating for Cultural Competence.* Prospect Heights, IL: Waveland Press.

Lieberman, A., & C. Lester. 2004. *Social Work Practice with a Difference.* Boston: McGraw Hill Publishers

Memorable quotes from Once Were Warriors. 2005. http://www.imdb.com/title/tt0110729/quotes

Miley K., M. O'Melia, & B. DuBois (2004) *Generalist Social Work Practice.* Boston: Allyn & Bacon

Selfhelp Therapy Group. (2005) http://www.helpyourselftherapy.com

Selfhelp Therapy Group. (2005) Self Test. http://www.sober24.com/

Smith, B. & B. Wilson. 1938 *The Big Book* NY: Alcoholics Anonymous World Service

U.S. Census 2000. http://AmericanFactfinder/factfinder.census.gov/home

Worksheet

1. The Harm Reduction Model has increasingly become an option in working with substance abuse and presents an approach that is a departure from the traditionally preferred 12-step approach of AA. It is important for social workers to understand this newer model and discuss both alternatives, as well as potential others, with clients. Describe both the 12-step program and the Harm Reduction Model in a way that explains the advantages and disadvantages of each. Which model do you believe is most effective? Why?

2. In reading this case, I was struck by the fact that clients of this agency knew the directors and managers and felt comfortable in contacting them with any concerns. The author notes that the concerns expressed in this way actually were addressed. How do client problems, issues, and concerns reach the executive director or administrator of your agency? Do you think that the system is effective? What could be done to improve communication between consumers of services and those who administer and develop programs?

PART THREE

Workbook

This text has presented a process called cultural immersion for the attainment of cultural competence, which can be applied to any population with whom you are working, and to any setting. Mastery of this process provides a portable, clear, and thorough method for attaining a measure of cultural competence with any population. In addition, a process has been also included through which the cultural competence of any agency setting and any program and services can be assessed and evaluated for its cultural competence with any selected population. Because self-evaluation is the cornerstone upon which true cultural competence must be built, a method for examining cultural competence through the social work processes at any level of practice has also been suggested. An evaluation of agency, programs and services, and personal competence in the context of the NASW Standards for Cultural Competence has also been suggested.

As noted in Part I, the basic structure for comprehensive knowledge acquisition and evaluation consists of two separate parts, knowledge acquisition about a specific population, and the application of that knowledge to an assessment process. Part II has provided some specific examples of populations, assessments, and self-evaluation, which illustrate the way in which this process can be utilized.

In this Part, the reader is asked to apply the learning to a population of choice. In effect, this Part will assist the reader to utilize the process developed in Part I by exploring a self-selected population, and will provide guidance with each step in the process. As each step in the process is completed, it is recorded in the appropriate section of the workbook. When all of the work is completed, the reader will have developed a personal population immersion and assessment similar to the studies in Part II with the population he/she has chosen as the focus of the cultural competence attainment effort.

> **Space is provided for recording information and processing. If additional space is required, the reader may insert extra pages with any appropriate section.**

The first, most essential step in this process is the selection of a population for study. Make a list below of all of the populations served by your agency. Your list can include populations which are focused around:

Race	Language	Ethnicity
Social Class	Sexual Orientation	Ability/disability
Immigration Status	Worldview	Religion
Worldview or Philosophy	Appearance	Region
Gender		

Populations Served by My Agency:

_____

_____

_____

_____

_____

_____

Mark or cross out all the populations on your list of which you are personally a member. These will be excluded from consideration.

As you study the remaining populations, it might be helpful to consider:

which population(s) are served in significant numbers by your agency?

which population(s) do you know least well?

which population(s) have you always had a special interest in?

which population(s) have you been least comfortable with, and why?

which population(s) do you associate with certain stereotypes, positive or negative?

which population(s) will be accessible to you in terms of books, films, individuals, and events?

Considering all of these and other factors, note the population you have selected as the focus of your work below.

Population Selected for Cultural Immersion:

_____

_____

Knowledge Acquisition through Cultural Immersion

Population's History and Major Milestones

An essential ingredient in cultural competence is knowledge of the collective history of your population, their experience in the United States and in their country of origin (if applicable), and the group's worldview as it has been influenced by historical experience.

Using history books, articles, the Internet, and any other appropriate resources, note important historical milestones and landmarks through which your population may define itself. To understand the current demographics (how many members, where they are located, etc.), you can access U.S. Census information online at factfinder.census.gov or at census.gov/main/www/cen2000.html.

History of _____ People

_____

_____

_____

_____

_____

_____

_____

_____

_____

_____

_____

_____

_____

_____

_____

_____

Immersion Experiences

In order to personalize what you have learned in the "history" part of your work, the next parts of the process involve learning about members of the populations' personal lives and experiences. There are several parts to this section, designed so that you may have an opportunity to explore and understand both some of the common threads in this population's experiences, and the very unique experiences of individuals as members of that population. The "common threads" will help you to understand some of the potentially general worldview, while the "unique experiences" will help you to avoid stereotyping.

Autobiography or Biography

Select an autobiography or biography about a member of your population. This should be a full-length book, so that you may gain insights about the individual over a broad span of time, through an immersion in personal life experiences.

Autobiographies and biographies selected by students in the past two years for this project are included below to assist you in locating an appropriate book. You may choose one of these, or explore your library and book store's holdings about the population you have selected. The population for whom the book was selected follows in parentheses.

AA World Services. 1984. *Pass It On: The Story of Bill Wilson and How the A.A. Message Reached the World*. New York: AA World Services (Members of AA).

Administrative Office for the Courts, Center for Families, Children and the Courts. *Can You Hear Me? A collection of poetry by Youth in California's Court System* (2003) *My Life: A collection of poetry by Youth in California's Court System* (2004) *What Gives Me Strength: A collection of poetry by Youth in California's Court System* (2005) (Parens Patriae Children).

Afghan Journal: An Intergenerational Afghan American Voice (2004):3:1 (Afghanis).

Albom, M. 1997. *Tuesdays with Morrie: An Old Man, A Young Man, and Life's Greatest Lessons*. New York: Doubleday (Elderly people).

Anaya, R. 1972 *Bless Me, Ultima*. Berkeley, CA: TQS Publications (Mexican Americans).

Angelou, M. 1969. *I Know Why the Caged Bird Sings*. New York: Random House (African Americans).

Anonymous. 1971. *Go Ask Alice*. New York: Simon Pulse (Teen Drug Users).

Armstrong-Coster, A. *Living and Dying with Cancer*. Cambridge: University Press (People with Cancer).

Atkin, S. B. 1996. *Voices from the Streets*. Boston: Little, Brown, & Co. (Urban Gang Youth).

Bacho, P. 1997. *Dark Blue Suit*. Washington: Univ. of Washington Press (Filipino Americans).

Bahrampour, T. 1999. *To See and See Again*. New York: Farrar, Straus, & Giroux (Iranian Americans).

Beer, E. H. 1999. *The Nazi Officer's Wife*. New York: Perennial (Jews).

Bonner, R. 1987. *Waltzing With a Dictator: The Marcos and the Making of American Policy*. New York: Times Books (Filipino Americans).

Brown, C. *A Piece of Cake*. (Commercially sexually exploited children).

Burns, B. 1998. *Shelter: One Man's Journey from Homelessness to Hope*. Tucson: Univ. of Arizona Press (Homeless people).

Burton, S. 1989. *Impossible Dream: The Marcos, the Aquinos, and the Unfinished Revolution*. New York: Warner Books (Filipino Americans).

Calloway, J. 1992. *We Were Soldiers Once*. New York: Harpertorch (Vietnam Veterans).

Canfield, J., M. V. Hansen, P. Aubrey, & N. Mitchelle, 1997. *Chicken Soup for the Christian Soul: 101 stories to open the heart and rekindle the spirit*. Florida: Health Communications (Christians).

Casanova, R., & S. Blackburn, 1996. *Each One Teach One*. New York: Curbstone Press (People in poverty).

Cheever, S. 2004. *My Name is Bill: Bill Wilson: His Life and the Creation of Alcoholics Anonymous*. New York: Simon and Schuster (People in AA).

Chetin, D. 1982. *Angel Island Prisoner*. Berkeley, CA: New Seed Press (Chinese Americans).

Chovil (personal website) *The Experience of Schizophrenia* (Chronic mental illness).

Cohen, L. H. 1994. *Train Go Sorry: Inside a Deaf World*. New York: Vintage Books (Deaf culture).

Cortez, J. 2004. *Sextile* New York: Gay Men's Health Project (Transgender people).

Crow Dog, M. 1991. *Lakota Woman* New York: Harper Perennial (First Nation people).

Dalai Lama, and H. C. Cutler, 1998. *The Art of Happiness*. New York: Riverhead Books (Buddhism).

Davis, S., G. Jenkins, & R. Hunt, 2002. *The Pact: Three Young Men Make a Promise and Fulfill a Dream*. New York: Riverhead Books (African Americans).

Desetta, A., and S. Wolin 2000. *The Struggle to be Strong: True Stories by Teens about Overcoming Tough Times*. Minneapolis, MN: Free Spirit Publishers (Transitional-Age foster youth).

Dixit, M. 2002. *Stories of Afghan American Women*. In http://www.Asianweek.com/20020517/feature.html (Afghanis).

Dorias, M. 2004. *Rent Boys: The World of Male Sex Workers*. (Male sex workers).

Douglass, F. 2001. *Narrative of the Life of Frederick Douglass: An American Slave Written by Himself*. New Haven: Yale University Press (African Americans).

Ehrenreich, B. 2001. *Nickel and Dimed*. New York: Henry Holt and Co. (Working class whites).

Erenreich, B. 2001. *Nickel and Dimed*. New York: Henry Holt Co. (Filipino Americans).

Erenreich, B. 2002. *The Global Woman: Nannies, Maids, and Sex Workers in the New Economy*. New York: Henry Holt Co. (Filipino Americans).

Feinberg, L. 1993. *Stone Butch Blues: A Novel*. Ithaca, New York: Firebrand Books (Transgender people).

Feinberg, L. 1996. *Transgender Warriors: Making History from Joan of Arc to Dennis Rodman*. Boston: Beacon Press (Transgender people).

Fiagiel, S. 1996. *Where We Once Belonged*. Auckland, NZ: Pasifika Press (Samoan Americans).

Flook, M. 1998. *My Sister Life*. New York: Random House (Teen prostitutes).

Guilbault, R. C. 2005. *Farmworker's Daughter*. Berkeley, CA: Heyday Books (Immigrant Latina youth).

Hagedorn, J. 1990. *Dogeaters*. New York: Penguin Books (Filipino).

Hansberry, L. 1959. *A Raisin in the Sun*. New York: Random House (African American families).

Hanson, D. 2005. *Room for J*. Edina, Minn: Beaver Pond's Press (People with schizophrenia).

Hardy, James E. 1994. *B Boy Blues* Los Angeles: Alyson Publications (African American men on the down low (MSM)).

Harrison, D. 2003. *Another Place at the Table*. (Foster Parents).

Hillard, D., K. Zimmerman, and K. Zimmerman, 2006. *The Spirit of the Panther* New York: Thunder Mouth Press (Native Californians).

Holcomb, R. K., S. K. Holcomb, and T. K. Holcomb, 1994. *Deaf Culture: Our Way*. San Diego: Dawn Sign Press (Deaf culture).

hooks, b. 2000 *All About Love: New Visions*. New York: William Morrow (African Americans).

hooks, b. 2000. *Where We Stand: Class Matters*. London: Routledge (African Americans).

Jamison, K. 1995. *An Unquiet Mind: A Memoir of Moods and Madness*. New York: Vintage Books (Consumers of mental health services).

Jones, E. 2003. *The Known World*. New York: Amistad (African Americans).

Kingston, M. H. 1975. *Woman Warrior*. New York: Vintage (Chinese Americans).

Kingston, M. H. 1977. *The Woman Warrior: Memories of a Girlhood Among Ghosts*. New York: Albert A. Knopf (Chinese Americans).

Kisor, H. 1990. *What's That Pig Outdoors: A Memoir of Deafness*. New York: Penguin (Deafness).

Knapp, C. 1996. *Drinking: A Love Story*. New York: Dial Press (Alcoholics).

Kozol, J. 1988. *Rachel and Her Children: Homeless Families in America*. New York: Fawcett Columbine (Homeless women).

Lee, H. 1996. *Still Life With Rice*. New York: Touchstone (Korean Americans).

Liebow, E. 1993. *Tell Them Who I Am: The Lives of Homeless Women.* New York: Free Press (Homeless women).

McBride, J. 1996. *The Color of Water: A Black Man's Tribute to His White Mother.* New York: Riverhead Books (Bi-Racial people).

McCourt, F. 1996 *Angela's Ashes: A Memoir/Frank McCourt.* New York: Scribner (People in Poverty).

Meade, M. 1928. *Coming of Age in Samoa: A Psychological Study of Primitive Youth for Western Civilization.* New York: W. Morrow (Samoan Americans).

Mior, K. 1997. *Polite Lies: On Being a Woman Caught Between Cultures.* New York: Ballentine (Japanese Americans).

Nestle, J., C. Howell, and R. Wilchins, 2002. *Gender Queer: Voices from Beyond the Sexual Binary.* Los Angeles: Allyson Books (Transgender people).

Paris, D. G., and M. Drolsbaugh Eds. 2001. *Deaf Esprit: Inspiration, Humor and Wisdom from the Deaf Community.* Salem, OR: AGO Gifts and Publications (Deaf culture).

Pryor, R. 1995. *Pryor Convictions: and Other Life Sentences.* Pantheon Books (African Americans).

Ramos, J. 2002. *The Other Face of America: Chronicles of the Immigrants Shaping Our Future.* New York: Harper Collins (Mexican immigrant day laborers).

Rodrigues, L. 1993. *Always Running.* New York: Touchstone (Latinos).

Sharlin, C., and L. Villa Nueva, 2000. *Philip Vera Cruz: A Personal Hiostory of Filipino Immigrants and the Farm Worker's Movement.* Seattle: Univ. Of Washington Press (Filipino Americans).

Shehyn, A. 2000. *Picture the Girl: Young Women Speak their Minds.* New York: Hyperion (Teenagers).

Siems, L. 1992. *Between the Lines.* Hopewell, NJ: The Ecco Press (Mexican Americans).

Simon, L. 2003. *Detour: My Bi-polar Road Trip in 4D.* New York: Washington Square Press (Mentally ill people in peer-based support groups).

Simone, N., and S. Cleary, 1991. *I Put A Spell on You: The Autobiography of Nina Simone.* (African Americans).

Smith, M. 1996. *Sanctuary Stories.* Tempe, AZ: Bi-Lingual Press (Latinos).

Tademi, L. 2002. *Cane River.* New York: Warner Books (African Americans).

Tan, A. 1989. *Joy Luck Club.* New York: Putnam (Chinese Americans).

Taylor, Q., and S. A. Wilson Moore, 2003. *African American Women Confront the West 1600-2000.* Norman: University of Oklahoma Press (African Americans).

Teen 1999. *Real Teens: Diary of a Junior Year.* Petersen Publishing Company, LLC: Scholastic Inc. (Teenagers).

Thompson, H. S. 1971. *Fear and Loathing in Las Vegas: A Savage Journey to the Heart of the American Dream.* New York: Random House (Drug addicts).

Toth, J. 1993. *The Mole People: Life in the Tunnels Beneath New York City.* Chicago: Chicago Review Press (Homeless people).

Tum, R. M. 1984. *I, Rigoberta Menchu: An Indian Woman in Guatemala.* (Guatemalan Americans).

Urrea, L. A. 1993. *Across the Wire: Life and Hard Times on the Mexican Border.* New York: Anchor Books (Mexican Americans).

Villanueva, M., and V. Cerenio, 2003. *Going Home to Landscapes: Writing by Filipinas.* St Paul, MN: CALYX Books (Filipino Americans).

Vincent, N. 2006. *Self-Made Man.* New York: Viking (Trangendered people).

Walker, L. A. 1986. *A Loss for Words: A Story of Deafness in a Family.* New York: Harper and Row.

Wallens, S. *Pushed.* (Bi-polar youth).

Zajdow, G. 2002. *Al-Anon Narratives: Women, Self-Stories, and Mutual Aid.* Westport, CT: Greenwood Press (People in AA).

Title of Book Selected: _____

Author: _____

Publication Data: _____

Major Themes: _____

_____

_____

_____

_____

_____

_____

_____

_____

_____

_____

_____

_____

_____

_____

_____

_____

_____

_____

_____

_____

_____

Film

While books convey through the medium of words, visual images can provide an immediacy of experience which is also very helpful. Select a film which is by, about, or specifically made for members of your chosen population. The film can be produced in another language, with subtitles, if this is appropriate. It may be a current film, or one available on DVD or VHS for home viewing, a documentary, or an educational film. Your school's video collection is also an excellent source of material for this part of the assignment, and can be accessed easily online.

A list of some of the films viewed by students in the past two years is included here as an example of the films that can be used for this section of your cultural immersion experience.

A Beautiful Mind directed by R. Howard (Mentally ill people in peer-based support groups).

A Day Without a Mexican, 2004, directed by Sergio Arau, Xenon Pictures (Mexican immigrant day laborers).

Antwone Fisher, 2002 (Transitional-age foster youth).

Apocalypse Now, 1979 directed by F. F. Coppola, (Vietnam veterans).

Born on the 4th of July directed by O. Stone, 1986, (Vietnam veterans).

Boys Don't Cry, directed by K. Pierce (Transgender people).

Boyz "N Hood (African Americans).

Candyman II: Farewell to the Flesh 1995, Polygram Video (African Americans).

Carved in Silence, directed by F. Lowe (Chinese Americans).

Complaints of a Dutiful Daughter (Elderly people).

Country Boys, Sutherland, David, Producer Boston WGBH (Working class whites).

Day Laborers, 1997, (Mexican Americans).

Deer Hunter directed by M. Cimino, 1978, (Vietnam veterans).

El Norte, directed by Gregory Nava (Refugees Seeking Asylum) (Guatemalan Americans).

Eve's Bayou, 1997, directed by Lemmons Kaci, Trimark Pictures (African American women).

Good Morning Vietnam, directed by B. Levinson, (Vietnam veterans).

Hell House (Pentecostal Christians).

Hoop Dreams (Teen boys).

In America, directed by J. Sheridan (People in poverty).

It Was a Wonderful Life: Hidden Homeless Women, directed by M. Ohayon (Homeless women).

Kandahar, 2001, directed by M. Makhmalbaf, (Afghanis).

Kids, directed by L. Clark, Trimark Home Video, Dates Unknown (Teen drug users).

Legacy, 1999, directed by Tod Lending (African Americans).

Looking for Mr. Perfect (Chinese Americans).

Looking Toward Home, 2003, directed by D. Kruzic, Amer. Film Institute: Visionmaker Video, Lincoln, Nevada (Native Americans).

Mad Love, 1995 (Bi-polar youth).

Man Facing Southeast (Mental health consumers).

Margaret Meade and Samoa NY: Brighton Video (Samoan Americans).

Maria Full of Grace (Latinos).

Mean Girls, directed by M. Waters (Teenagers).

Mi Familia, directed by G. Nava (Mexican Americans).

Mi Vida Loca, My Crazy Life (Urban gang youth).

Monster , directed by P. Jenkins (People in poverty).

Mulan, 1998, directed by T. Bancroft, and Cook, B., DVD Disney Films (Chinese Americans).

My Own Private Idaho, 1991, G. Van Sant, (Writer, dir., prod.) Idaho Productions (Male sex workers).

National Hero (Filipino Americans).

New Jack City (African American youth).

Normal (Transgender people).

Once We Were Warriors, directed by L. Tamahori (Members of AA).

One Flew Over the Cuckoo's Nest, directed by M. Forman (Mentally ill people in peer-based support groups).

Pharaoh's Streets, directed by J. Rothe-Kushel (Homeless people).

Platoon, 1986, directed by O. Stone, (Vietnam veterans).

Qallunajatut (Urban Inuk) 2005, directed by J. Weetaluktuk, American Film Institute: Isuma Distrib. International, Montreal, QC Canada (Native Americans).

Ray, directed by T. Hackford (African Americans).

Real Women Have Curves, directed by Cardozo (Mexican Americans).

Requiem for a Dream (Drug addicts).

Romero, directed by John Duigan (Refugees seeking asylum).

Saved, directed by B. Dannely (Christians).

Saving Face, directed by A. Wu, (Chinese Americans).

School Daze, a Spike Lee film (African Americans).

Separate Lives, Broken Dreams, directed by J. F. Kew (Chinese Americans).

Sideways (Native Californians).

Smoke Signals, directed by Chris Eyre (First Nation people).

Soul Food (African American families).

Sound and Fury, 2000, R. Weisberg, Prod. and J. Aronson Dir., Aronson Film Associates (Deaf culture).

Spring, Summer, Fall, Winter . . . and Spring, directed by K. D. Kim (Korean Americans).

Stand and Deliver, directed by R. Menendez (Mexican Americans).

Stella Does Tricks (Teen prostitutes).

Straight Outta Hunter's, 2003, directed by K. Epps, DVD Frisco Street Show (2005) (Residents of Hunter's Point, San Francisco).

Take It From Me, 2001, directed by E. Abt, USA: Pureland Pictures (Women on welfare).

Taxi Driver, 1976, directed by Martin Scorsese (Commercially sexually exploited children).

The Color Purple, directed by Steven Spielberg (African Americans).

The Daddy of Rock 'N' Roll directed by D. Bitton, Oaks, Pennsylvania: Music Video Distrib. (People with schizophrenia).

The Debut, 2000, directed by G. Cayajon (Filipino Americans).

The Fisher King, directed by T. Gilliam (Homeless people).

The Gatekeeper, directed by C. Frey, (producer and director) (Undocumented Mexican immigrants).

The Gospel, 2005 (African American religious practice).

The House of Sand and Fog, directed by V. Perelman (Iranian Americans).

The Joy Luck Club, 1993, W. Wang, A. Tan, R. Bass, and P. Marrkey, (Prod.) USA: Hollywood Pictures (Chinese Americans).

The Lost Weekend (People in AA).

The New Medicine, PBS Documentary (NICU families).

The Pianist, directed by R. Polanski (Jews).

The Wheel of Time by W. Herzog (Buddhism).

They Call Me Sirr, 2001, directed by Robert Munic, (African Americans).

To Live (Chinese Americans).

Tongues Untied, 1991 M. T. Riggs. MRT Productions (African American Men on the Down Low (MSM)).

Transamerica, 2005 Bastian (producer) and Tucker (director) USA: Belladonna Production (Transgender people).

Waiting to Exhale (African Americans).

When A Man Loves a Woman directed by L. Mandoki (Alcoholism).

White Oleander, 2002 directed by Kosminsky, Warner Brothers (Parens Patriae children) (Foster parents).

Who's The Man (African American).

Wit, directed by Mike Nichols, (People with cancer).

Film Viewed: _____

Director, Company, Year: _____

Major Themes: _____

Direct Immersion Experience: A Culture-Specific Event

Cultural-specific events provide an opportunity to experience an element of your population's experience in a very direct way. Ethnic fairs and festivals, religious services, gay or straight bars, support group meetings, and community meetings are examples of the kinds of events to select.

There are a number of levels of awareness that are important during your experience at this event. You will be observing the event and learning about the special traditions, group norms and expectations, and interactions among members of your group. You can also note their reaction to your presence: some groups will welcome an outsider warmly, others will engage in conversation and even ask you why you are there (it's good to be prepared with an answer!), others will take no obvious notice of your presence, while still others will leave a "space" around you.

Caution: Don't place yourself in a situation where you are uncomfortable—you may choose to do this activity with a classmate or a friend if you prefer, though it will dilute your experience somewhat. Select an activity at which you will be at least somewhat at ease—and *always safe.*

Date: _____

Event Attended: _____

Major Themes: _____

_____

_____

_____

_____

_____

_____

_____

_____

_____

_____

_____

_____

Personal Interview

The personal interview is your opportunity to have an in-depth, one-on-one contact with someone who has directly experienced some, or much, of what you have been learning. This personal experience may complement or supplement your reading, viewing, and cultural event experiences, or may provide a completely different kind of insight. You may choose to interview a classmate, a friend, someone you meet at the cultural event you have attended, or someone you contact for this specific purpose. *Always* share with your interviewee the purpose of your interview: you are attempting to learn all you can so that you can provide culturally competent services to all people who are a part of your interviewee's group, and assure them that their personal identity will remain confidential.

Asking someone to share their insights and story is a very personal experience for the person you are interviewing. It is important to acknowledge that, to always be respectful and attentive, and to maintain her/his confidentiality by disguising any identifying information during the process of writing about your experiences. Because of the power issues, confidentiality concerns, agency policy, and other possible issues, please ensure that you *do not* interview a client of your agency, or someone whose name and identity you have learned in the course of your work at your agency.

You might feel more comfortable if you prepare for the interview in advance by developing a list of questions that you think will help you gain insight. You may find that you will utilize all, some, or none of the questions, depending on the interests of your interviewee. However, preparing these ahead of time will help you be more comfortable and will provide the possibility of a framework within which to interview if desired.

Date of Interview: _____

Name of Interviewee (disguised as needed): _____

Major Themes: _____

_____

_____

_____

_____

_____

_____

_____

Summary And Synthesis

The "cultural immersion" you have experienced will have provided you with much new knowledge, experiences, and ideas about your chosen population. Hopefully, it will have given you an opportunity to address any biases or stereotypes you might have had as you entered this project and selected your population. You will have gained an overall understanding of your group's experiences, values, and worldview, and also an appreciation for the intra-group variation that distinguishes your population.

While it may be difficult, if not impossible, to describe all of the experiences you had and the things you learned, a summary will assist you in organizing your thoughts and ideas and will help to guide the subsequent assignment involving assessments.

Summary of Immersion Project: _____

_____

_____

_____

_____

_____

_____

_____

_____

_____

_____

_____

_____

_____

_____

_____

_____

_____

_____

_____

_____

Application of Cultural Knowledge

Assessing Agency, Programs and Services, and Personal Cultural Competencies

Assessing the Field Work Agency

Social agencies have a "culture" of their own, a culture that is often palpable to clients as they walk in the door. The culture is made up of both visible and invisible elements. Visibly, an agency can be welcoming, or unwelcoming, depending upon its location, accessibility, layout, decor, and staffing patterns. It can appear to reach out and embrace clients, or to hold them at arm's length. Invisibly, an agency's culture might include its hierarchy and organizational structure, the patterns of behavior and interactions of its staff, and the overt as well as covert attitudes of staff members toward the client population.

Some of these elements have an especial impact upon clients, whose perceptions are also influenced by their own cultural beliefs about, and attitudes toward, and previous experiences with help-seeking and social agencies. Several issues might have an especial impact on clients who must cross cultures in order to access services. Considering these in the context of the knowledge gained from the immersion experience will assist the reader in understanding the experiences clients from the population studied might have in accessing services from the field placement agency.

Name of Field Placement Agency: _____

Address of Agency: _____

Agency's Community

Simply walking around the agency's neighborhood can provide a great deal of helpful information. How can the "feel" of the neighborhood be described? What populations reside and work in your agency's community? In its catchment area? What other services, such as hospitals, community centers, schools, social agencies, etc., are available? What commercial services are available, such as grocery stores, banks, clothing shops, etc.? Are people in your selected population living and working in your agency's neighborhood?

Draw your agency's immediate community, indicating hospitals, schools, retail and social centers, social service agencies, and transportation routes.

_____

_____

_____

_____

Access

How do members of your chosen population get to your agency? Do they use public transportation, travel long distances, and cross ethnic and cultural boundaries in order to reach your agency? Obtain a map of your agency's catchment area (this will vary widely from small neighborhood to state and beyond). Include your map with this part of the assignment.

If people do not come to your agency, how are information and services accessed?

_____

_____

_____

_____

_____

_____

Receptivity

During hours when your agency is open to clients, walk through the front entrance, and into the waiting room. (If you are placed in a host agency, you may choose to explore either the social service department specifically, or the agency, school, hospital, etc. as a whole.)

Sit down in one of the chairs designated for clients and look around the room, noticing the decor, color scheme, furniture style, and anything else that catches your attention. Notice clients, the receptionist, and any other staff members, the noise level, the interactions between clients, and clients and staff. Look at the literature, brochures, or other material available to clients in the waiting room.

If you were a member of the population you have focused on, would you feel welcomed and comfortable? Do you see yourself reflected in the staff, in the decor or color schemes, in pictures on brochures? Are they available in a language and format that you can understand?

_____

_____

_____

_____

_____

_____

Administration and Staff Training

Agencies vary in the provision of training in cultural sensitivity, and may or may not include the group you have learned about as one of the focus points for diversity competence. From your personal experience with your agency, and from contacts with other staff members, are trainings, workshops, retreats, or other forums for discussion of diversity issues available to staff? With what frequency? Who is invited or expected to attend? Has there been a training that addresses the cultural issues of your specific population, or of populations, problems, and issues that can contribute to cultural competence with your population?

Does your agency employ members of your populations, both as professionals and as staff?

_____

_____

_____

_____

_____

_____

_____

Funding

In many instances, agency funding is directed at specific services with specific populations, or tied to reimbursements for services, rather than the training and recruitment of a diverse workforce. Does you agency's funding support training and hiring practices that enhance culturally sensitive services to your population? Does the funding allow for cultural variations in programs and services, such as literature available, types of programs and services funded, outreach, frequency of contacts, and other factors that might vary culturally?

_____

_____

_____

_____

_____

_____

_____

Staff Sensitivity

A vital ingredient of a culturally sensitive agency is the way in which staff members talk about, or act toward, people in the client population. You have had both formal and informal opportunities to observe both professional and support staff during your placement experience. Have you found that staff is sensitive and aware of special client needs, nonjudgmental, and respectful of the population you have studied? Are any stereotypes or "they" language used in regard to your population? Are staff and professionals sensitive in the levels of formality/informality of address they use with clients?

_____

_____

_____

_____

_____

_____

_____

_____

_____

_____

_____

_____

_____

_____

_____

_____

_____

_____

_____

_____

_____

_____

Agency Programs and Services

We have explored the more tangible and easily measured resources your agency utilizes to provide culturally congruent services to clients who are members of your population. In this next section, we will consider the ways in which agency programs are designed, administered, and evaluated, kinds and relevance of community outreach and involvement, and utilization of services by your population. Four criteria, effort, quality, effectiveness, and efficiency, will be used as guides to assist you in your evaluation process.

You may find some of the answers to your questions through direct observation, and others in consultation with your supervisor, colleagues, and executive director or administrator. You will also need to refer to your agency's mission statement, policies, program descriptions, and any follow-up or evaluative studies your agency has performed.

Effort

Has you agency made an effort to reach out to your population's community to secure input into program design, utilization, and administration? Are members of your population on committees within your agency that formulate and design programs, and is their input solicited in decision-making to develop culturally sensitive services?

_____

_____

_____

_____

_____

_____

_____

_____

_____

_____

_____

_____

_____

Quality

How are programs and services evaluated for cultural congruence and sensitivity to the needs of your population? Are members of your population involved in assessing quality of services? Do the services offered take into account cultural variations and cultural barriers that your population might encounter in accessing services through agency programs? Are eligibility criteria for service culturally sensitive to your population, or do they include criteria that clearly reflect the biases of the dominant society? How can (does) your agency enhance services to your population to take cultural differences into account?

_____

_____

_____

_____

_____

_____

_____

Effectiveness

Do the numbers of clients from your population being served by your agency reflect their numbers in the agency's catchment area? What is your understanding of the ways in which clients from your population feel about the quality and quantity of the programs and services available to them? Are there unmet needs that members of the population can identify for which no appropriate services are available?

_____

_____

_____

_____

_____

_____

_____

_____

Efficiency

Do your agency's programs coordinate well with other services that address the needs of your population? Has your agency reached out to community resources, set up linkages, and used alternative service delivery systems that are culturally sensitive to the needs of your population?

Describe some of your agency's referral sources and resources.

_____

_____

_____

_____

_____

_____

_____

_____

_____

_____

_____

_____

_____

_____

_____

_____

_____

_____

_____

_____

_____

Personal Cultural Competencies

The social work processes of engagement, trust, and relationship-building, assessment and problem definition, contracting and goal setting, intervention, and evaluation and termination can support the provision of culturally competent services to clients because of the inherent flexibility and adaptability that is built into them.

You can assess your personal cultural competency skills in working with your chosen populations using these processes as a framework, by describing the ways in which you might use your knowledge of your chosen population to ensure that your approaches to your clients are culturally competent.

Engagement, Trust, and Relationship-building

Knowing about the way in which your population expresses help-seeking, and the way help-seeking is considered within the population is essential to the early processes of engagement, trust, and relationship-building. It is also essential to understand cultural norms and expectations regarding eye contact, hand-shaking, touch, personal space and distance, empathic responding, and forms of address. There is often cultural variation in the expectations for direct advice-giving and guidance, and in the people and circumstances expected to be involved in decision-making. Familial and communal styles of decision-making and change efforts. Ethnographic interviewing can assist you in learning about your client's culture through his/her/their eyes, and thus increase your ability to provide culturally sensitive services.

From your experiences with your population, what are some culturally congruent approaches you might use to begin a relationship with a client and establish trust?

_____

_____

_____

_____

_____

_____

_____

_____

_____

_____

Assessment and Problem Definition

While some of the traditional social work assessment tools, such as the psychosocial assessment, the eco-map, the community assessment, and the strengths assessment might be applicable to many populations, there are also some assessment tools that can assist you and your client to understand and place issues within the client's cultural context. How can you effectively engage a client from your population in the assessment process? What are some assessment tools that might be culturally appropriate? How might your client identify, describe, and wish to address problems or concerns, grounded in group cultural norms, beliefs, and expectations? How might you assist your client to explore any areas of difficulty that might be grounded in the relationship between his/her/their cultural group and the dominant society?

_____

_____

_____

_____

_____

_____

_____

_____

_____

_____

_____

_____

_____

_____

_____

_____

_____

_____

Contracting and Goal Setting

It is especially important that overarching goals and objectives that are developed to meet client need be culturally appropriate. Goals and objectives that are not culturally congruent will have a relatively low chance of success. Success can be maximized by engaging the client fully in the process, and by using the client's language and terminology. Goals and objectives should also reflect values in the client's culture.

List three examples of culturally competent overarching goals which would be appropriate for your population.

1. _____
   _____
   _____

2. _____
   _____
   _____

3. _____
   _____
   _____

Select *one* of these goals, circle it for future reference, and develop three objectives which relate to your goal and are culturally congruent. Remember to state your objectives in language appropriate to your population, and include both a time frame and a measurement tool to enable assessment of progress.

1. _____
   _____
   _____

2. _____
   _____
   _____

3. _____
   _____
   _____

Interventions

Like overarching goals and objectives, the success of intervention strategies is very much related to cultural values and norms. Interventions should be developed within the client's cultural parameters, and should reflect culturally appropriate behaviors and tasks.

List five examples of culturally appropriate interventions for clients of your agency.

1. _____

_____

2. _____

_____

3. _____

_____

4. _____

_____

5. _____

_____

It is also essential to be aware of culturally inappropriate interventions. List five examples of interventions that would *not* be appropriate to members of your chosen cultural group.

1. _____

_____

2. _____

_____

3. _____

_____

4. _____

_____

5. _____

_____

Evaluation

The determination of success or failure of a social work intervention is very much grounded in the culture of the group. Focus may vary between the elimination of symptoms, the diminution of symptoms, problem solutions, external changes, or inner changes. In the culture you have studied, who in the society determines whether an intervention has been beneficial or successful? Clients may be dependent upon the judgment of family members, the community, or a community institution, such as a church or school, to evaluate success or failure. How might this be determined for members of your population?

_____

_____

_____

_____

_____

_____

Termination

Termination attitudes and practices are certainly as culturally sensitive as engagement attitudes and practices! Cultures vary greatly in their norms for termination: some terminate easily and impersonally, others tend to want to linger, still others to retain some contact. Some cultures also may desire to "normalize" the relationship by attempting to establish a social relationship or a friendship. What are some of the specific considerations—in time, manner, and degree—that your population may expect in the termination process? How would you assist the clients to terminate in a meaningful, culturally congruent manner?

_____

_____

_____

_____

_____

_____

_____

NASW Standards for Cultural Competence

Review the NASW Standards for Cultural Competence in the context of your chosen population, considering your field placement agency, the programs and services offered, and your personal cultural competencies

Using one or more of the Cultural Competence Standards, assess your agency, your programs and services, and your personal cultural competencies.

Standard(s) Selected for Review: _____

_____

_____

_____

_____

_____

_____

Agency: _____

_____

_____

_____

_____

_____

Program and Services: _____

_____

_____

_____

_____

_____

Personal Cultural Competencies: _____

_____

_____

_____

_____

_____

_____

_____

_____

In completing these workbook assignments, you have had the opportunity to gain direct personal experience in the process of attaining and applying culturally competent practice standards in social work. While you have focused specifically on one population for the purposes of this project, the *process* that you have learned is applicable in any setting. It is hoped that you will carry this process knowledge with you during the course of your career, and that you will find it helpful in the achievement of excellence in culturally sensitive social work practice.

Final Thoughts: _____

_____

_____

_____

_____

_____

_____

_____

_____

_____

_____

_____

_____

CREDITS

Pages 8, 11, 20–21, 34–35, 44–46: Selections from *Social Work Practice and People of Color, A Process Stage Approach*, 5th edition by LUM. 2004. Reprinted with permission of Wadsworth, a division of Thomson Learning: www.thomsonrights.com.

Pages 9–10: National Association of Social Workers, Inc., NASW Code of Ethics. Copyright © 1999.

Pages 9–10, 25, 55: Selections from *Culturally Competent Practice, A Framework of Understanding Diverse Groups and Justice Issues*, 2nd edition by LUM. 2003. Reprinted with permission of Wadsworth, a division of Thomson Learning: www.thomsonrights.com.

Pages 9–11, 18–19, 33–34: Selections from Green, James W. *Cultural Awareness In The Human Services: A Multi-ethnic Approach*, 3rd edition. Copyright © 1999 by Pearson Education. Published by Allyn and Bacon, Boston, MA. Reprinted by permission of the publisher.

Pages 11–13: National Association of Social Workers, Inc., NASW Standards for Cultural Competence in Social Work Practice. Copyright © 2001.

Pages 26, 32: Reprinted with the permission of The Free Press, a Division of Simon & Schuster Adult Publishing Group, from *Understanding Race, Ethnicity and Power* by Elaine Pinderhughes. Copyright ” 1989 by Elaine Pinderhughes. All rights reserved.

Page 31: Selections from *The Life Model of Social Work Practice* by Carel B. Germain and Alex Gitternan. Copyright © 1996 by Columbia University Press.

Pages 36–38, 43, 50–52: From Wynetta Devore & Elfriede G. Schlesinger *Ethnic-sensitive Practice With Families* (1987) Published by Allyn and Bacon, Boston, MA. Copyright © by Pearson Education. Reprinted by permission of the publisher.

Page 43: Selections from *Communicating for Cultural Competence* by James. W. Leigh, Copyright © 2001 by Waveland Press, Inc.

Page 312: The Twelve Steps are reprinted with permission of Alcoholics Anonymous World Services, Inc. (AAWS) Permission to reprint the Twelve Steps does not mean that A.A.W.S. has reviewed or approved the contents of this publication, or that AAWS necessarily agrees with the views expressed herein. A. A. is a program of recovery from alcoholism only — use the Twelve Steps in connection with programs and activities which are patterned after A. A., but which address other problems, or in any other non-A.A. context, does not imply otherwise.

INDEX

355

/